The Templar Code For Dummies®

Cheat Sheet

Templar Who's Who

Chaplains: The Catholic priests within the order.

Commanders of Knights, Houses, and Farms: Knights responsible for the specific operation of Templar holdings, under the Commanders of the Lands.

Commanders of the Lands: Administered Templar operations in the Holy Land regions of Jerusalem, Tripoli, and Antioch, which included castles, farms and Templar "houses" or *preceptories.*

Craftsmen: Farmers, cooks, masons, smiths, and other serving brethren who performed the day-to-day menial tasks of supporting the order. Some also took on a military role and were armed when needed (and were, thus, considered to be of higher rank), while others did not.

Draper: In charge of all clothing for the order.

Grand Master: The head of the order in both military and administrative matters. The Grand Master was elected for life and answered only to the pope

Knights: Noble-born Templars, groomed for battle.

Marshal: The Minister of War within the order, res...

Masters: Heads of the order within the provinces o... ...tland; Poitiers, France; Portugal; and Hungary.

Provincial Masters: Located outside the Holy Land, ...he administration of the banking side of the order, along with being European recruiters.

Seneschal: Second in command to the Grand Master.

Sergeants: Common soldiers, who held a lower rank because of their lowborn status.

Squires: The young attendants to the knights, who aspired to eventually become knights themselves.

Turcopoles: Turkish/Greek, Eastern Orthodox soldiers recruited as light cavalry or scouts, of lower rank than the Sergeants.

Under-Marshal: In charge of all equipment.

Templar Architecture

battlements: A castle wall's defenses, consisting of the walk wall along the top ridge, protected by the parapet.

concentric: This style of castle, favored by the Knights Templar, features a series of outer walls surrounding the castle. Attackers breaching one wall would find themselves suddenly trapped in a narrow alley confronting yet another inner wall.

donjon: A French word for the keep; *not* a dungeon as we know it today.

garderobe: The one thing everybody needed, the community toilet. It was a hollowed-out area in the castle wall, with a chute down to the moat or sewer pit.

gatehouse: The entry to the castle, usually secured by a drawbridge and a portcullis, and often defended by towers or turrets on either side of the entrance. The gatehouse is the easiest entry, the weakest link to all the castle's defenses, and, therefore, usually the most heavily fortified.

Great Hall: The primary social center of the castle. The Great Hall served as a ceremonial reception room and dining hall.

keep: A strong, central tower, either square or round; the place of last resort to hole up in when all other defenses have failed. Round towers were easier to defend with fewer blind spots, but square towers provided more conveniently shaped interior rooms.

The Templar Code For Dummies®

Cheat Sheet

Templar Architecture (continued)

moat: A ditch surrounding the castle. It was filled with water if water was handy. There was no need for crocodiles to keep waders and enemies out, because the moat was usually full of the castle's sewage P.U.

murder holes: Openings in the ceiling of the front gate, used for dropping large rocks, firing arrows, or pouring boiling liquid on the enemies' heads.

parapet: A crenellated wall of high and low vertical indentations, so archers could fire from the wall and then hide, simply by moving to one side or the other.

portcullis: The gate, usually made of iron, that could be slid down behind the drawbridge entryway.

postern gate: A secret back gate to the castle, usually well camouflaged. Used for sneaking troops out to surround the enemy, or to let spies and scouts come and go.

towers: Large, defensive structures placed at corners or strategic positions along the castle's walls. Towers could be square, round, or D-shaped. Round exterior walls meant greater visibility all around and were harder for attackers' ladders to rest against.

turret: A small, round tower. In some castles, turrets protruded out from the walls of the keep so archers could shoot down on enemies.

ward: The castle's interior courtyard; sometimes called the *bailey*.

Important Templar Dates

1000 B.C.	King Solomon's Temple built on Temple Mount in Jerusalem.
A.D. 638	Muslims conquer the Holy Land.
1095	Pope Urban II calls for the First Crusade.
1099	Jerusalem taken from Muslims. Priory of Sion allegedly founded.
1119	Founding of the Templars by Hughes de Payens.
1129	The Templar Rule is adopted at the Council of Troyes.
1139	Pope Innocent II exempts the Templars from all but papal authority.
1146	Second Crusade begins.
1187	The Battle of Hattin: Saladin and the Muslim army retake Jerusalem, killing 200 Templars.
1191	Third Crusade captures the port of Acre, becomes new Templar headquarters.
1192	Richard the Lionheart and Saladin agree to open Jerusalem to Christian pilgrims.
1202–1204	Constantinople sacked. Christian relics fall into hands of the Templars.
1291	Acre, the last Crusader state in the Holy Land, falls to the Muslims. Templars move to Cyprus.
1293	Jacques de Molay becomes Grand Master of the Templars.
1307	Templars arrested by Phillip IV (*le Bel* or "the Fair") in France on Friday, October 13.
1308	Edward II, under pressure from the pope, arrests all Templars in England.
1310	54 Knights Templar burned at the stake in France to compel remaining Templars to confess.
1312	Templar order dissolved by the Council of Vienne, transferring property to the Knights Hospitaller.
1314	Jacques de Molay and Geoffroy de Charney burned at the stake in Paris. Templars alleged to assist Robert the Bruce of Scotland at the Battle of Bannockburn. Phillip the Fair dies in a hunting accident. Pope Clement V dies.
1319	Order of Christ founded in Portugal by King Dinis as a new home for the Templars.
1446	Rosslyn Chapel construction begins in Roslin, Scotland.

For Dummies: Bestselling Book Series for Beginners

The Templar Code

FOR

DUMMIES®

The Templar Code

FOR

DUMMIES®

by Christopher Hodapp
and Alice Von Kannon

Wiley Publishing, Inc.

The Templar Code For Dummies®

Published by
Wiley Publishing, Inc.
111 River St.
Hoboken, NJ 07030-5774
www.wiley.com

WILEY

About the Authors

Christopher Hodapp is a Freemason and a member of the Masonic Order of the Knights Templar. He is the author of *Solomon's Builders: Freemasons, Founding Fathers and the Secrets of Washington, D.C.,* and his first book, *Freemasons For Dummies,* has quickly become the most popular modern guide to the ancient and accepted fraternity of Freemasonry. In 2006, he received the Duane E. Anderson Excellence in Masonic Education Award from the Grand Lodge of Minnesota, and the Distinguished Service Award from the Grand Commandery of the Knights Templar of Indiana. He has written for *Masonic Magazine, Templar History Magazine, The Philalethes Magazine,* and *The Indiana Freemason,* and he is a monthly columnist for *Texas Home Gardener.* Chris has spent more than 20 years as a commercial filmmaker.

Alice Von Kannon has been an advertising executive, a teacher, a writer, and even a greedy and villainous landlord. She studied film production at Los Angeles Valley Community College and history at California State University, Northridge, and she has worked for many years as a writer and broadcast producer. Alice has traveled widely in Europe and the Middle East and has written extensively on the subject of the Barbary Wars and the birth of the U.S. Navy. She is a member of the Order of the Grail, the fraternal body of the International College of Esoteric Studies. A history junkie beyond the help of intervention since the age of 14, her recent studies of Near Eastern religious cults and sects led to this, her first *For Dummies* book.

Hodapp and Von Kannon both live in Indianapolis, Indiana.

Dedication

For Steven L. Harris (1954–1999)

"He was a truly perfect, gentle knight."

Authors' Acknowledgments

Our deepest appreciation goes to the many friends and authors who unselfishly shared their knowledge and love of the Poor Fellow Soldiers of Christ and the Temple of Solomon with us.

To Stephen Dafoe, author of numerous books about the Order, and the editor of *Templar History Magazine,* who graciously acted as the Technical Editor of this volume.

To Rabbi Arnold Bienstock of Congregation Shaarey Tefilla in Indianapolis for his indispensable help in deciphering Hebrew, Greek, and Aramaic; to Father James Bonke and the Catholic Center of Indianapolis; and especially to Most Reverend Phillip A. Garver of *l'Eglise Gnostique Catholique Apostolique* for his incredible knowledge of Gnosticism, Martinism, Catharism, and all things esoteric.

To Nathan Brindle, Jim Dillman, Jeffrey Naylor, Eric Schmitz, R. J. Hayes and all the "Knights of the North" for their constant support and input.

To Andy Jackson, Larry Kaminsky and especially the Sir Knights of Raper Commandery No. 1, Knights Templar of Indiana.

To Tracy Boggier at Wiley Publishing for being a tireless champion of this book through a long and circuitous route to completion; to our indefatigable editor Elizabeth Kuball for bravely withstanding the onslaught of two of us this time; to Jack Bussell for his cheerful assistance, usually with absolutely no notice whatsoever; and to the entire *For Dummies* team that works behind the scenes to make this process simple.

And finally, to Norma Winkler, who has been a boundless source of help, support, confidence, and love.

Publisher's Acknowledgments

We're proud of this book; please send us your comments through our Dummies online registration form located at www.dummies.com/register/.

Some of the people who helped bring this book to market include the following:

Acquisitions, Editorial, and Media Development

Project Editor: Elizabeth Kuball

Acquisitions Editor: Tracy Boggier

Copy Editor: Elizabeth Kuball

Technical Editor: Stephen Dafoe

Editorial Manager: Michelle Hacker

Consumer Editorial Supervisor and Reprint Editor: Carmen Krikorian

Editorial Assistants: Erin Calligan Mooney, Joe Niesen, Leeann Harney, David Lutton

Cartoons: Rich Tennant (www.the5thwave.com)

Composition Services

Project Coordinator: Lynsey Osborn

Layout and Graphics: Carl Byers, Joyce Haughey, Shane Johnson, Laura Pence

Anniversary Logo Design: Richard Pacifico

Proofreader: Aptara

Indexer: Aptara

Publishing and Editorial for Consumer Dummies

    Diane Graves Steele, Vice President and Publisher, Consumer Dummies

    Joyce Pepple, Acquisitions Director, Consumer Dummies

    Kristin A. Cocks, Product Development Director, Consumer Dummies

    Michael Spring, Vice President and Publisher, Travel

    Kelly Regan, Editorial Director, Travel

Publishing for Technology Dummies

    Andy Cummings, Vice President and Publisher, Dummies Technology/General User

Composition Services

    Gerry Fahey, Vice President of Production Services

    Debbie Stailey, Director of Composition Services

Contents at a Glance

Table of Contents

Introduction

● ●

*Y*ou can tell a lunatic by the liberties he takes with common sense, by his flashes of inspiration, and by the fact that sooner or later he brings up the Templars.

—Umberto Eco

Last October, the two of us received some happy news; after a long process of outlining, cutting, pasting, re-outlining, meetings, major changes, and more meetings, our editor called to say that victory was ours. This somewhat unusual project had made it into the list for 2007; in fact, it would be out by June. We would be doing a project we cared about a great deal, *The Templar Code For Dummies*. Any author will tell you that this is always a thrill. But the next piece of news was a little unnerving. The official launch date for the project had been set for the following Friday, which happened to be Friday, October 13th.

For one brief moment, a chill of premonition slithered down our backs, like ice cubes at a frat-house party. After a few seconds of silence, we did what many people do when they have an uncomfortable moment of premonition; we both burst out laughing. It did help the shiver.

The chill we felt wasn't because we're particularly superstitious, at least, no more so than anyone else. It was something far more disconcerting than mere superstition. Because for anyone who knows the lore of the Knights Templar, Friday, October 13, 1307, was the date that the Order was rounded up all across France in one single day, by order of the French king, Phillip IV, to be indicted on various charges of heresy. In fact, this is sort of superstition in reverse, because the reason that Friday the 13th is considered an unlucky day, so the legend goes, is *because* of what happened to the Templars on that fateful date, seven centuries ago. Whistling in the cemetery, we decided it was the perfect launch date for the book.

That particular Friday was the 699th anniversary. By the time this book is on the shelves, it will be precisely 700 years since the Knights Templar were arrested, and seven centuries haven't dimmed the fascination people have with this mysterious, courageous, and singular brotherhood of knights.

What is known for certain about the Knights Templar is a story with a larger-than-life aura of myth, that finished in an abrupt and almost unbelievable tragedy. Founded in A.D. 1119 by nine crusading French knights, the Poor Fellow Soldiers of Christ and of the Temple of Solomon (known as the Knights Templar) shot across the political landscape like a meteor, vaulting from obscure guardians of pilgrims in Jerusalem to the most powerful and influential force of their age. They were fierce warriors, devout monks, and international bankers. Within half a century of their birth, they were men who walked with kings and advised popes, brokered treaties, and built castles and preceptories on a massive scale. Then, even more inexplicable than their rise came their fall, a harrowing plunge into arrest, trial, flight, and execution that shocked the medieval world, both East and West. The charges against them of heresy and sodomy were equally shocking, and are still debated by historians today.

In fact, theories about the Templars are hotter today than ever before. Historians, researchers, wishful thinkers, and dreamers have claimed that the Templars lived on after their destruction, placing them in Portugal, Scotland, Switzerland, Nova Scotia, and Massachusetts. They are alleged to have sailed pirate ships, founded banking dynasties, and given birth to the Freemasons. Their explorations in the Holy Land have led to speculation that they found the Ark of the Covenant, the True Cross of Christ's crucifixion, the head of John the Baptist, the Spear of Destiny, and the Holy Grail. They have alternately been described as pious guardians of the most sacred secrets of Christianity, and as heretical practitioners of occult and satanic rites. And more than one suicidal doomsday cult has claimed to be descended from the Templars, living in wait for the Intergalactic Grand Master's mother ship to enter low-earth orbit and beam them aboard.

In 2003, an author named Dan Brown published a modest sequel to a moderately successful mystery entitled *Angels & Demons*. Little did he know that he was handling fissionable material. *The Da Vinci Code* has sold more than 60 million copies in 44 languages, and is the eighth most popular book ever published. In it, Brown told the tale of the "true" nature of the legend of the Holy Grail. If you're one of the seven or eight people left on earth who haven't read it yet, allow us to spoil the ending for you. According to Brown, the Grail was not some humble cup used by Christ at the Last Supper, or even a golden, jewel-encrusted chalice. It was the bloodline of Jesus, a child born to Mary Magdalene from a union with Christ. The book tells of a mysterious organization that was created to keep the secret, and to protect the offspring of Christ and Mary down through the centuries. And that group, through a succession of plot twists, was — you guessed it — the Knights Templar.

Dan Brown undoubtedly set out to tell a good story, but he couldn't possibly have known that he was writing what would become a worldwide phenomenon. How could he have known that his book would cause millions of people to reexamine their own beliefs and those of their neighbors, inspiring thousands to make pilgrimages to the sites of his book in France and the United Kingdom, in search of a sign or symbol that would reveal some hidden truth to them? He might not have intended it, but, whether by chance or fate, that's exactly what happened. And curiously, in spite of what many alarmed religious leaders feared, the result has been a greater interest in the origins of Christianity, and a whole world of readers whose faith seems to have been strengthened by what they've found.

Brown, like so many others, looked at the Knights Templar and was intrigued by what he saw. The unanswered mysteries and outlandish legends surrounding them didn't just spring out of nowhere, or even out of Mr. Brown's fertile imagination. The Templars have been a pillar of Western mythology for centuries, and there's no end in sight for the world's obsession with the Poor Fellow Soldiers of Christ and the Temple of Solomon.

About This Book

We wrote this book to assemble the vast, outlandish, popular, and confusing lore of the Knights Templar into one convenient volume. The first four parts of the book strictly tell the Templar story; their rise, their fall, and the forces at work in the world that gave them birth. If you first encountered this stuff in *The Da Vinci Code,* you can go straight to Part V; that entire part is devoted to the questions raised by the novel, including the bloodline of Christ, the "sacred feminine," and the mysterious relationship between those concepts and the Templars. It's a unique approach, but it should give you a great overview of the Templars and their world, as well as a definite leg up at the office holiday party when somebody wants to talk your arm off about the Black Madonna Cult or the Council of Nicaea.

We're both writers, both history fanatics, and both obsessed with the Knights Templar. While other people may loll about, wasting their vacations broiling on the beaches of Cancun or falling down the ski slopes of Aspen, history cranks like us spend our free time taking off every year for the backcountry of France and Britain, Portugal, and Turkey, up at dawn every day to strap on a backpack and go sweat our way up another ruin. *We* know how to have a good time. Who wants to spend a vacation lolling on the beach with an umbrella drink in his hand?

We're hoping that in this book, all that sweat paid off. Together we've stood in the prison cell of Jacques de Molay, last Grand Master of the Knights Templar, reading the messages scratched onto the walls by the imprisoned knights. And together we've stood on the Île de la Cité in the shadow of Notre Dame Cathedral in Paris, where de Molay was burned at the stake for the amusement of the crowd that was, to the vindictive king's disappointment, sullen rather than boisterous.

Generally, people in the 14th century enjoyed a good burning or hanging or quartering, but no one was indulging in any satisfaction on that tragic day. The Templars had been the most formidable knights of Europe, brave warriors as well as monks sworn to a life of poverty, chastity, and obedience.
No one gave up more for the sake of his faith than a Knight Templar.

Consequently, the Poor Knights, as they were sometimes called, had the respect of the entire Christian world, and even many in the enemy camp. When the brilliant soldier Saladin won back the Holy Land from the Crusaders, the prisoners he took who were to be beheaded at once, without question of ransom or the slave market, were the Templars. As far as Saladin was concerned, they were just too dangerous an enemy to be left alive. And never once did a Templar knight beg for his life. After the disastrous Battle of Hattin, they queued up in their hundreds to be slaughtered, each calmly waiting his turn.

Everyone knew the legends of their almost foolhardy courage, and everyone knew what the Templars had sacrificed in order to secure the Holy Land for the sake of Christian pilgrims, so that the souls of the men and women on this journey could be saved from purgatory or damnation. In fact, one particular biblical quote from John 15:13 was something of an unofficial motto for the Templars: "Greater love hath no man than this, that a man lay down his life for his friends." The general consensus of the somber crowd on that bleak execution day in 1314 has been the general consensus of most people ever since: that the Templars were getting a very raw deal, whether they had fallen victim to some Eastern heresy or not.

For us, ever since that prophetic launch date, we've had the feeling that the martyred de Molay could be looking over our shoulders, which made for two very nervous writers. More than anything else, we wanted to get it right. We think we have.

Conventions Used in This Book

We don't use many conventions in this book — why use conventions when you're talking about such an unconventional group of guys? — but we do use a couple:

- ✔ Any time we define a term for you, we throw some *italic* on it and put the definition nearby, often in parentheses. (We sometimes use italic for emphasis, too, because our editor won't let us type in all caps — something about sounding hostile.)

- ✔ Web addresses and e-mail addresses appear in a funky font called `monofont`. It's there so you can easily tell what to type in your Web browser and what to leave out.

When this book was printed, some Web addresses may have needed to break across two lines of text. If that happened, rest assured that we haven't put in any extra characters (such as hyphens) to indicate the break. So, when using one of these Web addresses, just type in exactly what you see in this book, pretending as though the line break doesn't exist. And if you *do* see a hyphen in a Web address, that means you're supposed to type it.

What You're Not to Read

You don't actually *have* to read *anything* in this book — we won't test you on it, we swear — but we know you won't be able to resist turning the page. When you do, you can safely skip anything marked by the Technical Stuff icon (see "Icons Used in This Book" for more on that). You can also skip sidebars (text in gray boxes), because they're not critical to your understanding of the subject at hand.

Foolish Assumptions

The Templar Code For Dummies was written for a lot of different people, but we make a few superficial assumptions about you, without even knowing you or asking your relatives about your most embarrassing moments. With luck, one of these descriptions fits you like a chain-mail gauntlet:

- ✔ **You know nothing about the Templars.** If so, the whole story is here: the Crusades from which they emerged; the Christian society back home in Europe and the strange combination of religions and cultures they were surrounded by in the Holy Land; their skyrocketing fame among the movers and shakers in Rome and the capitals of the world; their lavish wealth and their creation of the banking business; their mysterious reputation as the "Grail knights"; and their abrupt fall and destruction.

- ✔ **You know a little about the Templars.** If you've already studied some about the knights, this book will put it all in perspective for you. It covers the facts and the legends, from the plausible to the downright preposterous.

- ✔ **You first heard about this stuff in *The Da Vinci Code*.** *The Templar Code For Dummies* is the book you need to make sense of Dan Brown's connections between the Templars, the Priory of Sion, the Holy Grail, and the sacred feminine. As good as *The Da Vinci Code* is, what Brown wrote wasn't a new theory — it's been around for a while — and he left a lot out of the whole picture. In this book, we explore what the connections really are and where they might have come from.

- ✔ **You are either a Christian or an interested bystander.** Especially if you're a Catholic, or just wonder what they say about all this hullabaloo, we clue you in on the Church's position on the Templars, Constantine, Opus Dei, celibacy, Black Madonnas, and killer albinos.

- ✔ **You are a Freemason.** If so, this book is an essential. The fraternity of Freemasons has a modern Order of Knights Templar, and though they don't profess a direct descent from the original 12th-century knights, an awful lot of claims have been made over the years about the Templar origins of the Masons. There's more to the Templars than what the Masonic version says, and in this book we clear up the confusion.

How This Book Is Organized

If you sped right past the Table of Contents without bothering to signal, go back and take a look. You'll see this book is divided into six easily digestible slices. Feel free to read them in any order. We don't care. Really. Here's what you'll find inside.

Part I: The Knights Templar and the Crusades

You can't tell the players without a program, and you can't understand the Knights Templar without knowing a little bit about the Crusades. In this part, we give you the overall lay of the Templar landscape. In Chapter 1, we set out the road map that leads from Jesus and Mary Magdalene to the Templars and the Holy Grail. In Chapter 2, we cram hundreds of years of crusading history into one densely packed, whirlwind tour of mucking about in the Holy Land. Finally, in Chapter 3, we trace the very beginnings of the Order as protectors of pilgrims, through their incredible rise in power and prestige as the bankers, landlords, and ecclesiastical fat cats of the Christian world.

Part II: A Different Kind of Knighthood

This section is the red meat of the Templar story — who they were, what they became, how they got whacked, and who did it to them. In Chapter 4, we give you a rundown on the harsh daily lives of the men who chose to become these warrior monks. Chapter 5 examines their annihilation just two centuries later by a king, a pope, and possibly their own successes and excesses. Chapter 6 takes a closer look at the accusations against the Order made during their trial, and pieces together the evidence that was used to make the case — from the serious and creepy, to the outlandish and cockamamie.

Part III: After the Fall of the Templars

In this part, we pick up the trail of mythology that followed the destruction of the Templars. Chapter 7 takes a closer look at what we *do* know about the Templars after their arrest, trial, and convictions, as well as what we *think* we know. Chapter 8 examines the possibility that the fraternity of Freemasons crawled out of the ashes of the Order, along with taking a peek at the modern-day Masonic Knights Templar. And in Chapter 9, you discover some other, lesser-known groups that claim to be the 21st-century heirs to the Templar legacy.

Part IV: Templars and the Grail

The Knights Templar and the story of the Holy Grail were twin sons of the same mother, born out of the Crusades. This part explores the Grail myths of the West, their connection to the Templars, and the place of the knights in the new Grail-mania brought on by *The Da Vinci Code.* Chapter 10 goes back to the beginning to examine the very first Grail stories, their links to both Christians and pagans, and how they led to the ideas of chivalry, courtly love, and King Arthur. Chapter 11 discusses the Grail myth of the 21st century, the supposed bloodline of Christ, starting in the B.D.B. (Before Dan Brown) era with the first modern researchers who proposed the startling notion that Jesus had a wife. From there the tale heads to the south of France, to the mysterious hill town of Rennes-le-Château, and to the legends of the Cathars, who play a major role in the Grail stories of the past and present.

Part V: Squaring Off: The Church versus the Gospel According to Dan Brown

If you picked up this book because *The Da Vinci Code* was the first place you'd ever read about the Templars and you wanted to find out more, you may want to turn to this part first. For every Christian reader who found new interest in the history of his faith, there was another who was upset or angered by Dan Brown's alternative theories of his alleged "true" story of Christianity. And the Catholic Church wasn't exactly thrilled with Brown's version either.

Dan Brown said that his famous novel was a fictional account based in fact, so this part examines the historical claims put forth in *The Da Vinci Code.* Chapter 12 looks at Dan Brown's version of the Knights Templar as the warrior wing of the secretive Priory of Sion, their survival, and their ongoing secret mission to protect the bloodline of Christ. Chapter 13 explores Brown's many assertions about the history of women before and after the Christian era, the Church's real historical attitude toward women, and some surprising aspects about Christian women and the sacred feminine. Chapter 14 presents the amazing behind-the-scenes politics in the creation of the Bible we know today. We delve into the significance of the Apocryphal biblical books, and the story behind the recently discovered Gnostic Gospels that have caused many to change the entire structure of their faith. We fearlessly tread on the role of celibacy in history and in the Church, and its survival into the present day. We finish with the place of the Knights Templar in the newly emerging picture of Christianity, and the latest theories of Templar influence on the survival of these alternative gospels and the secrets they contain.

Part VI: The Part of Tens

This part of the book cuts to the chase and taunts travelers, tourists, treasure-trove hunters, and tall-tale tellers with tantalizing tidbits and Templar tchotchkes. (Please, make him stop.) Chapter 15 explores ten possible candidates for the location of the Holy Grail. Strap on your backpack, grab your camera, and strike out for the ten must-see Templar sites in Chapter 16. Chapter 17 points you in ten different directions to start hunting for the hiding place of the fabled Templar treasure: long forgotten gospels, secret documents, gold and silver, the fabled Ark of the Covenant, or even the Holy Grail itself.

Icons Used in This Book

You'll find the following icons lurking in the margins of this book. Beyond just giving you a little scenery to gaze at, they help you find what you're looking for and navigate the potentially scary parts.

The Grand Master was the head of the Knights Templar, the Mr. Know-It-All of the Order. He was in charge of both military and spiritual matters, and it was a tough job. That's why he's wearing a helmet for protection. He helps sort out pesky issues about the Templar origins and rules.

This icon marks key points that are vital to understanding the Crusades, the Templars, the Grail myth, or other truly important topics. Don't skip these!

This icon highlights stuff like additional data, explanations of obscure rituals and practices, or other information that may interest you, but can be ruthlessly skipped over without missing the important themes of the chapter.

This one points out handy tidbits and topical advice.

This icon alerts you to subjects specifically having to do with topics from works of Dan Brown. If *The Da Vinci Code* is what piqued your interest in this book, these are the hot topics to look out for.

When it comes to the Templars, there are many conflicting sources of misinformation and fantasy masquerading as history. This little icon alerts you to those tantalizing bits of speculation, romantic wisps of wishful thinking, or burgeoning cartloads of crap.

Where to Go from Here

The best news you've heard all day is that this is not like a textbook. The genius of the *For Dummies* series is that it's designed so you can come and go as you please. If you want to know it all, get all the hot dates, and find the secrets to cutting in line at the bank, start at the title page and read until you hit the back cover. If you prefer, you can skip chapters that don't interest you without hurting our feelings. Does the prospect of reading about the Crusades make your head throb like you're at a Bow Wow concert with your kid sister? If so, skip Chapter 2. Want to know why your grandfather has a sword in the attic that says he's a Knight Templar, even though he can't wear armor with his bad knee? Head over to Chapter 8. Want to know where the Holy Grail might be hiding so you can grab a pickax and get right to work chopping through some old church floor? (Don't get caught.) Go directly to Chapter 15.

Part I
The Knights Templar and the Crusades

The 5th Wave   By Rich Tennant

Oh, for God's sake, Richard! It's a couple of mice in the basement stealing grain. Quit making a crusade out of everything!

In this part . . .

This part begins, appropriately enough, with a general overview of the Knights Templar — who they were and what they believed in, as well as a condensed version of the symbols, accomplishments, and legacy of the Poor Fellow Soldiers of Christ and the Temple of Solomon.

You can't tell the story of the Knights Templar without at least a nodding acquaintance with the turbulent period of bloodshed known as the Crusades, so buckle your seat belt for Chapter 2, which is the top-speed, full-blast, high-gear version of the medieval wars in the Holy Land. We start with the Very Big Picture — the battle between the Christian West and the Islamic East — and then narrow down to the Holy Land itself — the prize that both sides were after. Then we zoom in even closer in Chapter 3, to the incidents on the road to Jerusalem that gave birth to the Knights Templar, the most powerful force in Christendom, and how their meteoric rise to the halls of power and the splendor of gold catapulted them to a dizzying height.

Chapter 1

Defining the Templar Code

• •

• •

Thus in a wondrous and unique manner they appear gentler than lambs, yet fiercer than lions. I do not know if it would be more appropriate to refer to them as monks or as soldiers, unless perhaps it would be better to recognize them as being both. Indeed they lack neither monastic meekness nor military might. What can we say of this, except that this has been done by the Lord, and it is marvelous in our eyes. These are the picked troops of God, whom he has recruited from the ends of the earth; the valiant men of Israel chosen to guard well and faithfully that tomb which is the bed of the true Solomon, each man sword in hand, and superbly trained to war.

—St. Bernard of Clairvaux, *In Praise of the New Knighthood* (1136)

*I*n A.D. 1119, the Order of the Poor Fellow Soldiers of Christ and the Temple of Solomon formed in the wake of the First Crusade, and the world had never seen anything quite like them. They were knights, dedicated to the same unwritten, medieval, chivalric code of honor that governed most of these fierce, professional fighting men on horseback throughout Europe and the Holy Land. But they also took the vows of devoutly religious monks, consigning themselves to the same strict code of poverty, chastity, and obedience that governed the brotherhoods of Catholic monks who spent their ascetic lives cloistered in monasteries. These were no mercenaries who fought for money, land, or titles. They were Christ's devoted warriors, who killed when it was necessary to protect the Holy Land or Christian pilgrims.

The Templars became the darlings of the papacy and the most renowned knights on the battlefields of the Crusades. They grew in wealth and influence and became the bankers of Europe. They were advisors, diplomats, and treasurers. And then, after an existence of just 200 years, they were destroyed, not by infidel warriors on a plain in Palestine, but by a French king and a pliant pope. In the great timeline of history, the Templars came and went in an astonishingly brief blink of an eye. Yet, the mysteries that have always surrounded them have done nothing but circulate and grow for nine centuries.

In this chapter, we give you a quick tour of who the Knights Templar were, and the two seemingly contradictory traditions of war and religion they brought together to create the first Christian order of warrior monks. We also discuss the meanings of the codes they lived by, both the code of behavior that governed their daily lives and the secret codes that became part of their way of doing business.

Knights, Grails, Codes, Leonardo da Vinci, and How They All Collide

Everyone loves a mystery. Agatha Christie wrote 75 successful novels in a career that spanned decades, with estimated total sales of over 100 million. Her stories remain a fixture in the bookstore, as well as in film and television. But Agatha Christie always neatly wrapped up the mystery by the end of the story. The historical mysteries examined in the tale of the Templars are far more complex, and it's rarely possible to tie them up with a ribbon and pronounce them solved.

Interest in the Templars, the Holy Grail, and various mysteries of the Bible have something in common with lace on dresses or double-breasted suits; over the course of the last couple of centuries, the mania will climb, reach a peak, then recede into the background, consigned to the cutout bin of life, to be picked up, brushed off, and brought to rousing life once more by a new generation with a fresh perspective.

The bare facts are simple. After two centuries of pride and power, the Templars went head to head with the dual forces that would destroy them — the Inquisition, and the man who used it as his chief weapon, Phillip IV, called Phillip the Fair, king of France, whose nickname definitely described his looks and not his ethics.

In the heresy trials that followed, the Templars were often accused of being *Cathars,* a form of Gnostic Christianity that was deemed a heresy by the Catholic Church. We explain Gnosticism in greater detail in Chapter 14, but speaking simply, the Gnostics were dualists, believing that the world was a place of tension between good and evil, light and darkness. The Templar Code may best be defined in the same way — a dual ethic, with two meanings: the decidedly unspiritual violence of the warrior knights on the one side, contrasted with the devoutly spiritual nature of religious life as monks on the other. The most common image signifying the Templar Knights was that of two Templars, armed for battle and riding the same horse together (see Figure 1-1). It was the perfect shorthand for both their fierceness in fighting, and the vow of poverty they lived by.

Christopher Hodapp

You'd be hard pressed to find a more important and enduring myth in the Christian West than that of King Arthur, his Table Round, and the quest of his knights for the Holy Grail. The Templars were always another pillar of Western mythology, side by side with the Holy Grail legends. The two fables cross constantly along the way, and the many parallels between the Templars and the story of Arthur and the Grail, the parable of a man's reach exceeding his grasp, may explain, at least in part, the continuing hold of the noble Templar legend on the Western imagination, seven centuries after the destruction of the Order.

And then Dan Brown wrote a book called *The Da Vinci Code,* and people's perceptions of the Knights Templar, and just about everything in their world, changed almost overnight. The Templars were described as sinister gray eminences, dark powers behind the throne, keepers of the true Grail, the most dangerous secret of Christianity. Nowadays, truth can be almost anticlimactic. Yet the truth of the Templars is anything but a bore. It's a story of the highest in the land brought low by greed and envy, of Crusader knights and Islamic warlords, of secret rituals, torture and self-sacrifice, and mysteries that still beguile the historians of the Middle Ages and beyond.

Right now, we're living in a time when interest in the Templars is at an all-time high, and the reason for it is the intriguing way that all these mysteries, and many more, weave in and out of one another, touching, drifting apart, and then coming together again: Templars, the Grail, the Gnostic Gospels, the Dead Sea Scrolls, the Spear of Destiny, the heresy of Mary Magdalene as the wife of Jesus — they're all tied to one another, with all the same players, in all the same events. The Templar story begins 900 years ago.

The Poor Fellow-Soldiers of Christ and of the Temple of Solomon

Yep, that's the full name of the Knights Templar. This name changes here and there, depending on the translation. Obviously, St. Bernard and the others who gave the order this final moniker wanted to make sure that everything about them but their shoe size was reflected in their title.

The Temple of Solomon

The origin of the temple that makes up the name of the Templars is King Solomon's Temple, described in the Old Testament books of 2 Chronicles and 1 Kings. It was believed to have been constructed in approximately 1,000 B.C. by the wise Solomon, son of King David.

The temple was the most magnificent monument to man's faith constructed during the biblical era. Its innermost sanctuary, the *Sanctum Sanctorum,* was built to hold the Ark of the Covenant, which contained the sacred words of God — the tablets Moses was given that contained the Ten Commandments. (The temple complex occupied what is known as the Temple Mount in Jerusalem, dominated by the Islamic Dome of the Rock; see the first image in this sidebar). It was destroyed by the Babylonians in 586 B.C.

Israel images / Alamy

A second temple (see the second image in this sidebar) was rebuilt on the same spot by Zerubbabel in 516 B.C. after the Jews had been released by the Babylonians 70 years before. This Temple was of a slightly different design and was extensively renovated and enlarged by King Herod the Great in 19 B.C. (This is the temple that Jesus threw the moneylenders out of, described in Matthew 21.) The Second Temple was destroyed by the Romans in A.D. 70 during the Jewish rebellion.

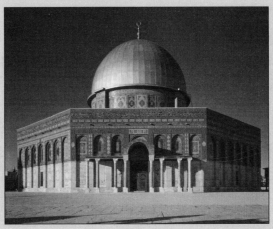

Scala / Art Resource, NY

The Templars were granted the area of Jerusalem's Temple Mount, former site of King Solomon's Temple (see the nearby sidebar "The Temple of Solomon") as their Holy Land headquarters. This is where the term *Templar* originated.

The Templars soon had a nickname, simply the Order of the Temple. Then later came Knights Templar, as well as White Knights, Poor Knights, and just plain Templars.

Defining knighthood

Templar Knights started life simply as knights. The word *knight* carries with it so much mythological baggage that it may seem a ridiculous question, but just what is a knight, anyway?

You probably think you know all about knighthood, because you've seen Sean Connery, Orlando Bloom, and Heath Ledger each play one. Well, actually, if you have, then you do already know quite a lot. The Hollywood treatment of knighthood and its rituals has been right more often than it's been wrong, which is an amazing thing from an industry known the world over for its cavalier contempt for historical accuracy.

Roman origins

The concept of knighthood is an old one. The word itself — whether it was *knight* in English, *chevalier* in French, or *ritter* in German — simply means a cavalry warrior, one who did battle from the back of a horse instead of clomping along in the mud with the infantry. In the beginning, this didn't necessarily make him a person of higher rank than an infantryman. The cavalry warriors of the Roman army were called *equitatae,* a pretty squishy word that just means "mounted."

The medieval knight

The cavalry knight of the Middle Ages grew into a powerful force as the centuries passed. And the knight was inseparable from the feudal system in which he lived. As with everything else in Europe, Rome had a hand in the creation of the feudal system. This feudalism, from its very inception, was essentially a contract. The knight and his own vassals made various promises to their lord, to pay taxes or to serve him in wartime for a certain number of days each year, often 40 days, while the lord also made various promises.

Knights were proud and powerful men, with squires and servants, and so on, but their influence shouldn't be overstated. Where the feudal chain of power was concerned, knights were close to the bottom, at least at first. A *knight errant* was a knight who had no lands, a little higher than a paid mercenary. For the knight errant, his first goal was to gain lands in battle, and he fought in the hope of being granted a fief by his overlord in gratitude for services rendered. Eventually, this knightly rank and vow of service became hereditary, and with these inherited titles came land and greater privileges.

A strange development in the history of knighthood was that these warriors, who were not necessarily of noble birth or great wealth, were great military leaders. As a result, the nobility became envious of this "lower class" of men, and became knights themselves. Later orders of knights, Templars included, always preferred their knights to be at least the petty nobility to be a part of their groups, to lend them greater prestige. By this time, sons of earls, dukes, and even kings proudly bore the title of *knight.* Eventually, it made economic sense for the nobility to be knights — it was an expensive way of life to buy horses and equipment, and working slobs didn't have the kind of leisure hours needed to train themselves for battle.

The decline of the knight

After the fall of Rome, battle tactics changed quite a bit in the following centuries. With the development of body armor, a mounted knight became a far more powerful adversary than a much larger number of men on foot, and knights formed the power core of armies in the way foot soldiers once had. Socially, the feudal system lingered for centuries. But the real end of knighthood, military knighthood, came with changing military tactics. More than any other factor, the development of greater speed, power, and accuracy in the bow and arrow would spell the doom of the knight in the field.

Flipping the bird: The sign of victory

Like many coarse and vulgar Americanisms that have gone worldwide, if you travel in England, you'll see people from cabbies to pub brawlers use a classic American gesture of defiance — arm extended, fist closed, middle finger pointing in solitary contempt into the air. But this is a relatively recent development, the U.S. pollution of a much funnier British hand gesture. As late as *The Benny Hill Show* or the terrifically funny *Carry On* movies of the 1960s, you see the British using their own, centuries-old method of "flicking thine enemy the royal bird." The English version looked more like a victory sign — once more, arm extended, fist in the air, but with two fingers up, the index and middle finger. This gesture has a noble, if mythical, history. In several battles with the French, the British military discovered that their most valuable force against a superior number of mounted knights was their skilled archers. The technology of armor-piercing arrows was getting better all the time. And so, the government unleashed a program of training the peasantry in archery, with prizes awarded, clubs formed, and such, to try to make it fun, as well as a point of national pride. They succeeded. All across England, at dusk on the village green after the day's work was done, men practiced their archery, every day. At the Battle of Agincourt in 1415, British archers as a military force reached their peak of rapid fire, power, and skill, bringing down thousands of French mounted knights and winning a battle in which they had been greatly outnumbered.

Consequently, the French cooked up a counteroffensive. Whenever a British foot soldier was captured in battle, the first two fingers of his right hand were amputated, so that he could never again draw a bow. For centuries afterward, when British soldiers wanted to razz the enemy, they would raise their two fingers high up into the air, with a "you didn't get *mine,* you froggy so-and-so" attitude, usually accompanied by colorful raspberries and shouts about the morals of the French soldiers' mothers. During the dark days of the Blitz in World War II, when Hitler's rockets rained down on London, killing thousands, it became, once more, a treasured symbol of British defiance. That's the legend, anyway.

By the late 16th century and the development of field artillery, the warrior knight of the Middle Ages was already more of a mythic figure than an effective force on the battlefield. Though some still rode horses and wore armor, and hereditary knighthood continued to be passed from father to son, the legendary knights of the crusading period were already the stuff of moldy tapestries and mythic tales.

Defining monasticism

Monasticism grew out of an idea as old as knighthood. In even the most ancient pagan faiths, there were legends of monks and hermits, men who separated themselves from society, living in caves or the out of doors, in order to achieve a closer relationship to the spiritual. Despite the fact that monks live in communities, the word *monasticism* comes from the Greek word *monachos*, which means "living alone," in reference to these lone hermits who inspired it. Not just Christianity, but Hinduism, Buddhism, Taoism, and Jainism (a peaceful Indian sect of ascetics) all practice monasticism. Organized Christian monasticism goes back at least as far as the fourth century. As the ideal picked up speed, it formed into the more common orders we know today — the Benedictines, the Franciscans, the Dominicans, and so on. But the name of the game was the same for all. Though each order had its own character, patron saint, and principle type of devotion (as in aiding the sick, teaching, or being strictly a "contemplative" order, devoted to prayer), all monks lived a bare and vigorous existence.

Both jobs — knight and monk — were definitely enough to keep you busy. They were also about as opposite in their goals, actions, and beliefs as two occupations could be; monks were not even allowed to carry a weapon, no matter how dangerous was the pagan territory they were sent into to spread the gospel to the barbarians, mostly the descendants of the Visigoths and Huns who'd brought down the might of Rome. Nevertheless, rather than fight, monks were expected to die for their faith if necessary. Moreover, they were expected to die well, because first impressions are so important where nonbelievers are concerned.

Warrior Monks: Their Purpose

What made the Knights Templar unique in history was that they decided to take on both obligations, knight *and* monk. They would be warriors for God, sworn to a life of poverty, chastity, and obedience. It was a startlingly new concept to the Christian West, and there was a great deal of resistance to it at first. But the idea seized the imagination of the charismatic figure of the Cistercian Order, St. Bernard of Clairvaux, who pushed it through the ecclesiastical bureaucracy.

And so, by papal command, the Order of the Poor Knights of Christ and the Temple of Solomon was born. They were also given, in a series of papal bulls, powers and privileges that had never before been extended to any single arm of the Church. (A *papal bull* is an official statement-of-position document issued by a pope, named for the *bulla,* or round wax seal, affixed to the document.) The Templars were, in effect, now answerable only to the pope in everything they did. But, like most things in life, that power came with a price.

In the recent wave of books and movies featuring Templars, one thing seems to come across above all else: They were loaded. Everyone seems to know that there's a lost Templar treasure out there. But this had nothing to do with the way a Knight Templar lived in the day to day. In the Middle Ages, faith was woven into the fabric of life in a way that would be nearly impossible to explain to the modern, secular mind. Only the life of a person in a religious cult would come close, and even that is a flawed comparison. In this medieval world of faith, laymen gave up all sorts of things for the sake of their belief in

God. Monks, priests, and nuns gave up a great deal more: love, marriage, children, freedom, luxury, and any sort of self-indulgence, down to the smallest, most inconsequential comforts.

But few gave up more for the sake of his faith than a Knight Templar. We discuss the daily life of a Templar in more detail in Chapter 4, but for the time being, suffice it to say that the wealth belonged to the order and most decidedly *not* to any individual knight. At that time, the holiest of men and women lived a life of *asceticism,* a constant state of self-denial. The quantity and quality of food was extremely limited; the Templars were allowed the luxury of meat three times a week on the theory that, as fighting men, they needed it. But eating it wasn't much fun — for monks, nuns, and Templars, meals were taken in silence, generally while scripture was being read. The monastic day was roughly divided into four-hour sections, called the Liturgical Hours, or the divine office, the seven Catholic hours being *Matins, Lauds, Vespers, Terce, Sext, None,* and *Compline.* Each one represented another trip to chapel, for Mass or prayers or readings from Scripture and the Church fathers. Even a good night's sleep was interrupted for a trip to the chapel to pray. No personal possessions were allowed under any circumstances; all that these people owned were the clothes on their back. Visits to and from family were discouraged, because it tied a person to his old life. A Templar was even expected to have light in his private chamber at all times, to prevent even the accusation of hanky-panky.

Some other monastic orders had stricter rules for daily life, but they certainly weren't risking their lives in battle. Along with giving up a wife and children, possessions, and freedom, Templars were also expected to give up their lives fighting for the faith. A Templar was not allowed to retire from the battlefield, even to regroup, unless the enemy had a three-to-one superiority. Whenever Crusader knights went into battle, the highest casualty rates were always among the Templars.

There were perks, of course, here and there, particularly for the officers of a commandery. In the Holy Land, there were few higher in the new kingdom of Jerusalem than the Grand Master of the Knights Templar. He advised the court in all matters — foreign, domestic, and military. The Templars walked with popes and kings, their courage and their honesty never questioned, which is what made their breakneck fall from grace so much more shocking.

A vow of nine crusader knights

We cover the concept of pilgrimage in more detail in Chapter 2. Here, we must explain one thing: The other two major monotheistic faiths — Judaism and Islam — both practiced the obligation of pilgrimage to holy places. Although pilgrimage isn't written down in Christian ritual, it was no less important to medieval believers. Almost since the beginning, pilgrimage was considered a way to save a soul in peril. And Jerusalem was ground zero for Christians, the holiest of holies. Medieval mapmakers referred to it as the "navel of the earth," the center of all things. When the Holy Land was in the hands of the Christian Byzantine Empire, this was no problem. The roads were hazardous, yet people generally got there alive. But when the property was stolen by waves of Islamic Seljuq Turks in the 11th century, pilgrims were risking life and limb to get there. They were attacked on the road constantly, not only by the Turks, but by various unsavory bands of thieves and cutthroats. Going in groups didn't help; the brigands were a lot tougher than the people who had come to pray at the Church of the Holy Sepulchre.

After the First Crusade, Jerusalem was back in the hands of Christians for the first time in four centuries. But afterward, the majority of the knights went home, back to their feudal obligations. There were barely enough men to garrison the city; there were none to protect the countryside.

One lone knight of Champagne named Hugues de Payens decided that there was something gravely wrong here. What good did it do to take back the Holy Land, if it was still too dangerous a place for pilgrims to visit? With the help of his brother in arms Godfrey de St. Omer of Picardy, they gathered together seven more knights, probably in the year 1119, and vowed to patrol the road from the coast to Jerusalem, in order to protect the Christian pilgrims. What made this vow remarkable — absolutely unprecedented in Christian history, in fact — was that they promised to live as monks as well. Theirs was the holiest of missions, and they decided that the drinking, whoring, and brawling of the typical knight was not appropriate for them. Instead, they voluntarily chose to live by the monastic rule, swearing poverty, chastity, and obedience, on top of the vow to put their lives on the line each day to see Christian pilgrims safely to Jerusalem.

The Templar order grew, though we have no figures from such an early period. They applied for official recognition from King Baldwin of Jerusalem, which he granted eagerly, offering them the plum quarters of the Al-Aqsa Mosque on the Temple Mount, just opposite his own palace. The Christians did not call this place Al-Aqsa, but rather the Temple of Solomon. From here came the various legends of the Temple of Solomon that would forever be associated with their name.

Don't leave home without it: The Templars' role as international bankers

After a time, the Templars decided that simply protecting pilgrims physically wasn't quite enough. Anything that they did to make the whole process easier was an act of grace. And the biggest problem pilgrims had was making safe passage carrying the money they needed to cover them for the long period of time that they'd be gone from home.

The Templars also became something of a travel agency for pilgrims, recommending routes and carriers, offering aid for injured or lost travelers, and even providing security vaults in which pilgrims could store their most precious valuables until they returned. Even kings availed themselves of this service; King John of England once gave over the Crown Jewels to the Templars for safekeeping, during one of the many and various periods in which he felt his position on the throne to be a bit shaky.

Templar banking was born, and it was a godsend to knights and pilgrims traveling such a distance. Out of it was created the West's first international banking system, a system not dissimilar from the one we have today.

Templars could help a Christian who wanted to mortgage his property to pay for his journey, giving him the cash, and then setting up various holding companies to help insure for the knight on Crusade that he didn't find his property bought out from underneath him before his return.

Say, for example, that you've decided to go on a pilgrimage to Jerusalem. You're probably going to be gone at least a year. No matter how simply you travel, you're going to need access to funds on your journey, and particularly on your arrival. But the state of the roads to Jerusalem, not to mention the routes by ship, with the toughs and uglies hanging out at the docks, would make carrying your money on your person an unbelievably stupid thing to do. With the help of the Knights Templar, a pilgrim could travel with relatively little cold hard cash in his money belt. He could deposit his money at his local Templar commandery or preceptory, which were the Templar centers of Europe and the Near East. At the height of their power, there were an astounding 9,000 of Templar properties in Europe alone (although, admittedly, not all were preceptories). After making the deposit, a pilgrim was given a check. On the way to the Holy Land, he could present this check at any Templar preceptory and withdraw some or all his money.

They were definitely a full-service bank, and it's easy to see from these services that the Templars very soon found themselves indispensable in the day-to-day lives of nobles, merchants, and landowners in the 12th and 13th centuries. And as the *Crusader States* (the four Latin states founded by the Crusaders in the Holy Land at the beginning of the 12th century) became a fixture in the Near East, the Templars were there, negotiating, brokering treaties, helping the kings of Europe to deal with the Saracens who seemed so alien to them. The Templars knew the language and the culture of Islam, and they got very buddy-buddy with many Muslims as the centuries passed. Too buddy-buddy, according to the Inquisition, who used the Templars' knowledge of Eastern customs and faiths to build a case that their pure Christian faith had been "tainted" by this exposure to the infidel. Chapter 5 features a detailed discussion of this business of the "Syrianization" of the Frankish knights, and even more so of the Templars, a process that occurred over two centuries of contact with the exotic cultures of the East.

Builders

Last but far from least, the Templars were builders. Many of their European preceptories were acquired properties, farms, and manor houses willed to them by the devout. But along the frontiers in Palestine, in Spain, and even in the Baltic, the Templars built magnificent commanderies to hold the Christian borders against the Muslims. These commanderies were like cities, and they had it all — chapel, armory, barracks, training grounds and classrooms, as well as equipment for fortification.

Although some of the commanderies are no longer in existence, many still stand, like Tomar in Portugal or Atlit in Syria. They are a testament to Templar skill as architects and masons. In fact, one of the more common theories linking the Freemasons to the Templars is the fact that Templars had the best stonemasons in the world working for them, and Freemasonry grew out of the great medieval guilds of the stonemasons. Countless other secret societies throughout history have either been accused of being Templars, or have proudly claimed a tie that may or may not exist. (For more on these various theories of Templars in other secret societies, turn to Chapter 8.)

Templars in Battle

The Grand Master of the Knights Templar was a very important man in the war councils of the Kingdom of Jerusalem, as well as the other three Crusader States. The Crusader armies organized in Western Europe were a motley crew — true feudal knights in service to a crusading lord; the peasant vassals underneath them, who knew little of war but were tossed in to flesh out the troops; paid mercenaries in the service of the particular king or warlord on Crusade; and last but not least, the sea of pilgrims who drifted into the Holy Land during all the Crusades, the least militarily skilled of all. Men literally dropped by the local Crusader holdings in places like Acre after their arrival in Palestine, to see if they could pitch in and help for a few months, as if it were a barn raising. The Templars, with their skill and courage, were the cream at the top, as well as the glue that held this chaotic assortment together.

The legend of Templar superiority on the battlefield was no myth. In 1177, King Baldwin IV of Jerusalem and a force of 500 troops were pinned down by the Muslim warrior Saladin's army of 26,000. A contingent of just 80 Templars arrived to assist Baldwin. Through surprise and shrewd battle tactics, the Christian forces attacked Saladin at Montgisard. Saladin was forced to retreat with less than 3,000 of his soldiers left. The Templars were revered for their policy of being the first to take up the battle and the last to retreat.

The Templars, and the Frankish knights in general, depended more than anything else on the tactic of the mass charge, "the irresistible first shock," as it was described by chronicler Anna Comnenus, daughter of the Byzantine emperor. Unfortunately, it wasn't the well-ordered charge of our own times. The Turks were lighter and quicker, as well as being excellent horsemen. In other words, if the target of the charge could get out of the way quickly enough, the charge could degenerate into a disorganized mob moving too quickly to be reined in, like a Roman candle that couldn't be called back. When that happened, the enemy was often able to encircle the knights for a counterattack. The charge had to be timed just right, so that it routed the main body of the enemy, and not a phony one deployed to draw them in. If it did so, it was usually devastating. The infamous Frankish charge was feared throughout the Near East, and the Templars were usually in the lead.

The most annoyingly effective Muslim tactic was to use their first-rate horsemen, quick and lightly armed for mobility, to harass the enemy while the enemy was on the march. This could go on for days at a time. The Turks loved to attack from the rear, a very effective ploy until the Templars began organizing lines with a powerful rear guard. The men hated the harassing rain of arrows that came, they said, like flies to cause them misery. There is evidence that, as time passed, the Templars moved forward with attempts to refashion the Christian army with some Eastern tactics. It's a shame so many of the crusader kings were suspicious of the Templars and their "foreign ideas," obstinately marching off their own way to destruction.

Betrayed, Excommunicated, and Hunted

There is one more generality about the Templars that is often tossed about, and that's the simple fact that, with the loss of the last Christian possessions in the Middle East, usually dated at the fall of the city of Acre in 1291, the Knights Templar had lost their raison d'être, the purpose for which they were formed. The problem with this theory is that, by that time, at the end of the 13th century, the Templars had undergone quite a metamorphosis, from a small band of fanatical Crusaders, to an unimaginably huge and influential organization of international bankers and diplomatic middlemen who had military commanderies and preceptories from London to the Slavic countries of the East, and all throughout the Mediterranean basin.

Yet, there's no denying the fact that as the gilded luster wore off the Crusades, they became an investment in money and blood that the nations of Europe were no longer willing to make, because they were back to their old habits of making war against each other back home. It probably seemed to the Templars' enemies to be just the right time to bring the Poor Knights to heel — and to steal their vast wealth in the process.

So where'd everybody go?

It's true — after the order was outlawed by Pope Clement V in 1312, the Templars did drop off the radar map of history. As for where they went, it probably wasn't the same place for all of them. Many people offered refuge, such as the kings of Spain and Portugal, who created knightly orders to fight the Moors on the Iberian peninsula that strictly existed as a refuge for Templar knights. If Phillip the Fair didn't want these skilled warriors, the kings of Aragon and Navarre certainly did.

But there are dozens of theories about where the rest of the Templars went, and where the vast resources of their international operation disappeared to. Chapter 7 discusses the lost Templar treasure, which probably isn't lost at all, and presents several pretty disappointing answers for what probably happened to it. But that doesn't end the mystery. The Templar treasure of legend was the contents of the Templar commandery in Paris, their home office, as it were. The Templars were predominantly French knights; they became the virtual treasury of the French government in 1165. But there were lots of other commanderies and lots of other treasures, and all vanished without a trace. Chapter 17 takes a look at where some of the swag may have gone, so get out your shovel and your metal detector, and take a look.

The riddle of Templar symbols

Like all special, secret, or elite organizations or brotherhoods, the Templars had a wide variety of symbols and codes that helped to bind them together, as well as to hold them apart from the commonality. At places throughout this book, we discuss Templar secrets and rituals, but for now, here are two of the most common Templar symbols: the Dual Knights (see Figure 1-2) and the Chi-Rho Cross (see Figure 1-3).

Figure 1-2:
The symbol of the Dual Knights.

Scala / Art Resource, NY

Figure 1-3:
The Chi-Rho Cross, or *labarum,* made up of the first two letters in the Greek word for Christ.

There is no question that, for a Templar, the symbol of the Dual Knights was the most important one to the Order, and the oldest. Other symbols changed over the years; this one did not. It was a seal (upon which the statue in Figure 1-1 was based) picturing two knights riding on one horse, a symbol of the poverty and brotherhood of the Order. Other medieval symbols, like the Tetragrammaton (the four Hebrew letters that symbolized the unspeakable name of God; see Figure 1-4) or the Chi-Rho Cross would be used by other organizations. But if you see two medieval knights on one horse, you're looking at a Templar artifact.

Figure 1-4:
The Hebrew Tetragrammaton, the unspeakable name of God.

All legends aside, the Cross that Constantine saw in the sky just before battle that converted him to Christianity was the Chi-Rho (pronounced like the Egyptian city Cairo) Cross. It consists of an *X* overlaid with a skinny *P* inside, often surrounded by a round or oval cartouche. Though the cross we know today was already taking over, the Chi-Rho Cross remained very popular with Templars. The Chi-Rho also flourished once again by the Renaissance. The symbol comes from the first two Greek letters in the word *Christ;* it's sometimes called the *labarum,* the word for the banner Constantine carried into battle that bore this icon. Other Christian symbols used similar logic, such as the IHS or IHC symbol, from the first three Greek letters in the name *Jesus.* The most famous organization that uses the Chi-Rho Cross today is the Jesuits of the Catholic Church.

Templars in the 21st Century

Thanks to a wide variety of books and films, the Templars live on, almost as vibrantly as they did in the Victorian era, when the fascination with them was at its peak. As always, the Templars are tied to that other myth known to every English schoolboy, the Holy Grail. The Templars were the Grail knights, and as Grail theories change over the centuries, the outlook on the Templars changed along with it.

Templars and the Grail quest

To tell the truth, despite humanity's fascination with the Grail, it had sort of gone out of fashion in the last few decades. From medieval troubadours to Celtic bards, Victorian poets to Hitler's SS, many and various cultures have had a love affair with the Grail. But the post–World War II generation seemed to look on it as a relic of the distant past. John Boorman's sumptuously gorgeous film *Excalibur* was the last time that a big money movie took the Grail legends seriously, instead of putting some post-modern occult twist on the story, or playing it for straight comedy, Monty Python–style. Those with a special interest in medieval history, or in the occult, as with the growing community of Wiccans and New Agers, have always had a special fascination with the Grail. But for the most part, it wasn't a very popular myth anymore.

Then *The Da Vinci Code* shambled into your nearest bookstore, and suddenly, without any PR behind it, the book was a smash, and the Grail was all over the place again, as it has been so many times in the past. That's the measure of a truly great myth: It may wax and wane, but it's always there to be picked up and reinterpreted for a new generation. Right now, amateur history buffs, seasoned archeologists, and various university- and privately-funded associations are questing for the Grail as never before. And many of them are convinced that the key to the discovery of the Grail lies in the history of the Templars, the Cathars, and many other organizations featured in this book.

Templars and the fringe

Yes, we know. We're going to get called "judgmental," "close-minded," and "dogmatic," not to mention the ever-popular "blinded by orthodoxy." Or perhaps just willing stooges of the new world order. But we may just as well come right out and say it — the Knights Templar and the lunatic fringe have had a love affair going on for years. The birth of the Templar cock-and-bull industry occurred in 1798, with the publication of a book by a Frenchman named Cadet de Gassicout, called *The Tomb of Jacques Molay.* De Gassicourt, like everyone else in France, was standing amid the blood-soaked wreckage left behind after the French Revolution, trying to figure out how it all happened. There just had to be *somebody* to blame. Finding a scapegoat is, in essence, what de Gassicourt did.

Thanks a lot, Sir Walter Scott

Dan Brown's *The Da Vinci Code* is only the latest book to create renewed interest in the Knights Templar. Another book, written two centuries ago, almost single-handedly rescued the Templars from obscurity. Unfortunately, it cast the order in a less than admirable light.

Sir Walter Scott's *Ivanhoe* (1819) told the tale of Richard the Lionheart's return to England from the Crusades, and the evil plotting of his brother John to keep him off the throne. The story revolves around the character of Wilfred of Ivanhoe, a knight who was on Crusade with Richard, and his rival Brian de Bois-Guilbert, a decidedly impious Templar knight.

Ivanhoe was unimaginably popular in England and the United States in the early 1800s. Apart from creating the modern legend of the character of Robin Hood, the book created an international mania for all things medieval, and was instrumental in spreading the cultural movement of Romanticism in literature. It was unquestionably responsible, in part, for the profusion of fraternal orders that sprang up all around the world in the 1800s, patterning themselves after medieval knights.

The American satirist Mark Twain was less than enthusiastic. In his 1883 memoir *Life On The Mississippi,* Twain places the blame of the U.S. Civil War firmly at the feet of Sir Walter Scott and *Ivanhoe.* According to Twain, Scott

> set the world in love with dreams and phantoms; with decayed and swinish forms of religion; with decayed and degraded systems of government; with the sillinesses and emptinesses, sham grandeurs, sham gauds, and sham chivalries of a brainless and worthless long-vanished society. He did measureless harm; more real and lasting harm, perhaps, than any other individual that ever wrote.

Absolutely everyone read *Ivanhoe,* and its tales of the knights so enthralled Southern society with its lofty titles of nobility and florid prose that it truly did affect the writing, speech, and social attitudes of the Southern aristocracy. Twain railed that Scott's influence

> made every gentleman in the South a Major or a Colonel, or a General or a Judge, before the war; and it was he, also, that made these gentlemen value these bogus decorations. For it was he that created . . . reverence for rank and caste, and pride and pleasure in them. . . . Sir Walter had so large a hand in making Southern character, as it existed before the war, that he is in great measure responsible for the war.

Scott followed *Ivanhoe* with *The Talisman* (1825), which told the tale of King Richard in the Holy Land. A key character was the wise, virtuous, moral, and heroic Muslim warrior, Saladin (see Chapter 5). As in *The Da Vinci Code,* the facts didn't get in the way of a good story — again, the Templars were made the bad guys. Scott's fictional version of the Crusades, in which the 11th-century Muslims are kind, peace-loving pacifists attacked by thickheaded, brutish, kill-crazy Christians has enraged historians for almost 200 years, yet it influences popular perceptions to this day.

For men like de Gassicourt, who thought of themselves as being civilized, finding someone to blame was essential, just so they could all go on looking into the shaving mirror every morning. De Gassicourt found his scapegoat in two places — the Templars and the Freemasons. Actually, as far as he was concerned, it was one place — they were, in his mind, one and the same. His theory was that the Templars, excommunicated and scattered, spent five centuries plotting their vengeance on the French crown. To get it, they founded the brotherhood of the Freemasons, and then awaited their opportunity to kill the king and take their vengeance, raining death on thousands of Frenchmen in the process. Contrived, unfounded, unprovable, and, for want of a better term, daffy, it nevertheless captured the imagination of a large portion of the public, that portion that had always had suspicions about the secret brotherhood of the Freemasons. The books came thick and fast throughout the 19th century, following in de Gassicourt's footsteps. They were all very popular.

Which brings us to the present, and a dynamic that hasn't changed much in two centuries. The books out there with wacko theories about the Templars could fill a warehouse, running the gamut in their absurd conjecture, from Templars using a "death ray" from the Ark of the Covenant to win the Battle of Bannockburn for the Scots, to the Templars as shape-shifting reptilian aliens, left here eons ago by visitors from another planet. The shame of it is that the work of serious historians like Malcolm Barber, Stephen Dafoe, and Helen Nicholson can get lost in this avalanche of horse manure. So, when interesting speculation exists, as in books like *Holy Blood, Holy Grail* or *The Templar Revelation,* we present this information *as speculation.* As for the rest, it gets mentioned once in a while. You know, just for laughs.

Chapter 2

A Crash Course in Crusading

In This Chapter

▶ Uncomplicating the Byzantine: Discovering the causes of the Crusades

▶ Introducing the medieval Y1K crisis

▶ Nation-building in the Holy Land

▶ Counting till you run out of fingers: Crusading by the numbers

*Y*ou can't understand the Templars without understanding the upheaval that gave them birth: the Crusades. This series of wars isn't just the stuff of dusty history books. The Crusades are featured in today's newspaper on a fairly regular basis.

After the attacks of 9/11, one former and one sitting U.S. president each put a very large foot in their even larger mouths, and both on the very same day. George W. Bush made the blunder of referring to the war on terrorism as a "crusade," while Bill Clinton felt compelled to "apologize" for the Crusades, which had occurred four centuries before Columbus set foot in America. Both were chastised, but not nearly hard enough.

The Catholic pope was the juiciest target of all, when he made a pretty boring speech in September 2006 on "reason and faith." In his address, Pope Benedict XVI quoted from a lot of sources. Unfortunately, one was a 14th-century Byzantine emperor named Manuel II, repeating part of his conversation with an unnamed "learned Persian," on the subject of Islam's practice of conversion by force, forbidden in early Islam, but encouraged later during periods of conquest. The pope quoted it to show just how old the argument is, that faith can't be forced, but must come from reason. In his own glue-footed way, he was getting his licks in against the free-thinkers of the 18th-century Enlightenment, two centuries too late. But the quoted put-down of the Muslim faith set off a firestorm of protest in the world of fundamentalist Islam, with imams from Cairo to Mogadishu calling for the pope's head, literally.

All this brouhaha over wars that happened nine centuries ago seems incomprehensible to Americans; we have a hard time remembering who was vice president in the last administration. This chapter clarifies some of the vague facts you may know, and lets slip some startling ones you may not, about the series of wars between East and West, between Muslim and Christian, that history calls the Crusades.

Getting a Handle on the Crusades

The dictionary says that any "vigorous cause," taken in concert to end an injustice or abuse, is a crusade. But historically, the word *crusade* generally means any war of the Christian West to gain control of the Holy City of Jerusalem, as well as other sites associated with the life of Jesus Christ. For most people, some very definite images come to mind when they think of the Crusades — some true, and some the product of myths and movies. The real Crusades, the ones closest to that image, lasted about two centuries, from 1096, until the loss of the last Crusader possessions in Syria in 1291.

The First Crusade is pretty easy to understand, but as the centuries unfolded, the Crusades became more complicated. Historians can't even seem to agree on how many Crusades there were, or how many years the crusading impulse lasted. Sir Stephen Runciman, the respected medieval scholar, sets the number at five in his three-book history of the Crusades. But some say there were really only four. Other say six, and still others go as high as eight. Sir Stephen dates the end of the Crusades as 1291, with the fall of the city of Acre, the last Crusader possession in the Holy Land. But some historians claim that the Crusades didn't end until the late 14th century, and others contend they went on into the 16th and 17th centuries, right up to the doorstep of the Age of Enlightenment.

So, if the chaotic jumble of the Crusades has always confused you, reading this chapter should make you sound like a pro to family, friends, and history professors alike. The first part of the chapter covers the cultural forces that led to crusading. The second part explains the whys and the wherefores of the very important First Crusade, and of the seven Crusades that followed. Or the six. Or maybe the four. At any rate, dive in and get the straight facts on the Crusades — all of them. Sir Stephen would be proud of you.

So, what is a crusade anyway? Is a crusade any war between the Christian West and the Islamic East, or is it something more? For some historians, it's like the infield-fly rule in baseball: Only an umpire can call that batter out. And only a pope can proclaim a real and legitimate Holy Crusade.

Oddly enough, Islam has the same problem, today more than ever before. It's a similar muddle resulting from definitions — just who has the right to declare jihad, when, and why? *Jihad* is something of an abused word. It simply means "struggle" — sometimes an inner, spiritual one; sometimes an outer struggle against an enemy. Nowadays, when people hear the word *jihad,* they think of an Islamic declaration of war against the West, the Muslim version of a Crusade. And when they hear the word *fatwa,* they think of a Muslim cleric putting out a hit on someone, like author Salman Rushdie, who's been deemed an enemy of the faith, despite the fact that a *fatwa* is simply a declaration of canon law, something like a papal bull. At one time, the real power to proclaim a *fatwa* or a *jihad* generally lay with the sultan of the Ottoman Empire and his religious leader, the Mufti of Istanbul. (The Byzantine capital of Constantinople was renamed Istanbul by its conqueror and sultan, Mehmed II, in 1453.) Until the fall of the Ottoman Empire during World War I, the overwhelming majority of the world's Muslims lived in the empire or one of its client states.

Simply defined, the Crusades were a group of military campaigns that began late in the 11th century, sanctioned by popes and conducted in the name of Christianity. The original goal of the Crusades was to protect the Christian Eastern Orthodox Empire of Byzantium from invading Muslim forces, and to recapture Jerusalem and the Holy Land from Islamic forces who had invaded and captured the city in A.D. 638.

A Snapshot of the 11th Century

To comprehend the domino theory that led tens of thousands of European Christians to wake up one morning and set off on a 10,000-mile stroll to the Holy Land and back, you need to understand how society was set up at the time. The whole idea of crusading may strike our modern minds as being pretty barbaric, not to mention bloodthirsty and arrogant. But the Crusades, as well as the political, spiritual, and military issues that gave birth to them, are way too complicated to be dismissed with a quick hipshot.

Of course, looking at the key players and the main events, there's plenty of ignorance, fanaticism, and brutality to go around. However, in the case of the fanatical and brutal Crusades, lots of things were going on at the dawn of the 11th century that seemed to lead the people of Europe, almost naturally, into this centuries-long conflict with the Islamic East.

Fealty, fiefs, and feudalism

At the dawn of the crusading era, Europe was organized in a *feudal system.* Feudalism is like a chain of command, an iron bond of what was called "fealty," rising up from the serfs, who did most of the work, all the way to the king.

Fealty comes from the Latin word for "faithfulness," and in essence that's what it means, though a better definition would be "obligation." In the feudal system, each man was a vassal to the knight or earl or duke above him, which meant that he owed his overlord the obligation of fealty — meaning taxes or tribute in time of peace, and men and weapons in time of war.

One of the effects of feudalism is that these self-same barons, earls, and dukes became petty princelings, with a great deal of power. This is the essential problem with the system, as far as building a nation is concerned. Feudalism created powerful lords and a central authority, usually a king, who often isn't quite powerful enough to control them — if there's a king around at all.

So, you've got petty wars between petty kingdoms, dukedoms, and fiefdoms; a lousy centralized government that can't create anything even resembling an infrastructure, like passable roads; and roving bands of lawless criminals and out-of-work mercenaries preying on anyone crazy enough to travel from one place to the next. It would seem that any king in 11th-century Europe would have enough to deal with without worrying about what was going on 5,000 miles away, yet the crusading impulse took root in the soil of feudalism.

Pilgrimage

In the 11th century, pilgrimage was hardly a new idea. Since very nearly the dawn of Christianity, the concept of pilgrimage had been an integral part of the faith. It was also occasionally a penance given to major sinners. You can only make someone repeat so many Hail Marys before the punishment loses its impact.

Though there were dozens of destinations for pilgrims, three were the most popular; clerics sometimes referred to them together as the *Axis Mundi,* the spiritual axis of the world:

  ✔ **Rome:** Rome is the home of the Holy See and of numberless Christian relics and sites, like the prison cell of St. Peter and the place where St. Paul was executed.

  ✔ **Santiago de Compostela:** This city in northwestern Spain was home to a chapel that contained the bones of St. James the Great, both an apostle and a Christian martyr. The city was sacked in 997 by the Umayyad vizier and general Muhammad Ibn Abu Amir al-Mansur, the commander of Moorish Córdoba, which did not endear the Muslims to the Christians of Europe.

  ✔ **Jerusalem:** The greatest pilgrimage site was Jerusalem; it was the centerpiece to all the holiest shrines of Christendom. It was also the hardest one to get to, so it was considered the most powerful balm for the soul of pilgrims.

This business of making pilgrimages was a serious one, particularly considering the fact that travel was so difficult and dangerous. "Roads" were little more than cattle tracks. The Romans had built far better ones, ten centuries before; in fact, many of these were still in use, despite being overgrown and in poor repair. Inns and monasteries, where food and a place to sleep could be had, were far apart and miserably uncomfortable. Plus, a thousand or so years ago, the trackless distances between towns were infested with wild animals, and travelers were in danger of attack from wolf packs, boars, and other even more unusual animals, such as *aurochs* (similar to buffalo, but with a nastier disposition). Worse than the savagery of the animal kingdom was the savagery of man, in the form of the pitiless thieves and cutthroats lurking around every bend and behind every stand of shrubbery.

The difficulty of travel makes it all the more remarkable that most of the pilgrims to Jerusalem and other holy sites were not wealthy, but rather were simple peasants, dressed in coarse brown wool, carrying all their worldly possessions in a gunnysack called a *scrip* slung over their shoulders, and usually holding a staff and wearing a simple wooden cross. They chose to make the journey for a wide variety of reasons. Sometimes they were seeking forgiveness for their own sins, and sometimes they were making the journey for a loved one whom they feared was in purgatory. Sometimes they were headed for a shrine to cure their own illness or that of a family member, and sometimes they were simply pious and devout, determined to see the site of Christ's crucifixion before their death.

The nobility, too, went on pilgrimages, although a bit more comfortably. Sometimes pilgrimage was their sentence of penance for their sins, as in the case of Count Fulk III ("the Black") of Anjou. The count had very much earned his dark nickname, having been a sinful man with many crimes on his conscience. When he reached middle age, and the grave yawned before him, he asked for a penance that would be the price of forgiveness for all his sins. Legend has it that he fainted when the sentence was passed. He was ordered to endure a *triple* Jerusalem pilgrimage, which was the worst thing his priest could come up with. He was forced to make the journey on foot, three times from France to Jerusalem, or a total of 15,300 miles. On his third arrival in the Holy City, barely able to stand, he was lashed through the streets of the Way of the Cross as a grand finale, dragged on by the monks each time he fell.

Along with the spiritual potency of a pilgrimage, the story of Fulk also highlights the power of the clergy, over high and low born. Even kings stood before the papal palace in sackcloth and ashes, sometimes for days on end, in the rain or snow if the pope were lucky, in order to have the dreadful judgment of excommunication lifted from them. They held in their hands the scissors and the rod, symbols that they were willing to be whipped or shorn, at the pope's pleasure. In the days before Martin Luther, you just didn't mess with Holy Mother Church.

Y1K: The end of days

The year A.D. 999 was a terrifying one for the Christians of the world. Respected theologians had been predicting for some time that the world would come to an end in the year A.D. 1000, which was precisely 1,000 years after the birth of Christ. Looking around themselves throughout the 900s, the virtuous saw a world packed to the brim with sin, violence, greed, and apostasy. A good deal of it was in the very bosom of the Church, with a line of popes throughout that century that were far worse than merely incompetent — they were downright heretical, Machiavellian, and unbelievably sinful. Between A.D. 872 and A.D. 1012, more than a third of those on the papal throne died violent deaths, usually at the hands of their successors. To the faithful, they were anti-Christs, masquerading as popes. It seemed clear that the world was mired in the "abomination of desolation" Jesus had spoken of in Matthew, a quote from the prophecy of Daniel concerning the signs pointing to the end of the world.

On the night of December 31, 999, Christians stood in frightened silence, filling St. Peter's in Rome inside and out, while Pope Sylvester II prepared a special midnight Mass. Many of the worshippers were face-down, their arms spread to form a cross, waiting for the end of the world. Women fainted, old men succumbed to bad hearts, and it was, in general, one of the darkest nights of the soul mankind has ever endured.

But the sun came up on January 1, as the sun has a habit of doing. Which, of course, brought on the time-lag two-step. Maybe it wasn't 1,000 years after the *birth* of Christ. Maybe it was 1,000 years after the *crucifixion* of Christ. Or maybe it was 1,000 years after the destruction of the temple in Jerusalem. Or maybe the numbers were out of whack because of the differences between the old Roman calendar and the present Julian calendar.

The upshot was that "millennial fever," the fear that the world would soon end, lagged on throughout the tenth century, and on into the 11th. Perhaps a quick stroll down memory lane, to New Year's Eve of 1999, will make it a little easier to understand the general aura of fear and unease during the millennium. After all, times change, but people don't. Come on, you remember the hysteria over Y2K. The headlines ran the gamut, from warnings that folks might have a little trouble accessing their bank accounts by ATM, to terrifying predictions of nuclear apocalypse. In the United States, the authorities tried hard to keep a level head in public, but their advice on what to do to prepare for Y2K had a reasonable tone that just couldn't hide the uncomfortable fact that the government was telling its citizens to store canned food and bottled water, set aside an extra sum of cash, and have plenty of batteries on hand. And maybe we should get Dad's old pistol down from the closet and make sure it still works. Or buy a $5,000 space heater that runs on gasoline so we don't freeze to death in January. Or maybe just build ourselves a nice, dry, fallout shelter in the basement.

These same millennial fears of doom had an effect on the period leading up to the Crusades. Pilgrimages increased throughout that nervous era, and any interruption of Christian access to the shrines of their God would have been looked upon with grave seriousness by the Church, as well as the Christian peoples of Europe. To a Christian pilgrim, being barred from the Church of the Holy Sepulchre or the Way of the Cross was a worse crime than murder, because far more than his life was at stake — his very soul was on the line. Perhaps this fact makes the ideology behind the Crusades a little easier to understand.

The Spanish ulcer

Napoleon Bonaparte once made an ill-considered attempt to bring the Iberian Peninsula into the French empire. As the conflict wore on, Napoleon called it his "Spanish ulcer," a galling sore that wouldn't heal, but just kept bleeding him of men and money.

Spain presented a similar nagging sore in the 11th century. After the death of the Prophet Mohammed in A.D. 632, his followers swept out of Arabia at warp speed, converting the population to Islam by fire and sword. In less than a century, they had carved out a vast empire, one that extended from Spain to the steppes of Central Asia. When they had the Berber nations of North Africa in their pocket, it was an oh-so-easy jump across the Straits of Gibraltar into southern Spain, a leap they made in the year A.D. 711. From that time forward — in fact, for the next six centuries — Spain would be a battleground between the forces of the Christian north and the Islamic south, and the Mason-Dixon line between them shifted more often than the San Andreas fault. At the peak of Arabic power, Christian forces were hanging on to a tiny strip of property, chiefly Aragon and Navarre.

The wave of Arab conquests that flashed over Spain in 711 moved on, across the Pyrenees, and deep into the heart of Gaul (present-day France). At last they were turned back by the French king Charles Martel, grandfather of Charlemagne, in his stunning victory over the Saracens at the Battle of Poitiers in 732. For several centuries afterward, Europe seemed willing to look on Spain as simply a wall to keep Islam from going any farther. But continued Islamic-Christian wars there coincided with an unnerving cultural development in Spain. Various mystical and heretical brands of Christianity were growing, as well as melding their ideas with Islam, both of which in their turn were being influenced by other heretics, Sufis and Coptics and Maronites, as well as by the growing communities of Sephardic Jews, who'd been arriving since the conquest of Jerusalem by Titus in the first century. All this free-thinking and fusing of faiths really scared the Church, and every fresh Islamic conquest brought these heresies closer to their doorstep.

The Abbey of Cluny was in Saone-et-Loire in France, and its monks became a powerful force within the Benedictine order. It was the influential monks of

Cluny who first began floating the idea of offering "warriors of Christ" salvation instead of a salary if they would take back Spain from the Moors. Templar historian Juan Garcia Atienza called it "a dress rehearsal for the East."

By 1064 Pope Alexander II was issuing "collective indulgences" to Christian knights in Spain; he had the full support of Cluny in the person of his chancellor, Hildebrand, an influential Clunaic monk and scholar who would one day be pope himself, as St. Gregory VII. Eventually, these papal dispensations on a small scale led to the first Crusade Bull, issued by the newly-elected Urban II in 1089, granting dispensation to knights who fought to recapture Tarragona in northeastern Spain. Urban II, incidentally, had also once been a monk of Cluny. Drafting "warriors for Christ" doubtless wasn't ethical, but tactically speaking, a glance at a map of the Mediterranean basin in the 11th century makes the shaky position of Christianity and the West crystal clear.

Figure 2-1 is a map of the entire area of the Mediterranean basin just before the Crusades. The Muslim onslaught that poured out of Arabia in the seventh century had swallowed up startling amounts of real estate, Christian, Persian, and pagan. The speed of these conquests was in the same vein as Alexander or Napoleon or Hitler. The Mediterranean had once been teeming with lucrative trade from East to West and back again, but Muslim corsairs were making trade impossible. It doesn't take a cartographer or a military genius to see that Christian Europe was being roped in. Soon, all that the forces of Islam would have to do was tighten the noose.

The war in Spain, the battleground between East and West, became the precursor to the Crusades, the bony finger pointing to the next war that was bound to break out, sooner or later. The losses in Spain for Christians painted a very gloomy picture of what could happen elsewhere in medieval Europe.

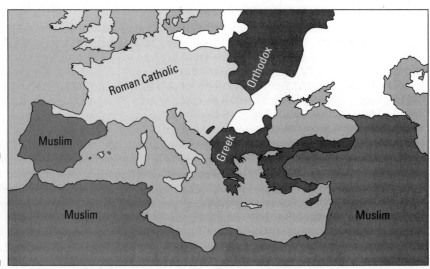

Figure 2-1: Europe and the Mediterranean in A.D. 1000.

The dilemma of the second son

The annihilation of whole towns and villages by the bubonic plague was still three centuries off in the future, and in the 11th century, Europe was undergoing a steady increase in population. For that reason, it's important to understand the meaning of the ten-dollar word *primogeniture,* the system of inheritance that was dominant throughout the feudal period. For any man of noble rank, everything — his title, his money, and his lands — went to the eldest son in the family. It may seem unfair, but the reasoning behind it was that it kept the fief or holding together, instead of breaking it up again and again through the generations until there was nothing left that was worth inheriting.

Unfortunately, this left second sons in a dicey position. Like the vice president of the United States, everyone knew what he was there for — he was the spare, in case war or pestilence carried off the firstborn. But in a time of rising population, families often had more than one, or even more than two, sons who survived to adulthood. Therefore, the typical medieval question was, "Whatever are we to do about Harry (or John or Phillip or Irving)?" He had a right to stick around in the household after the death of his father, and to be provided with at least a subsistence living from his elder brother. But for many knights, or simply proud young men, this was an intolerable situation in which to live, and they were usually gently but firmly encouraged to leave the nest, in order to keep jealousy and internal squabbling to a minimum.

Many younger sons of the nobility chose the Church as their profession; in fact, doing so was quite common, because it was a way that even a moderately intelligent young man of good family could achieve his own rank and respectability. It's interesting to note just how coolly and clinically the Church understood the second-son dilemma: It was common practice, if the elder son were killed without having had any sons of his own, for the second son of the family to be released from his vows to Holy Mother Church so that he could return home to take up his earthly burden.

Feckless younger sons who were allergic to the discipline of the Church might choose to live on as dependants, despite the potential for humiliation. And handsome younger sons might marry well, perhaps a wealthy widow, in order to acquire a fiefdom of their own.

The final route to personal fulfillment for a second son was foreign adventure and conquest, if and when the opportunity presented itself. This despite the physical danger, and the very real possibility that he'd never see his homeland again. But as the 11th century drew to a close, another route to personal achievement for the second son was born, one that melded knightly opportunity with Christian grace — he could take the Cross, and become a Crusader. With the dawn of the age of crusading, the noble calling of serving God was added to the already potent blend of the opportunity to achieve personal wealth and military glory in a faraway and exotic foreign land.

Piracy and trade

This last is probably the easiest cultural factor to explain. At this time, there was a rising middle class in Europe. This business class would endure plague, war, and calamity, and just keep coming back for more. The wealth of this brand-new class was based on one thing more than any other: trade. By the time of the First Crusade, Arab pirates on land and sea were making trading expeditions very difficult and dangerous. The Silk Road, the 4,000 mile caravan route between Rome and the great Chinese city of Xi'an, with a large stopping-off juncture in the Levant, had been an artery of merchandise and ideas from East to West and back again since ancient times. Now it belonged to the Turks, and was no longer safe for business travelers. Meanwhile, the Mediterranean was becoming an Islamic backyard swimming pool. As the borders of Christian Europe shrank, their world becoming ever smaller, it was clear that something had to be done.

The First Crusade: A Cry for Help, a Call to Arms

Pope Urban II got a very unusual letter in 1095, while he was in Italy at an ecclesiastical conference. It was from the Emperor Alexius Comnenus, ruler of the Byzantine Empire. There was never any more than a polite civility between Catholic Christians in the West and Orthodox Christians in the East. In the last century in particular, a tiff over the Frankish Norman invasion of Byzantine territories in the south of Italy had set off a skirmish between the pope of Rome and the patriarch of Constantinople, one that ended in mutual excommunication and a formal schism.

But the Emperor Alexius was asking Pope Urban to put aside those differences, and stand together as Christians to face an oncoming horde of Islamic Turkish warriors, the Seljuqs. In A.D. 1071, at Manzikert, Alexius had lost a major battle to the Seljuqs, who then took huge chunks of his empire, including Persia, Syria, and Palestine, before turning north to nest at Nicaea, on Alexius' very doorstep. Urban II was one of many theologians who had dreamed of reconciliation between the two halves of Christianity. The timing must have seemed heaven-sent to him.

Meet the Byzantines

Most people don't know very much about the Byzantine Empire, and it's little wonder. The art, the architecture, and especially the religious icons of Byzantium are so very foreign to Western eyes that it makes their long and complex history seem even harder to understand. Many times, in U.S. history classes, textbooks go directly from the Fall of the Roman Empire to the Middle Ages, with perhaps an all-too-brief stop along the way to mention the *other* half of the old Roman empire, the half that *didn't* fall — at least not for another ten centuries, when the Ottoman Turks overran the old empire in A.D. 1458.

For centuries, Westerners seemed to feel that there was a corruption at the core of Byzantium. The Byzantines had a reputation, right or wrong, for opulent decadence, serpentine court intrigues, and poison-in-the-wine-cup politics. The very word fell into the language of the West as a generally unflattering adjective. To say that a politician has the twists and turns of a *byzantine* mind still is no compliment.

But as far as the Byzantines were concerned, they weren't some offshoot or weird eastern outcropping of the Roman Empire. They *were* the Roman Empire, period. All through its history the Roman Empire had contained a natural dividing line between the eastern and western halves, one that was eventually recognized by creating two emperors — one in the Latin West, the other in the Hellenic East. So, as far as the Byzantines were concerned, the western half of the Roman Empire may have dropped the ball, but *they* hadn't.

The Byzantines were essentially Greek in character, while Europe was essentially Latin. As is so often true, everywhere in the world, cultural differences spring up from a difference in language.

No matter how different their churches or their vestments looked, the Byzantines were Christians, with the same essential belief system as Catholicism.

Go East, young man!

When Alexius sent his call for help to Pope Urban II, the pope had several very good reasons to answer it:

- ✔ It was simply an ethical question of universal Christian unity.
- ✔ That unity seemed more important in the face of Muslim encroachments, from the Spain to the Black Sea.
- ✔ These Muslim incursions were now menacing the Christian West, not only emotionally in their invasion of the Holy Land, but politically and militarily, in Islam's wildfire spread across the steppes of Asia to Constantinople, literally the gateway to the West. Worst of all, the Seljuq Turks were robbing and killing Christian pilgrims, as well as blocking access to Christian shrines.

Urban convened the Council of Clermont on November 18th, 1095. Most of the Catholic bureaucrats who attended were churchmen of the south of France. A series of canons were to be voted upon, including an important one on the subject of the *Truce of God*. This was a peace movement in France, an attempt to limit violence between feudal lords, and to protect the clergy and other travelers from being preyed upon on the roads. It was a movement that Urban very much favored, as well as an issue that becomes even more important later, in the story of the birth of the Templars. This was the perfect opportunity to present Alexius's plea.

At the close of the Council, Urban had a chair brought outside to an open field where he had invited a gathering of the entire city to hear an important papal announcement. He explained Emperor Alexius's predicament, and offered a *plenary indulgence* (the remission of all penance for sin) to anyone willing to go East and aid the Byzantine emperor in fending off the infidels. He wanted the Truce of God extended to *all* endangered Christians making their pilgrimage to the Holy Land.

Historians have no reliable record of exactly what was said, but Urban definitely moved his listeners with his eloquence and idealism, and he managed to hit a collective nerve in the larger-than-expected crowd. Apparently, he spent a good deal of breath on the knights of France, reminding them of what knighthood had once meant in terms of chivalry and piety, and then delivered a verbal lashing to them for having become robbers, murderers, and blasphemers. He wanted them to turn that violent energy to a noble cause — freeing the Holy Land from the heavy hand of the Muslim invaders.

It seems likely that even the pope was astonished at the overwhelming reaction to his speech. Nothing on this sort of scale had ever before been proposed. Legend has it that people in the crowd began shouting over and over again, *"Deus volt! Deus volt!"* meaning "God wills it!" It must have seemed a little like a rock concert, as the faithful immediately began tearing up strips of cloth, to pin them to their clothing in the shape of a cross. The concept of "taking the Cross" was born, for men, women, and even children. It wasn't a nodding up and down of heads, a few huzzahs, or even a general chorus of agreement — it was a literal stampede.

Urban had not envisioned this mass response. He tried his best to set reasonable limits on who could, and who should, make the journey. He forbade the elderly or the infirm, pleading that only fit young men take the Cross. Surprisingly, he also asked that married men consult with their wives first. And, if a wife wished, she could go along with her husband. Many did so, adding to the chaos of Crusader "armies" that looked like straggling columns of refugees.

France, being the most stable and powerful country in Europe at that time, would be the chief player in the First Crusade. England was still trying to pick up the pieces after the Norman invasion of A.D. 1066, while Spain was already fighting for its life in its own battle with Islam, which came to be called the *Reconquista,* the retaking of Spain. But the knights who could go, the Franks as they came to be called (because French was their common language), were all completely won over.

Preparations for the grand adventure began at once, with everyone packing, making arrangements for someone to watch the house, and muttering "tickets, passport, money" over and over again. The Church helped in any way it could, from holding mortgages on the property of Crusaders, to making them untouchable by civil courts — *their* lawbreaking would be handled by softball ecclesiastical courts.

Peter the Hermit

It was not Pope Urban, however, but an itinerate preacher named Peter the Hermit, who opened the floodgates to anyone of any age, sex, or condition to march with him to Constantinople. He is surely one of the oddest figures in history, especially for a man who would have so much influence on the events to follow.

These unarmed and untrained hordes of people set out at once for Constantinople, without waiting for the Crusader knights, in a mass exodus often called the "People's Crusade" or the "Peasant's Crusade." They followed Peter the Hermit and his chief lieutenant, Walter the Penniless. This last was an apt nickname, because all these unruly, unarmed, and untrained people were short of money and supplies, racing headlong to disaster.

However, Peter did have one talent, albeit not a military one. As he preached his way through Europe, he gathered up several trunkloads of gold. Although it came from many supporters, it also seems Pete had a gift for extorting money out of the Jews of Europe. The Jews of this period had a reputation for being moneylenders, which was not entirely born of the rampant medieval anti-Semitism, but out of the fact that Jews in medieval Europe had very few ways to earn a living. They were forced to live in *ghettos,* the area of each large city set aside for them, and walled off to the main, Christian part of the city. Jewish physicians were renowned, and this often allowed them to cross over the wall. But Jews were not allowed into any of the trade guilds, and consequently, they could not earn their living in any of the typical professions of the period, such as masons or carpenters or blacksmiths. Moneylending became a way that Jews could earn a living, particularly because Catholics were forbidden to practice what was called "usury." And so was born the repulsive myth of the money-grubbing and usurious Jew, with hoards of gold stashed away in his mattress. (The Knights Templar would later find a loophole around these rules and become the first international bankers; see Chapter 4.)

So, with about 25,000 Christians marching behind him, who's going to tell the old hermit that they really aren't interested in making a donation? Of course, these masses of people caused nothing but trouble along the way, even occasionally setting off a major battle. In the Hungarian city of Semlin, for example, an argument with a tradesman over the price of a pair of shoes erupted into a full-scale riot, then a battle, claiming the lives of over 4,000 people in the city.

The meanderings of Peter the Hermit illuminate one very important fact of crusading: that the lack of centralized authority in government under the feudal system was reflected in the same lack of organization of the Crusades. There was no single leader, no organized place of embarkation, and no central clearinghouse for weapons and supplies, not to mention information. As word of the Crusade was spread over Europe, the Christian West ambled its way to Asia Minor in ragtag bands, with no connection to one another apart from a determination to rendezvous at the gates of Constantinople. It's difficult to grasp what 25,000 Christians on the march in one party must have been like. Many would die on the journey, and many would simply give up in despair, too short on food, supplies, and men to continue the journey. Entire contingents of thousands of Crusaders sometimes disappeared, never to be seen or heard from again.

Get out the beer, we're here!

Nearly a year after his distress call, a horrified Alexius woke up one morning, wandered out to the stoop in his jammies, and found an unimaginable mob of Christians headed for his doorstep, nearly as frightening as the Turks. There were not only thousands of armed soldiers, but also their women, children, squires, servants, donkeys, hunting dogs, and various and sundry whatnots. It must have been something to see. According to the 12th century chronicler William of Tyre, Alexius had expected a small, well-armed force of Christian knights, just to help out. What he got was a horde the size of the population of Racine, Wisconsin.

Still, Alexius graciously met with Peter the Hermit, giving him gifts and thanks. But when the locals began to complain of thievery and trouble, he asked them very politely to cross the Bosporus and make camp on the Asian side, in the remains of a fortress there called Civetot. Small groups were let into the city each day to tour its wonders, while the rest remained on the other side, completely vulnerable. The Turks, having word of their arrival as well as their position, mounted a devastating attack that all but wiped out the entirety of Peter's "army." It was the first full-scale disaster of the Crusades, but hardly the last.

In August of 1096, the main military force of the Crusaders moved out for the East. By April of 1097, all of them had arrived, by various routes. There were many lords and knights, but the following were the principle players: Hugh of Vermandois, who was the brother of King Phillip I of France; Godfrey de Bouillon, along with his brothers Eustace and Baldwin; Bohemond of Taranto, a battle-hardened Norman warlord; Raymond de Saint-Gilles, the Count of Toulouse, who assembled the largest force of armed men; and Robert of Flanders, another powerful Norman warlord, who also happened to be the brother of the king of England, William II Rufus.

It was a vast army assembled before Constantinople. Alexius, who'd already dealt with Peter the Hermit, now had the time to try to absorb the pandemonium he had unleashed with a simple letter asking for a bit of help. But, as recorded in the fascinating journals of Alexius' daughter, Anna Comnenus, he felt a little threatened by this combined force of over 4,000 mounted knights, and about 25,000 infantry — as well he might. After all, Alexius was himself a usurper, and he knew how easily a throne could be taken. Therefore, before anyone set off to battle any Turks, he asked for a parley with the principle leaders above, and then asked each of them to take a solemn oath that any lands they conquered that had once belonged to Byzantium would be returned to Byzantium. After a short huddle and a little grumbling, all three knights knelt to give their solemn vow. Only Raymond of Saint-Gilles would make any serious attempt to stick to their bargain.

Forward ho!

That uncomfortable business aside, everyone seemed chummy once again, and the official First Crusade started out fairly well. The Christian army, together with a contingent of Byzantine forces, marched on the city of Nicaea, taking it with relative ease. The city was promptly handed over to the Byzantines, as promised. Next they headed south and east for the great prize, the city of Antioch, in present-day Syria. Since Roman times, Antioch had been one of the most populous and powerful cities in the Levant.

The *Levant* is simply another term for the Holy Land, usually the important coastal areas. It comes from Old French, *levaunt,* the word for "rising," a metaphor for the sun rising in the land of the East.

Now Antioch was a Christian city in the hands of the Seljuq Turks. To reach it, they had to slog their way through the miserably hot, dry, and mountainous region of Anatolia. On the way, they faced a major attack by the Turks on their advance guard and won a great victory, sharpening their appetite.

The Christian and Byzantine army arrived at Antioch on October 20, to begin a very long and grueling siege. When the Emperor Alexius never showed up to help them, as he had promised, the feelings against him began running very high. They took the city in the spring of the following year, and by agreement, Bohemond took charge of the city. It would remain with his descendants for two centuries.

There was by now a great restlessness amongst the crusading army, and a general desire to move on and to get the job done. Raymond de Saint-Gilles, Count of Toulouse, led the army south, toward the ultimate prize of Jerusalem.

The massacre of Jerusalem

The Christian army that arrived at the gates of Jerusalem on June 7, 1099, was considerably reduced in power from the army that had arrived at Alexius' doorstep two years before. Casualties, epidemics, and those who'd just drifted away left them with roughly 1,500 knights of cavalry (perhaps less) and about 12,000 foot soldiers — still a considerable force.

The Crusaders began the construction of siege towers and scaling ladders, ignoring the frequent catcalls and raspberries from the Muslims guarding the walls of the city. The guards laughed as the entire Christian army, led by their priests, would walk the whole parameter of the city, finishing on the Mount of Olives to hear services from Peter the Hermit, who was just as incendiary as ever, despite the thousands he'd led to their deaths.

The fighting began in earnest on July 13, and by July 15 Godfrey de Bouillon had taken a section of the city's walls. The north gate was opened, and the army poured through to take the city. And after the city was theirs, be it a holy city or not, the Crusaders gleefully did what the Assyrians, the Babylonians, the Romans, and the Turks had done there before them: They massacred everyone in sight whom they deemed an enemy — in other words, anyone who wasn't a Christian.

At the Tower of David, the noble Tancred, the nephew of the not particularly noble Bohemond, escorted the governor and his entourage from the city in safety, promising that the al-Aqsa Mosque would not be touched, and no reprisals taken. It was a promise he couldn't keep — in fact, the slaughter had already begun.

For the Christian Crusaders, this moment in history was something else altogether. The massacre in Jerusalem was a hypocritical betrayal of everything their faith had taught them. In the 11th century, most people couldn't read, so the largest part of what they knew about their own religion had come to them from the words of priests and churchmen, many of whom put their own self-serving twist on Christ's teachings. One tenth-century pope burned several Franciscans at the stake for having preached the "heresy" that Christ and his apostles lived in poverty.

Islam's warrior heritage

The massacre in Jerusalem has long formed a centerpiece of Crusader legend. They slaughtered the Muslims, despite the many beliefs of Christianity that are held to be true by Islam, as well. Jesus was the great prophet preceding Mohammed, the last prophet. But Islam is a very different religion, one founded by a constant soldier; it was a warrior's faith and a warrior's code, and their attitude about massacres was a bit different.

In A.D. 638, when Omar of the Umayyad caliphate captured Jerusalem, many a Christian there had cause to rejoice. All of Palestine contained many Christian sects considered heretical by the Byzantine emperor, and they had been persecuted under his rule. But during the next peaceful century, the Umayyads brought order and tolerance. Christians were allowed access to Jerusalem and were allowed to worship as they pleased. A century later, the Abbasid caliphate of Baghdad drove the Umayyads into Spain and took the Near East. They disliked Christians, and many suffered under their rule, but things did settle down. The Abbasids got along very well with the Nestorians, their favorite brand of Christian. But three centuries later, the arrival of the newly-converted and warlike Turkish Muslims, the Seljuqs, spelled the end to any tolerance of Christians. They believed in the Five Pillars of Islam — belief in God and Mohammed as his prophet, prayer, fasting, the giving of alms to the poor, and pilgrimage to Mecca. But every warlike passage of the Koran and the Hadith became the special code of the Turks. (The Hadith is a body of the sayings and acts of the prophet, set down for the most part two or three centuries after his death; it is just as holy to Muslims as the Koran.)

"Know that Paradise is under the shade of swords," were the words of the Prophet Muhammad. "When you meet the unbelievers in the battlefield, strike off their heads . . ." (Koran 47:5). The Koran repeatedly calls unbelievers "the vilest of creatures" (Koran 8:65), leaving no doubt that their slaughter will not weigh heavily on the Islamic conscience. Therefore, Muslim warriors (as well as Persian warriors, Mongol warriors, and Berber warriors, not to mention a dozen others) had many times taken part in such massacres following a victory, in Egypt, in Cyprus, in Armenia — in fact, all over the East. In the medieval world, slaughter of the defeated seemed to be every bit as expected as a wrist carnation on a prom date. For these proud warriors, their own holy book, the Koran, permitted them the option of slaughtering unbelievers, particularly if they refused to convert — they were to "slay the unbelievers wherever you find them" (Koran 9:5).

When Muslims conquered a city, the citizens had three choices — convert, die, or pay the *jizyah,* which was a heavy tax on unbelievers. The ceremony of payment by the *dhimmis,* or unbelievers, was incredibly demeaning and generally included body blows and slaps on the face, or outrages to their women. "The dhimmi has to be made to feel that he is an inferior person when he pays, he is not to be treated with honor." They were generally made to dress in clothing identifying them as non-Muslims, and were subject to endless laws and edicts that increased the feeling of humiliation. Of course, in other instances, the prophet was far more blunt: "Kill any Jew that falls into your power," for instance. This quote is part of a long story in the hadith about Jewish perfidy in general — Mohammed had expected the Jews of Arabia to convert, and when they did not, he grew less tolerant of them. In keeping with this sentiment, Muhammad personally ordered the execution of between 600 and 900 Jews in Medina in a single day.

Yet Christianity was not, at its core, a warrior's faith, and the words of the gentle carpenter from Nazareth would hardly inspire the slaughter of the innocents. Despite the fact that the romanticized image of the Crusaders would come into fashion again and again over the course of the centuries, there was always a tension between Christian *lore* and Christian *belief.* It was a tension that would worsen in many ways after the 15th century, when the miracle of Gutenberg's printing press would soon put a Bible, in the everyday language of the people, into the hands of anyone who wanted to read it.

Though some of these knights were more savage than any foe, others, like Godfrey de Bouillon, were educated men who knew the words of the Bible. They would carry a heavy burden of guilt over the spilling of an ocean of blood in the City of God. It is a guilt that has remained with Christians to the present day.

A relief army from Egypt attempted to reach the city, but they were defeated by the victorious Christians. Now Jerusalem and the Palestinian territory surrounding it were in the hands of the Crusaders, without doubt.

The founding of Outremer

Despite the massacre at Jerusalem, and despite the chaotic disasters of the "People's Crusade," the First Crusade is really the only one that could be called a tactical success. The military goals of the leaders had been met, their targets taken, and Christian access to the shrines of their God ensured. As at the close of all wars, there was a general desire at that point to go home, and it didn't seem to occur to most of the army that they couldn't just walk away from their conquest and expect it to remain open to Christians. Like the proverbial dog that catches the car he's chasing, they had the city by the bumper, with no idea what to do with it.

And so the powwows began. There was a strong sentiment that government in the city should be in the hands of the clergy, which many of the remaining knights saw as a tactical folly, because the city was still surrounded by enemies. At last, the respected Godfrey de Bouillon was elected to govern, at least temporarily, and he took the modest title of "Defender of the Holy Sepulcher." Many Christians still felt that the governance of the Holy City should be, like the Vatican, in the hands of the Church, an open city for all faiths. But a year later, on Godfrey de Bouillon's death, his brother Baldwin was called back from Edessa, and was crowned King of Jerusalem in November of 1100. For good or ill, the Crusader States, sometimes called the Latin States, were born.

Actually, there was another name for this new nation, one that isn't heard as often. They called it "Outremer," and though it sounds like a mythical land at the center of the earth in a Jules Verne story, Outremer was simply an invented French word for a faraway kingdom across the sea (*mer* being French for sea). And when wistful and homesick citizens of Outremer spoke of home, they called it Citremer, implying the civilization, or *les cités* (cities) across the sea.

Four kingdoms made up the Latin States:

- **The Kingdom of Jerusalem**

- **The County of Edessa:** This was to the north, in present-day Syria, and was populated mainly by Armenians and Syrians. The kingdom was established by Godfrey's brother Baldwin, by means fair and foul that are still debated by Crusader scholars. When Baldwin became King of Jerusalem, he gave Edessa over to his cousin Baldwin Le Bourg.

- **The Principality of Antioch:** It was ruled by Bohemond, the Norman warlord. After he was captured by the Muslims in 1100, it was given over to his nephew Tancred. They replaced the Greek patriarch with a Latin one, and bristled Christian sensibilities in the predominantly Greek, Syrian, and Armenian Eastern Orthodox population.

- **The County of Tripoli:** It was founded by Raymond of Toulouse, who began the siege of the city in 1102, after his part in the failed Crusade of 1101. After his death in 1109, this kingdom was taken by Raymond's descendants, creating a new baronial house.

Islamic politics were a mess at this time, and it wasn't until the arrival of Saladin on the scene, nearly a century later, that Muslims began pulling their oars in the same direction. But the Christians knew they couldn't count on Muslim factionalism as a defense forever. They began at once to build a line of defensive forts, many of which still exist. The Knights Templar and the Knights Hospitaller were a very important part of this building boom (see Chapter 3).

Let's Give It Another Shot: The Second Crusade

A powerful Muslim warlord named Zengi of Mosul came out of the north in the mid-12th century, attacking Damascus first. In 1144, Zengi overran the County of Edessa, massacring the Franks and the Christians of the city. Pope Eugenius III issued a papal bull calling for another Crusade, and the war was on again.

There's one fact to remember about all the Crusades that would follow the first: All were trying to imitate the success of the First Crusade, and for the most part, all of them failed. The pope abused his powers in later centuries by proclaiming a "crusade" against temporal powers that were giving him a headache, or, more commonly, against factions of Christianity that he considered "heretical." These "Crusades" were not popular, and they ended by lowering the prestige of the Church.

Like the sinking of the *Titanic*, the marriage of George II to Caroline of Brunswick, or the 1972 Super Bowl, the Second Crusade was one of those grand and epic failures that leaves people hooting from the cheap seats, giving off Bronx cheers, despite the dignity that Bernard of Clairvaux brought to the whole affair.

Two powerful kings got on board for the Second Crusade: Louis VII of France, and Conrad III, emperor of Germany. Although the Third Crusade would be known as the Kings' Crusade, the Abbot Bernard had drafted some impressive bluebloods into this debacle.

Arriving at Constantinople late in 1147, each king would face major defeats at the hands of the Turks. Conrad had brought with him a slew of nobles from Germany, as well as the King of Poland and the King of Bohemia, and none of them was any help whatsoever.

Conrad, in strange territory, was too proud to listen to the sound advice of the Byzantine Emperor Manuel, disdaining his recommendations on routes and supplies. As he waltzed his main force past Nicaea into the heart of Anatolia, his men weary and his supplies running out, he may just as well have been wearing a KICK ME sign on his back. He was attacked by a large Turkish force on October 25, and his army was virtually annihilated. Conrad gathered together the pathetic remnants of his forces and retreated to Nicaea.

Louis didn't do much better. He had brought along his wife, the remarkable Eleanor of Aquitaine. She was related by blood to several of the powerful families of the Latin States. Shrewd, powerful, and immensely wealthy in her own right, she would be the wife of both the French king and the English one, and two of her sons would go on to become kings themselves. (For more on Eleanor of Aquitaine and her Court of Love, see Chapter 10.)

Even after Conrad's humiliating defeat, Louis could still put a staggering 50,000 men into the field. Unfortunately, his marriage to Eleanor was sinking into the squabbling and accusations of adultery that would be its finish, and this had a great effect on his ability to think tactically. Louis stubbornly ignored the shrewd advice of Eleanor and her uncle, Prince Raymond of Tripoli, that he should attack the city of Aleppo, which was the center of power for the Crusaders' new principle enemy, Nureddin, the son of Zengi. Digging in his heels, Louis refused to listen to either of them, and finally decided, for reasons unclear and probably capricious, to attack Damascus.

Unur, who was the Turkish commander of Damascus, was also afraid of Nureddin, and may well have been made an ally had Louis not had the bad taste to lay siege to his city.

The campaign was bungled all around, and on July 28, after a mere five-day siege, news came that Nureddin was approaching. Louis and his forces retired with their tails between their legs, looking incredibly foolish. This disaster, born out of a family squabble, led to bitter accusations of treachery all around. Louis went home in a huff, leaving the Latin States, and his wife's family, to fend for themselves.

A dynamic new Muslim force

With the death of Nureddin in 1174, the Muslim forces of both Egypt and Syria fell to his tactically brilliant protégé — the mighty Saladin (for more about Saladin, see Chapter 5). Unfortunately, in that same year, Nureddin's principle enemy, King Amalric also died, leaving the Franks in a dynastic mess.

Amalric's 13 year-old son, Baldwin IV, succeeded, but he had leprosy. With his death eminent, two parties began to form around the deathbed — one headed by the young king's sister Sibyl and her husband, Guy of Lusignan, a newcomer to the East, and the other around the "old" baronial families, including Raymond III of Tripoli. It didn't help Frankish nerves that their urgent appeals to Pope Alexander III for help had gone unanswered. In March of 1185, when the young Baldwin IV died, Raymond of Tripoli became regent for Sybil's son, Baldwin V. But when Raymond died in 1186, the faction around Sibyl had its way and hastily crowned her queen. She, in turn, crowned her husband, Guy.

So, the Franks were already near to civil war when Reginald of Chatillon, lord of Kerak and Montreal, broke the truce they'd had with Saladin by attacking a caravan. Saladin proclaimed jihad against the Latin Kingdoms. In 1187, he crossed the Jordan River and took up a position on the other side. The Crusaders had mobilized about 38,000 men, with about 1,200 in heavily armed cavalry, a larger force on horseback than the enemy, although Saladin probably had as many as 50,000 men.

The new king, Guy of Lusignan, would not exactly prove to be a tactical genius. Ignoring the wise advice of the old campaigners, who were certain that Saladin was baiting a trap for Guy in the city of Tripoli, the king led his men, who were exhausted from a long march, with not enough food and water, straight into Saladin's trap. This was the battle at the Horns of Hattin, (an extremely important moment in Templar history; see Chapter 5). It was one of the worst defeats ever suffered by the Frankish forces. The foot soldiers broke and ran, causing chaos in the cavalry, and Saladin's final charge finished them. The king's life was spared, but Saladin ordered many executions, including the instant decapitation of Reginald of Chatillon, who'd attacked Saladin's caravan, and the execution of every Templar or Hospitaller knight he could lay hands on, at least 200 of them. Saladin feared these warrior monks as he feared no others, and the rules of the game did not apply to them. As for the rest, it was the usual — highborn were ransomed, lowborn sold into slavery. At this point in time, there was really no military force left for the Kingdom of Jerusalem.

Jerusalem falls

Saladin moved quickly, taking Tiberius, and then charging up the coast to take Acre. By September of 1187, he had most of the major Latin strongholds, including all the ports south of Tripoli except Tyre. There were only a handful of men to defend Jerusalem, and, on October 2, Saladin took the city. He wanted ransom rather than death. Inhabitants who could pay it were allowed to leave freely. Several thousand of the unredeemed poor were sold into slavery. Most who elected to stay were Syrian or Greek Christians. Later, he let some of the Jewish population back in. By 1189, Saladin was pretty much the lord of all he surveyed.

The news of the fall of Jerusalem reached the West even before the archbishop who had been sent by the Franks to appeal for aid. The new pope, Gregory VIII, promptly obliged with a crusade bull, calling for fasting and prayer as well. One quick recovery was made by Conrad of Montferrat, Baldwin V's uncle, who put together a small force of Italian ships and took back the city of Tyre from Saladin, while he was busy marching on Jerusalem. The following year, Saladin released his prisoner, Guy of Lusignan, the king of Jerusalem, and, ominously, Montferrat would not submit his fealty. The Latin barons were still sniping at one another when the prayed-for ships appeared off Acre, bringing supplies and the joyous news that a new army was on its way.

The Third Crusade

There is a very definite aura around the Third Crusade, one that resembles the star power without a decent script that erupts into a big-budget Hollywood flop-buster. All style and big budget, no substance.

Insofar as the players are concerned, the Third Crusade is definitely the most famous of all the Crusades, but truth to tell, it didn't accomplish much. It did restore the Latin States, sort of. It left them well-enough fortified to linger on for another century, which isn't much of a victory, considering this Crusade's size and splendor.

Cecil B. DeMille

In 1935, Hollywood's most powerful director, Cecil B. DeMille, was working on his latest over-sized epic, *The Crusades.* He received a letter from an Islamic citizen's group, worried over his portrayal of Islam in his film. DeMille certainly had the power to file it in the circular, if he'd chosen to. But being a gentleman of the old school, he arranged a prescreening for the group, in order to ensure that he'd done nothing to offend them. At that "work print" stage, he would be able to alter anything that they found objectionable.

When the lights came up after the movie, Mr. DeMille found a roomful of people who were perfectly happy with his film. Actually, they were *delighted* with his film. In fact, they asked to see it again. When *The Crusades* had its initial run in Cairo, it played for an astonishing *three years.* And when DeMille went to Egypt to film *The Ten Commandments* in 1957, he was fawned over by no less a fan than President Gamal Abdel Nasser, who gushed that *The Crusades* was his favorite film, and as a boy he'd seen it 20 times.

This isn't at all hard for a historian to understand. DeMille was a very well-read man, and he'd been raised on the Crusader stories of the 19th century. In those stories, the larger-than-life figure of Saladin was a man of heroic proportions. He was the epic figure of an enemy worthy of a knight's steel — courageous and courteous, honorable and proud, with a deep spirituality that was matched by his skill as a warrior. This gave the troubadour tales an aura of tragedy; had Richard and Saladin been born on the same side, they would doubtless have been friends. As it was, the relationship between these two mythic figures was something of a mutual admiration society. In DeMille's film treatment of the Third Crusade, there's no question at all that the brave and noble Saladin, played by the handsome actor Ian Keith, comes off a whole lot better than Henry Wilcoxon's loutish and lunkheaded Richard. In fact, Richard very nearly loses the girl to Saladin's charms. This is hardly a case of fanatical Western Christians demonizing a Muslim.

Well, perhaps one other thing was accomplished. The Third Crusade became the wellspring for the West's most enduring myths and legends of Crusader knights, their ladies fair, and their Muslim enemy. This was the Crusade of Richard the Lionheart, Saladin, Robin Hood, and the evil Prince John. Unfortunately, these deeply engrained myths can overshadow truth.

Lately, a lot of books about the Crusades are skewed by what's called "revisionist history," a good thing so long as people aren't blinded by a new, but equally unchallengeable, orthodoxy. As the pendulum swings in the opposite direction, and Crusaders become the bad guys, certain aspects can be particularly annoying. These works often suggest that the people of the West have always seen Muslim leaders like Saladin in a negative light. Nothing, absolutely *nothing,* could be farther from the truth. Saladin was a legendary figure in Western mythology, sharing the stage with Richard the Lionheart. (See the nearby "Cecil B. DeMille" sidebar for more.)

The celebrity crusade

Here are the bare facts of the Third Crusade, starting with a list of the kings who dropped everything to answer the pope's appeal. It was definitely the *Hollywood Squares* of the Crusades:

- **William II of Sicily, known as William the Good,** in contrast to his father, who had been called William the Bad. Sicilians let you know what they think of you.

- **Frederick I Barbarossa, fabled emperor of the Holy Roman Empire,** who came at the age of 70, despite the fact that he'd been feuding with the pope off and on. He crossed Hungary into Byzantium with the largest Crusader force ever assembled. In 1190, he reached Iconium, after defeating a Turkish army on the way. He then crossed into Armenian territory, but on June 10, while riding ahead with his bodyguard, he was drowned fording a stream. His death broke the spirit of the German army, many of whom turned back, but smaller contingents kept on, under his son Frederick of Swabia, and Leopold of Austria. Saladin had been a little discomfited at the thought of facing the legendary Frederick in battle and thought his drowning an act of God.

- **Phillip II Augustus, king of France,** son of Louis VII, and perennial enemy of Richard.

- **Henry II of England,** who took the Cross but died before he could go, in 1189, passing the ball to his eldest son, Richard the Lionheart. The British and French were feuding with one another over territorial claims of the English in France, but they arrived together in 1190, three years after Hattin. In 1191, they laid siege to Acre.

Richard did stop along the way to conquer Cyprus. In all fairness, the renegade Comnenus there, Isaac Comnenus, was holding both Richard's sister Joan and his fiancé Berengaria as hostages, after they'd been shipwrecked there on the way to join Richard. It was a small event of the Third Crusade, though in later years Cyprus would prove to be a valuable tactical possession for the West.

Richard and Saladin

A month after the siege began, Acre fell to the Crusaders. The arguments started about ten minutes after the kings passed through the gates. Saladin seemed to be trying to dance out of signing a surrender agreement, and Richard massacred a couple thousand Muslim prisoners as a result.

This Crusade developed into something of a grudge match, since both forces were roughly equal, and both commanders, Richard and Saladin, tactically brilliant. They also had enormous respect for one another as adversaries. Both could be ruthless, and both had an unusual and singular sense of honor that seemed to mirror one another's, far more so than in the testy relationship between Richard and the other Christian kings. Consequently, the war was a stalemate; a diplomatic solution was needed, but both proved to be lousy diplomats. At last came the Treaty of Jaffa in 1192, which left the Franks in control of the coast from Acre to Jaffa, and gave Christians access to Jerusalem.

Tactically, the Third Crusade failed to retake Jerusalem, its principle objective, but it did take Acre and secure enough of the coastline to keep the Latin States going. Richard also conceded to the majority of the Latin barons that King Guy should be deposed, and he endorsed Conrad of Montferrat, who was assassinated soon after, another scandal that would involve the Templars in accusations of collusion with the Islamic cult of the Assassins (see Chapter 5). Guy was given the governorship of the new possession of Cyprus, which he managed not to screw up.

Unfortunately, Richard and Saladin, by that time, seemed to need each other in some way in order to function. Saladin died six months after the treaty was signed. Richard, himself very ill, was shipwrecked on his journey home. (It's easy to see why the Crusaders eventually left the business of sea transport to the Venetians.) Later, Richard fell into the hands of Leopold of Austria, who had not forgotten Richard's slights to him at Acre. He was held hostage until the English people could raise enough money to sooth Leopold's hurt feelings.

The Final Curtain

It's probably not fair to say that nothing of much importance happened in Crusades number 4, 5, 6 and 7. But the fact is, nothing of much importance happened, at least, not until the finale. Also, despite all that death and dysentery and derring-do, nothing much happened that is of great importance to the Templar story that we don't cover in far greater detail in Chapter 5 on the fall of the Templars. So, what follows is a miniaturized, encapsulated, freeze-dried, and vacuum-packed version of the last four important Crusades.

The Fourth Crusade

If the Second Crusade was a disaster, the fourth played out like a darkly comic farce. Pope Innocent III tried to recapture the glory days of the First Crusade but made his biggest mistake in 1199 when he hired the Venetians, the trading lords of the Mediterranean, to ferry his army across to the Holy Land. Venice had once been a colony of Byzantium, and there was bad blood between them. Once again, as always, the Crusaders wanted to break the Cairo/Syrian axis by attacking Cairo, but Venice had close trading ties with Egypt.

Before long, the wily Venetians were running the show, talking the two chief knights of the Crusade, both of whom were married to Byzantine princesses, into overthrowing the emperor of Byzantium instead. The combined Latin and Venetian forces sacked Constantinople and set up their own government. When the pope tried to stop them, he was told to butt out.

It was the ugliest and most ignoble of all the Crusades. Chaos reigned, with no heroes in sight. Saladin was dead, and Muslim alliances were falling apart. In Europe, occasional outbreaks of mass hysteria resulted in tragedies like the "Children's Crusade" and the "Shepherd's Crusade," in which thousands of innocent children marched off to Constantinople with the pope's blessing, ending up dead or in the slave markets of the East. Meanwhile, the nobility was growing disenchanted with the whole mess.

The Fifth Crusade

Pope Innocent III was of the "if at first you don't succeed" school of military planning. In May of 1218, he fast-talked the emperor of Germany into a Crusade, even dusting off the old plan that had failed twice before — attack and take Cairo, break the Egypt/Syria axis, and use the city as a bargaining chip to get back Jerusalem. It was an eight-year debacle. Many times the Egyptians were ready to make peace and a compromise, but the papal legates along for the ride kept interfering in military matters, and it all ended in a lot of blood spilled for nothing.

The Sixth Crusade

Civilization and common sense actually triumphed in this Crusade. Pope Gregory IX sent the German emperor to make war in Egypt, and instead he brokered a ten-year peace with the equally wise sultan of Egypt. Not a drop of blood was spilled, and warmongers on both sides were deeply disappointed. About five minutes after the peace ran out, early in 1239, the newly powerful Kwarezmian Turks invaded the Levant. Eventually the Egyptians joined them, and together they sacked Jerusalem in 1244.

The Seventh Crusade

Sacking Jerusalem was always an invitation to war with the Christians. In 1245, the truly brave and noble French king, Louis IX, drafted Pope Innocent IV into helping *him* put together a Crusade, reversing the process for once. He tried twice to take back the Holy City and was finally captured by the Muslims. When he was ransomed back in 1254, he was too weak and ill to fight any longer.

By 1260, two powerful new forces were slugging it out, using Palestine as a battleground:

- ✔ The Mongols who were sweeping out of the East
- ✔ The new dynasty of Mamluks out of Egypt, former slave-bodyguards of the sultans who were devastating warriors

Baybars, the Mamluk sultan of Egypt, who is still a great hero in the Islamic world, drove out both the Mongols and the Franks, reducing the Crusaders to a few fortified coastal cities. He massacred the inhabitants of all the cities he took, on the flimsy pretext that they had aided the Mongols.

In what's often called the Eighth Crusade, poor Louis IX, still weak in health, felt guilty over all the massacres that wouldn't have happened if he had succeeded. He returned in 1270, though he could get no other king to accompany him. Both Louis and his son died in Egypt within the year, and the army lost more men to fever and dysentery than to war. Louis's brother Charles evacuated what was left of the army, and when a small force of English knights arrived to relieve him (the Ninth Crusade?) they were too late. So everybody went home, where they probably should have stayed to begin with.

In 1274, at the Council of Lyon, Pope Gregory X called for another Crusade to rescue the Holy Land. He got dead silence in reply, punctuated by a few cricket noises. European kings were now in debt up to their eyeballs, most were at war or planning to be with one another, and they were all sick of pumping money into the Middle East. By 1291, the Mamluks conquered the last Crusader stronghold of Acre on the Levantine coast, massacring anyone left alive. The era of the Crusades was finished.

Chapter 3

The Rise of the Knights Templar

*I*n the Middle Ages, magical thinking was simply a normal part of life, a shared view of the world. People believed that witches would sink if you threw them into the water, that base metal could be turned to gold, and that comets were an ominous portent of some sort of disaster. They also believed that kneeling at the tomb of Jesus could cure disease or erase a past sin.

The concept of pilgrimage is an old one. It's based on a human foible that may not make any sense, but it just comes with the rest of the equipment. People have a tendency to believe that an object or a place can hold within it some sort of ectoplasmic essence of a person or event. And nowhere is this more true than in regards to religious faith.

It was the misfortune of Christian pilgrims that so many of the important sites of the faith were in the perpetual war zone of the Middle East. There were about 50 understaffed years between the victory of the First Crusade that established the Latin States, and the arrival of reinforcements in the Second Crusade. There were very few knights to protect the cities they'd taken, much less to patrol the roads to get there. But the pilgrims kept coming, the numbers steadily increasing. They often carried all their wealth in their *scrip,* a sort of a backpack, to have access to money during a journey that could take a year and more. Sometimes they weren't even certain of the route they should take to get there. But they trusted in God to protect them. In other words, they meandered into a war zone with a cross pinned to their breasts and a target painted on their backs.

This chapter discusses the plight of the pilgrims, and how, in 1119, a French knight named Hugues de Payen felt called by God to help them. He put together a force of nine knights who vowed to keep the roads of the Holy Land safe. They vowed as well to live as monks, promising poverty, chastity and obedience. It was an unprecedented act for warrior knights that would have enormous repercussions on history, when these nine impoverished soldiers were catapulted to the pinnacle of the medieval world. They would be known to history as the Knights Templar.

The Perils of Pilgrimage

The roads were dusty, the terrain was mountainous, and the climate was inhospitable. For anyone accustomed to the rolling green pastures of Sussex or the lush alluvial farmlands of the Loire, the landscape would have seemed as alien as the surface of the moon.

The passage east, with its bone-dry, crystalline air; its painfully blue sky; and its stunted and twisted scrub brush scattered across miles and miles of waste ground — this was the Route of the Pilgrims, the road from Jaffa on the coast to inland Jerusalem that most Christians took to reach the sites sacred to their faith. Far more about this place than just its climate was inhospitable. It was a supremely dangerous road to travel, alone and unarmed. It's often said of any journey that the last mile is always the longest — nowhere was this truer than on a pilgrimage to Jerusalem. After surviving the hazards of the barbarous roads of Europe and the perils of crossing the sea, after traveling thousands of miles, the last 40 miles were the most dangerous of them all.

There were two common routes for a pilgrim traveling from Europe to the East. One was a land route, which began by heading, from wherever you were, toward the Mediterranean, through the south of France and the north of Italy, up and around the coastline of the Adriatic, following the old Roman road along the Danube, then again southeast, through the Slavic nations to the Bosporus. From there it was a game of leapfrog: Nicomedia to Tarsus, Tarsus to Antioch, Antioch to Tripoli, then finally to Jerusalem. Most pilgrims would stop off at major points, particularly Constantinople, to see the dazzling sights of the "Rome of the East." This path to Jerusalem, though long, was the one most commonly taken by the poorest pilgrims, because they could walk the entire way, without paying for passage. If one could afford it, a donkey was a great help on this route.

The other way from Europe to the East was by sea. Typically, pilgrims set out in the spring, heading for the coastal towns of Italy or southern France. After passage was arranged, they took a ship across the Mediterranean, usually island-hopping, stopping in at Sicily or Crete, then Rhodes or Cyprus, to take on water and supplies. The feluccas, with their distinctive triangular fore-and-aft sails, and other, smaller square-sailed ships that plied the Mediterranean were lean, lightweight, fast, and maneuverable, but they couldn't carry enough water to make it all the way across the Mediterranean Sea. Their captains felt safer keeping land in sight.

Generally, they sailed directly east from Cyprus, and at Syria they turned south, moving down the coast until they docked at one of the common drop-off points — Acre, Jaffa, Beirut, or Tyre, depending on political and weather conditions at the moment, or the convenience of that particular ship. By the 13th century, the most common point from which to leave Europe was definitely Venice. The Venetians were by then the greatest commercial power on the Mediterranean, and there wasn't anyone or anything that they wouldn't take on to make a profit. In fact, though early pilgrims came to depend very much on the Knights Templar, who were the closest thing on this journey to a string of banks and travel agents, as the years passed, Venice stepped in to fill the breach. And they got it down to a fine art. Fifty golden ducats would buy you a package trip, including your fare from Venice to Jaffa and back, and tours of the most important sites on arrival.

The route by sea became more popular as the Crusades approached. The stretch through Asia Minor on the route by land had once belonged to the Byzantine Christians, but by the 11th century the Seljuq Turks were all over it, and of the many groups who were a potential threat to pilgrims, the Seljuqs were the worst.

Why bother?

So, you ask, why bother with the whole thing? A fair question.

Jerusalem is a holy city for all three of the world's major monotheistic faiths — Judaism, Christianity, and Islam. For the ancient Jews, the pilgrimage to Jerusalem for Passover each year was part of the bedrock of their faith. Remember that, in ancient times, most Jews did not live any farther from Jerusalem than the countryside surrounding it. In fact, it was forbidden to sacrifice anywhere but the Temple on the Mount. The *Diaspora* (the scattering of the tribes of Israel) changed Judaism to a great extent, making it more cerebral, less tied to a physical temple. Nevertheless, each year, devout Jews still prayed at their Passover Seder, "Next year in Jerusalem."

Pilgrimage (the *hajj*) was also an ingrained idea for the Muslims. At least once in his lifetime, every devout Muslim was — and is — expected to travel to the city of Mecca, and take part in the Kaaba ritual there during the holy month of Ramadan; this is one of the five pillars of the Islamic faith. Apart from the hajj, any pilgrimage to any spot sacred to Allah is held to be a holy act for the faithful.

Christianity is the only one of the three religions that does not specifically lay out the need for pilgrimage in its rituals and dogma. Yet, pilgrimage was no less sacred to a medieval Christian. And Jerusalem was no less a holy city for the Christians. This was the land where Christ had walked. It was the city of his final ministry, of his crucifixion, burial, and resurrection. What it would mean for medieval Christians to stand in the holiest of holies, the Church of the Holy Sepulchre, the very tomb of their risen Lord, is difficult for the modern, secular mind to grasp fully.

St. Helena discovers it all

Christians had been making pilgrimages since before the Gospels were written down. But there's no question that one very powerful and determined woman brought about the virtual exodus of Christian pilgrims to Jerusalem of later centuries. Her name was Flavia Iulia Helena, now known as St. Helena, the mother of the emperor Constantine the Great, the first Christian emperor of Rome. She would leave an imprint on Christianity nearly as important as her son's.

In A.D. 327, at the spry age of 72 Helena traveled to the city of Jerusalem to see the Holy Places of her newfound Christianity before she died, guided by no less a personage than the patriarch of Jerusalem (some sources say she was as young as 53 or as old as 79). It is said that she consulted with many advisors, and then, like a Byzantine, post-menopausal Indiana Jones, set out to discover the site of Golgotha, the place of Christ's crucifixion. Beneath the cistern of a pagan temple to Aphrodite, she uncovered the remains of three wooden crosses. According to legend, she determined which had been the crosses of the two criminals and which the cross of Christ by laying an old woman who was very ill on each one of them. Needless to say, the cross of Christ was the one that cured her.

Helena returned with the True Cross to Constantinople, where her son would put it in a place of honor, crowning the last of four enormous arches that led to the entrance of the new capital he was building. He also returned a piece of it to Jerusalem, to be placed in a new church, the Church of the Holy Sepulchre, that he decided to have built over the spot. In fact, after hearing his mother's tales of the holy sites she'd seen, he passed a decree opening the treasury for her use, and the dowager empress spread it across Palestine as seed money, to build churches in all the most important holy sites.

Wherever they landed, or from whatever direction they'd come, pilgrims ended up on the coast road of the Levant, funneled toward the city of Jaffa. And running north to south along that road, strung across the coast like pearls on a harem princess, were the legendary trading cities of the eastern Mediterranean. Most had been founded by the trading empire of the Phoenicians, ten centuries before Christ. There were the famed twin cities of Sidon and Tyre, as well as Beirut, Jaffa, Acre, and Tripoli. Here Christian pilgrims were met with what must have seemed every race and creed of mankind; Berbers of North Africa, Persians from the mythic East, Arabians and Greeks, Ethiopians and Turks, all of them part of the clamor of commerce that had been thriving there for centuries, through wars and plagues and various changes of ownership. To someone who'd never been outside the confines of his village in France or Germany or England, it must have been an overwhelming experience.

These Christian dogs will buy anything! — The lucrative trade in "holy relics"

It all began with two famous remnants of the death of Christ. The first, the Holy Spear of Antioch, was found beneath the city's citadel by a monk named Peter Bartholomew who was certain it was the spear used to pierce Christ's side when he was on the cross. The Norman knights who'd just taken the city had more important things on their minds, but the monk wouldn't back down from his story. In fact, he believed it so strongly that he underwent a trial by fire to prove the spear was real — and died. Although, in the end, there are several Roman spears (at least four) that have as good a claim as any other of being the true spear. The second was the True Cross itself, object of endless conjecture, searching, and zealotry. Christian belief was absolute that touching the Cross could cure the sick and wipe away sin. At first, the sharp-eyed Arab traders of Palestine were at least a little wary, though they soon discovered that gullible Christian tourists would shell out for just about anything — old lumps of iron that became nails from the cross, the toe bone of St. Catherine, the finger bone of St. James, the sandal strap of John the Baptist, the tassels of Salome.

When the greedy and unethical knights of the Fourth Crusade carved up the Byzantine Empire, one of the first things they got their hands on was the True Cross, breaking it up into as many pieces as possible, and distributing it, like everyone's fair share of the peanut brittle, to all the knights and bishops present. After that, there wasn't a toothpick from Belgrade to Hamburg that didn't come with a provenance claiming was it part of the True Cross. Actually, there is some fairly respectable scientific evidence that many of these are the genuine article. At the very least, the relics held in churches and museums and private collections the world over came, for the most part, from the same tree. Many religious scholars have attempted to prove that, if they were all put back together, they still would not constitute enough wood to form even one cross large enough to hang a man from. Yet, considering the loopier aspects of the relics trade, it's impossible not to laugh over the words of the Protestant reformer John Calvin. "There is no abbey so poor as not to have a specimen [of the True Cross] . . . if all the pieces that could be found were collected together, they would make a ship-load. Yet, the Gospels testify that one man was able to carry it."

When they reached Jaffa, pilgrims turned east to cover the short, final distance cross-country to Jerusalem. Their first view of the city would have been of the shimmering globe of the Dome of the Rock, which they could see from the crest at the monastery of St. Samuel, the hill that was known as *Montjoie,* the joyful hill at the journey's end. The average pilgrim was particularly thrilled if he'd managed to survive the journey in one piece.

Medieval muggers

Brigandage, what nowadays we would call either a mugging or a carjacking, was a constant problem on the back roads of Europe. But that problem was unimaginably worse on the desert roads of Palestine. At one time, all of it had belonged to the Byzantine Empire, the surviving, eastern half of the Roman Empire, and a certain amount of order was kept by the legions and the city patrols of the emperor. But in 1071, a key year for the Templar story, the Byzantines were shown to the world to be a gilded and hollow shell of a once mighty empire, when they were annihilated at the Battle of Manzikert by the invading hordes of Seljuq Turks out of the steppes of Asia.

The Seljuqs were a violent tribe to begin with, before they conquered the city of Baghdad and were, in the process, converted to Islam in the late eighth century. Afterward, their radical Sunni brand of Islam went west along with them, combining religious fanaticism with an already characteristic mercilessness. When the Seljuqs swept westward out of Asia, even their fellow Sunni Muslims got out of the way.

After the arrival of the Seljuqs in Asia Minor, these incidents of brigandage were more numerous, and more deadly. Crusader forces kept Jerusalem safe, but when you were outside the city walls, all bets were off. Distant areas like Galilee, close to cities held by the Turks, were particularly dangerous. For example, in 1119, the year the Templars were formed, 700 pilgrims were attacked by Saracens on their way to visit the River Jordan at Easter. Three hundred were killed, and 60 more whisked off to the slave market. This was not a minor irritant — it was a major problem. And there's a good chance that this was the final straw that led to the formation of the Knights Templars.

Due to the many upheavals of Palestine over the centuries, not to mention the persistent lack of any local authority to keep order, the roads of the Holy Land were always teeming with shady characters of every race, color, and creed. Small bands of out-of-work mercenaries hunted together, as well as deserters from the various armies who'd marched through over the years, the Persians and the Arabs, the Byzantines and the Crusaders. Throw in some cutthroats who'd jumped ship at one of the Levantine ports, a few local sheep herders who were looking for ways to augment their income, and then add just a dash of the bully boys who simply love their work, and you've got the most villainous witch's brew of thugs, vandals, rapists, thieves, assassins, pickpockets, sadists, and reprobates to ever blacken the pages of history.

Just who is a Saracen, anyway?

When you read the journals and letters of medieval travelers to the Holy Land, you see the term *Saracen* a lot. To these Europeans, it was a blanket term, one that referred to Arabs, Turks, or Syrians, and just about anyone else who was a Muslim. *Turk* is another term that comes along often, especially a little later in history. Although modern scholars have sometimes tried to paint the word Saracen as some sort of racial slur, it really wasn't. These people didn't read the *New York Times* over coffee. They knew little enough about the geopolitical realities of their own countries, much less the complex weave of races and nations that made up the fabric of the Near East in this period.

Even if they'd wanted to go straight and turn over a new leaf, Palestine wasn't the place to do it. No matter what the Bible says about the land of milk and honey, this was a land laid waste, crippled by poverty and drought. So why, you may ask, didn't they roam off to look for greener pastures? Willie Sutton famously said, when he was asked why he robbed banks, "Because that's where they keep the money." For these sharks, the flow of pilgrims down the road to glory was a smorgasbord. These pilgrims were often old or weak, as well as naive and starry-eyed, carrying their cash and all the rest of their earthly possessions, their eyes fixed on the eastern horizon instead of their money belts. It was like ringing the dinner bell.

And now, after Manzikert, the thieves, pirates, and cutthroats behind every rock and around every bend were reinforced by the Seljuqs, who were essentially organized and well-armed thieves, pirates, and cutthroats.

Where'd everybody go?

The First Crusade (see Chapter 2), called by Pope Urban II in 1095, was really the only Crusade that achieved its stated goal. The Crusaders had defeated the Turks and taken for themselves the territory of the Levant, which was the tactically and economically important coastline of the eastern Mediterranean. By the year 1100, the four Crusader States, or Latin States, of the Holy Land had been formed (see Figure 3-1). One of the most respected of the knights who'd fought the campaign, Godfrey de Bouillon, was made "Defender of the Holy Sepulchre," essentially the king of Jerusalem in everything but title. Afterward, everybody had a good meal on Godfrey, and then decided they were ready to go home. Well, after all, they hadn't come to do any nation-building.

All at once it dawned on the lords of the First Crusade that they had a dilemma: How were they going to hold this land they'd taken, so that it didn't fall back into Turkish hands about 15 minutes after they hit the road? It was a continuing problem with warfare in the Middle Ages. Under the feudal system of the day, the knights who held fiefdoms under any particular lord were bound to give over a certain number of armed men for any of the lord's campaigns, a number generally set by the size and wealth of the fief in question. But there was a time limit to this service, because the knight's principle objective was to hold and work the land he'd been given. Very often, the amount of time owed for military service was a mere 40 days a year. That system was fine if your principal enemy was the duke whose lands adjoined yours. But for a Crusader knight, 40 days would just about have gotten him to the port of Brindisi in Italy. Clearly, this system wasn't going to work very well in an expanding Christian universe.

Slowly, as kings became wealthier and more powerful, the professional standing army of paid mercenaries would be born. But at this time period, standing armies simply didn't exist for the warlords of the First Crusade. In fact, when the Knights Templar came along, many historians consider them to have been the first standing army in Europe since the age of Rome. Of course, *this* standing army didn't stand their ground because they were paid to. These men would give up their homes and commit themselves to loneliness, poverty, and perpetual warfare for their love of Christ and their hope of salvation.

After the mass exodus of Crusaders back to Europe, it's estimated that as few as 300 knights and perhaps as many foot soldiers remained to garrison Jerusalem. For this skeleton crew who remained behind, it was to their good fortune that the Muslims of the period were too busy fighting one another to make a major, concerted attempt to dislodge the Christians. There was a grave and bloody line in the sand between the Sunni Muslims of the north and east, like the Seljuq Turks or the caliphs of Baghdad, and the Shiite Muslims of the powerful Fatimid Caliphate in Egypt. They despised one another as heretics, and the wars between them, both large and petty, kept them employed for the next 40 years. In fact, it seemed to successive rulers of the Crusader states that this dividing line between the Muslims to the northeast and the Muslims to the southwest would always serve to protect them, and they quite deliberately made various pacts with first one and then another Islamic lord, playing them off of one another. The Crusaders' worst nightmare, an axis forming between the two Islamic worlds that could surround and strangle their new nation of Outremer (their term for the Latin States) was another century away.

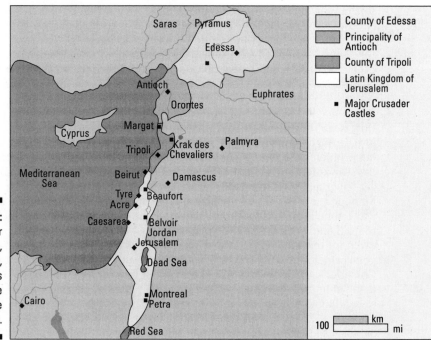

Figure 3-1: The major cities, counties, and castles during the time of the Templars.

REMEMBER

In fact, the four Latin States would have been there for nearly 50 years before the arrival of the first serious threat to their existence, in the form of the Muslim warlord Zengi of Mosul. At that point, around 1144, they sent out an SOS, and the Second Crusade was put together. They had taken Jerusalem in July of 1099, but the first major reinforcement of Crusader knights from Europe didn't arrive in the Holy Land until 1147.

Yet, during this period between the First and the Second Crusades, the pilgrims came once again, not in dribs and drabs, but in waves. They were used to dangerous territory — it was the common experience of all Europeans who risked travel, but the treacherous roads of the East were even worse than the ones they'd left behind. For safety's sake, they often traveled in groups, sometimes fairly large ones. But this really didn't help much if they were part of a caravan of ragtag men with little or no battle training, herding their women and children with them — especially not in the face of a massed attack of ruthless Turkish warriors. Jerusalem was taken, and Jerusalem was held. But in reality it didn't make much sense for the Crusaders to have bled to take the Holy City, not if the average pilgrim couldn't survive the journey to get there.

A New Knighthood

Two fabled knights finally decided that something had to be done about it. They were Hugues de Payens, a noble knight from the Champagne region in France, and Geoffrey de St. Omer, a Flemish knight from northern France. Legend has it that the two knights were so poor upon their arrival in the Holy Land that they shared a horse, the origin of the famous symbol of the Knights Templar (see Chapter 4).

"The Poor Knights of Christ"

Between 1119 and 1120, Hugues de Payens and Geoffrey de St. Omer gathered about them seven fellow knights whose thinking was similar to their own. They called themselves the Poor Knights of Christ (or more formally, the Poor Fellow Soldiers of Christ), and their mission would be to protect pilgrims on the road to Jerusalem.

Their actions were not entirely without precedent. Across Europe in the 10th and 11th centuries, poverty and political anarchy — two forces that will always breed lawlessness and thievery — were widespread. By the late tenth century, it was becoming somewhat common for small confraternities of knights to take it upon themselves to support and guard a particular shrine or monastery that was in danger from the nomadic bands of outlaws that controlled the roads in the backcountry. They bound themselves to one another for the sake of their avowed purpose. This effort was a strictly volunteer one, something that a knight with the time or the opportunity undertook for the sake of his Christian faith. During the Crusades, this basic idea became even more popular, the creation of a shared fraternal experience that gave one particular group of knights a common identity.

This was essentially how the Poor Knights of Christ were born, in a volunteer effort to protect and to aid Christian pilgrims. But what made these men remarkable was the length to which they were willing to go for the sake of their faith. The natural desire to return to their homes was put aside. More importantly, they discussed it, and then took it upon themselves to swear to the vows of a monk as well as a knight. These were the vows of St. Augustine, promising poverty, chastity, and obedience. No church or brotherhood had asked this of them — it was a sacrifice to their faith that they made of their own free will.

Legend has it that Baldwin II, King of Jerusalem at that time, was quite taken with the idea, and the first two young French noblemen, Hugues and Geoffrey, took their vows before the king and the patriarch of Jerusalem on Christmas Day in 1119. A few weeks into the new year, all nine knights gathered together at the Council of Nablus, north of Jerusalem, and were formally accepted by the clergy meeting there.

The Knights Templar

King Baldwin was thrilled and handed over a portion of the Temple Mount, around the area of the Al-Aqsa Mosque, to the knights as their new home. The Crusaders always called Al-Aqsa the Temple of Solomon, though whether from a stubborn denial of an Islamic presence there or simple ignorance that it had been built as a mosque is debatable. Regardless, the area given to the Poor Knights of Christ was believed to be the ruins of the temple, and they became known as the Poor Knights of Christ and the Temple, or more simply, the Knights Templar.

It was sometimes said of the Poor Knights that their pride was their undoing, but in those first lonely years in the desert, there was no arrogance or vanity in this sacrifice. They had chosen a harsh and dangerous life, not to mention an ascetic one, and there was no one around to applaud. But as time passed and the legend grew, this additional sacrifice of taking holy orders was an act that would ennoble them in the eyes of their contemporaries. To voluntarily give up gambling and whoring, drinking and pillaging —the most cherished pastimes of any knight — was an act without precedence in the history of the faith.

The Temple Mount: Ground zero for Jews, Christians, and Muslims

The Temple Mount, the low hill in Jerusalem, is the most sacred place on earth for the Jewish faith. It is also, without doubt, the most hotly contested, blood-soaked piece of ground on earth. It stands on the site upon which Abraham was prepared to sacrifice his son's life for his faith, before God stayed his hand, and promised him the hill and beyond for a nation of his descendants. But after making war with the Babylonians, the Seleucids, and numerous other invaders, Jerusalem was stamped flat by the Romans in three major wars that strung out through the first and second centuries A.D. The Temple Mount stood barren and abandoned. At the Wailing Wall, the last remnant of the great temple, Jews mourn the loss of it to the present day.

In the century after the conversion of Constantine in A.D. 321, Jerusalem had been a Christian city. It remained one until the rise of the Persian Empire (modern-day Iran), which invaded Palestine, laying siege to Jerusalem and taking the city in A.D. 614. Roughly 60,000 Christians were slaughtered. The new young Byzantine emperor, Heraclius, defeated the Persians at the Battle of Nineveh in 627. The Persians had taken the remnants of the True Cross, as well as other Christian relics, back to their capital as prizes of war. Heraclius, in the year 630, rode through the gates of Jerusalem in triumph, returning the True Cross to its home in the Church of the Holy Sepulchre.

At this point, Jerusalem began to change hands more often than the government of Italy. In the seventh and early eighth centuries after Christ, a warrior of Mecca named Mohammed created a new religion and converted the whole of the Arabian peninsula, before he set out to conquer the rest of humanity, all in the space of ten years. After the death of Mohammed in 632, his followers poured out of Saudi Arabia, mowing down any armies, large or small, who got in their way. To the astonishment of the world, both East and West, the armies of Islam stormed North Africa, knocked out the mighty Persian Empire, and then began to devour all the Near East — including Jerusalem. Jerusalem's conqueror, Caliph Omar, prayed on the Temple Mount and then ordered the construction of a mosque — later replaced by the Al-Aqsa Mosque — to honor Mohammed, who was said to have had a dream on this spot in which an angel promised him his ascent to heaven.

Still, for the next few centuries, as far as Jews and Christian pilgrims were concerned, the whole thing could have been a lot worse. It's true that the Muslims claimed the Temple Mount as Islam's possession, and proceeded to pave it over like a pork-barrel governor spending out a fat federal highway grant, only to lay out another, larger mosque, the Dome of the Rock. But for the time being, Christians and Jews living under Muslim rule could still go to their shrines and pray to their God. For Mohammed, the other three monotheistic faiths — the Jews, the Christians, and the Zoroastrians (the Persians had been Zoroastrians) — were called the People of the Book, and were treated better than pagans, who were killed at once. If the People of the Book chose not to convert, they had to live under a system called *dhimmitude,* a state of second-class citizenship in a Muslim country that included high taxes and some occasional, humiliating razzing. But they could still worship as they pleased.

But by the ninth and tenth centuries, the sun was setting on the once-powerful Umayyad Caliphate of Omar, which was followed by the Abbasid dynasty. The next overlord to take Palestine and southern Syria was one of history's complete nut cases, the ruler of the Fatimid Caliphate of Egypt, which was reaching its peak of power and dominance.

(continued)

(continued)

His name, in a very abbreviated version, was Abu Ali Al-Mansur, alias Al-Hakim bi-Amr Allah (Arabic for "Ruler by God's Command"). He became the sixth caliph of the Fatimid Shiite dynasty of Egypt in 996. But Al-Hakim is far more commonly known as the "Mad Caliph," and with ample cause. If not an out-and-out psychotic, he was at the very least the worst sort of bipolar problem child. His mood swings were remarkable; sometimes he was doing the work of an enlightened ruler, feeding the poor and founding universities; other times, he was persecuting one faith or another, and ordering all the dogs in the nation to be killed because he was annoyed by the sound of barking.

Although he was raised by a Christian mother, he later converted to Islam. More surprisingly, the chief targets of his eccentric cruelties were Christians. For ten years he passed one vindictive ordinance after another against them, moving up to looting and burning at least *30,000* Christian churches in his realm. He topped it off in 1009 by burning the Church of the Holy Sepulchre in Jerusalem, which lies just to the west of the Temple Mount. He later magnanimously gave the Byzantine emperor permission to rebuild it. He hated Jews, as well, and his actions against them were in a similar vein.

However, in 1016, he committed a majorly dumb move — he declared himself to be a divinity, ordering all Shiite mosques to pray to him as they did to Allah. This one was more than the Sunnis could take. The Abbasids had faded, but Sunnism was experiencing an upsurge in power under the rule of the Seljuq Turks. They were appalled at this apostasy by a Muslim ruler. As far as Al-Hakim was concerned, he was simply delivering the good news, and was miffed to no end by the reaction to his divinity of his Muslim brothers. In a snit, he rescinded all his laws against Christians and Jews and gave them freedom to worship once more. He even put Christians and Jews at his court and paid to rebuild some of the churches and synagogues he'd burned.

He had hoped, of course, to get under the skin of the Sunni Muslims. Unfortunately for him, he got a little *too* deep under their skin. Hakim disappeared without a trace while taking an evening stroll on February 13, 1021. Some said that he had ascended into heaven, but most of the more pragmatic sort believe that he was assassinated by his Sunni enemies, who had the help of his sister, the princess Sitt al-Mulk, who despised him. Luckily for Islam, this left him no time to turn on his new enemies and burn down the mosques on the Temple Mount.

Today the fighting continues over this small piece of real estate (about the size of two football fields). Muslims will allow no historical digging to take place on the site of either holy site. Recently, an attempt by Jewish archeologists to get round this by tunneling far beneath the Dome of the Rock, in search of remnants of Solomon's Temple, has caused nothing but street riots and bloodshed. For more on the Temple Mount, check tomorrow's newspaper.

Logic as well as history tells us that these men were extremely poor, living a marginal existence in the unforgiving backcountry of Palestine, disdaining any spoils of the victor of the sort their fellow knights had taken, before turning tail to head for home. The Templars would stay in the wilderness, like their hero John the Baptist. They would stay, and they would continue the fight.

Their force was small, but it's important to remember that, at this junction of history, the mounted and armed knight was a formidable enemy, worth more than a dozen foot soldiers. However, despite the fabled power of a mounted knight, there's no denying the fact that nine was a rather paltry force, especially to cover all the 40-odd miles of ground between Jerusalem and the Mediterranean coast.

Keeping their oath

So now, the Knights Templar, all nine of them, had taken upon themselves a job of unimaginable difficulty and complexity: They were going to keep the roads in and out of Jerusalem safe. To do it, they were going to need more than courage, skill, and money. There's a certain naiveté in this vow that's heart-warming, but disturbing. It's one thing to believe you have God on your side; it's quite another to jump off the roof in order to test God's fidelity. Jerusalem and its surrounding precincts had been the site of one calamity after another, including invasion, siege, civil war, religious conflict, blood feuds, brawls, mass executions, betrayals, sneak attacks, street riots, and a general level of incessant belligerence that would have made Saddam Hussein feel right at home.

In other words, what might seem on the surface a simple mission could, and did, get really tangled up by the grim political realities of the Holy Land. The Templars were idealists, but Jerusalem had swallowed up many an idealist before their time.

A Simple Mission Creates a Powerful Institution

Historians don't know very much about the early years of the Templars. From their formation in 1119, they must have been at least attempting to increase their force; it simply stands to reason. Yet there is no record of how many knights patrolled the Route of the Pilgrims over the course of the next ten years. We do know that by 1125, when their founder, Hugues de Payens, set sail for France to seek money and converts, there were enough Templars for him to take a small number of knights with him, and to leave behind a force that would continue the job.

Digging in the temple

One of the prevailing stories told about the early days of the Knights Templar has to do with their headquarters on the Temple Mount. There is an area directly under the southeast corner of the mount, where the dirt falls away to reveal rooms carved into the rock itself. It is commonly referred to as Solomon's Stables, but it is unlikely that it existed before Herod rebuilt the Temple. And it wasn't really used as stables until the Crusaders arrived. In actuality, it's sort of a subbasement to the Temple Mount, extending the support for the flat area above it. This area has been associated with the Templars and has been the source of much speculation in recent years.

Here's the way this line of enquiry usually goes:

> Nine knights could never credibly hope to protect the entire city of Jerusalem, *so* . . .
>
> They had to have another reason for creating this cover story, *so* . . .
>
> They arranged for the King of Jerusalem to give them this seemingly worthless bunch of rooms under the Temple, *so* . . .
>
> They could dig up King Solomon's buried treasure that the previous 2,000 years' worth of invaders had never managed to find before them.

And, goes the rest of the theory, when they had the treasure in their grasp, Hugues trotted off to Rome to arrange for papal immunity from all secular laws; they cashed in on the vast wealth they found (or the mysterious secret knowledge they discovered — it's told both ways). Whatever it was, it made them the most powerful force in the world.

Dan Brown, among other speculative researchers, has long claimed that the templar HQ was in Solomon's Stables. The truth is that the Templars really *did* use the stables as, well, stables. Their living quarters and the offices of the order were above, in what is now the al-Aqsa Mosque.

We discuss the various permutations of this legend in Chapter 7. What's important to this stage of the Templar's real history is that no one actually knows just what *did* go on in the first decade of the their mission in the Holy Land.

A windfall of money and power

As any aspiring actor can tell you, sometimes, after years of fruitless labor in dinner theaters, performing in bit parts without recognition, it only takes meeting one important person at one important moment to create an "overnight" sensation. Sometimes it only takes a word in the right ear.

For the Templars, the right ear came along in 1120. Fulk V, the count of Anjou, was very definitely a player. Not only would he one day be king of Jerusalem himself, but he very cleverly arranged the marriage of his son, Geoffrey Plantagenet, to Matilda, daughter of the English King Henry I. After a very ugly civil war in England, his grandson would sit on the English throne as Henry II, first of the Angevin line of kings, more commonly called the Plantagenets. Between the holdings of his grandfather and his wife, Henry II would own more French territory than did France's king. Count Fulk's blood was bluer than blue, and he was a political force in both France and England.

Fulk came to Jerusalem in 1120, met Hugues de Payens, and was deeply impressed, both by the Order and its mission. He asked to be made an honorary Templar, and because the knights were desperately poor, he pledged them a yearly sum in support. The seed was planted. Through the influence of Count Fulk with his powerful friends, other nobles stepped up to the plate to help the Poor Knights. These friends included a man of great importance in the Templar story, Hugh, count of Champagne.

Hugh had visited the Latin States twice in the previous 15 years, and on the second occasion he'd been accompanied by Hugues de Payens as one of Count Hugh's vassals. Hugh held court for Champagne in the city of Troyes, which would become something of a home city for the Templars. It's very near Payens, and in fact, it's been speculated but never proven that Hugues was also a kinsman of the count of Champagne. When the count returned to the Holy Land for the last time, in 1125, he himself became a Knight Templar.

For the Poor Knights, Hugues de Payens's trip to France in 1127 would have great consequences. He was sent by the king of Jerusalem to achieve several diplomatic aims for him, as well as to secure for the Templars a more formal recognition by the Church. Hugues was successful in all his missions, but the most important thing to happen to him in France was his meeting with Bernard of Clairvaux.

Bernard of Clairvaux

Bernard was without doubt the most influential theologian of his day. He reformed the fledgling Cistercian Order and made it his own, an order with a structure different from any other in the monastic world. His stature as a theologian would see him canonized in 1174, and he is now more properly known as St. Bernard. He was a man of ecstatic, passionate faith, and apparently an accomplished public speaker, who swayed his audiences with the power of his beliefs. Bernard had a great friend and supporter in Hugh of Champagne, and through him gained a thorough understanding of the situation in the East. Bernard also understood the tactical situation for the Templars because it is probable that André de Montbard was not only one of the first of the nine Templar knights, but also Bernard's uncle. With all his passion for the monastic life, Bernard did not kid himself into thinking that what the Latin States needed were more monasteries. He knew and understood the dangerous military situation.

For the next two years Hugues de Payens would travel in the highest circles of France and England, even attending the aforementioned wedding of Matilda to Geoffrey Plantagenet. Land grants and monies were coming at him from all sides — gifts of nobles both petty and great. In England, he established the first Templar preceptory in Europe, at what is now the north end of Chancery Lane, in an area of London that still bears the name Temple Bar. It's not far from the magnificent Templar church inside the Inns of Court. Hugues also traveled as far as Scotland and Flanders, spreading the word about the Templars and seeking donations. Despite his successes, the upcoming Council of Troyes was always in his mind, as he attempted to prepare for the most important moment of his journey.

The Council of Troyes

By the opening of the Council of Troyes (the capitol of Champagne in France), in 1129, Hugues de Payens was a shoo-in. In fact, the Templars were a comet streaking across the medieval sky, absolutely unstoppable. Before the council of high churchmen, de Payens gave a straightforward speech about the founding of the Order, its goals, and the religious structure of its days — both at the Temple base and when they were abroad. Afterward, Bernard and his assistants drew up what came to be called the Latin Rule of the Templars, consisting of 72 regulations that would form the core of the Rule of the Templars, although it would be added to several times. With Bernard at the helm, the Rule followed many of the patterns set down in his own rule for the Cistercian Order of monks.

This original core is often referred to as the Primitive Rule, to separate it from later additions, especially the Hierarchical Statutes that were added around 1165, mostly dealing with obligations and privileges of Templar officers. In the end, it would come to 686 articles that covered every conceivable aspect of the Templars' daily lives. (For more on the daily life of the Templars, see Chapter 4.) They were to wear white habits to signify their purity, while lesser officers, such as sergeants, squires, and other brothers in support positions, were to wear dark brown or black. The Primitive Rule was a handbook for a lifestyle that was extremely grim and austere, highlighted by silence at meals apart from Bible readings, no possession of *any* personal property, no visits from women, discouraged even if they were of the knight's family, and incessant sessions of prayer based on the cycle of matins, prime, vespers, and so on, which was called the *Hours,* the structure for chapel in any monastery.

There were only two meals per day, meat no more than three times per week, an overwhelming emphasis on work and prayer, and admonitions of any laughter, horseplay, close friendships, or even the sight of the opposite sex. Vanity was discouraged to such a degree that the Rule even discussed the limit on permitted decorations on a knight's arms or bridle. One of the calls to prayer, *matins,* even broke the sleep of the Templars in half, calling them to appear at chapel at 4 a.m., and then return to their beds for a little more sleep. All in all, it must have been a joyless, oppressive existence, like one interminable dirge.

Division of labors

The hierarchy of the Order was also established at the Council:

- ✔ **Grand Master:** Elected by the Order, not appointed. The Grand Master was answerable only to the pope.

- ✔ **Knights Templar Masters:** Sort of the area vice presidents of the Order. There was a Master for each nation or regional area.

- ✔ **Preceptors:** Four or five were assigned to assist the Grand Master and the "regional" Masters. It is the Latin word for "commander."

- ✔ **Priors:** The fighting knights themselves.

In addition, each knight had a sergeant assigned to assist him in combat, who rode into battle sharing the knight's horse. In a battle, the sergeant was to dismount and act as a foot soldier to protect his assigned knight. Sergeants and each knight's personal priest wore black or brown robes. All other members of the Order wore white.

Battle rules

The Templar knight went into battle in state-of-the-art protective gear: a chainmail *coif* over his head, a steel helmet or cap, a shield, a straight broadsword, a mace, a lance, a dagger, and sometimes a smaller knife.

The knights would ride to the scene of the battle with their sergeant. The sergeant would dismount, and the knights would then charge the enemy with a lance in one hand and a shield in the other. At the last minute, the lance would be thrown at an oncoming enemy, and the sword would be drawn for closer combat.

Behave yourselves

The Order had strict rules of conduct (see Chapter 4). No one was forced to remain in the Order, but anyone who quit had to turn over his Templar robe within two days, so he could no longer dress like one of them. Templar proceedings and rules were kept secret (not unusual for the period — the Knights Hospitallers and Teutonic Knights of the same period had similar rules). No scandals were tolerated. When punishments were meted out, they were frequently done in public, so the citizenry could see that proper justice was done.

Opposition to the Templars

Despite their sacrifices in the name of grace, many conservative theologians wrote passionate treatises against the notion of monks who were also warriors.

The ups and downs of medieval warfare

Their force was small, but it's important to remember that, at this juncture of history, the mounted and armed knight was a formidable enemy, even without the support of foot soldiers. Men who were not well-trained soldiers, but rather the dregs of the desert, would not have wanted to face a Frankish knight wielding an axe or broadsword; they were cautious warriors, but skilled and fearless. The Frankish warriors were justifiably famous for their ability to carefully arrange horse and foot soldiers on the battlefield, which is one reason the Turks loved the tactic of attacking from the rear and upsetting their carefully organized apple cart. The Franks were well versed in the tactics of the heavy charge with drawn lances, but the Turks had faster, lighter horses and their archers could pick off the knights from a distance.

Over the course of the next three centuries, the tactical advantage of armored knights would begin to fade throughout the world, as archers became more skilled and their arrows more deadly. Historians often cite the Battle of Agincourt in 1415 as the finish of mounted and armored knights. In that battle, Henry V of England, who was invading France to put forward his claim to the French crown, won a stunning victory over the French, deploying his 6,000 men against a force of over 20,000. Though his tactics were brilliant throughout, it was the power and skill of his deadly archers that won the day. Like the dropping of the atom bomb or the first use of artillery, it was one of those turning points in military history that was quite a shock to the system. Dirty and ignorant English peasants had brought down the cream of the French nobility, and warfare would never be the same again. Still, this growth of the power of archers was already happening by the 13th century, as can be seen in the tactical disaster of the Battle of Hattin, a major loss for the Templars.

Mounted Frankish knights could fire arrows, but the Turks were much better at it, with an incredible rate of fire, even turned backward in their saddles to take out pursuers—the origin of the term "parting shot." (For more on the Battle of Hattin, see Chapter 4.)

A monk was a person who was never, under any circumstances, permitted to arm himself. When sent on a mission to convert pagans, he was expected to die rather than take up arms, even in self-defense, and thereby show with his courage the truth of his Christian message. In response to all the grousing, Bernard wrote *In Praise of the New Knighthood,* outlining the virtue of holy war with a persuasiveness that's a little chilling.

In spite of the rhetorical eloquence of Bernard's tract, remnants of opposition remained. They wouldn't just be checkmated. In fact, they were about to be slam-dunked.

The Explosion of the Order

After the Council of Troyes, something remarkable happened. The 12th century was not exactly the communication age. It was a time when Crusaders' letters to loved ones could take months to arrive, if they arrived at all, a time when pilgrims could be swallowed up by the East, never to return, with the folks back home never knowing what had become of them. Yet, in this age of isolation and lack of information, the legend of the Poor Knights who guarded the pilgrims to the Holy Land sped across Europe with astonishing speed. There is little doubt that a great deal of this was due to the unceasing work of Bernard of Clairvaux, who preached the Templar cause wherever he went. But there was really more to it than that. In the medieval world, people loved a good story, especially one that contained epic elements of faith, revenge, courage, and the eternal struggle of the everyman to choose between good and evil. The story of the Poor Knights had it all, and it was a tale that gripped the imagination of 11th-century Europe.

New gifts

In short order, Europe turned into a five-alarm love-fest for the Templars. The nobility of Europe lined up to give lavish gifts to the Templars:

- ✔ England donated lands in Herefordshire, Essex, Lincolnshire, and Buckinghamshire
- ✔ King Lothar III ("the Fat") gave a castle at Supplingenberg in northern Germany
- ✔ Spanish counts in the frontier region of Urgel gave castles in Grañena and Barberà in Catalonia
- ✔ French nobles gave over land in Baudiment, Carlat, Dole, Foix, Laon, La Rochelle, Nice, and Richereches.

France's King Louis VI got so concerned at the amount of property being tossed to the Templars that he finally put his foot down and proclaimed that French towns and castles could no longer be signed over to the Order, no matter *who* owned them.

Eyes of the pope

When Bernard of Clairvaux was on the move, the Templars experienced an explosion of growth that was stunning to the Christian world. From 1139 to 1145, six different popes issued a series of pronouncements that gave the Templars remarkable and singular powers.

The popes of the 10th and early 11th centuries were a pretty sorry lot, including "holy men" like the teenaged John XII, called the "Caligula of the Papacy." He gambled, spent money like water, turned the Lateran Palace into a whorehouse, and was killed by a jealous husband when caught in bed with the wife in question. Worse, many of these tenth-century popes had been violent men;

in fact, between 872 and 1012, a third of the popes who ruled the Holy See met a violent end, often at the hand of the next pope in line. Many popes of the great families of Italy had bastard children who followed them onto the papal throne as if they'd been Hapsburgs or Windsors.

Pope Gregory XII, St. Gregory, set out to change all that. He went to work on lust, luxury, and simony in the Lateran Palace. But because of the scandals of the past, theologians were very sensitive about the subject of violence committed in the name of Christ.

Yet, the purity and purpose of the Templars won over a long line of popes. When Hugues de Payens died in 1136, he left behind an Order far more prosperous, respected, and famous than the one he'd founded. It fell to the next Templar Grand Master, Robert de Craon, also known as Robert the Burgundian, to consolidate and increase those gains. And brother, did he manage it neatly and quickly. Apparently, he believed in going straight to the top. The powers he envisioned being granted to the Templars could only be the gift of the pope of Rome.

Within three years, he'd secured from Pope Innocent II the first of three papal *bulls* (documents stating the pope's position on some subject or other, given the weight of a command under canon law) that would give the Templars unprecedented powers and independence. *Omne datum optimum,* the first and most important of these bulls, was issued on March 29, 1139. It basically put the Templars above the mortal strain, making them answerable in their actions only to the pope. It recognized their officers and system of governance, approved the gifts given them, and exempted the knights from paying any tithes. It allowed them their own inner clergy of priests, chaplain brothers who were there strictly to hear their confessions and perform mass. They were permitted to hear the divine office in their own chapels. Templar knights had the power to give the last rites and absolve sin, even of a priest.

This bull was the foundation. Two more, from two upcoming popes, simply added to those powers. The bull of Pope Celestine in 1144 urged priests to raise money for the Templars and offered penances for any person or organization that gave money to the Templars. A year later, Pope Eugenius III's bull for the most part backed up the other two, with a few perks added. Eugenius was making it clear where he stood. And one more thing — if Templars were accused of having committed a crime, they could not be tried by the secular authority of any nation, but only by an ecclesiastical court.

The Templars had become "untouchable."

International Bankers

In the Middle Ages, and for some reason most particularly in the 10th and 11th centuries, many scandals rocked the Catholic Church, scandals that were very often sexual in nature. If they weren't sexual, then they prominently featured that other devil's tool, money. It would be the 15th century and the arrival of the Borgia popes before the Holy See was brought as low as it was by some of the 10th- and 11th-century popes mentioned earlier in this chapter. Apart from that, nearly every major Catholic order, from the Benedictines to the Franciscans, had some sort of scandal, large or small.

All but the Templars. No matter what was said about other orders, the Templars had a reputation for purity, purpose, and rigid self-restraint. It was for this reason that the accusations that rained down on the Templars out of the blue in 1307 — charges of heresy, sodomy, and extortion — were so difficult for most people to believe. There was really only one gripe that people had with the Templars: that they were money-grubbing. They always, *always* had a hand out, palm up, pleading for more donations. However, in defense of the Templars, one thing really needs to be said. Apart from the enormous and impressive Templar Commanderies in the capitals of Europe, their other Commanderies and Preceptories were generally fairly modest, although expensively numerous. Most of the money was being poured into holding the Latin States. It paid for the construction of the enormous Templar fortresses that ran all along the hostile borders of the four major Crusader states. Their avowed purpose — to defend Christianity and to protect its pilgrims — got more and more expensive with each passing year. Running an international operation of this size and scope was incredibly costly.

We must make one more point about the Templars as bankers for the sake of fairness: The fact was, they'd gotten involved in the banking business to begin with in order to help pilgrims to the East. This was a world in which, if you needed enough gold or silver to last you through a six-month or a year-long journey, you had no choice but to carry it with you, and pray you had the wherewithal to guard it. Otherwise, you were likely to find yourself in the middle of nowhere, thousands of miles from home, begging for your supper. Not a pretty picture.

But the Knights Templar came up with an absolutely brilliant solution to this constant problem. And the structure of this solution is one of the reasons they needed such a large number of Preceptories in Europe and the East. The Romans had some interesting systems of money transfer, and yet it's more than fair to say that it was the Knights Templar who invented the idea of international banking. It was a godsend to any and all who were traveling for any reason, and especially those traveling on a pilgrimage. The beauty of the system was its simplicity.

Check, please

Anyone, knight or squire, merchant or pilgrim, could take the money he'd put together to go East and deliver it into the hands of the nearest Templar preceptory. There, he would be given a piece of paper stating the amount of his deposit. Then, whenever the need for money arose, he could present this paper at the preceptory nearest him, and withdraw some or all of it, receiving a new paper stating the adjusted amount he had with the Templars. In later chapters, we discuss the Templar use of secret codes and ciphers. For the time being, it's interesting to note that even these cheques were written in a code based on Latin. This way, even if the cheque were to fall into the hands of a thief, he would be exposed as such the moment he tried to present it at a Templar commandery and claim the money as his own. It was a brilliant system, and it worked like gangbusters, solving a major problem for those on the road East. Essentially, it was an American Express traveler's cheque. And for God's sake, you didn't dare leave home without it.

From the highest to the lowest born, money in coin was a hard-won commodity in the Middle Ages. Even today, people are aware of the amount in their savings account or the size of their paycheck, and would notice any suspicious discrepancy on the spot. But for two centuries, the people of Europe, of every rank, handed their money over to the Templars without thinking twice. This fact in and of itself is a powerful argument for the esteem in which these knights were held. No one doubted that his money would be in good hands when dealing with these noblest of Christ's soldiers.

Building boom

A vow of poverty is one thing, but there's no denying that as their reach extended across the Holy Land and Europe, the Templars needed to have castles and fortifications to protect the money pilgrims deposited, to house their growing numbers. As a result, the Templars hired indigenous stonemasons to help them design and build these great castles and chapels, a few of which survive today.

The knights, like most who went off to the Crusades, were generally illiterate, and there were no skilled architects or masons among them. So, the Templars would hire local builders, who introduced Byzantine and Muslim design into their projects. The distinctive round churches for which the Order became famous was said to be a copy of the Church of the Holy Sepulchre, which was, in turn, a Byzantine design.

When the Templars fanned out across Europe, they had no desire to train new architects and foremen, so they undoubtedly brought these foreign building types and methods to a largely rough and rugged Western countryside.

Imitation, the Sincerest Form of Flattery

The Templars were unlike any religious or military order that had existed before it, and their eventual lofty position as "the untouchables" within the politics of the Roman Church was unmatched. It didn't take long for other knights to seek similar privileges and powers.

The Knights Hospitaller

A Benedictine abbey had been established in Jerusalem by merchants from the Amalfi area of Italy in 1050. Thirty years later, a hospice was opened next to the abbey for the care and comfort of pilgrims. A soldier (or merchant — accounts vary) named Gerard Thom arrived in the Holy City in about 1100 and was placed in charge of the hospice. The Blessed Gerard, as he came to be known, is credited as the founder and first Grand Master of the Order of the Hospital of St. John of Jerusalem, or more simply, the Knights Hospitaller.

In 1121, the Hospitallers' second Grand Master, Raymond du Puy de Provence, peddled his strong family influences with Rome into new prestige for the Order. Over time, as the riffraff went home, leaving dedicated knights behind to protect and defend the Holy Land, the mission of the Hospitallers expanded to include not just running a hospital, but the creation of a well-trained and disciplined fighting force as well. Raymond built an infirmary next to Jerusalem's Church of the Holy Sepulchre, along with transforming the growing Order into a respected military force. Thus began a rivalry with the Knights Templar that would last until the Templars' fall, and beyond it.

The Hospitallers adopted a uniform that was the inverse opposite of the white mantles of the Templars. They wore black surcoats, emblazoned with the eight-pointed *Amalfi cross* (later called the Maltese cross when the Knights moved their headquarters to the Island of Malta; see Chapter 4).

What made the Hospitallers unusual was the division of duties within the Order. Some knights engaged in military battles and the defense of the Holy Land, but others were dedicated to healing the sick and wounded. Like the Templars, they were given the extraordinary position of being answerable only to the pope, and misbehaving members of the Order could only be tried in papal courts, making them essentially immune to the laws of the countries in which they resided.

Also like the Templars, the Hospitallers had massive holdings throughout the Holy Land and Europe. Their London headquarters were just up the road from the Templars, and they too had Commanderies and Priories.

When the Templars were arrested, tried, and disbanded in the 1300s, their rivals, the Knights Hospitaller, were the principal beneficiaries of their misfortune: The Hospitallers were handed the vast majority of Templar property, though not the Templar gold. (For more about the Hospitallers' later role in the Templars' fate, see Chapter 5.)

The Knights Hospitallers were eventually forced from the Holy Land, moving their headquarters first to the Greek island of Rhodes, and then to the

Mediterranean island of Malta, where they became known as the Knights of Malta. They survive today as a modern chivalric organization (see Chapter 9).

The Teutonic Knights

The Order of the Teutonic House of Mary in Jerusalem, or more simply, the Teutonic Knights, arrived later on the scene in the Holy Land than the Templars and the Hospitallers. Mostly made up of German knights and priests, the Order was formed in 1190 in the port city of Acre. Their mission was to establish a hospital for German pilgrims during the Third Crusade, the bloodiest period in the entire history of the Crusades. Christian forces lost 7,000 men in the first major battle against Saladin at Acre in 1189, and the city was under siege for another two years. The curative brothers of the Teutonic Knights and their hospital had their work cut out for them.

In 1198, the Knights received new marching orders from the pope. They were to take on a more militaristic mission and defend Jerusalem. Though never as far-reaching or rich as the Templars or Hospitallers, the Teutonic Knights were still a force to be reckoned with, and their holdings included vast lands in Italy, Greece, and especially Germany. When the Holy Roman Emperor Frederick II was crowned King of Jerusalem in 1225, the Teutonic home team from Germany was raised to new prestige.

As sort of a cross between the garments of the Templars and the Hospitallers, the Teutonic Knights wore a white surcoat with a black cross on the breast.

Because the Templars and Hospitallers were answerable only to the pope, the Teutonic Knights wanted similar status, and in 1224 their *Hochmeister* (Grand Master) petitioned Pope Honorius III for just such a position. Unlike the Templars and the Hospitallers, the Teutonic Knights turned into swords-for-hire in Europe and became embroiled in politics, military actions, and forced Christian conversions in Hungary, Poland, and Prussia. They took their role of religious knights seriously and set about converting or killing pagan Slavs, Poles, and Prussians. They even attempted an invasion of Russia in an attempt to convert the Orthodox Catholics there to Roman ones.

In 1237, they absorbed the Livonian Brothers of the Sword (see the following section), and their sovereign rule extended over Prussia, Latvia, Estonia, and the costal areas of Poland — essentially most of the eastern shore of the Baltic Sea.

The Teutonic Knights clung to their vast holdings and power right up until the 16th century, long after their mission in the Holy Land was forgotten. In 1525, the last Hochmeister of the Order embraced the Protestant movement of Martin Luther in Germany, converted to Lutheranism. The newly named Duchy of Prussia became the first Protestant state. Interestingly, the Order survived and allowed both Catholic and Protestant members. (For more information about the modern Teutonic Order, see Chapter 9.)

Livonian Brothers of the Sword

The trouble with being a big, successful, international group of warrior monks is that everybody thinks they can do it, too. Such was the case of the Brothers of the Army of Christ of Livonia, which loosely based its rules on the Templar model. The difference was that this group ditched all that bothersome reverence and piety stuff and just concentrated on the more exciting killing bits.

Formed in 1202 in Estonia, the Brothers of the Sword didn't mess with marching to the Holy Land. They sprung up to convert pagans in northern Europe in the area around the Baltic Sea. Unfortunately, they didn't have the discipline of the other more famous orders, and they certainly didn't have the pope's immunity from secular authority. They were for all intents and purposes slaughtered in 1236 by a large force of Lithuanians, and the Order was absorbed into the Teutonic Knights after a brief 34-year lifespan. The Order managed to remain its own self-governing division within the Teutonic Knights into the 1500s.

Up Where the Air Is Thin: The Templars Reach Their Zenith

By the 12th century, the Templars were one of the most popular organizations for the nobility to endow, either in life or in death. In fact, in a coup that left people gap-jawed and stunned, the Templars had become so close to King Alphonso I of Aragon that, when he died without an heir in 1131, he willed a third of his kingdom to the Templars, and a third to the Knights Hospitaller. The *Reconquista,* the battle of Catholic Spain to take back the Iberian peninsula from the Moors, was a battle that had gone on for centuries, ever since the Arabs had swept across the Straights of Gibralter in 711 to invade Spain. It had gone very well for Alphonso since about 1118, so much so that he was having difficulties protecting the land he'd gained from being reconquered right back again by the Moors. He set up several confraternities of knights to aid him in this effort, though none was expected to take holy orders. He hadn't had a great deal of success with this plan, and so hoped that the powerful knights of the Latin States could cope with the problem.

But let's face it — when people start leaving their *kingdoms* to you, there's bound to be some jealousy and backbiting, human nature being what it is. Like the tale of a legal nightmare in Charles Dickens's *Bleak House,* the legal wrangling over such a bequest went on for nine years. The Templars settled for less than they'd been bequeathed, just in order to get on with the thing. But it was still an unprecedented windfall, causing resentment on the part of some of the crowned heads of Europe and the East.

All three papal bulls concerning the Templars were important, but there was one small exemption that, in the end, proved far more powerful than the others.

Templars were given a papal exemption for the purpose of moneylending. For several centuries, Jews had been the principle moneylenders in Europe, for two reasons:

- ✔ The Catholic church of the Middle Ages had declared usury to be a sin.

- ✔ The Jews were a people apart, object of ceaseless prejudices, one of them being that Jews were not allowed to join any of the medieval labor guilds.

As the Templar banking organization grew, helping pilgrims to travel more safely to the Holy Land, they began taking on other banking tasks, as well. Their squeaky-clean ethics and their meticulous record keeping were a big plus in this endeavor. Not only merchants and knights, but nobles and kings began borrowing from the Templars, or using their vaults to store valuables during unstable times. Just sentimental little things, like the Crown Jewels of England. For the Second Crusade, Louis VII borrowed money for the mission from the Templars. From there it grew into a family tradition, until, by the late 12th century, the Templars were the de facto treasurers of the French royal family. Other kings began to depend on them, though not to the degree of the French kings.

The pope, too, depended heavily on the financial services of the Templars. It was an admirably modern system, with careful records kept, receipts given, and regular statements sent out to important clients. The Templars got innumerable perks in return, and in many cases were trusted to both collect various taxes and to take them to the Holy Land. Apart from actually being a pope or a king, they were about as high as high ever gets.

They say when you sup with the devil, eat with a long spoon. We would suggest that when conjugating with royalty, you'd be safer with an even longer sword. The power given over to the Templars was staggering, unmatched by any other medieval organization. But with wagonloads of money changing hands, it was probably only a matter of time before the Templars came to grief. Royalty of the Middle Ages had a persistent habit of making promises they had no intention of keeping, while they resented the poor schmuck left holding the promise — not to mention their discomfort with anyone who was the keeper of too many dangerous royal secrets.

Part II
A Different Kind of Knighthood

The 5th Wave   By Rich Tennant

"Sometimes I forget...Are we supposed to be
warrior-monks or monk-warriors?"

In this part . . .

This part is the heart of the Templar story. Chapter 4 takes you inside the secret universe of a Templar preceptory, to experience the daily life of a Templar knight, the harsh and demanding Templar Rule, the organization of a Chapter House, and the grueling ritual that was the ordinary routine for these warriors of God. The story follows the Templars to the battlefield, where their strict adherence to the code made them the most courageously exposed — and the most feared — warriors of their age.

At the height of their power, the only direction left to go was down. Chapter 5 shows how Fate laid heavy blows on the Order, the loss of the Crusader states, the shock of their arrest and trial, the torments of the Inquisition, and the tragedy of an unimaginable end. Chapter 6 undertakes a little cold-case detective work, by taking a look at the accusations made against the Templar Order — and the likelihood of truth in any of them.

Chapter 4

Living in a Templar World

*I*f you've done any reading about the Templars, you've probably heard lots of rumors. Chief among them was that they were incredibly wealthy, with holdings in the billions (with a *b*), the most powerful investment bankers in Europe. We'll let you in on a little secret — it's all true. But there's so much more to tell. In order to gain a real picture of the Knights Templar, you need to look at the day-to-day life of the Order.

In this chapter, we describe how the Order was organized and governed on a day-to-day basis. We explain the harsh, everyday life of a typical Templar warrior monk and what was expected of him from the Order. And we wrap up with an examination of the many symbols that are associated with the Templars.

A Standard Unlike Any Other

If you didn't take a closer look, you could get the wrong impression about the Templar Order — you could easily assume that their title of the Poor Knights of Solomon was nothing but the worst sort of hypocrisy. The Templar *Order* was wealthy beyond measure; the individual Templar *knight* was anything but rich. The Templars lived in what a historian might call "extreme monastic asceticism." We would call it, well, squalor. And it wasn't even a messy squalor, apart from the various droppings of the barnyard animals all over the place. You have to actually *own* something before that something can end up lying around in messy piles.

All money from tithes and properties, all gold or possessions of any sort, belonged to the order as a whole. Everything was held communally, without any wealth in the hands of an individual. If a Templar was given a gift as reward for some service, he had to turn it over to the Master. If some small trinket or gift of remembrance was given to a knight by his family, he had to have the Master's permission to keep it. He couldn't even trade something to another knight without getting permission first. If a knight were given money to buy something for the community, he had to return every penny he didn't spend. In fact, if a Templar was found to have money on his person or amongst his things after he died, he was refused burial in consecrated ground. According to the Templar Rule of Order of Conduct, his body was to be thrown to the dogs. If his hidden money was discovered after his burial, he was dug up and *then* thrown to the dogs. You just didn't mess with these guys.

In the medieval world, a great deal was expected of a Christian, even an everyday churchgoer. A priest or monk was expected to make a greater commitment still, and a Crusader knight was expected to risk his life for his faith. But no one made a greater sacrifice for his faith than a Knight Templar. He was expected to live in absolute poverty, with no personal possessions apart from his weapons and the clothes on his back. He was expected, like a monk, to give up any and all sexual pleasure, and do without the comfort of a wife and family. But a monk was not expected to make war for his faith — and a Templar was. In fact, a monk was not even permitted to carry arms, and if he found himself in a war zone by an accident of fate, all he had to do was duck, cover, and pray until the calamity passed. No such luck for the Templars.

A Templar was expected to risk his life on Crusade in the same fashion as any other warrior knight. Actually, he was expected to take a much greater risk. In order to live up to the Templars' reputation, a Templar knight was forbidden to retreat from any battlefield unless the enemy had at least a 3-to-1 superiority over them. An ordinary Crusader knight could use tactics, and he could retreat to regroup if he saw any danger of annihilation. A Templar had to carry into battle with him the heavy burden of being God's chosen warrior. Which meant, of course, that a very large percentage of Templars were carried off the battlefield on their shields, never to see their homes again.

The Templar Rule

Eventually, nearly 700 rules governed the life of a Knight Templar (expanded from the original 72 rules drawn up at the Council of Troyes). Those rules covered every subject imaginable, and the level of nitpickiness is absolutely staggering. Basically, a Templar couldn't spit without being told how much to spit, how high, how far, at what time of day, and how many times a day.

Templars lived by the holy rule of the Cistercian monks, with a weighty ency-clopedia of added rules tacked on just for them. The Cistercians were a rela-tively new order of monks who had organized in 1098 in Dijon, France. (Yes, where the mustard comes from.) What made the Cistercians — and, by exten-sion, the Templars — different for their period was that they organized them-selves to follow the strict rules of conduct set down more than 500 years before by St. Benedict.

Benedict had been the son of a Roman nobleman, but in his early 20s, he moved to the countryside and lived out a hermit-like existence in a cave for three years. He determined that only by hard work, extreme poverty, and iso-lation could he best clear his mind to contemplate, serve, and understand God. His example became the classic definition of monasticism. His written guidelines for the monastic life — the Rule of St. Benedict — was not for everyone, not even for all devout servants of the Church. He believed that religious people needed to have social contact. But he also believed that a very small, special group of people in society had what it took to live a strict, isolated life solely dedicated to God.

Patterned after St. Benedict's example and the even tougher rules of the Cistercians (who thought the Benedictines had it easy), the Rule of the Templars was put together over the course of a century, which is why it sometimes contains an annoying amount of duplication. But the first draft was probably written, for the most part, by the Templars' first powerful spon-sor, Bernard of Clairvaux, who would become St. Bernard after his death.

Over and over again in the Rule of the Templars are certain general rules regarding the overall carriage and behavior of a Templar. A Knight Templar was not to laugh to excess, or to indulge in practical jokes or horseplay; he was to remain silent whenever possible, and was not to raise his voice, except to be heard on the battlefield; he was not to indulge in any displays of anger; he was not to gossip, about anyone or anything. During the period from late afternoon until Mass the next morning, they observed the Grand Silence, and no talking was allowed. Even apart from the Grand Silence, Templars are told that "to talk too much is not without sin," and "idle talk and wicked bursts of laughter" were forbidden.

Even the Templar knight's spartan diet was very rigidly controlled, and when he was in the field or roaming around in the Holy Land, he was expected to adhere to it as much as possible.

Apart from all these generalities, there were some pretty unbelievable specifics. And they stemmed from the doubly demanding organization of the Order.

Warriors and monks

Crusading knights took vows that were already tied to the teachings of the Church. Although there was no *exact* set of rules for all knights, generally the code of Christian chivalry included

- ✔ Believing in the teachings of the Church and its rules
- ✔ Agreeing to defend the Church
- ✔ Being true to your own country, your king, and your feudal lord
- ✔ Respecting and defending the weak, while fighting against injustice
- ✔ Waging ceaseless and merciless war on the infidel
- ✔ Pledging your word, your *parole,* with honor on pain of death

These were the general guidelines for the Templar knights as well. What made the Templars different was the addition of the vows of a religious order. The monastic life, for any order, required very stringent rules, and the combination of warrior/monk made for a doubly-heavy burden of duty and self-denial. Any man who joined them was making an amazing commitment, because the traditional vows of a monk were poverty, chastity, and obedience — three tough ones if ever there were.

Not all Templars took the rigid religious vows. Some were already married. They were called *Fratres Conjugati* (Married Brothers), and they simply signed up for a limited hitch and then went home to their wives. It was also possible to join for a set period of time and then be released, like joining the army today. And non-Latin Christians, often of mixed races, could join as sergeants. These "temporary" knights wore a black or brown mantle with a red cross, to clearly distinguish them from the lifetime members, as well as the knights of noble birth, who wore the famous white mantle, signifying their celibacy. Often, these short-timers were from rich and noble families. Serving in the Order was a form of what the Catholic Church called a *plenary indulgence,* meaning the forgiveness of sin in heaven with the payment of money down here on earth. The written indulgence you were given even covered sins you hadn't committed yet, which is a handy thing to have around the house. Often these lay brothers connected to the Order left them land or monies in their wills, adding to the Templars' wealth.

Templar do's and don'ts

In trying to understand what life was like for a Templar night on a day-to-day basis, it might be better to start with what he *couldn't* do, rather than with what he *could* do. The list of don'ts is a much, much longer list. On reading it for the first time, you may think that all the joys of life, even the simplest, were forbidden a Templar. It's even more depressing to think that all 687 rules were not yellowing documents lying around in the back of a closet — they were rigidly and precisely enforced, by a hierarchy of officers (see "Who's in Charge around Here?", later in this chapter).

Here are just of few of the more niggling and overbearing strictures under which a Templar had to live his life:

- A Templar was forbidden to eat meat more than three times a week, except at Christmas.
- A Templar knight was not allowed to decorate his horse, bridle, or saddle, particularly not with the gold or silver plaques that were popular in this period for other Crusading knights.
- A Templar was forbidden to have a lock, anywhere, on anything.
- A Templar was forbidden to stand as godfather for any child.
- Even though Templars were called to prayer in the middle of the night, they were forbidden to sleep in complete darkness, "so that shadowy enemies may not lead them to wickedness." There would be no hanky-panky in a Templar commandery.
- Falconry and all hunting for amusement were forbidden.
- Carrying any letters from home in your possession was forbidden. When someone wrote to you, the message was read to you, with the Master's permission.
- Even "excessive abstinence" was forbidden, because it indulged the sin of pride. Sometimes you just couldn't win for losing.

A Templar day planner

Not only was every form of behavior controlled, but so was every moment of the day. The Templars lived in godliness, hour by hour, and even minute by minute. The day was divided into 12 hours, and the night into 12 hours.

There were what were considered seven sacred (or *canonical*) times of day, each with its own Latin name: *Matins, Prime, Terse, Sext, Nones, Vespers,* and *Compline.* See Table 4-1 for a list of the canonical hours and what went on when.

Table 4-1	A Day in the Life of a Templar	
Time	*Sacred Hours*	*Activity*
2 a.m.	*Matins*	Brothers to join in prayers. Then see to horses and equipment, check in with their squires. Sleep till dawn.
6 a.m.	*Prime*	Morning mass.
9 a.m.	*Terse*	Prayers or quiet reading.
Noon	*Sext*	Mass if not heard earlier; then repair armor and equipment, pegs or tent posts, or other work followed by lunch. Knights eat at first seating, sergeants at second, while a chaplain reads aloud. Then go to chapel to give thanks, ask for Lord's help in tasks.
3 p.m.	*Nones*	Vigils for the dead, prayers for the needs of the Order.
Dusk	*Vespers*	Evening prayer, followed by supper.
Dark	*Compline*	A communal drink with all brethren, followed by prayer and the Grand Silence. Then check horses and equipment before bed.
8 p.m.	Bed	

This dreary schedule would change on Feast Days or Holy Days, sometimes for the better, sometimes for the worse — an incredible number of fasts were scattered throughout the schedule for the year. The bells calling the chapter to their prayers were never silent for very long. As you can see from the timetable, a knight wasn't accustomed to being able to get eight hours of sleep at one time. The time of *Matins,* the middle-of-the-night prayers, could change from season to season, or from one chapter house to another, but generally speaking, a knight had to get up halfway through the night to pray and to check over his gear, particularly in the field. Because he was only permitted a hard, narrow cot, one blanket of wool, and one *bolster* (pillow), and he had to wear his clothes and boots while sleeping, it's not likely that he was sleeping that deeply anyway. Also, these *Matins* prayers were silent. The Grand Silence had to be obeyed from *Compline* until *Prime* the next morning.

Templars ate twice in a day — once at *Sext,* and again after *Vespers.* There was one bowl for every two knights which they ate from together. Curiously, the point was so that they could keep an eye on each other and make sure each brother knight ate enough, and didn't engage in "undue abstinence." They did drink wine, but they were supposed to dilute it with water. Drunkenness would not be tolerated (although in the waning years of the Order, the term "drink like a Templar" was a common description of being on an all-night bender). The meals were anything but gourmet fare, but what was perhaps even more difficult for the talkative sort was the fact that chatting over a meal was absolutely forbidden. The knights ate in silence, while a clerk or chaplain brother read aloud from the Bible. Every meal. Every day. A Templar ate to keep his body functioning for God, not to enjoy the cuisine or the company.

The length of their *surcoat* (the long, cloth tunic worn over the top of their armor or chainmail) and hair were specified; types of shirts and styles of shoes approved and forbidden; even the various shades of white used in their surcoats were addressed. To be away from all this fun and games, particularly for more than one night, required the permission of the Master, just like a sophomore needing a hall pass to go to the bathroom.

No women allowed

Women were cut utterly and completely from a Templar's life, and he was expressly forbidden any contact with them. He was not allowed to kiss a woman under any circumstances, even if she were his mother or sister. Kissing a woman was considered unseemly and could "rouse dangerous passions." Any carnal contact with a "sinful woman" carried one of the harshest penalties in the Order — the knight's habit was taken from him, he was paraded in chains to be shamed before his brothers, and then he was kicked out of the Order for all time.

The pride and the power

You may be thinking that only some sort of masochist would want to take on this life. But there were compensations, strange as some of them may seem today. For a devout Christian, being the lords over such a faraway place, the place where Jesus Christ lived and preached and was crucified, was an exciting life. And wherever they walked, these knights were given more than admiration — they inspired awe.

Templars walked with popes and kings, their shining humility and piety untouched by the many scandals that were demeaning the papacy and many of the other monasteries and nunneries in this period.

Masters of a Templar chapter or the Grand Master of the Temple were given extraordinary powers, because they had the complete trust of men in power. They often had *plenipotentiary power,* meaning the right to bargain in the name of the pope or the king with the enemy. They also had the right to hear confessions and offer absolution if a priest was unavailable (for example, in a time of plague).

One pleasant thing, apart from a love of God, is a constant theme that runs through the Templar Rule — the care of sick and elderly brothers. Despite the oppressive silence between brothers, the lack of fun or laughter, the Master expected these men to bond closely to one another, in war and in peace. Templars took a great deal of pride in their willingness to protect one another, and never to desert each other on the battlefield.

Punishment and penance

What good is it if you have rules, but no form of punishment? The Rule of the Templars also set out types of penance and punishment to be meted out to members of the Order who broke the rules. These weren't unusual — most monastic orders set down similar kinds of guidelines.

When a member was charged with breaking the rules, he was summoned to a meeting of everyone in the Commandery. The charges were read out, and the offending brother was expected to confess his sins. When he did so or, more rarely, mounted a defense, he was escorted from the room, and the assembled brothers determined his punishment, or in the case of a serious offense, referred the case for a trial.

Among other offenses, a Templar knight could be stripped of his rank (called *loss of habit*) for fighting with a fellow brother, hurting a fellow Christian in anger, losing or killing a slave or a horse, having sex with a woman, or defacing the Templar uniform.

A Templar could be expelled from the Order (called *loss of house*) and sent off to serve as a Cistercian monk for committing sodomy, heresy, treason, or cowardice on the battlefield; for murdering a Christian; or for bearing false witness against a brother. The belief was that life as a warrior was a privilege, and being sentenced to a period of solitude and reflection would aid in the offending knight's reformation and teach him piety and obedience — along with putting him in a nice quiet place away from the commandery.

Who's in Charge around Here?

Every organization has to have its hierarchy, but the Templars' was unique. In this section, we cover some of their principal officers — these guys come into play in any discussion of the Templars in war or peace.

These offices were called *bailies,* meaning something entrusted to someone. It's the root word for the more familiar term of *bailiff.*

Grand Master

This office was for life, and the Grand Master was in charge of the entire Order, worldwide. Throughout history, a couple of men retired from the position of Grand Master, with the pope's permission, but for the most part, dying was the only way out of the job.

The election for Grand Master was held in the East, at the Templar headquarters. It would have been impossible to leave the office empty long enough to wait for emissaries of the Western chapters to go East and vote, and so those commanders simply prayed for a worthy outcome.

There was a reason that the election of the Grand Master was a worrisome enough matter to need their prayers: The Templar Grand Master was a very important person politically. The Templars spent the bulk of their time in the Holy Land (roughly the modern nations of Israel, Lebanon, and Syria), and they knew the language, tactics, and attitudes of the Muslim enemy. This knowledge, in combination with their premier skills as warriors, made the input of the Templars very important in any council of war or peace. When new regiments of knights and soldiers arrived at Acre, which was the Templars' principal port, the first man they wanted a powwow with was the Grand Master, and sometimes the Grand Master of the Knights Hospitallers, as well. (The main mission of the Hospitallers was to care for the wounded, as guarding the pilgrims had been for the Templars.) Though it was well known in later years that the Templars and the Hospitallers were great rivals, in the early days of the Crusades they appeared to work together and fight together very well.

Master and Commander

The Master and Commander was the local commander in charge of the commandery. He had complete command in the field.

Seneschal

The Seneschal was the right-hand man for the Master and was sometimes called a Grand Commander. In peace, the Seneschal administered all the lands belonging to the chapter house. In war, he handled the movement of the men, the pack trains, the food procurement, and other issues of moving an army.

Turcopolier

This officer was the third in line militarily. He was in command of the light cavalry and the Sergeant brothers.

Marshal

The position of Marshal was a very important one on the battlefield: The Marshal was in charge of all arms, as well as all horses. He was very much a military man, and a Master would usually consult with him, as well as the Seneschal and the Turcopolier, before making any final decisions on tactics.

Under-Marshal

The first officer under the marshal, the Under-Marshal was in charge of the lesser equipment, bridles, padding for saddles, barrels of water, and other supply problems. He held a very important position in battle, because he held the *piebald banner,* a flag at the head of all, to keep stragglers together.

Standard Bearer

Also called the Confanonier, the Standard Bearer was in charge of the squires. He was their paymaster, their disciplinarian, and the man who checked over their very important work of keeping the knights' horses and weapons in good order. He didn't actually "bear the standard" in battle — he marched in front of the banner and led his marching column.

Knight

The knight was the backbone of the battlefield. Knights were the equivalent of the cavalry. A small force of knights was very powerful, skilled in warfare, clad in armor, able to take on a large number of foot soldiers. Only a man whose father and grandfather both had been knights could become one, and if he were caught lying about his lineage, the penalty was severe. No *bastard* (illegitimate) son could be a knight.

The knights dressed in the famous white habit, adorned with a red cross. There was no mistaking a Templar knight on the battlefield. Hair was cut short, but knights were forbidden to shave their beards, probably in keeping with the Muslim belief that a beard was a sign of greater masculinity. No sense giving your enemies a reason not to respect you.

Sergeant

Usually from a lower social class than the more noble knights, the Sergeant was still a light cavalry officer, the chief support officer for the knight. Sergeants dressed in a black tunic, and a black or brown mantle, often with a red cross.

Treasurer

The Treasurer's duties are clear — this was the guy who kept the books.

Draper

The Draper was in charge of all the clothing and bed linen of everyone in the Order. He also had the power to oversee everyone of every rank, and to chastise them if their clothing was not proper for their position, or if anything decorated it, such as a collar of fur on a knight's white robe or mantle. The Draper was sort of like the fashion police.

Squires

Squires were the young men who, just like in the movies, were there to assist the knight in any way possible, from polishing his weapons to feeding his horses. The difference for a Templar Squire is that this was often a hired position, especially in the first hundred years of the Order. It was only later that many Squires were there specifically to test themselves and their mettle, and to climb to the order of knight.

Lay Servants

Lay Servants could run the gamut, from masons brought in to do building or repair work, to personal servants, to an officer. The hierarchical statutes of the Templar Rule laid out precisely how many of such servants each officer was allowed to have. For a Templar to have too many would be a sin of pride.

Chaplain brothers

One of the most important positions within a Templar commandery was that of the Chaplain brother. The job came with many delicate layers of meaning underneath. He was sort of the internal priest for the Order. He had the power to hear confessions and to give absolution for sins. In fact, Templars were forbidden to say their confession to *anyone* else without a *papal dispensation,* which simply means special permission from the pope. This is a very important point, because in effect, what the pope did was to make the Templars spiritually, as well as politically, independent from the rest of the Church. They were not answerable to local clerics or bishops, but only to the pope.

The Templar Commandery: Medieval Fortress and City

When he was not on Crusade, or on some other mission for the Order, a Templar knight generally lived in a place called a *commandery* or *preceptory.* This was a complex of buildings that formed a small Templar city, often built around a military stronghold that had either been built by the knights or been given over to them to guard.

The usage of both of these terms interchangeably emphasizes two of the purposes of the Templar stronghold. As a *commandery,* it was the military outpost for the Latin States (the nations founded in the Holy Land by the Crusading powers), as well as an armory and a defensive stronghold. The word *preceptory* implies one of its other duties, which was as a school, a place to train new recruits for the Order.

City within a city

At the height of their power, the huge tracts of land held by the Templars in major European cities like London or Paris was nothing short of astonishing. They were self-contained communities within already established cities, with their own local government, municipal infrastructure, law-enforcement, treasury, building and maintenance crews, and food supply.

The signature round churches

Not every Templar church was round like the one that survives today in London, but many were. The distinctive round Templar churches were designed to pay homage to the Church of the Holy Sepulchre in Jerusalem, and they had a definite Eastern influence. Templar commanderies from Hungary to Portugal to the South of France feature these gorgeous medieval curiosities of construction. The Templars were enthusiastic builders and developed much of their architecture from Byzantine examples. They were unlike anything the Europeans were constructing.

It's simply a matter of good luck that one of the loveliest and best-preserved of them is not, like so many other Templar sites, in a difficult place for a typical tourist to find. It is easily situated in the heart of downtown London.

The area where the Templar Church (see Figure 4-1) is located is still called Temple Hill, in recognition of the fact that the 5 square miles around it were once Temple property. After the dissolution of the Templar Order in 1307, the area became a magnet for attorneys. It is now the odd and unique area of London called the Inns of Court, a huge, labyrinth complex of brownstones that is office and home for the city's lawyers and law students. But be careful when you go to take a look — the Inns of Court are considered private property, and the huge doors set in the brick walls surrounding it are only open during certain hours of the day.

Figure 4-1: The Templar Church in London is one of the best surviving examples of Templar architecture.

Christopher Hodapp

In the floor of the round nave are full-sized stone effigies, the burial place for the knights and lords who donated the land to the Templars. It's difficult to believe the church was bombed by the Nazis during World War II — it has been extensively restored as a breathtaking architectural time capsule.

Symbols of the Templars

A wide variety of insignias, emblems, flags, seals, and other images have been attributed to the Templars. The general image most often applied to the Order is an image of two knights riding the same horse, which was visual shorthand that symbolized both their poverty and their ferocity. In reality, the Templar Rule said no knight could own more than three horses, but knights were forbidden to share them — a situation where Christian charity had to give way to military practicality. And there is no shortage of irony that, in spite of this image of poverty, the Templars went on to become the richest religious order in the world.

Different meanings have been attached to the symbol of the two knights over the centuries, but the duality of the symbol can be seen as representing the Templars' roles as both warriors and monks, poor individually but rich as an order, or, as was alleged after their arrest and trials, a symbol of homosexuality — all of which seem far from the mark of the original meaning.

The red cross

When the Crusades began, the term "to take the cross" really meant what it said. Pilgrims, princes, knights, and paupers took strips of red cloth and sewed them to their clothes in the shape of a cross. So the red cross was not strictly a Templar symbol.

The cross officially adopted by the Templars in 1146 is the Cross of Jerusalem (see Figure 4-2). What makes it distinctive are the lines making up the cross that are of even length (unlike the more common crucifix with a longer vertical line). It is believed that the Templars adopted this form of cross after seeing it in Coptic Churches, an Eastern Orthodox branch of Christianity founded in Egypt.

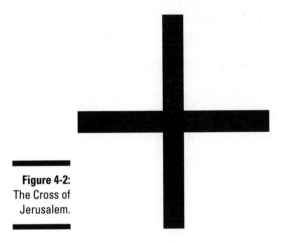

Figure 4-2:
The Cross of
Jerusalem.

The cross pattée is similar, in that the horizontal and vertical lines are of
equal length, but they are thicker, and the ends are splayed out, supposedly
resembling a lion's paw (see Figure 4-3). A similar design was used by other
Orders such as the Knights Hospitallers during the same period, usually
appearing in white on their black mantles. And it survived into the 20th century as the German and Prussian Iron Cross medal.

Figure 4-3:
The cross
pattée.

A related symbol that is often attributed to the Templars, the Maltese Cross (see Figure 4-4), is also slightly different. It became the symbol of the Knights Hospitallers in later years when they changed their name to the Knights of Malta (or their more proper name today, the Sovereign Military Hospitaller Order of St. John of Jerusalem of Rhodes and of Malta). Its ends form eight points, which are said to symbolize the eight beatitudes of Christianity, spoken by Christ in the Sermon on the Mount (Matthew 5–7): "Blessed are the poor in spirit, the meek, those who seek justice, the mourners, the merciful, the clean of heart, the peacemakers, and the persecuted." And you just thought it was a cool design.

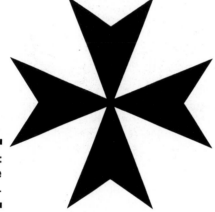

Figure 4-4:
The Maltese
Cross.

The Beauséant

Banners and flags have always been important on the battlefield, both as an easily seen rallying point for troops, as well as a handy identifying device so you didn't kill your own troops. The banner of the Templars was called the *Beauséant,* which some claim meant "be noble" or "be glorious."

The banner itself was a black square over a white square, and it is theorized that this symbolized the concept of "darkness to light" (see Figure 4-5). The black stood for the sinful, secular world, and the white for purity and goodness. In later years, the red Templar cross was added to the banner.

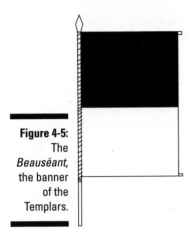

Figure 4-5:
The
Beauséant,
the banner
of the
Templars.

The Templars took the flying of the Beauséant in battle very seriously. Ten brothers were assigned before a battle to protect the banner, and there were harsh punishments for losing it, dropping or defacing it, failing to fly it while knights still fought, or using its flagpole as a weapon. It was also forbidden for Templars to retreat from a battle if the Beauséant was still flying. No wonder the Templars were always last to retreat from battle — they got punished if they stopped flying the flag during the battle, and punished if they stopped fighting while it still flew!

Skull and crossbones

The symbol of the skull and crossbones has long been believed to be an image tied to the Templar Order, but this one is probably more legend than fact. The flag flown by pirates known today as the Jolly Roger has long been claimed to have been flown by Templar ships after the arrest and elimination of the Order in 1307. Because the knights were on the run, so the tale goes, they had no country and no allegiance to the Catholic Church. The skull has long been a symbol of mortality and death, and these former knights would have doubtlessly mourned the deaths of their brethren and of their Order. No country would give them sanctuary, so they had no choice but to become pirates. Well, okay. It could be true.

The first association between the Templars and a skull seems to be in the equally legendary story of the Skull of Sidon. (Here we go again.) *This* story goes that a Templar knight broke his vows and fell in love with a woman. When she died, he was so lovesick that he dug up her body and had carnal relations with the corpse. A voice spoke to him afterward that told him to return to the grave in nine months, where he would find a son. When he did so, all that was in the grave was a skull on top of two crossed leg bones. The same voice told him to guard the skull and it would protect him and bring him good fortune. He did so, and it is said that by merely showing the magic head to his enemies, they would retreat in fear. Not exactly a heartwarming tale of romance.

The story actually predated the creation of the Templars, but by the 1300s, it had been attached to them anyway. When the Templars were tried for heresy, it formed the basis of one of the many accusations against them — namely, that the knights worshipped an unholy head of some kind. The story varied, and some believed they were, in fact, worshipping the head of John the Baptist, or of their first Grand Master, Hughes de Payens. And then there could have been another one, called Baphomet. (For more about this head-worshipping business, see Chapter 6.)

The problem for the Templars when they went to trial was that they had done a pretty good public relations job of circulating stories like these to frighten their enemies. Unfortunately, when they lost their favor with the Church, these creepy, occult, and unquestionably heretical stories came back and were used against them as proof that they were up to no good.

When the Freemasons created an order of Masonic Knights Templar in the 1700s, their ceremonial aprons featured a skull and crossbones, and the symbol was also used on the headstones of their deceased members. (For more about the Masonic Templars, see Chapter 8.)

By the way, in case you wondered, the term *Jolly Roger* is thought to have come from a red flag flown by French ships, referred to as a *jolie rouge*. The current term is probably a combination of an English mispronunciation of the French term and the obvious description of the grinning skull.

Chapter 5

The Poor Knights Crash and Burn: The Fall of the Templars

• •

In This Chapter

▶ Reaching the pinnacle: Templar perks make dangerous enemies

▶ Getting comfy with heretics

▶ Laying waste the dream: The arrests, the Inquisition, and the trial by fire

• •

*F*ace it: Of the 20th-century dictators, Stalin had better posters, but Hitler had snappier uniforms. What Mussolini had no one has figured out yet. All of them, at some point in their rise to power, orchestrated lightening coups, against either one-time friends who were now enemies, or outspoken political opponents.

The most famous was known as the Night of the Long Knives. In the early 1930s, Ernst Röhm had been Adolf Hitler's closest friend. Röhm was the brutal overlord of a three-million-strong band of street thugs called the SA, or the "Brown Shirts." With his help, Hitler rose from the leader of the Munich street rabble to the newly elected chancellor of Germany. But by then, Röhm was an unpleasant reminder to Hitler of his rude beginnings, and Röhm's openly flamboyant homosexuality, orgies included, was becoming an embarrassment to the Nazi Party. Röhm had to go.

So, on Saturday, June 30, 1934, after weeks of planning, Hitler had the entire leadership of the SA rounded up — hundreds of them. They were put to death with pitiless efficiency. Röhm was shot in his cell by the SS as he shouted out one last "Heil Hitler!" Hitler had met the dawn tense and uncertain, but he ended the night with a Cheshire grin.

Although many news stories at that time, in the western press, of course, called these ruthless blitzkrieg tactics "unprecedented," they were wrong. There was nothing new about them at all. More than six centuries before, at dawn on October 13, 1307, Phillip IV of France, tense and uncertain, was waiting for word from his hordes of officers all over France who were, at that moment, arresting every Knight Templar they could lay their hands on. This chapter covers the events of that day, from the jealousy and intrigue that led to it, to the tragedy that followed.

The Seeds of the Fall in the Nature of the Order

Any powerful outfit, from the Palestine Liberation Organization (PLO) to the Walt Disney Company, has to stay on its toes insofar as enemies are concerned. Money and power will always draw plots and takeover attempts like a magnet. But the Knights Templar made for a particularly tempting target, for a variety of reasons related to the politics of the Middle Ages and the nature of the powers they had been given.

Though the White Knights, as they were sometimes called, had been born as warrior-monks, the fact was that as time passed, they changed into something entirely different. These Poor Knights were running an enormous and incredibly wealthy organization, one that walked with popes and bargained with kings. Later on in this chapter, in the "Money: The root of all evil" section, we provide a more detailed tally of Templar businesses and assets. For the time being, suffice it to say that, although the Templar mission never changed, the Templar character, as an organization, had changed drastically since its inception in 1119.

Yes, the Templars were still the protectors of the shrines of the Holy Land. But that purpose, as well as the expense of that purpose, had caused an evolution in the Order as a whole. By the 13th century, it was difficult for many to remember what their original purpose had been, particularly in Europe, where the problems of holding on to the Latin States weren't exactly staring people in the face day to day. It didn't occur to most Europeans who were dealing with the Templars as bankers or brokers that they were piling up money here to send over there. Micromanaging their literally thousands of preceptories across Europe was often the face of the Order to the people of the West.

Consequently, when the last of the Latin States of the Holy Land folded, in 1291, there were definitely some hard feelings in Europe. Wasn't saving the Holy Land the job of the Templars? Isn't that what they collected all that land and loot for? It didn't seem to matter that the Templars fought on, virtually alone, battling literally to the last man in their fortresses across the Levant. And it didn't seem to matter that there was little interest on the part of the kings and prelates of Europe in putting together another Crusade to hang on to the Christian lands. As far as the kings of Europe were concerned, seven trips to the well were more than enough, thank you very much.

Of course, as warriors, the courage of the Templars was never questioned. Templar knights were not allowed to retire from the battlefield, even for the tactical purpose of regrouping forces, unless they were facing at least a 3-to-1 superiority of enemy strength. When captured, they were beheaded by the hundreds before denying their faith. Yes, they were fierce, daring, and courageous fighters. But the truth is, they weren't always tactical geniuses. And when an angry West went looking for a scapegoat, these tactical errors, as well as errors in judgment or diplomacy, were blown far out of proportion by the enemies of the Order in the Christian community.

A little independence goes a long way

Today, nothing is comparable to the power that the Catholic Church had in the Middle Ages, before the Protestant Reformation. Even the Internal Revenue Service can't burn you at the stake, although they'd love to if they could.

Up until the Protestant Reformation in the 15th and 16th centuries, popes had weapons that could checkmate any king. They could excommunicate anyone, high or low, and had on many occasions excommunicated kings when they got too far out of line. Popes also had the power to put an entire nation under a *papal interdict,* meaning no marriages, no baptisms, no funerals, and a very frightened public. Some of the most powerful kings in history bent their knee to the pope, quite literally.

To the unending annoyance of their enemies, the Templars had nothing to fear from any of these papal powers. They were, in effect, the pope's personal God Squad, and if the pope was the most powerful figure in medieval Europe, then it naturally follows that the Templars were the most powerful organization in Europe. Even after their most humiliating defeats and losses, Pope Innocent III issued several new edicts concerning Templar powers and privileges, going so far as to reissue the papal bull *Omne datum optimum* (meaning "every best gift"), which had been the most important one in establishing the Templars' powers to begin with. It seemed a rather pointed thing to do; everyone in Europe and the Holy Land was being told that nothing had altered Templar status. One reason for this is crystal clear.

In the Latin States of the Holy Land, there may well have been four kings and four kingdoms, but the glue holding the whole thing together was the Templars. There were other military orders, the Hospitallers, and even lesser ones like the Teutonic Knights or the Hospital of St. Lazarus. But the Templars were by far the most important to the military stability of Palestine. Without them, the nobles of the Latin States, despite their blue blood, would have been royalty in name only — paper kings and queens, jostling for a place at the head of the line to get on the fastest ship for home.

Money: The root of all evil

One of the papal perks enjoyed by the Templars was the dispensation that allowed them to practice *usury*, the medieval word for lending money and making a profit off it. The practice had begun for the Templars in a rather sidewise fashion, because they were already charging a fee for accepting the deposits of pilgrims and then letting them make withdrawals on their long journey. They were also helping knights who wanted to go on Crusade by holding mortgages on their property for them. It was a very short step from there to lending money, and the pope allowed them to take it. For the rest of Christian Europe, usury was strictly forbidden by the Church — that's why most of the moneylenders in Europe were Jews. They were barred from the guilds, and couldn't work in most of the professions open to Christians. This became a great rationalization for the longstanding European habit of hating the Jews. But as time passed, some of that hatred, for the very self-same reason, fell on the Templars. It was inevitable. After all, does anybody love the bank that holds the mortgage on their house?

Money had never been any part of the equation for the founders of the Knights Templar. On the contrary, their first vow was one of poverty. Hugues de Payens, the Order's founder, had eventually traveled to Europe and received grants of land and money to help fund his work in the Holy Land. That was how the early Templars viewed money — as a gift of the high and the mighty to pay for their holy mission. Beyond that, they had no part of it, any more than they had any part of drink, women, or luxury. But when their holy mission to protect pilgrims became wrapped up with protecting the pilgrims' money, then money intruded itself upon their spiritual state. The act of transferring money safely from Europe to the East and back again turned the Order into something that Hugues de Payens could never have envisioned. They became a large, influential, multinational corporation.

Even defeats didn't seem able to touch the Templars. Whenever things went wrong in the Holy Land, it meant another influx of Crusaders, more people who needed the banking services of the Poor Knights. But the Templars were coping with a wide variety of problems through the 13th century that affected this vital aspect of their Order, because the entire period was doing a monetary downhill slide. We won't go into detail concerning multilateral trade, the doctrine of laissez-faire capitalism, or economic determinism. If you need help falling asleep, rent the film *Meet Joe Black*. But there is one key thought on economics to take with you from this discussion, and that's the fact that history is, in general, inflationary.

Money is worth less and less as time passes. Of course, history is turned upside down by disasters like the 1929 stock-market crash, catastrophes that in ancient times were usually brought about by plague, invasion, and war. They drop the bottom out of everything, before the inflationary process starts all over again.

The 13th century was a time of creeping inflation. Money was getting tighter all the time. In order to pay the ever-increasing costs of building and maintaining the enormous commanderies on the frontiers in the East and in Spain, the Templars had to channel their inner Ebenezer Scrooge. Every penny possible had to be squeezed none too gently from every property and every potential donor. For that reason, it was a period in which the Knights Templar gained a reputation for both greed and stinginess, not to mention whorishness, because of their selling away many of the rights of a Templar to anyone who donated enough cash. This included the right to be buried in a Templar cemetery — now *there's* a perk! Still, the entire rap was probably undeserved. It's simply that the average person of that time only saw the money-managing and donation-hunting side of the Order. They really could have no conception of the financial burdens under which the Templars were trying to operate.

Huge tracts of land

Most of the feudal holdings of the Knights Templar in Europe were in France, followed in number by Italy, England, and the northern, Catholic half of Spain. The Templars had a little property in Germany, but the far greater amount of land grants there were given over to the Teutonic Knights.

Without a doubt, their most pervasive presence, as well as their largest number of holdings, was in France, which was home to the largest percentage of the knights. The Paris commandery, with its beautiful tower (see Figure 5-1) and its rich vaults, was definitely their number-one priority. The Templars had nothing less than a city within a city, surrounded by crenellated defensive walls that were 26 feet high. It's heartbreaking that not a stone of it remains standing today. Because the Templar keep was used during the French Revolution to imprison King Louis XVI and Marie Antoinette before their execution, Napoleon had the tower torn down, to insure that it didn't become some sort of shrine to the persona non grata royal family. Most other Templar buildings suffered the same fate through the centuries. But in its prime, the Templar commandery at Paris was the principal bank, and in time it became the de facto exchequer, for the French crown.

Figure 5-1:
The Paris Temple, dominated by its *keep,* or central tower.

Cracks in the Armor

The botched Second Crusade of 1145 is important to the story of the Templars. After all, nobody wants to take credit for a military debacle. In fact, it's far more typical of human nature to start shopping around for someone else to blame, particularly where the delicate vanity of generals who are also kings is concerned. There were four general/kings on this trip, the principal ones being Louis VII of France and Conrad III, emperor of Germany. The kings of Poland and Bohemia came along just for the change of scenery. None of these men wanted to hear about the fact that they knew nothing of the terrain, and nothing of the language, customs, or tactics of their Turkish enemies, not to mention their glut of stupidity about their own Byzantine allies. When those allies, as well as the kings and nobles of the Latin States, tried to advise these arrogant gentlemen, they got a sour look and a deaf ear for their trouble. So, when the inevitable happened, and Louis and Conrad suffered major, humiliating defeats at the hands of the Seljuq Turks, everyone started sniffing around for a scapegoat. After all, these were mighty Christian kings, and they no doubt had God on their side. There *had* to be another reason for this inexplicable failure.

Getting a little too chummy with the heretics

For many, the "other reason" became the cozy relationship of the military orders, principally the Templars, with the "godless infidels" of the East. Both Louis and Conrad had been shocked by the level of placid acceptance with which the kings of the Latin States treated their mostly Islamic subjects. The Frankish knights had grown very comfortable with the diversity of the natives, and so long as the peace was kept and the taxes paid (taxes that had not changed since the overlords were Muslims rather than Christians), they were content to let each man find God in his own way. The major "heretical" Christian sects were left alone as well.

All the Templar Grand Masters in the East had an officer in their entourage who was a secretary for Saracen affairs, a position of great importance. Some Templar knights began to study Arabic. Many of the one-time mosques that had been captured by Christian knights and turned into churches retained an area where Muslims could continue to come to pray (see Chapter 2). To the Templars, this seemed to be merely a respectful accommodation; to the newly arrived Europeans headed for the Second Crusade, it was appalling. In his book *The Knights Templar,* Sean Martin relates the story of an ambassador from the Turks who came to Jerusalem to meet with the Templars. The Templars turned over to the ambassador a small chapel in the Al-Aqsa Mosque in which to pray. When a fresh-faced Frankish knight, shocked at this apostasy, tried to stop the ambassador from praying, he was literally dragged away by two exasperated Templars.

From a modern perspective, the actions of these Templar knights seem civilized, polite, and tolerant. To medieval European eyes, it seemed that the Knights Templar had been blown off course, turned from their unblemished Christian faith because of their tolerance for the faith of others. Stories like this one made their way across Europe with the knights returning from the Second Crusade — or at least with those knights who had survived the military incompetence of their leaders. Slowly but inexorably, a general suspicion about the Templars and the purity of their faith was growing in certain influential minds in the West, particularly in France.

The Second Crusade limped to a conclusion with an attempt to take the city of Damascus that was an abysmal failure, and a tactical disgrace. Because it was a concerted effort, with forces of Louis, Conrad, and the king of Jerusalem, it does seem a bit of a stretch to blame the Templars for it. But that blame game was becoming part and parcel of an interesting cultural shift that was occurring among the Frankish Christian nobles and military orders who were running the show in Outremer.

As with colonial Americans, who started out as British as Earl Grey tea, and ended up founding their own nation, the Frankish knights of Outremer were beginning to merge, slowly but steadily, with the Islamic culture around them.

Socializing with Saracens

French historians sometimes call this new culture of Outremer (French for "land across the sea") *la nation Franco-Syrienne,* and this is as good a name as any. The Frankish knights and nobles who lived in Outremer employed Syrian physicians, cooks, artisans, and servants. When not on the battlefield, they began to wear the comfortable Eastern dress more suited to the climate, and their diet, heavy on the readily-available fruits of the area, became Syrianized, as well. Their homes were designed by Eastern architects, or by Franks who were influenced by them, and featured fountains and mosaic tile floors, high ceilings, open spaces, and glass windows to let in the Mediterranean sunshine.

Even more astonishing to the Westerners of this period, the Franks began to bathe regularly, the full soap-and-water treatment. They indulged as well in other Eastern customs, from dancing girls at dinner parties to professional mourners at funerals, which was a staple of Eastern culture. And, of course, the shared enthusiasm of Islamic and Frankish nobility for hunting, hawking, and horses made for lasting friendships between men of both cultures. It's little wonder then that, in several later instances, Muslim and Frankish warlords banded together to fight off a common enemy, such as the Mongols.

Intermarriage

There is also no question that, greater than all the influences we list was the intermarriage that was becoming ever more common as time passed. Of course, any woman who married a Christian knight had to become a Christian herself. In those days, in both camps, a woman would always adopt the religion of her husband. But the cultural influence was still there. And as far as many fanatical Catholics were concerned, because it was extremely rare for a Latin knight to "turn Turk" and become a Muslim, the far more dangerous influence on the citizens of Outremer came from the heretical Christians that were dominant in that part of the world, various Gnostic and nonconformist sects that were viewed through the same lens of suspicion as the Muslims by the West. These, too, would have a mind-expanding effect on the citizens of Outremer.

So, where were the Templars in this stewpot of cultural diversity? Why they were out front leading the way, of course, as they had been nearly from the beginning. Needless to say, the chaste Templars couldn't intermarry with the Syrians, but in every other respect, they were creating a new brand of Templar knight, the Eastern Templar knight, who'd served in the Holy Land his whole life through and knew it like a well-loved book.

Templar bashing: The latest game from the Holy Land

Meanwhile, tales of Templar greed and pride had begun to circulate in the highly-charged atmosphere of the late 12th century. The Second Crusade had been a disaster; the Third Crusade had yet to arrive. Although a heartbreaking number of the histories and chronicles of this period have been lost, there is some surviving Templar griping that we can read today, from what would seem at first an unlikely source.

In 1170, William of Tyre, archdeacon of Jerusalem, complained that, though the Order had begun well enough, as holy men devoted to duty, they were soon, in his words, "neglecting humility." William was Franco-Syrian through and through, born in the Holy Land, and a very influential figure at the court in Jerusalem. In his chronicle of Outremer, he groused that the Templars had "denied obedience to the Patriarch of Jerusalem," to whom William claimed they owed their very existence (they owed their existence to the king, not the patriarch), and that, as their possessions began to multiply, their power got out of hand. He crabbed that their "wealth is equal to the treasures of kings." Though he didn't go into detail, he accused them of having gained that wealth, at least in part, by "taking tithes from God's churches," as if they'd literally picked his pocket. He summed up that they had "in general made themselves exceedingly troublesome."

This sort of bellyaching was an ominous sign of things to come, and it highlights a difficult burden that came with the Templars' high position: Being warriors as well as churchmen, and part of an influential group of men, they made enemies in political, military, *and* ecclesiastical circles.

Speaking of enemies, in this same period, throughout the last half of the 12th century, relations between Amalric I, the King of Jerusalem, and the Knights Templar were particularly lousy. The Templars had at one time played a major role in most Christian military actions, but they felt that Amalric was using them unwisely. During this period, they began to pull back from full cooperation, at least with the king of Jerusalem. It was not without cause.

Amalric had concocted an especially harebrained scheme to capture Egypt, thinking political chaos there would make his plan a cakewalk. Not only did his own mission fail miserably, but while he was away with the army, his biggest enemy, Nur al-Din, the Sultan of Halab, took the golden opportunity to attack the Christian city of Antioch. Bohemond, prince of Antioch, was in charge of the few forces left. He chose, like Amalric, to ignore the Templars' sound advice to play a waiting game, and his ill-considered attack cost a substantial number of Templar knights their lives. A year later, Amalric, in a fit of childish rage over the Templar surrender of a very small cave/fort in the Transjordan to the overwhelming forces of Nur al-Din, had the 12 Templars who gave him the news hanged like common criminals.

By that time, it looked like Templar relations with their own king were worse than with the Muslims. So, in 1168, when Amalric was putting together a much larger force to attempt to take Egypt again, the Templars refused point blank to have any part of it.

Playing politics

This brand of independence, an attitude that openly said, "We know the situation, and we're not going to blindly follow this idiot down the road to ruin," was bad enough when dealing with the Frankish nobles of Outremer. It was even worse in coping with what the Templars had increasingly begun to perceive as "outsiders."

Realizing the absolute necessity of keeping an alliance from forming between Damascus and Cairo was something the Templars thoroughly understood. They were extremely adept at the power politics of the various Muslim states. This was often decried by Crusaders fresh off the boat as "arrogance," which fueled tensions in Europe between knights and Templars. One story about this tension will do, but remember, this isn't one of a dozen stories — it's the same story, that could be told a dozen times.

In 1239, as a ten-year treaty for Jerusalem was about to run out, Pope Gregory IX started beating the bushes among the rulers of Europe for another Crusade. They didn't exactly rush forward to take the Cross. In fact, the only poor dope he got to help out this time was a moderately important French noble named Theobald, Count of Champagne.

It wasn't exactly the 25,000-strong army of the First Crusade. It was the sort of small force that would straggle in throughout the life of the Latin States. The count had dropped everything, filled with Christian zeal, to defend the Holy Land from the infidel, with his life, if necessary. That was what he'd expected, in the simplistic view of Europeans — a straightforward conflict of good versus bad, black versus white, Christian versus Muslim. What he got instead was a cold, hard dose of the Byzantine politics of the Near East.

He was, like Louis and Conrad in the Second Crusade, simply incapable of grasping the complex strategies, the *realpolitik,* of the situation. Encouraged by the Templars, the lords of Outremer had made an alliance with the Muslim ruler of Damascus; they would help him in his war against the Egyptians, and in return he would see to it that certain lands that had been taken from the Franks after the Battle of Hattin, including the Templar fortress of Safad, would be returned to them. The Templars needed the return of Safad if they were to secure Outremer. Theobald couldn't understand that the Templars were trying to take the most advantage they could from the unraveling situation in the Islamic world. The brother of Saladin, the powerful Egyptian warlord al-Kamil, had just died, and the entire Muslim world was in a mad scramble to grab the biggest chunk from out of the power vacuum. Unfortunately, one of Theobald's knights, Henry, the Count of Bar, decided he'd play a little power politics with the big boys. Thinking to take advantage of the death of al-Kamil, he decided to attack Egypt himself. The Templars warned him that the forces were far too strong for him to take on. He blithely ignored them, and his entire force was wiped out at Gaza. Of course, the blame in Europe fell, not on the count for his idiocy, but on the military orders, particularly the Templars, who'd failed to support him.

A new and deadly enemy: Saladin

There were others who understood the necessity of alliance between Damascus and Cairo. A new enemy would route the Christians, create a Damascus/ Baghdad and Cairo axis, and stand as the greatest adversary the Frankish army ever faced. His name was Salah ad-Din Yusuf Ibn Ayyub (meaning Joseph, Son of Job, Righteous of the Faith) known to us as Saladin (see Figure 5-2).

Figure 5-2: Salah ad-Din Yusuf Ibn Ayyub, better known in the West as Saladin.

Classic Image / Alamy

The author of *The New Concise History of the Crusades,* Professor Thomas F. Madden, brings a fresh perspective to many of our society's myths about the Crusades. He believes that, Western politicians and teachers notwithstanding, the Crusades were a very small blip on the very large radar screen of Arabic and Turkish history. In other words, they hadn't been stewing about it, working themselves up into a lather over the course of the last 700 years. That attitude began in the late 19th century, when the Western colonial powers brought their Crusader legends with them to the East. After all, the history of Islam is incredibly complex, jammed with wars, treaties, and personalities in conflict. The Crusades were truly a minor footnote, a brief period of Christian colonization that left behind nothing in the way of cultural change when the Franks were finally driven out of the region. The first Arabic-language history of the Crusades wasn't even published until 1899.

In that same year, when Germany's Kaiser Wilhelm II was on a tour of the Middle East, he sought out the tomb of Saladin. What he found shocked him: a neglected, crumbling, and forgotten wooden tomb tucked away in a small outbuilding of a garden beside the Great Mosque of Damascus. The Kaiser had been raised on romantic tales like Sir Walter Scott's *The Talisman,* just like most of the young men of his age, and he positively worshipped the figure of Saladin. He paid for a new mausoleum from his own pocket, a beautiful marble tomb in the medieval style with scrollwork that has a Byzantine flourish. On a bronze wreath he inscribed, "From one great emperor to another." Other sites in Damascus seem to back up the assertion of a Saladin long forgotten by his own people. The most beautiful monument to Saladin in Damascus is a magnificent statue of him on horseback, literally riding his horse over a helplessly and comically splayed-on-the-ground King Guy and Reginald de Chatillon. It wasn't built until 1992.

Saladin was a popular figure, not in Eastern, but in Western history. He has occupied that place of honor in the West for some time, from the songs of the Provençal bards to the 19th-century Sir Walter Scott bestsellers that paint a noble and sympathetic portrait of both Islam and Saladin, while Richard the Lionheart comes off as something of a brute, albeit an admirable brute. But the most interesting aspect of this argument is the reason for Saladin's virtual eradication from Arabic histories — the uncomfortable fact that he was a Kurd.

His father, the head of a respected Kurdish family, had been in the service of the warlord Zengi, as well as his uncle, Shirkuh, who was in charge of Zengi's forces that were conquering Fatimid Egypt. Though Saladin had a deeply spiritual bent of mind, after he was made a soldier, his rise to power was meteoric and brilliant, his skill on the battlefield soon catapulting him to a position second only to his uncle's. Shirkuh had two principle opponents in the struggle for Egypt, one being Amalric, the king of Jerusalem, the other the vizier and commander for the Fatamid Shiite caliph of Cairo, named Shawar. After the death of his uncle, Saladin ordered the assassination of Shawar, and by the age of 31 found himself the Sultan of Egypt. Technically, he was still a vassal of Nur al-Din. But with his overlord's death in 1174, Saladin came into his own, leading a small and disciplined force into Syria to take Nur al-Din's place, while retaining his hold on Egypt. In one of the greatest feats of his reign, he announced to the Shiite Egyptians that from that point on, they would be Sunni Muslims. Shiites were and are incredibly devout Muslims, but over the course of the next few years, a slow and steady course, Saladin replaced their faith with his own, and managed to keep his head in the process, principally through the force of his personality. He was particularly slick with the ideological use of jihad — the first Islamic leader to turn this aspect of the faith into a unifying core of fanatical anti-Christian belief that overcame sectarianism. Saladin was everything and more that every Crusader had ever dreaded in his worst nightmares — a tactical genius who now had both the Shiite and the Sunni nations under his banner, and the Crusader States by the throat.

Understanding Islamic sects

The Templars had a thorough understanding of the various Islamic sects; unfortunately, the kings of Europe arriving for the Crusade didn't want to hear about it. In fairness, the reason for the major split between Sunnis and Shiites is confusing to non-Muslims. It wasn't because they didn't see Mohammed or the Koran the same way. Even today, apart from slight differences in their customs, styles of prayer, and so on, the essentials of their beliefs are the same.

The split started because Mohammed died in 632 without a son or a designated heir. *Shiite,* in Arabic, means "party of Ali," highlighting that this was, in its beginnings, a political issue. Ali was a cousin of the Prophet's, an orphan who was raised in Mohammed's home, and eventually married Mohammed's daughter Fatima. Shiites cite numerous incidents in the *Hadith* (Koran commentary with sayings and stories of Mohammed) that they say make it clear that Mohammed wanted Ali to follow him as *caliph* (the spiritual and temporal leader of the faithful).

But the Sunnis felt that Abu Bakr, the powerful uncle of Mohammed as well as his second convert, was far more suited to rule. The Bakr side won. Essentially, this is the argument behind the split, though other differences have grown up over the centuries. Sunnis thought the best man should rule, while Shiites fervently believed, and still believe, that only the holy bloodline of Mohammed has the right to rule over Islam. Sunnis offered up a concession to Shiite feelings and, in both sects, the descendants of Mohammed are known respectfully as either *sayyids* or *sharifs.* But it's interesting to think that, if seventh-century Muslims had just been a little less chauvinistic in their thinking, then the rightful heir would have been Fatima, Mohammed's daughter, and none of this mess would ever have happened.

After the death of Abu Bakr, Fatima's husband Ali became caliph, the fourth caliph of Islam. But when he was murdered in 661 by a rival who took the caliphate for himself, a fervent party of followers rallied to Ali's son, Husayn. Husayn and his small army were annihilated by their opposition at the Battle of Karbala in 680. Karbala, in Iraq, is a place of pilgrimage for Shiites, and one of their holiest times of worship is called *Ashura,* which commemorates Husayn's death. Before the establishment of the month-long daily fast of Ramadan, all Muslims observed the fast of Ashura. Most of the holy days of the Islamic calendar are shared by both

(continued)

(continued)

sects, but Ashura has become a special time for Shiites, usually lasting ten days. Two aspects of this fast drive Sunnis nuts:

✔ During Ashura, Shiites defy Mohammed's law against any graven or painted image, and they include representations of the Battle of Karbala in their worship (not to mention the fact that Shiites often display images of Ali in their mosques and homes, even on bumper stickers or hanging from rearview mirrors).

✔ Shiites observe Ashura with extreme emotionalism. First-aid stations have to stand by, because Muslim men, apart from pulling at their hair and beating on their breasts in grief, also go so far as to practice ritual self-abuse, cutting at themselves with razors, whipping themselves, and so on.

The great majority of Muslims are Sunnis; it's sometimes called Orthodox Islam. Shiites are considered the breakaway sect. In very general terms, Sunnis look on Shiites as pain-in-the-neck heretics, and Shiites look on Sunnis as oppressors. Shiites have picked up dualist, Gnostic, and mystical elements over the years, particularly in small and even more mystical sects such as the Isma'ilis, the Sufis, and the Druze, that sprung from the Shiite movement. (For an explanation of Gnosticism, see Chapter 7.) Islam has had its own "Spanish Inquisitions" over the centuries, and Shiites have often been murderously suppressed. In Sunni-dominated countries, Shiites pay an additional (and substantial) tax as part of their *dhimmitude,* their defiant status as "heretics."

Islam has no priesthood as the West understands the concept, but the imams are the closest thing to it. Another major difference between the sects is in the power and position of the imams. For Sunnis, the imam is the respected and wise prayer leader. For Shiites, he is infallible, without sin, all-knowing in the hidden meanings of the Koran, and with a

mystical connection to God. Shiites also have a "messiah" belief, that one day an imam above all others will come, the *Mahdi* who will bring the world justice and salvation.

If you talk to Sunni Muslims, particularly of the middle and upper classes, you will often get a glimpse of their attitude about the mysticism and emotionalism of Shiites. It's the attitude a Madison Avenue–type New Yorker may have for a fundamentalist Christian in the Smoky Mountains who wrestles snakes or speaks in tongues. It's not fair, of course, but there it is — one more cultural difference that seems to be growing worse in the Middle East. Even Americans often equate *Shiite* with *terrorist.* Although it's true that both the radical Hezbollah and Hamas movements are made up of Shiites, Osama bin Laden and al-Qaeda, for example, are Sunni. Radical Islamic fundamentalism doesn't glue itself only to one sect.

The majority of stable governments in the Middle East are Sunni — Egypt, Saudi Arabia, Jordan, and Kuwait, for example. All these nations have a Sunni majority in their population, as high as 95 percent. All are fearful of fundamentalists in their midst who want to bring down the Sunni regime. For example, President Hosni Mubarak in Egypt is virtually at war with Shiite fundamentalists, a silent but very bloody war, as he tries to stabilize the country and save its $7-billion-a-year tourist industry. All these Sunni presidents and kings fear and distrust the single nation in the region that is controlled by radical Shiites — Iran. Iran is the only Shiite nation in the region and has been since the 16th century. The U.S. State Department will tell you, in its diplomatic nomenclature, that Iran is a far more "destabilizing influence" than Iraq. In other words, Iran has been exporting radicalism and violence for years. Their president, Mahmoud Ahmadinejad (elected in 2005), routinely delivers speeches laced with anti-Semitism, anti-Americanism, and open calls to violence.

Confused Westerners now find themselves trying to sort out the mess. For many years, Iraq had been a country with a large Shiite population ruled over by a Sunni government. After the fall of Iraq's Sunni dictator, Saddam Hussein, in 2003, the Shiite majority came to power, and an all-out civil war quickly broke out. When the new Iraqi government hanged Saddam Hussein on December 30, 2006, the first day of the *Eid ul-Adha,* a holy day of sacrifice and atonement, much was made of this in the Western press, with assertions that President George W. Bush had chosen the date as a deliberate slight to Muslims. But in Iraq, everyone knew who was jabbing whom. The date was chosen by the new Shiite-dominated government because *their* celebration of Eid ul-Adha on *their* calendar did not begin until the day *after.* This was only one of a string of dismal and violent tit-for-tat incidents that have grown ever more bloody, and it's doubtful that the strife in Iraq between the two sects will end anytime soon. (For a detailed but clear and easy-to-read outline of the various sects of Islam and their history, see *Islam For Dummies* by Malcolm Clark [Wiley].)

Saladin was a man of a deep and thoughtful nature, pious and clean living, generous to friends, ruthless to enemies, courteous and kind to the helpless, and without doubt the most brilliant military tactician of the 12th century. For this reason alone, his showdown with Richard the Lionheart and the crusader kings of the West was the stuff of legend. It remains so to the present day.

Despite being Islamic, the Kurds have their own language, their own dress, and their own culture. For centuries, the Turks, Iranians, and Iraqis (both Sunni and Shiite Muslims) have oppressed the Kurds and pressured them to assimilate. Because of this unceasing, centuries-old hatred of the Kurdish people, it does seem to make sense that Saladin would be tossed into the ashcan of Islamic history, until he was rediscovered, along with the Crusades, by early-20th-century Arabs eager to use the Crusades as a metaphor for all "Western imperialism."

The Treacherous Kingdom of Jerusalem

The East, both the Christian Byzantine East and the Islamic East (all of which would one day become the Ottoman Empire), has always had a reputation for assassination politics. It seems to have been an unfortunate backlash to this process of Syrianizing the Latin States that the Franks picked up on this as well, and pretty quickly, too.

Ethics by Borgia, politics by Shakespeare

By the last half of the 12th century, the Kingdom of Jerusalem was a land of epic bloodletting over politics, with noble families warring one another. In fact, it's amazing that Shakespeare passed it by. If he'd lived another ten years, he could've gotten a half-dozen more plays out of it. Talk about Lady

Macbeth! There were at least three of them to every noble family of Outremer. It was a "pellet with the poison's in the vessel with the pestle" kind of place, a land of secret decoder rings, bedroom alliances, and political rivals lured to a bloody death down a darkened alleyway.

It's strange to think that all this drama was founded after the First Crusade by Godfrey de Boullion, a man so pure he was absolutely no fun to party with. If Godfrey could have seen what he'd spawned out of a simple desire to bring a little order to the shattered city of Jerusalem, he'd probably have packed up bag and baggage for home. His progeny, great-grandnieces and great-grand-nephews, were all stock characters from some dark melodrama.

There was the pathetic Baldwin IV, the Leper King, who died at the age of 24, and spent the last ten years of his life surrounded by a pack of wolves waiting for him to drop. Desperate for some family feeling, he asked his mother, the Dowager Queen Agnes, to return to the court. After giving her husband Amalric three children, she'd been annulled by him for a variety of reasons, including her legendary inability to keep her knees together. She took her lovers by the gaggle, and when she was through with them she maneuvered them into positions of power to back up her party at court. Should anyone cross one of her former lovers, he was usually poisoned, or mysteriously slipped a knife between the ribs on a deserted back street.

Agnes's daughter Sibylla learned her own double-dealing at mama's knee. She'd already been widowed and was engaged to another lord, when she fell in lust with the handsomest and most worthless man at court, a petty noble named Guy of Lusignan. After her brother Baldwin's death, she plotted a palace coup against the regent, Raymond of Tripoli, who had a party of his own, naturally, and bargained her way to the throne with the skill of a Borgia pope. In a slippery scheme worthy of a carnival midway bunko artist, she soothed the ruffled feathers of the nobles at court, who had no objection to her as queen, so long as her husband was not king — they had no intention of bending a knee to a boob whose greatest assets were his blonde hair and square chin. At their insistence, Sibylla divorced her husband, asking for a single concession in return: that she could choose her next husband herself. Her request was granted, grudgingly. Imagine their delight on the day of her coronation, when these duped nobles were presented with her choice for a husband. Surprise! It was her ex-husband, Guy of Lusignan! She had, indeed, drunk duplicity in her mother's milk.

Historians sometimes go looking for a good guy in all this sewer diplomacy. Raymond of Tripoli often gets the nod. (In the film *Kingdom of Heaven,* Jeremy Irons plays a thinly veiled Raymond.) Yet, despite his wisdom and his courage, Raymond in all likelihood had his chief rival for the position of regent assassinated. It was the spirit of the age. These guys were not above using the notorious Assassins, a sect of murderous Islamic mystics, to do their dirty work for them. Raymond's own father of the same name was taken out by the Assassins in 1150.

As far as the military orders were concerned, there were only two things that were always a certainty:

- ✔ That they would be backing a political party
- ✔ That whoever the Templars were backing, the Hospitallers would be on the other side

But the biggest mistake the Templars made was in getting involved with any of this treachery and gutter depravity to begin with. Of course, that ideal makes no concession to human nature. The Frankish nobles of Jerusalem were a little island unto themselves, months away from the capitals of Europe. Like people on a desert island after a shipwreck, they're going to get involved with one another. Besides, being Grand Master of the Templars was a position of great temporal as well as spiritual power. It was inevitable that that power wasn't going to lie about unused.

Unfortunately for the Templars, their greatest defeat, from which they never really recovered, was brought about, at least in part, by their *danse macabre* with the slimy politics of the noble families of Outremer.

The horns of Hattin

The Battle of Hattin was fought on July 4, 1187. It was a blow to Templar pride from which they would never recover, the catalyst to a chain of events that would lose the city of Jerusalem for the Christians. And every step along the way was led by Gerard de Ridefort, Templar Grand Master.

In the preceding section, we say that historians tend to look for "good guy, bad guy" labels for figures of history. If there was a bad guy in all this, unfortunately, it was Gerard de Ridefort, Grand Master of the Knights Templar. With all the past Grand Masters who had spoken Arabic, been smooth negotiators, and been expert diplomats, it's sad to think that he was in charge at the most crucial moment of Templar history. He was a furious and impatient warrior, hawkish, arrogant, with a personal hatred for Raymond of Tripoli that blinded him to what was best for the Frankish army. Politically, he was backing King Guy and Queen Sibylla. And unfortunately, not only did he have great influence on the young King Guy, but de Ridefort's closest ally was a murderous and dishonorable liar named Reynald of Chatillon.

Reynald of Chatillon (confusingly referred to as Reginald in some books) was something of a maniac, and he screwed up everything he touched. He was no fit company for the king or de Ridefort. On a lighter note, he'd been imprisoned for ransom once by the Muslims, a common practice with a captured lord. After 16 years, no one liked him well enough to put together the ransom money, and so the exasperated Muslims let him go. Afterward, he ran around from then until his death, starting wars everywhere he went, breaking treaties, killing Muslim pilgrims, pillaging caravans that were traveling under a pass from both Saladin and the king of Jerusalem, and in general single-handedly making an all-out war with Saladin inevitable.

It was a war that Saladin was more than ready to fight. He had the power of both Damascus and Cairo behind him, an Islamic first, and he possessed an army of about 25,000. In this summer of 1187, he was moving south, victory after victory under his belt, obviously headed for Jerusalem. On the Sea of Galilee, he took the city of Tiberius, the property of Raymond of Tripoli, who at that time was in Acre at a council of war. Word arrived in Acre that Raymond's wife, Eschiva, was leading the defense of the city with the small force of knights at her disposal. Even so, Raymond pleaded for caution. The king ignored him, taking instead the advice of his friend Gerard de Ridefort, who said they should march at once.

King Guy, he of the Brad Pitt looks, had had several golden opportunities in the previous two months to take on Saladin when their numbers were roughly equal, and he'd blown them all, dancing around the enemy instead of engaging them. He was already getting a reputation as a coward, which was totally unfounded. He wasn't a coward; he was an incompetent. He had a tendency to believe with absolute faith in the last person who'd talked to him. The man had a hard time deciding what to have for breakfast, much less when and where to engage an enemy as dangerous as Saladin.

But now, on the long, dry march to meet Saladin and relieve the Countess Eschiva, decisiveness was an absolute necessity. It was Raymond himself, once again, who pleaded with King Guy to be cautious, to find water and supplies before attacking. His wife could handle the Saracens for the time being, of that he was confident. But the temperamental Gerard de Ridefort argued relentlessly that the time was now and the place Tiberius. Raymond pleaded at least for a night attack, when the broiling July heat would not have the opportunity to steam-cook his knights. This advice, too, was ignored.

Throughout their march, each day they were harassed by the skillful archers of Saladin. They'd been out of water for two days when they met the forces of Saladin at Hattin, a small village near a dormant volcano, whose sunken center left two peaks on either side like the horns on a bull. They had the high ground, and the road to Tiberius was before them, as was the glistening and potable water of the Sea of Galilee. But standing between the two was the army of Saladin, blocking the way to all that blue, clear water. It was nearing dark and the Franks camped, while Saladin's men began a slow process of ringing them in, starting a series of brushfires below that drifted up to choke the Franks, making them even more miserable. By dawn, when the charge began, it's said that many small groups of knights were bearing down on the Muslims like madmen, headed not for the enemy, but for the water.

When the battle was done, and the Christian defeat humiliatingly complete, Saladin ordered every Templar and Hospitaller knight to be killed, forcing

Gerard de Ridefort to watch. It's also said that he had a party of Sufis with him, peace-loving Islamic mystics who'd never handled a sword. Saladin ordered them to kill the knights, and the Sufis, too frightened to defy him, did their best, hacking at the knights who were on their knees on the ground, taking six and seven agonizing blows to behead them.

Saladin captured both Guy of Lusignan and, to his delight, Reynald of Chatillon. They were both brought into Saladin's tent by their guards. There is an old Islamic custom for the conquered: If the lord intends to let you live, he will offer food and drink; if not, he will kill you. Saladin smoothly offered King Guy a drink of water. When Guy politely turned to give a drink to Reynald, Saladin demurred, saying succinctly, "I did not offer the water to *him.*" And then he beheaded Reynald himself, with his razor-sharp scimitar, to the horror of the king. Saladin then turned, still completely calm, and told King Guy to finish his water.

In October of 1187, a victorious and virtually unopposed Saladin took the city of Jerusalem. Europe was shocked and appalled by the loss of the holy city, although you may wonder why they should have been. Surely, enough deputations from the Latin States pleading for help in the previous three decades had warned them of this dire possibility. But it did galvanize them enough to send along the Third Crusade, which was the last Crusade in many respects — the last to have any success, as well as the last to involve all of Europe. Saladin and Richard the Lionheart would spend those years of 1188 to 1192 in a sort of lovers' waltz, neither gaining any permanent tactical advantage. When Richard finally left, Outremer was relatively secure. But Jerusalem remained Saladin's possession, with treaty rights to pilgrimage given to Christians. Oddly enough, neither man lived long once the Crusade was over. It was as if, without one another, they'd lost their identity and their will to survive. War was just no fun anymore.

The final curtain

Outremer settled down after the treaty with Saladin, but there would only be a few decades of relative peace. By the middle of the 13th century, matters were going from bad to worse; by the end of the century, everything was crumbling around them. That absolute necessity of keeping the northeast and the southwest from attacking together was never a possibility again. Turks and Mongols poured in from above, ruthless Mamluk warriors from below, using Outremer for a battleground. The Turks overran Jerusalem in 1244, and proceeded to decimate any Christian relics they could find. The Church of the Holy Sepulchre was burned to the ground, one more time.

By 1268, Antioch fell, and the Templars reluctantly withdrew from the Amanus March, a large area to the north of the city that they'd held since the 1130s. Prince Edward of England arrived and brokered a ten-year truce with the Mamluks, but the attempts to put together a Crusade during this breathing space were a mess, mostly due to — you guessed it — more dynastic squabbling over the throne of Jerusalem. By the early 1280s, there was civil war in Tripoli as well as the kingdom of Jerusalem, which looked a lot like fighting over the last martini at the bar while the *Titanic* is going down. An embattled Tripoli fell to the Mamluks in 1289.

The pope scraped together a "Crusader" force that arrived in 1290; it was a collection of thieves, brigands, and opportunists, of the sort that the Templars had been formed to protect pilgrims from to begin with. Ten minutes after they got off the boats at Acre, they caused a bloody street riot over a dispute with some Muslim traders, which gave the Mamluks an excuse to put the city to siege. Since the loss of Jerusalem, Acre was the heart of the Templar universe. The Templar Grand Master, Guillaume de Beaujeu, fought with skill and suicidal courage for two months, until the Mamluks broke through a wall on May 18. De Beaujeu ran toward the fighting, not wearing his armor, and was killed in the melee. In the harbor, ships were already carrying refugees to the Templar holdings on the island of Cyprus. The Mamluks offered the marshal of the Templars a truce to evacuate his forces, but it was only a ruse. They fell on the Templars who were attempting to leave and slaughtered them. Late on the night of May 25, the Templar commander of Acre sailed for Cyprus with the Templar treasury. The rest fought on, to the last man.

Soon, it would seem that the Templars were going through Grand Masters as if they were Kleenex. After the death of de Perigord in Gaza and de Beaujeu at Acre, the commander of Acre who'd rescued the treasure, Theobald Gaudin, was elected Grand Master by the Templars remaining in their Levantine stronghold at Sidon. They had hoped for fresh reinforcements from Cyprus, but instead they were told to evacuate the entire coast. By then it was a game of dominoes; Sidon fell, then Haifa, then Tortosa, and finally the legendarily impregnable Atlit, which fell on August 14. The new Grand Master, Theobald Gaudin, did not survive another year.

The last Crusader

At a chapter meeting on Cyprus, the new Templar headquarters, Jacques de Molay (see Figure 5-3), at the age of 50, was elected Grand Master of the Knights Templar. This may seem the very definition of living in a fool's paradise, a small group of tattered survivors electing a new Grand Master, after having lost the entirety of the Holy Land. But keep in mind two things:

- ✔ **Hope, for them, was anything but dead.** They'd suffered their worst defeat, but there's no doubt that visions of another massive Crusade danced in their heads as the next obvious objective.

- ✔ **With all the controversy and all the infighting, the Templar knights were still enormously respected and trusted figures.** And they were still men who lived an incredibly joyless existence, stripped of all life's pleasures, in order to serve God.

Figure 5-3:
Jacques de Molay, the last Grand Master of the Knights Templar.

JACQUES DE MOLAY, chef des Templiers
(XIIIᵉ SIÈCLE)

Dark Clouds Converge over France

After the evacuation of the last of the Templars to Cyprus, Jacques de Molay took a ship for France, to meet with the pope and various nobles, in an attempt to put together another Crusade. His first meeting would be with Clement V, the new pope, and he had high hopes for success, especially because they were countrymen. He couldn't, at this point, have known of the dark forces that were assembling against him behind the scenes.

King Phillip "The Fair"

King Phillip IV of France was one of the most remarkable figures of the period, a king so forward-looking and modernistic that he seemed to have been born out of his time and place. Chicago in the 1930s should have been his time and place. The only difference between this guy and Al Capone was the cheap pin-striped suit.

Most French kings had nicknames, and some don't translate very well. Everything sounds better in French (always remember that *pâté de fois gras* in English means "smashed liver fat"), so maybe they sound odder to our hopelessly Anglo-Saxon ears — Chlodion the Hairy, Childeric the Lazy, Pepin the Short, Charles the Simple (not to be confused with Charles the Fat or Charles the Mad). On and on it goes, from the Bald to the Stammerer to the Do-Nothing. So you'd figure Phillip the Fair must have been a pretty good guy. However, and you can take this to the bank, Phillip the Fair was nicknamed for his good looks, not his ethics.

Kingship was the ultimate power trip in the Middle Ages, and all kings have had their little eccentricities. Phillip the Fair's eccentricity — in fact, his obsession — was money. In the course of his reign, one lousy decision after another was brought about by his mania for gold, and his belief that enough of it would make of him a great king, and of France a great nation. Phillip's monumental avarice knew no bounds of decency or fear of consequence. It's true that he left the nation larger than he found it, but this wasn't through the usual route of conquest; he *bought* new towns and counties (Quercy, Beaugency, and Montpellier). Like some sort of spend-happy trophy wife of an overage millionaire, he seemed to believe there was nothing, absolutely *nothing,* that money couldn't buy. And, in a dark portent of things to come, what he couldn't buy, like the town of Mortagne in Normandy, or Tournai in Flanders, he simply stole, after trumping up phony charges against the rightful owners. It was a tactic he would use again and again.

One of his most notorious schemes left the nation on very shaky economic ground. He cooked up a plot to recall all the coinage in France, melt it down, and then reissue it with the same printed value, skimming off a substantial portion of gold for himself. As any high school student of economics could have predicted, it caused a disastrous devaluation of the currency, which led to hunger, unemployment, and rioting in the streets. Which is not to say that he didn't do it again, because he did.

Phillip entered into one nasty intrigue after another to get his hands on someone else's money. An honest robber would have used a gun. Instead, Phillip hid behind the skirt of the power of his royal position to trump up charges against any group in the land that seemed to have a little bit of green. It began with the Lombards.

The Lombards were Italian bankers living in France to do business there. The word was that Phillip had borrowed from them, heavily. Suddenly, the wealthiest among them had various charges brought against them that had them expelled from France. The king, of course, kept their goods and money. Finally, tiring of shooting ducks one at a time, he had all the remaining Lombards expelled, and swooped in to gather up their money, too.

Next, in 1306, he turned his sights on France's Jews, a group that few Christians were willing to risk their own lives to defend. Many of the Jewish moneylenders of France had done fairly well in the previous two centuries, and, of course, as with the Lombards, it was rumored that Phillip was personally in hock to them. Charging that they "dishonored Christian custom and behavior," he expelled them from France, stealing their money and belongings, without letting a penny between the floorboards escape him.

Looking back, it seems obvious that Phillip's actions against the Lombards and the Jews were practice runs, simply to see if he could pull it off. Because by that time, he clearly had another organization in his sights, one with fabled wealth. Enough gold, Phillip thought, to make even him feel secure.

Pope Clement V

Unfortunately for the Templars, a papal disaster was brewing, a political and religious mess that no one could ever have foreseen. It would be the final blow, the one from which they would not recover. Catholics often refer to it as the Babylonian Captivity. Nowadays, it's usually called the Avignon Papacy or the Great Schism. Either way, an atom bomb by any other name still blows everything to bits.

Phillip and his personal henchman Guillaume de Nogaret had been in severe conflict with the then-reigning pope, Boniface VIII. The pope had declared that the king of France had no right to tax Church property, and the king had, obviously, disagreed. De Nogaret kidnapped an important French bishop, and the pope had come out swinging over it. He issued a papal bull proclaiming that kings must be subordinate to the Church, and that popes held ultimate authority over both spiritual and temporal matters on earth. To make sure they got the message, Boniface excommunicated Phillip and de Nogaret. Phillip answered his challenge by sending the brutal, devious, and bad-tempered de Nogaret at the head of an army to meet up with Italian allies and capture the pope. Boniface was, indeed, kidnapped and held for three days. After being beaten to a pulp, he was released; a month later, he died. The French king had proved just who was subordinate to whom, and he didn't mind a little papal blood on his hands. Pope Boniface's successor, Pope Benedict XI, lasted only a year in office, poisoned, it was said, by de Nogaret.

But there had been diplomatic difficulties to suffer for killing two popes. Consequently, King Phillip decided it would be easier to just buy one. He began procuring cardinals, pulling strings behind the scenes until the number of French cardinals in the Vatican's College of Cardinals was equal to the Italian ones. They then obligingly elected his handpicked candidate, Bertrand de Goth, making him Pope Clement V. The city of Rome was in turmoil, and the safety of the Vatican was in question. So, it didn't take much to convince the new French pope that his life would be in serious danger by living there. Clement obliged by staying in France, having his ceremony of investiture in Lyons. He remained in France, and in 1309 moved the Holy See to the city of Avignon (which was actually owned by the king of Sicily at the time), right on Phillip's back doorstep, where he built a new papal palace.

Two miters aren't better than one

Phillip's tactic, buying a pope and then virtually holding him prisoner if he tried to get out of line, would cause the worst breakdown the Catholic Church ever endured. After Clement's death, seven popes would reign from Avignon, anti-popes according to the College of Cardinals at Rome that was off electing its own popes the whole time. Confusion and chaos ran rampant in the Christian world, and nobody knew which pope to follow. The breach was healed at last, in 1417, but by that time, the papacy, and the Church as a whole, had suffered such a loss of legitimacy that it was a major factor in the success of the Protestant Reformation.

Clement had everything Phillip wanted in a pope: He was puny, weak, new in the job, and owed everything to his French king. Now was the time for the boldest move of Phillip's reign — the arrest of the Knights Templar.

The setup

Phillip had to set the snare just right. His aim was to destroy the Templar Order and confiscate all their treasuries and properties in France, but he had to achieve it legally. The one surefire way was to accuse them of crimes so heinous that, if proved, no one would dare come to their rescue. It was no good to simply accuse the Grand Master or a handful of leaders. It had to be all of them, and he had to find a way to make the charges stick. And he had to be quick about it, because battle-hardened Templar knights were already returning to France, partly because of tensions on Cyprus between the Templars and the island's king. Phillip needed no more knights to cope with.

King Phillip's audacious plan was to arrest every Templar in France, charge them with heresy, and exact immediate confessions from them by torture, before the pope or anyone else could protest on their behalf. By making the charges religious in nature, Phillip would be seen not as an avaricious thief, but as a noble servant of God.

Jacques de Molay had been called out of Cyprus to Poitiers, France, for the purpose of discussing a new crusade to retake the Holy Land with the new pope. For almost two years, he shuttled back and forth between the pope and King Phillip, essentially stamping out various diplomatic fires, such as the proposal to merge all the military orders.

In June of 1307, de Molay rode into Paris at the head of a column of his knights, with a dozen horses laden with gold and silver, to begin the financing of the new Crusade. For the next several months, Phillip treated the aging Grand Master with interest and diplomacy, and de Molay believed he and the Order were at a new turning point. He didn't know how right he was.

October 1307: An unlucky Friday the 13th

The end began at dawn on Friday, October 13, 1307. The sealed order to Phillip's Seneschals and bailiffs had gone out a full month before. It was accompanied by a personal letter from the king, filled with lofty prose about how heart-rending it was to be compelled to do his duty, while detailing frightening accusations against the Templars. The letter would have had an eye-popping effect on the king's men, and their secrecy was undoubtedly assured. The sealed arrest order was not to be opened until the appointed day.

At this time, France was the most populous nation of Europe, even including Russia. And it was no tiny country either, no Luxembourg or Monaco. France took up more than 40,000 square miles, an enormous area to cover from the back of a horse. Yet Phillip IV managed to carry off his own Night of the Long Knives, in a country without telephones, trains, or automobiles. It was a stunning piece of work. Hundreds of the king's men simultaneously opened letters all over the country ordering them to converge on every Templar castle, commandery, preceptory, farm, vineyard, or mill.

It was shockingly effective, instantly chopping off the head of the Order. Phillip obviously had a hit list of the most important knights to nab. Accounts differ wildly, but the most respected ones agree that 625 members of the Order were arrested in the first wave (for more details of the numbers of Templars arrested, see Chapter 6). These included the Grand Master; the Visitor-General; the Preceptors of Normandy, Cyprus, and Aquitane; and the Templars' Royal Treasurer.

The vast majority of the literally thousands of Templar properties in France were small manors and farms, tended by as few as two or three aging brethren. Often, a small preceptory with a few serving brothers and the occasional aged knight was all there was to meet these armed bailiffs of the king. The average age of those arrested was 41. They were not, as a rule, the cream of the Order's hardened fighting force, and many of those tending these unfortified properties were in their 60s and 70s.

The Templars were put into isolation, and immediately subjected to the gruesome tactics of medieval interrogation on the very first day of their arrest. The technique of the *strapaddo* was common. It involved binding the victim's wrists behind his back, passing the rope over a high beam, pulling him off of the ground, and suddenly dropping him, snapping his arms and dislocating his shoulders. Stretching the victim on the rack was another favored method. Perhaps the most horrible was coating the victim's feet in lard or oil, and then slowly roasting them over a flame. More than one knight was handed the tiny bones that fell from his burned feet by his gleeful torturers. Subjected to these agonies, the overwhelming majority of the knights confessed to every charge that was put to them.

The Accusations

The original charges against the arrested Templars were:

- ✔ Denying Christ, and spitting or urinating on the cross
- ✔ Denying the sacraments and having contempt for the Mass
- ✔ Worshiping idols, referred to in most cases as either a cat, or a head of various descriptions, during rituals that were kept secret
- ✔ Engaging in homosexual acts of kissing each other on the lips, navel, or the base of the spine while naked, and other forms of sodomy
- ✔ Acquiring property and profit by illegal or immoral means

By June of the next year, the Grand Inquisitor in Paris presented an expanded list of 127 accusations against the Order, but these original charges formed the essential core of Phillip's flimsy case. (For more detail on the accusations, see Chapter 6.)

The Confessions

Phillip's goal was to arrest all the Templars, subject them to torture immediately, and exact confessions from them *on the very first day*. He knew that the pope would be livid over his actions, and that Church officials would be wary of agreeing to the kinds of interrogations Phillip had in mind, so time was of the essence. He wanted to hand Clement V a stack of confessions so damning that the pope would lose his stomach for siding with the Order.

The pope reacted just as Phillip had planned. His outrage over the arrests turned to dread and resignation as the "evidence" was presented to him. Phillip leaned on Clement to issue papal arrest warrants all across Europe, which were largely ignored or skirted around by other monarchs. Very few show trials went on outside of France, and there were no cases (outside of the tortured knights in France) of Templars who admitted to the charges of heresy.

In an outburst of courage and remorse, most of the arrested Templars subsequently recanted their confessions, and proclaimed to Church officials that their statements were made under the pain of torture and threat of death. To intimidate the remaining Templars, Phillip ordered 54 of the knights to be burned at the stake in 1310, for the sin of recanting their confessions.

In 1312, Clement finally decided to end the situation at a council in Vienna. Just to make certain the decision went the way he intended, Phillip stationed his army on the outskirts of the city. The pliant pope officially dissolved the

Order, without formally condemning it. Clement was as mushy as usual. All Templar possessions apart from the cash were handed over to the Knights Hospitaller, and many Templars who freely confessed were set free and assigned to other Orders. Those who did not confess were sent to the stake. Phillip, ever the cheap gangster, soothed his loss of the Templars' tangible assets by strong-arming a yearly fee from the Hospitallers, to defray his costs of prosecuting the Templars.

The End

By 1314, both the pope and public opinion had abandoned the Knights Templar. The four senior Templar officers in Phillip's custody had been waiting in prison for seven grim years. All of them were old, the youngest being Geoffroy de Charney, who was almost 60. Jacques de Molay (see Figure 5-4) was in his 70s and had spent four years in solitary confinement. The four men were finally led onto a platform in front of Paris's Notre Dame Cathedral to hear the charges and make their public confessions. The charges were read, and two of the men accepted their fate of perpetual imprisonment and were led away.

Figure 5-4: Jacques de Molay and Geoffroy de Charney are burned at the stake on the tiny Île-des-Juifs in Paris. King Phillip watched from his palace across the river.

Mary Evans Picture Library / Alamy

But Jacques de Molay and his trusted follower Geoffroy de Charney did not follow suit. Weakened with age and imprisonment, de Molay shouted in a voice that startled the assembly that he and the Templars were innocent of all the charges. They were returned to their cells at once, while Phillip called together his council and quickly pronounced sentence, using the insane logic of the Inquisition; if they had recanted their confessions, then they were considered "relapsed heretics," and the penalty was the stake.

Late that afternoon, de Molay and de Charney were led to the place of execution, which was a tiny isolated island adjacent to the Isle de la Citè, called the Île-des-Juifs (Island of the Jews). The condemned men could see Notre Dame Cathedral in the east, but the site was not chosen for their view. Rather, it was chosen so that King Phillip could enjoy the entertainment without leaving his palace just across the River Seine.

Each man was stripped down to his shirt and tied to the stake. Jacques de Molay, with unbelievable courage, asked not only that he be turned to face the Cathedral, but that his hands be freed, so that he could die at prayer. His request was granted. The two men were roasted alive by the Inquisitional method that began with hot coals, so that their agony could be prolonged as much as possible. It was dusk on March 18, 1314.

When the Pont Neuf was built, the Île de Juifs was joined to the rest of the Île de la Cité, and today there are not one but two plaques near the bridge to commemorate this event. Jacques de Molay did not go to his God in silence. Instead, he died defiantly shouting his innocence and that of the Templars, calling on King Phillip and Pope Clement to meet him before the throne of God in one year's time, where they would all be judged together. Creepily enough, both men, relatively young, would be dead within the year. One month after the death of de Molay, Pope Clement V, age 54, died, it was said, of cancer. Phillip the Fair, age 46, died in a hunting accident probably brought on by a stroke. He died on November 29, 1314, managing to get in just under the wire.

The gruesome death of Jacques de Molay is the last act of the Templar story. At least, the last act of the accepted, scholarly story of the Knights Templar that is told, in names and dates, between the covers of the history books. But in reality, his death is only the beginning. It's the beginning of the *myth* of the Knights Templar, which is the maelstrom around which an endless stream of fact blended with speculation swirls, unabated.

Chapter 6

Cold Case Files: The Evidence against the Templars

A quick glance through a *TV Guide* will prove that the public has gone absolutely bonkers over television shows that feature autopsies, and usually at dinnertime. Terminology that was once confined to homicide cops and medical examiners has now insinuated itself into the American idiom. We'd love to sound high-minded and say we're above all this gory ambulance chasing, but we'll break down and admit it: We have a favorite ourselves. Despite the heart-stopping dramatic tension and boffo special effects of a show like *CSI: Miami,* it's the straightforward documentary style of A&E's *Cold Case Files* that has captured our hearts — and not just for the comforting presence and soothing voice of producer Bill Kurtis. It's because of the fascination of seeing real cops at work, patiently digging for evidence with a dogged determination to see justice done in a case that can sometimes be three or four decades old and has been long forgotten.

Maybe the passing of seven centuries *is* asking a bit much, but we'd love to turn these guys loose on the case of the Knights Templar. So much of the evidence used against the Order smelled like yesterday's cod when it was delivered up; by now, it stinks to high heaven. Not to mention the tactics of the Inquisition, that were strutted through the courtroom disguised as evidence. Come now. There's not much that people won't admit when they're being branded with hot pokers.

So, even though we haven't got a badge, we're going to take another look at the case against the Knights Templar and the evidence that sent them to exile, prison, or the stake. In this chapter, we let you know whether it would hold up under the cold and clinical examination of modern forensics.

The Chief Accuser

Nowadays, prosecutors like to hold a few charges back when dealing with a serial killer or a career criminal, so that, if one of the charges pending gets blown because of a Miranda glitch or a loss of evidence, one of the others can be pulled out of their pocket, thereby keeping the little creep in jail. King Phillip's tactics with the Templars were just the opposite, and though they were despicable, they were also effective. The idea was to simply rain down the charges, like overheated basketball fans throwing hot dogs and beer cups at opposition players — so many charges that, as soon as one was addressed to the best of their ability, another was instantly poured on, before the accused could even catch his breath.

When an accuser has motives of his own, plus a hidden agenda, it makes him a legitimate target for a defense attorney. And doubtless King Phillip would have been fried to a golden brown by an attorney, if the Templars had been fortunate enough to have one. As it is, we have to question a dead witness. Difficult, but not impossible.

As we establish in Chapter 5, Phillip was a man who'd have sold his own mother, if he could have gotten a single golden livre out of it. After all, he'd already done this twice before. Both the Lombards (Italian bankers) and the Jews had been recently expelled from France after a series of charges were made against them, their property confiscated by the crown. Oddly enough, in an age that was rife with anti-Semitism, both the pope and the Templars protested his brutal treatment of the Jews, and Phillip proved with his contemptuous lack of a reply that he didn't give a tinker's dam. This is called *modus operandi* by lawyers — the man's method of doing business. In other words, if a guy has already strangled two women with a pair of pantyhose, he makes for a great suspect when you find another woman strangled with panty hose. Score one for the defense.

Point two on the subject of modus operandi. In 1302, Phillip levied a tax on the Catholic clergy of *one-half* of their income. Many a king had attempted to tax the Church, but no one had ever tried to pull a heist like that. Enraged, Pope Boniface VIII issued a papal bull, *Clericis laicos,* proclaiming that no one had the right to tax the Church without the pope's permission, and he promptly excommunicated Phillip. Again.

This set off an all-out war between Phillip and the papacy, one that the king would eventually win. With jaw-dropping gall, Phillip had Boniface kidnapped, pressured, then beaten to a pulp by his murderous henchman, Guillaume de Nogaret. The pope died soon after. Phillip never stopped telling himself that the man was a heretic, and that he'd done the world a favor. But the incident shows that Phillip didn't care about the holiness of his adversary when he was on their scent. Score two.

In 1305, Phillip's queen, Jeanne de Navarre, died under shady circumstances, and there were rumors that he'd had her killed. Only gossip, of course, but sometimes gossip is a valuable tool in assessing character, because it says what people are *willing* to believe about you, whether it's true or not.

After Jeanne's death, Phillip applied to the Templars to join the Order, now that he was a widower — a curious move, tactically speaking. He may have even meant it. He actually volunteered to abdicate in favor of his son, which would leave him free to take the title *Bellator Rex* (Warrior King) and to lead the Templars, combined with the other military orders, into one powerful order of the Knights of Jerusalem in retaking the holy city. (Like many, he held the military orders responsible for the loss of the Holy Land, and so the idea being noised around all over Europe of merging the Orders may well have made his mouth water, in terms of the temporal and spiritual power that he would achieve as its head.)

When de Molay turned him down, Phillip may have felt that the man was standing between him and his glorious Christian destiny. On the other hand, Phillip was a master of propaganda, and it's entirely probable that he was simply making a big show of public piety. It would make it that much harder later for someone to say he had a personal ax to grind with the Templars. After all, he'd wanted to become one, right?

Incidentally, to add insult to injury, the Templars insisted that Phillip pay off his substantial loans to them before discussing it further. He refused, and the loans remained outstanding.

Philip had twice devalued the coinage of France by recalling it and recasting the money with less precious metal in it, skimming some off the top. He was unquestionably in need of serious influxes of cash. In 1306, he had been forced to hide in the Paris temple from angry mobs who were rioting over the new currency. Many people have speculated that it was at this key moment that Phillip saw the vast Templar treasury and determined to have it for his own. Though the story may well be a myth, it could just as easily be true, because of what happened next.

The Paris temple was one of the largest repositories of wealth in Europe; it included much of the treasury of the French government. Shortly after his visit to the vaults, Phillip had a new treasury building constructed where the Louvre stands today. He transferred half of the gold on deposit with the Templars into this new facility; the other half was left in the hands of the Templars, who continued to handle some of their old jobs, like paying the French military, until their arrest.

Finally, the tale has always been told that, shortly after the arrest of the Templars, their treasury was found to be empty. Some say the treasure was a myth and never really existed, though we find this one hard to believe. The vaults of the Paris commandery could hardly have been a myth. The other far more common assertion is that, tipped off, the Templars spirited the treasure away before Phillip could get his hands on it. There is certainly an emotional satisfaction in believing this theory, though it has holes in it you could drive a truck through. There's little doubt that the not-inconsiderable wealth of the Templars in *other* commanderies was spirited away, but not Paris, right under the king's nose. The one theory of the treasure that doesn't seem to get much air time is that Phillip stole it, and then claimed that he'd found the vaults to be empty. It would have been far easier, because all he had to do was transport it a very short distance to his newly constructed vaults. There is evidence that Phillip almost immediately recalled the French coinage from the countryside and recast it once again, this time with the proper face-value weight of gold or silver. No one can say with certainty that an influx of precious metals for the new coinage had come from plundered Templar coffers — but it certainly came from somewhere.

Opening Move: An Illegal Arrest

By the very act of arresting the Templars, Phillip knew that what he was doing was illegal. Two centuries before, the pope had decreed that the Templars would enjoy immunity from arrest and prosecution in secular courts. Only ecclesiastical courts could try a Templar. It was Phillip's unscrupulous plan that if he struck quickly enough, and then *put them to the question* at once (the euphemism of the day for torture), he could cop some quick confessions. That way, when the issue was raised that he'd had no right to arrest them in the first place, he could respond with a sheep-eyed look of innocence, "But they're heretics and sodomites. They already admitted it. Are you trying to protect heretics and sodomites?" Yes, indeed, his trial runs had taught him every dirty trick in the book — including how to plot.

Phillip was a first-rate plotter. With probably between 1,500 and 2,000 knights across France to be arrested, all in one fell swoop (and a pretty spectacular one, as fell swoops go), literally hundreds f knights, sheriffs, bailiffs, messengers, and others needed to be informed in advance. Communication was slow, even on horseback, and France is one of the largest countries in Europe — nearly 500,000 square miles. It took days for orders from the king to be galloped from one end of the country to the other. Phillip's sealed warrants of arrest were issued on September 14, 1307, a full month before the Templars were to be arrested, and it's absurd to believe that no one peeked at them ahead of time. The Templars probably were not all taken without prior knowledge, which is an issue that becomes much more important in Chapter 7.

The numbers game: How many knights?

Despite legends and books claiming that as many as 20,000 Knights Templar were arrested on Friday, October 13, 1307, history doesn't back this up. Understand that *knight* meant a trained, armed warrior on horseback, but the vast majority of Templars were not knights.

In his *History of the Inquisition in the Middle Ages* (1908), historian Henry Charles Lea suggested that there were 15,000 Templars in France, and it has long been surmised that there were approximately 9 or 10 serving brethren in the Order for every knight. If that's true, that means 1,500 may have been knights. This seems to be close to what Pope Clement V himself believed; he surmised that there were 2,000 of them. Using that same 1-to-10 ratio, we come up with 20,000 Templars of all descriptions. That is not an unlikely guess, because they had an estimated 9,000 properties in France of varying sizes, from castles and manor houses down to rickety shacks on lonely vineyards. And if this sounds like a piddling number of knights for Phillip to fear, there may be truth in that — though two things should be noted:

- The toughest of the fighting knights were usually where they were needed, in the Holy Land and Spain, but knights made homeless by the defeats in the Levant were beginning to trickle back into France.

- Even a unit of 300 skilled, well-armed mounted knights, riding their powerful and steel-plated war horses, was quite a formidable force during a charge. Picture 300 Sherman tanks pouring down the hill toward you.

At any rate, there are 138 surviving court documents for members of the Order who appeared before the Grand Inquisitor, and only 14 were actually *knights*. Of the 546 defendants who testified in 1310, only 18 of them were knights.

One figure that comes up again and again is that all but 24 knights were arrested, and 12 of those who eluded capture at first were caught later, apparently a quote from Mathew of Paris — but no one says 12 out of *how many*. So of course, many people assume that means 12 out of 20,000. But logic dictates that Phillip had a hit list of specific knights or important Templars he was targeting, which is where the reference to the missing 24 probably comes from. Yet there are no precise figures that have survived to say just how many Templars Phillip's men really did arrest. And there would have been no point to clogging up the country's dungeons with lowly serving brethren who had no knowledge of the Order's official activities.

Anne Gilmour, in *Trials of the Templars in the Papal States and Abruzzi,* claims that 1,151 Templars were brought to trial between 1307 and 1311. If that's true, then somewhere between 14,000 and 18,000 Templars escaped arrest, and there can be no doubt that those numbers included hundreds of knights. So, there may very well have been as many as 20,000 combined knights, Sergeants, Squires, Chaplains, and other various and assorted serving brethren in France, as well as lay brethren, who were pretty much paid employees. But there were very few actual *knights* who would have been any sort of threat to Phillip.

Most important, it is simply a fable that every single Templar in France was arrested by Phillip.

The Charge Sheet

Because it was an absolute rain of accusations, from the bizarre to the dangerously plausible, it requires a good deal of elbow room to discuss them all. But one thing really needs to be said here and now about the mystery of the charges against the Templars: So many of the world's foremost scholars, and some lesser lights of academia as well, all seem to tap in to their inner attorney on the subject of the charges against the Templars. It's always phrased so carefully; the Templars were "*in all likelihood* innocent," the charges were "*most probably* false," and so on. It's as if they're all scared of a lawsuit, or afraid to make a definite statement, only to be proved a fool two years from now when someone digs up some grainy YouTube footage of an Aleister Crowley–style Templar orgy, complete with Satanic altar and ritualistic sex.

So, we'll just say it right here and now. The charges were false.

However, one problem with examining the charges one at a time is that, as the defiant Templars sat in jail, having denied the initial confessions that were wrenched from them under torture, the accusations just kept growing, until they reached an astonishing list of 127 items. In this book, we concentrate on the generalities of the initial charges. Most of the additional ones were variations on the same theme. And besides, although they were more overblown, the charges were so similar to the ones Phillip had made against the Cathars, and the Jews, and the Lombards, and Pope Boniface, and assorted wealthy individuals, that by now everyone knew the lyrics by heart. They only got weirder as they rolled along.

Considering the whiter-than-white image of the Templars, even the initial charges against them were nothing if not bizarre. The phantasmagorical aspect of the accusations has always given the whole affair a Salem-witch-trial air. You know, crazy teenaged girls who were getting the first attention they'd ever had in their dreary lives, falling down and foaming at the mouth, claiming they'd seen the milkman's wife make a cow fly. Here are the accusations. Make of them what you will. To us, they look an awful lot like a flying cow.

- ✔ **Phillip claimed that incoming Templar brothers, during their ceremony of initiation, were ordered to deny Christ, as well as Mary and all the saints.** He accused Templars of spitting on the cross or grinding a crucifix under their heel, as well as spitting or urinating on images of Christ or the cross.

- ✔ **Phillip claimed that Knights Templar bestowed "obscene kisses" on their new brothers, or the new brothers on the higher officers, including kisses on the mouth, navel, and buttocks.** He accused them of any and all acts of sodomy on one another.

✔ **Phillip claimed that Templar priests denied a belief in the sacrament of the Mass (the central pillar of the Catholic faith) and that they did not bother to consecrate the *host* (the wafer that became the body of Christ during the Mass), making a mockery of it.** He accused Templar Grand Masters of absolving brother knights of their sins when they had no authority to do so.

✔ **Phillip claimed that the Order taught that the blessed sacraments were only a show, a screen to be viewed by outsiders, and that the true worship of the Templars was reserved for something called *Baphomet*.** The supposed identity of Baphomet was all over the place, from a hanged cat to the mummified head of John the Baptist.

✔ **Phillip accused Templars of holding all their chapter meetings and ceremonies at night, so that no one could see the secrets of their true fashion of worship.**

✔ **Phillip claimed that the Knights Templar had abused the trust put in them in regards to the issue of money, that they were not giving the amounts claimed to upkeep Templar charities, and that they used extortion and other illegal means in accumulating their vast wealth.**

Initially, the first Templars arrested were brutally tortured, and the overwhelming majority of them confessed, including the Grand Master, Jacques de Molay. Soon after, these same men recanted their confessions, knowing that meant automatic conviction as lapsed heretics, and, undoubtedly, death.

By the twisted logic of the Inquisition, if a man confessed, even under torture, it was often felt that he was confronting his sin and was now ready for the repentance and punishment that would save his soul. The torture itself was *not* considered to be punishment — it was simply a tool that was used to mortify the flesh in order to free the soul from Satan's grip. The punishment varied, and it wasn't always death. But if a defendant confessed and then later recanted, he was considered a "relapsed heretic," beyond the redemption of God, and he was going to go to the stake. Even considering some of the more horrific death sentences of the day — like being hanged, cut down while living, and then butchered and castrated, or being drawn and quartered, torn into four pieces by four horses — death by fire was probably the most agonizing, and the most terrifying, of them all. Yet, after the humiliation of quick confessions by men who were the most courageous on earth, they were willing to face this horror to take back their confessions.

To tell the truth, the whole thing has always struck both of us as some sort of deal gone sour, and the scholar Malcolm Barber puts forward this theory. It's as if, in order to win, Phillip took a promise-them-anything-but-get-their-confessions route. They may well have been told while under torture that if they just confessed and then took their medicine (whatever concession to

Phillip that may have been), they would be forgiven and the whole thing would soon be forgotten. The unity with which they all proclaimed their innocence, so soon after the unity of confessing their guilt, really does fit that scenario. They went along and then found out Phillip wouldn't keep his end of the bargain, so they recanted, knowing that, in all probability, they were going to die anyway. It's one interesting possibility. But it doesn't address the issue of whether there was any truth to the charges to begin with.

So, beyond the obvious motive of greed, would Phillip have had any other motives for lying about the Templars?

Phillip IV was, if nothing else, puffed up with his own piety. For a man with so much innocent blood on his hands from the victims of his temper tantrums, he had a hugely inflated public image of saintliness. His letters to the pope and to the arresting Seneschals and bailiffs who actually hauled off the Templars were filled with the heart-rending, soul-searching exhortations of a tortured Christian conscience.

Like a pit bull with a law degree, nothing was as important to Phillip as being right. After his handpicked pope, Clement V, was installed on the throne of St. Peter, Phillip attempted to force the new, nervous pontiff to actually dig up the remains of his murdered enemy, Pope Boniface VIII, and try his bones posthumously for heresy. He was a man who loved to surround himself with a coven of lawyers, which in and of itself makes him easy to hate. He then took extraordinary pains to find legal and ecclesiastical loopholes that made his actions lawful in the eyes of both Church and State. Apart from that fact, there seems to be one more deeper, darker facet to his (and Nogaret's) outward fanatical piety: It was probably more than a hypocritical camouflage to cloak their true feelings.

There's a reason lie detectors aren't allowed to be used as evidence in most court cases: It's because some people can lie their heads off and still breeze through a lie-detector test. Some of them are just plain sociopaths, people who simply have no conscience. Others are a bit more complicated — they're people who are *narcissistic* (madly in love with themselves) and pathological liars. The lie they tell initially, in order to make the path easier for themselves, gets told again and again, and in a very short time, they come to believe the lie themselves. Based on the testimony of the people who were there, this does seem to be the case with Phillip and his chief henchman. After all, Phillip's grandfather was a bona fide saint of the Catholic Church, which is a heavy burden to live up to. It's entirely probable that his elastic ethics, combined with rationalizations of elephantine proportions, were the tools that made it possible.

The caliber of the witnesses

The caliber of the witnesses was pretty lousy, actually. You could almost see the money changing hands outside the court. One of the most important witnesses was a professional blackmailer and murderer, who was procured as a witness by a professional paid informant. This little rat fink was named Arnolfo Deghi, and he had done dirty work for Guillaume de Nogaret before. De Nogaret had risen to become a personal pet, negotiator, brown-noser, and finally chancellor. It was through Deghi that de Nogaret made contact with a renegade ex-Templar named Esquiu de Florian. Florian had once been the prior of the Templar preceptory in Montfaucon, but for reasons we don't know, he was busted from his position. So, he decided to get even by lying in wait for his Grand Master and stabbing him to death. He then hit the road to avoid his death penalty, ending up in Spain, where he tried to extort money from the King of Aragon by offering information that would allow him to confiscate Templar property in Spain, of which Florian would get a share off the top. There were no buyers in Spain, but he found one back in France.

Phillip was in need of a witness who could say he'd actually been there during closed and secret Templar meetings. Florian would do very nicely. And so, de Nogaret set up an elaborate farce to protect his king. He had powerful friends in his home city of Toulouse, especially in the prison, which is hardly surprising. He arranged for Florian and Deghi to occupy the same cell on bogus charges. Then, Florian, in a fit of repentance, could tell Deghi his tall tales of idol worship, sodomy, and witchcraft (leaving out the murder he'd committed, of course). Deghi, good Christian that he was, could pass this information on to de Nogaret. That way, the pious Phillip could have this information fall into his lap completely by accident, shocking him dreadfully, and forcing him to do something about it. Brother. How underhanded can you get?

With witnesses like these, we think little more needs to be said about the character of the men testifying against the Templars.

Dangerous foreign entanglements

Before addressing the charges, we need to make one more point, to try to make sense how such witnesses could be believed. Apart from financial improprieties, there was one thing drawing all these various allegations together. If you haven't yet read Chapter 5, understand that the Templars were coping with a very real vulnerability in their attempts to defend themselves. People generally believed that the Knights Templar, unlike the innocent boys back home, had been exposed to sinister, occult rituals and beliefs as they manned their posts at the far-flung edges of the Christian world. All the charges played to the superstitions of an incredibly provincial medieval public. The charges underscored an image of a Christian faith that had been tainted, compromised by its dangerous and incessant contact with the dark and evil forces of infidel or pagan sects.

This widespread suspicion was definitely an Achilles heel for the Knights Templar. They were as far-flung as geese, traveling through the wide and alien world, in an age when that sort of thing just wasn't done. Not only did they travel to the very edges of the Christian world, they lived there, on and beyond the frontiers of Western civilization. And in the process of defending and extending those frontiers, they were both diplomats and traders, dealing with the peoples of those lands of such exotic "otherness" that seemed so dangerous to Christian eyes. They'd already been accused of being far too clubby with the Muslims in the East, of being influenced by the alluring Moorish culture in the south of Spain, and of being sympathetic to the Cathars in the south of France. All these — especially the suspicion of chumminess with Muslims, Jews, and infidels — made the Templars an easy target for accusations of heresy.

Blowing Away the Charges, One by One

In this section, we examine the principal charges against the Order and see if they hold water.

Desecrating the cross

One of the most common psychological outrages used by Muslims against Christians while fighting each other in the Holy Land was the desecration of the cross. When Muslim forces took a Christian stronghold, their first act was to tear down any church crosses and drag them behind their horses, with Muslims spitting on them as they passed. Desecration of the cross was also a tactic used against Christian prisoners. Muslim captors often ordered their Christian prisoners to spit or urinate on the cross in order to win mercy.

Some researchers, attempting to take both sides, have suggested that the Templars may have acted out these dramas as part of their ritual in an effort to fortify the Christian resolve of new knights who may have been forced to perform such acts, if they were captured by the Saracens. Such rituals would have had to have been held in secret, because the outside world would have completely misunderstood the purpose of them. If true, the Templars performing such acts as a dramatic lesson would have been free of any actual desecration, though as Christians, it would certainly have made them uncomfortable, which of course would have been the purpose. This theory doesn't hold a great deal of water with us, but it's certainly possible. Anybody who's sat through any films made by the War Department for our boys overseas in the 1940s and 1950s has surely seen dumber things.

Ritual training aside, this accusation is nearly impossible to defend, because it suffers as much as the others from the problem of proving a negative — in a secret ceremony of initiation, with no witnesses, how do you prove that it *didn't* happen? However, we *can* address this charge using a little common sense, combined with a knowledge of Templar history. For example, after the infamous defeat of the Franks at the Battle of Hattin, Saladin decreed that all the Templar knights were to be put to death at once; no ransom, no slave market, no mercy at all for these holy warriors that he considered his most dangerous enemy. For the Arabs, whose royalty preferred the garrote, beheading was an ignominious death for traitors and infidels. But Saladin could take off a man's head in one sweeping stroke. This was too easy a death. To their horror, a small band of *Sufis* (a mystical sect of Islam that preaches peace and unity with the Divine) in the encampment was ordered by Saladin to do the beheading. To the uproarious amusement of the victorious soldiers gathered around them, the Sufis were making a complete mess of the executions, needing in some cases seven or eight blows to finally behead the knights. Despite the unimaginable anguish of the knights within that circle of laughing men, the Templars were not only lined up quietly, but virtually shouldering one another out of the way to be next, according to witnesses who were present. Does that sound like the behavior of men who did not believe in Christ? Would men who believed only in satanic self-gratification be that proud and eager to face their maker? Somehow we doubt it.

Denying the sacrament of the Mass

This charge is very similar to the preceding one, denying Christ, and it has within it the same difficulty of mounting a viable defense. Blessing sacramental bread and wine is something a priest would generally do in private, so there's very little opportunity to prove that the Templar chaplain had *not* blessed the Eucharist. Of course, once again, tampering with the Eucharist in some way was also a standard charge in witch trials and persecution of Jews. Several times in Europe in this period, large-scale *pogroms* (the beating and murder of Jews and the destruction of their property) were caused by an urban legend that Jews had somehow desecrated the Eucharist; one riot started over the accusation of a Jewish baker having substituted bread that had been baked with the blood of Christian babies. Absurd, certainly. But again, it played to the fears and superstitions of the crowd. Nobody was supposed to tamper with the Eucharist. But like the bulk of the charges against the Templars, there was not a single shred of evidence to back up this ridiculous assertion.

Sodomy

This charge didn't get thrown into the stewpot just to add a piquant spice of scandalous sex to the trial. For one thing, it was thrown in to make sure that the Templars burned. Sodomy equaled a death sentence, period. In folklore, sodomy was always tied to devil worship. Country people knew for an absolute fact that the "Musselmen" (Muslims) practiced sodomy. Sodomy, by definition, was just about any deviant sexuality, which meant, to the Church, any sex that didn't have procreation as its ultimate goal. Make babies, or keep yourself buttoned up.

If historical records are any indication, getting away with homosexual activity was strictly a pastime for kings. We know of many royals in Europe, from Edward II in France to Richard the Lionheart, who far preferred sex with men to women.

Andrew McCall, in his book *The Medieval Underworld,* an examination of the lives of outcast groups in the Middle Ages, discusses the attitudes toward homosexuality in the days of Greece and Rome, which ran the gamut from a grudging tolerance to open acceptance. But by the Middle Ages, the idea of homosexuality was tied completely to the concept of profanity or demonology, which is why the two most common words used in addressing it are *abomination* and *sodomy,* both words that were loaded with the baggage of heresy. For the common people, on the other hand, homosexuality could be a hanging offense, and the same was true in Islamic culture, despite European beliefs to the contrary. For the most part, Sunnis and other Islamic sects abhorred homosexuality, and the punishment was death.

Holy Mother Church endured an eruption of various sexual scandals in the 13th century, from the pope on down the line to the Benedictines and the Dominicans. But never, not *once,* did anyone find any reason to investigate the Templars. It was a common joke of the day that the Knights Templar were too obsessed with money to have any desire left over for sex. Nevertheless, might there have been homosexual contact among some of the Knights Templar? Certainly. It would be naïve to say otherwise. The modern Catholic Church has had more than its share of humiliating publicity over the actions of a tiny handful of its priests placed in positions of trust. Likewise, it is not a stretch of the imagination to believe that there were certain preceptories that may have had a more conducive atmosphere to private homosexual practices than others. Punishments for it in some ecclesiastical courts, where men understood the loneliness of monastic life, were sometimes mild, and could include anything from a penance to expulsion, if the guilty party seemed to be unrepentant, or a repeat offender. Yet in the case of the Templars, there are records concerning a case of three brethren who were "well acquainted" with each other. One was killed, another died trying to escape, and the third spent the rest of his life in irons. The Templars obviously didn't look on it as a trifling offense.

This is doubtless one more reason Phillip made sure to combine the accusation of sodomy with implications of devil worship. It's especially apparent in the charge of the kiss on the backside of the master, *le besa de derrier,* a ritual still practiced by many advertising executives. Again, both nobles and peasants supposed it to be an essential part of all Black Masses and Satanic worship, which assured a death sentence.

Embezzlement

Oddly enough, although this was the least lurid charge, it was in many ways the most shocking, and even seven centuries later, it's the easiest one to refute. The men who handled money for the Templars were incredibly meticulous. They all knew that any whiff of financial improprieties would be the end of them. It's true that the greatest bulk of Templar financial documents, and others as well, were destroyed on Cyprus, whereas Hospitaller documents survived, leaving them with no burden of assumed guilt to live down, even to the present day. (Yes, they still exist, as the Knights of Malta; see Chapter 9.) However, a great number of Templar financial documents still are available to historians, due to the wide reach of the organization. None of them contains any hint of impropriety. Oh, you had the occasional dissatisfied customer, who claimed that mistakes had been made, and that there was more money in his account than he'd been credited. That's only natural. But all these small whirlwinds were quickly and efficiently worked out to the satisfaction of all parties.

The Templars had been the bankers of the French crown for two centuries, and again, never was there an accusation of fiddling by any of the kings before Phillip. Apart from that, they did a great deal of banking for the Vatican, as well, and those sharp-eyed gentlemen were nobody's fools. Still, the Templar reputation for honesty and exactitude had never been questioned. There was no desperate Templar money-crunch, either, that may have driven them to embezzlement. All the treasuries from the East had been moved to safer ground, by men who risked and often gave their lives to do so. Does it really seem likely that, after two centuries of working to maintain their trusted position with the high and the mighty, they would suddenly start dipping fingers into the till after 1300, for no reason at all?

Baphomet

We saved the weirdest one for last. This thing about Baphomet has been endlessly debated, down through the ages. Historians who believe it may have had a basis in fact have said it could have been the head of John the Baptist, tying the Templars to the Johannite heresy, or maybe it was the head of Hugues de Payens. The purpose of the charge was crystal clear: Idol worship was another witchcraft-related accusation brought against the Order. But no one has ever managed to determine just what, exactly, was the origin of this particular allegation. The stories of the various witnesses were growing more and more bizarre, and so Phillip's interrogators could "suggest" just about anything, and the agonized knights would have admitted it. As a result, the descriptions varied wildly. Some claimed they worshipped the bearded head of a man, one said a head with two faces, while others said it was a cat. Some claimed it was a skull, while still more described it as a horned demon. But, like the rest of the charges leveled against the Order, outside of France, in countries where the knights were not tortured, no such admission was ever made.

Still others said the secret ritual had paid homage to a skull. But the presence of a skull — or a whole lot of skulls — in a religious building in the medieval period was by no means any proof of witchcraft, heresy, devil worship, or even cool Halloween décor. The skull was a symbol of mortality, which every man was urged to keep in mind at all times. A plaque outside of the subterranean catacombs of Paris today reminds visitors, "Happy is he who is forever faced with the hour of his death and prepares himself for the end every day." Europe is dotted with chapels and churches whose walls, columns, and archways are made up of the skulls and bones of hundreds of years' worth of clergy and parishioners. It's a cheery décor.

You'll find skulls on headstones, often accompanied by the wings of angels carrying the skulls to heaven, which is hardly an image of evil. Equally important was the use of the skull as a reminder of the sin of vanity. A king, a pope, a blacksmith, and a supermodel all look the same when the flesh falls away. So it would not be out of the ordinary if the Templars had skulls prominently displayed in their chapels or preceptories. Of course, worshipping them would have been another matter.

Where the accusation gets dicey concerns the legend of the mystical Skull of Sidon (see Chapter 4 for lots more detail on this story). Never mind that the myth of a magical skull mixed up with necrophilia predated the Templars. The story had circulated among their Muslim enemies that the Templars were in possession of it, and that it had powers that protected them and brought them victories on the battlefield. Unfortunately for the Templars, such fairy tales designed to frighten their foes didn't sound so fairy-tale-ish to the Inquisition.

But the inquisitors kept beating on this business of idol worship, especially of a cat, which is right out of the witchcraft interrogation playbook. Cats — either live ones or sculpted idols — were commonly referred to as objects of worship in secret occult rituals. Fear of cats was a longtime medieval superstition, and (dog lovers take note) the killing or tormenting of cats was a popular pastime during the period; it was even a regular component of certain feast days in the French calendar. Cats were believed to be connected with Satan and sorcery, so compelling the Templars to admit to cat worship was a clear admission of heresy. Again, such nonsense was never substantiated outside of France, where torture was not applied.

For centuries, researchers have battled over the origin and meaning of Baphomet. The name came up occasionally during the confessions of the tortured knights, in connection with the subject of idol worship. The most common suggestion has been that the word is a variation of Mohammed (*Mahomet* in Latin), the prophet of Islam. The most logical supposition is that the interrogators wanted to allege that the Templars in the Holy Land had been corrupted by their association with Muslims. The unintended hilarity is, of course, that Muslims forbid any kind of idol worship themselves, to the point where most Islamic art contains no depiction of any living person, plant, or animal. Whether Church or French inquisitors actually knew that is doubtful but largely academic. What was important to them was the tie to infidels and the confession of idolatry.

The Indian author Idries Shah suggested that Baphomet may actually have come from the Arabic word *Abufihamat,* which means "Father of Understanding." If that's true, it could have referred to a statue of Christ, or a head-shaped sculpture representing Christ, John the Baptist, their founder Hughes de Payens, or any number of other symbolic fathers.

What Baphomet *doesn't* seem to have meant is what it has come to represent in modern times: the winged, goat-headed, cloven-hoofed demon that commonly appears on Tarot cards (see Figure 6-1). Nineteenth-century French mystic Eliphas Lévi came up with the drawing for his book *Dogme et Ritual de la haute Magie* in 1854. Although Levi claimed Templar origins of his mystical figure, testimony from the trials describes no such thing.

Figure 6-1:
Baphomet
as depicted
in the 19th
century by
Eliphas Lévi.

Heads up: So what was it?

If there was any "head" at all that was being venerated in Templar ceremonies, it would most likely have been the sort of thing found in Catholic and Eastern churches all over Christendom: a reliquary. The trade in holy relics was a hot one, and the world was filled with teeth, jawbones, tibias, fibulas, phalanges, and metatarsals of a universe of blessed saints and martyrs. One old, dry bone looks much like another, so elaborate containers called *reliquaries* were often made of gold and silver to house and protect them. But all this specula-tion presupposes that the forced, tortured confessions of the Templars had any basis in fact in the first place. We believe that the similarity of stories told from one Templar to the next was because of the suggestions of the inquisi-tors' questionnaires, and not by some secret, shared ceremony of the Order.

So if the witnesses couldn't even agree on what Baphomet is, then it would tend to prove the charges false. A modern judge would have thrown the whole mess out of court and threatened to file charges with the French Bar Association if they dared bring it to him again. But Pope Clement V, Phillip's personal pope, was propelled by no such qualms over the quality of the evidence. It's interesting to note how many times he disagreed with Phillip — but when push came to shove, everyone knew who was in charge.

The Pope Knuckles Under

The Order was not arrested en masse by the forces of the pope or the Catholic Church. The action was officially ordered and carried out on October 13, 1307, by King Phillip IV. And though Pope Clement had only been in office for two years, and was already regarded as a tool of Phillip, he did seem to be truly outraged that the Templars had been arrested in violation of his sole papal authority over them — and he said so.

A word about torture and the Inquisition

The question that passes through the modern mind when it comes to the torture and burning of those accused of religious "crimes" is obvious: What can possibly be construed as remotely proper about a religion based on the gentle philosophies of Christ torturing confessions out of people?

In crimes against Christianity, so the reasoning went, men may have lied to cover their guilt, but their souls knew the truth. Only when the Christian was dragged to the edge of Hell and forced to confront an eternity of damnation would the conscience, a part of the soul, triumph and tell the truth. That was the ecclesiastical reasoning. In actuality, most people would confess to anything if enough pain was inflicted on them over a long enough period. It's goofy to think that it never occurred to them that the "confession" they got was only given to get them to stop; in fact, this was the principle argument against torture, an argument used by later incarnations of the Inquisition and by the kings who refused to resort to it.

It's unfortunate that, mostly because of the horrors of the Spanish Inquisition, torture is bound together with the very word *inquisition,* as well as with Catholicism. The Inquisition was often merely one of many Catholic bureaucracies, and its purpose was to insure that the rituals of the Church remained on target, particularly in far-flung regions, such as Ireland, where local customs and not particularly well educated priests may have allowed ritual to be influenced by pagan or other beliefs. People are usually surprised to learn that the Inquisition still exists today, renamed the Holy Office in 1908, and finally, in 1965, the Congregation for the Doctrine of the Faith.

The powers of inquisitors were first given to the new order of Dominican monks in the early 13th century. Their specialty was to argue theology with the Cathars, the most popular heresy in France. In the south, it was becoming more popular than Catholicism, and St. Dominic's idea was that, if they were going to run around the countryside living an ascetic life, arguing Biblical points, the Dominicans would do the same and win the argument. Of course, fairly soon, they decided that if they couldn't win the argument, they'd simply burn them at the stake. Thus was born one of the darkest aspects of the Inquisition, the Albigensian Crusade, when Simon de Montford led the king's soldiers south to wipe out the Cathars. They were killed by the tens of thousands. (We discuss the Cathar beliefs in Chapter 14.)

The Templars had strong ties to the Cathars. Many Templar knights came from the Languedoc, and many of the high officers of the Order had been born into the most important Cathar families of the Languedoc. Local priests who tried to stop the violence being committed against

(continued)

(continued)

their friends and neighbors were accused of being secret Cathars, and often ended up before the Inquisition themselves. At the least, priests and bishops who objected were barred from their own churches for refusing to implement the rulings of the Inquisition.

Torture was a common feature of ancient and medieval justice; it was not by any means peculiar to the Catholic Church. Church officials did not authorize it for use until the 1250s under Pope Innocent IV, and there were rules about what could and could not be done. Bloodshed and mutilation were prohibited, as was the outright torturing to death of the accused. Naturally, these restrictions resulted in imaginative devices and methods designed to skirt the loopholes. For instance, slowly roasting a man's feet off cauterized the wound and didn't shed blood, and it didn't kill him, either.

Religious interrogation procedure during this period usually followed a pattern: First, the stern threat of death by fire; second, confinement to mull that one over; third, a kindly visit from a member of the clergy to attempt to reason a confession out of the accused; and then, finally, torture.

At first, the Church ruled that two witnesses had to be produced against the accused, and neither could be a convicted heretic. These pesky annoyances were dispensed with by the mid-1200s.

The important part to remember about medieval torture was that it was not considered to be punishment, as ridiculous as that sounds.

Torture was used to elicit the confession, and the punishment was decided after the confession was made. The rules of the Catholic Inquisitors were that the accused could only be tortured once. That was circumvented by simply adjourning the session and starting up again, for days at a time. And, of course, any new evidence found was cause for new charges and a new session of torture was permitted.

In most cases the practice of torture was forbidden to members of the clergy. This meant that the hands of the Church were innocent of actually having exacted such agonies on the accused themselves. Better to let a king or noble's henchmen do the dirty work.

However, one more point made the Templar trial different from those that had come before: There is no question whatsoever that the French king, and not the Inquisition, was calling the shots. The representatives of the Inquisition were, for the most part, there to lend an aura of legitimacy to the whole sorry affair.

Of course, don't think that the Catholic Church has been the sole practitioner of torture against those accused of religious crimes. Protestants gleefully practiced similar activities against heretics in England, Germany, Switzerland, North America, and elsewhere, with special treatment for — you guessed it — Catholics, all through the 1700s. Unfortunately, a stop in at the Amnesty International Web site produces a list of nations that still use torture as part of their "judicial system."

It's interesting to note how many times, particularly in the beginning, that Clement disagreed with Phillip. When word first arrived that Phillip was looking into certain accusations against the Templars, Clement reacted with disbelief. When he found out about the arrests, which he in all probability did not know were coming, he reacted with fury. And when he discovered that his noble Templar knights were being put to torture, he reacted once more with outrage. But as time passed, from the arrests of 1307, to the final executions in 1314, Clement would express fewer and fewer opinions of his own. Phillip began keeping him as close to the vest as possible; in fact, there were times when sharp-eyed critics said it looked like Clement was virtually under house arrest. Yet, he tried to play the game, to act as though he believed the charges to be true, before he finally dissolved the Order.

The reason: propaganda. Phillip was exquisite at it; he clearly understood how to manipulate public opinion. He had done it before with Pope Boniface VIII, until no one really questioned that the dead pontiff was anything but a crook and a heretic. He had achieved it with the Templars in a very short time, by making their tortured confessions public. And so, to keep him in line, he turned his dark talents on Pope Clement, by circulating stories that he had engaged in blatant nepotism and financial chicanery. When Clement held a papal council to determine the fate of the Templars, Phillip sent along his army to camp just outside the city, for, you know, "protection."

Secretly Absolved

In August 1308, almost a year after their arrests, Pope Clement had his own investigation of the Templars conducted privately at Chinon, and the results are contained in a document known as the *Chinon Parchment*. In it, the agents of the pope detail their interviews with Grand Master Jacques de Molay and four other knights.

Three of the men admitted to being asked to spit on and denounce the cross, as part of their secret initiation rites. One admitted to seeing a head revered as an idol. None admitted to the charges of sodomy.

When the interviews were concluded, the cardinals absolved the knights of their sins, lifted the order of excommunication, and reinstated them to receive the sacraments of the Church. But the results of the papal investigation were not made public. Clement V did nothing to release the knights from prison or to stop Phillip from having them burned as heretics six years later.

Part III
After the Fall of the Templars

The 5th Wave   By Rich Tennant

CURRENT EVOLUTION OF THE KNIGHTS TEMPLAR

"I'm from Knights Temporarys. Someone here contract for a warrior-receptionist?"

In this part . . .

*I*n this part, we pick up the cold trail of Templar fact, and follow it to the birth of Templar mythology. Jacques de Molay, the last Templar Grand Master, was burned at the stake seven centuries ago, and since that time, the legend of the mysterious Order has never died. Instead, it has merely changed shape to fit each new century and each new storyteller.

Chapter 7 takes a closer look at what we *do* know about the Templars after their fall, as well as what we think we *might* know, following the trail of myth to the land of hucksters and crackpots, and what they *say* they know. Chapter 8 examines the very real possibility that secret rituals of Freemasonry grew out of the surviving remnants of Templars on the run, and Chapter 9 takes a peek into other modern societies that claim a legitimate Templar lineage, as well as groups that have patterned themselves on the Order.

Chapter 7

Templars Survive in Legend and in Fact

*L*egend has it that the end of the Knights Templar was only the beginning. Almost five centuries after the execution of the Templars' last known Grand Master, Jacques de Molay, the French Revolution erupted.. King Louis XVI and his family were arrested and thrown into the dungeon built by the Templars so long ago. On January 21, 1793, King Louis was led to the guillotine in Paris's Place de la Revolution, stripped of his honors and titles by the new Republic. Citizen Louis Capet was pushed against the bascule, and his body was tilted forward, face down. His neck was secured in the wooden lunette to hold it firm and straight. And then, to the cheers of the mob, the sharpened steel blade dropped, cleanly severing the former king's head from his body with chilling efficiency.

When Louis's head rolled into the basket, so the story goes, someone rushed forward from the crowd. Grabbing the head and holding it aloft, he yelled, "Jacques de Molay, thou art avenged!" The death of the Templars had finally been repaid by the death of the French monarchy.

Except that it didn't really happen. The story wasn't true, but it was important, because this was the dawn of the modern conspiracy-theory movement. And the Templars were smack-dab in the middle of it.

This chapter is a whirlwind tour through the surviving myths and legends of the Knights Templar. In most cases, we try to separate fact from plausible conjecture, wishful thinking, and four-alarm codswallop.

The Templar Fleet

The most common legend about the survival of the Templars has to do with their fleet of ships. The tale usually is spun that, when the knights were all arrested on Friday, October 13, 1307, King Phillip's men rushed into the Paris vaults to find that the vast collection of loot stored there had been secretly spirited away. Phillip's whole reason for seizing the knights had come to nothing. His evil plans were thwarted, and the knights sailed away from France with their treasure safely packed on their fleet of ships, which slipped from their moorings and vanished into the mists of time and legend. Golly.

Sailing up the Seine

Several books and many Web sites refer to a fleet of ships departing Paris on the night of October 12 laden with Templar treasure. The term *ship* may be more grandiose than you're thinking. The Seine runs right through the heart of Paris. It flows northeast and spills into the western edge of the English Channel at Le Havre, but although it has been a commercial artery since Roman days, it is not deep enough to handle large ships. More important, the medieval city of Paris hugged the river, and the king's palace was in the middle of it, on the island called the Îsle de la Cité — a perfect vantage point for spotting any unusual dockside activity. And surely some civic-minded soldier or citizen who was preparing to help arrest the Templars on the 13th would have raised an alarm if they had noticed the ships trying to leave the day before.

La Rochelle

The most commonly touted escape route of the Knights has long been claimed to be the port city of La Rochelle, about 300 miles from Paris. During the trials, Jean de Chalon testified that Gerard de Villiers, Preceptor of the Paris temple, had fled the country with 50 horses and 18 ships. The Templars did indeed have ships, but again, surely someone on the king's side, privy to the arrest order, would have noticed streams of Templars making their way to La Rochelle, as well as unusual activity on the docks around the Templar ships. There is no record of such a mass exodus.

The story of some massive Templar fleet leaving La Rochelle is certainly flawed, but that's not to say that Templar ships couldn't have set sail *before* October 13. The order had shipping interests all throughout the Mediterranean and up and down the Atlantic coast. One massive movement of ships would surely have been spotted, and the king's officials notified. But a ship here, a galley there, some disguised knights hiring a merchant ship some other place, all managing to slip from their docks before the night of the arrest — these are all highly possible scenarios. But some estimate that 2,400 members of the order managed to flee the country. That's an awful lot of men to just slip off in a dinghy or two.

So where'd they go?

Nevertheless, the Templar ships did go *somewhere,* even if it wasn't overnight. There are no records of a large number of ships handed over to the Hospitallers (or snatched by Phillip, for that matter). The bulk of their navy was bottled up in the Mediterranean Sea, and ships for use there were not built for arduous voyages in the open Atlantic. They undoubtedly had ships at their headquarters in Cyprus, along with ports in Italy, France, Spain, and Portugal. But these were generally smaller transport vessels that hugged the coastline, without much provision for, well, provisions. Trips around the Mediterranean were kept pretty short, island hopping from Rhodes to Sicily to Cyprus and so on. And if a flotilla of fleeing Templar ships *did* try to pass westward through the straits of Gibraltar around the time of the arrests, someone would have seen them and it would have been reported to Spain or Portugal's king, to the pope, or to Phillip himself. There were no such reports.

As for having 18 galleys that may have left from La Rochelle, history doesn't back that up either. In shipping records from La Rochelle of the period, there is no record that the Templars *had* 18 galleys, much less that all 18 were at La Rochelle. Reports in the years leading up to the arrest seem to imply that the Templars (and the Hospitallers, for that matter) actually had very few large ships — some suggest no more than four — and hired more from merchant shippers when needed.

Still, the rumors persist that the knights packed their ships with gold and sailed away, never to be seen again.

Talking Treasure

Over the centuries, the legend of the Templars' lost treasure has grown and taken some peculiar side trips. Visions of heaping chests of gold and jewels being smuggled out the night before their mass arrests are romantic, but is there any evidence to support such notions?

The surprise arrests happened only in France, and the intent of King Phillip was clearly to cut the head off of the Order by clapping its principal commanders in dungeons so fast that they would have no chance to flee or hide anything. And the story has circulated for centuries that the Paris treasury, in particular, was the prize that Phillip wanted most. But we examine that one in a little more detail.

Cold, hard cash

It has been said that Phillip saw the treasury when he had been hiding out in the Paris Temple after he had been chased through the streets by an angry mob. He had devalued the gold and silver coins by recasting them with less precious metal than their face value, and the economy was a mess. But what is curious about this contention is that Phillip's own government was using the Paris Temple as its treasury, making the Templars the official government exchequers. The Templars were politically neutral, well defended, and considered to be scrupulously honest. The one thing that French kings could count on was that their crown jewels and silver and gold reserves were safe when they were in the Templars' vaults.

But Phillip was quickly gaining a reputation as something of a ganef where money was concerned, and his most recent shenanigans with devaluing the currency were but one example. Shortly after the cowardly incident in the Templars' basement, Phillip ordered a new official government treasury building to be constructed on the banks of the Seine, where the Louvre stands today. When it was completed, he had the bulk of the French holdings transferred from the Templar vaults to his own, where no one could keep tabs on it. All he left in the care of the Templars was enough reserves to be used to pay French troops, and he continued to allow the Templars to administer these accounts.

When the mass arrests happened, Phillip had given strict orders for the arresting officers to take an inventory of every Templar commandery, preceptory, farm, vineyard, or hut, so a snapshot record would exist of all their holdings. If he was going to steal from them, he wanted to know exactly what he was getting. But when they came to the Paris Temple, the vast treasure Phillip had seen was gone. Supposedly. We have no one's word but a greedy, crooked French king's that the Templar treasury was empty. Moreover, the survey concluded by Phillip in 1308 revealed that the Templars' property was "unkempt and ruinous," with no evidence of wealth or luxuries. The Templars lived the life of peasants.

Yet, shortly after the arrest of the Templars, Phillip *again* recalled all the gold and silver coins and had them recast with the proper weight of metal. And all this happened shortly after he had built a new treasury and arrested the Templars. More important, there was no independent accounting or security watching over that new treasury.

Remember that when the trials ended and the pope dissolved the Templar Order, he decreed that their property would be handed over to the Hospitallers. Phillip certainly knew that that day would come, and the last thing he would have wanted was to hand over piles of loot. The vast majority of the Templar wealth was in property, not liquid assets, and Phillip couldn't hide castles, vineyards, and houses. But he certainly could have hauled gold, silver, and cash out of the Paris Temple across the way to his own treasury, and claimed that the Templars had fled with it. Consider this: After finding the "treasure" missing, Phillip certainly didn't put out an APB for it, close the borders, call out the navy, and give chase. And with all the torturing of knights going on in dungeons across France, the one question no one put to them was, "Where's the swag?" Possibly because Phillip knew right where it was all along.

Treasure more mystical than cash?

So, what if we're not talking about treasure in the sense of gold bars and silver coins. What if the real treasure of the Templars was more mystical, mythical, and magical?

Some people have long contended that the Templars had discovered esoteric knowledge in the Holy Land that revealed the secrets of life, the universe, and everything. They believe that the first nine long years the Templars spent in relative obscurity after their founding were consumed by digging under the Temple Mount, the site of King Solomon's Temple, where they found the Ark of the Covenant, mystical scrolls, the head of Christ or John the Baptist, the Holy Grail, or other equally exciting items. Others have claimed that the Templars were in possession of Gnostic knowledge, and certain "secret" gospels left out of the Bible. More recent claims have been made that the Templars possessed evidence of certain mysteries, the most recent being *The Da Vinci Code*'s central thesis that Jesus had been married to Mary Magdalene.

One curious supposed clue appears in Chartres Cathedral in France. The Templars had close ties to Chartres, which they had helped to construct. At Chartres is a column carved with an unusual scene of the Ark of the Covenant, loaded on a cart, obviously being transported somewhere. Over the years, some have claimed that this single carving depicts the original Knights Templar who started the order in Jerusalem, after discovering the Ark buried under the Temple Mount and moving it to France. This particular legend goes on to say that the Templars knew in advance of their pending arrest in France in 1307, and sent the Ark away. They took it, so the tale goes, to Scotland, where it was eventually buried beneath Rosslyn Chapel. (Of course, the Chartres carving may just be depicting Moses hauling the Ark around in a wagon, too.)

The Scottish Legends

In 2001, Arthur Herman wrote a delightful book called *How the Scots Invented the Modern World: The True Story of How Western Europe's Poorest Nation Created Our World and Everything in It.* Face it: Scottish people believe this is all true. And so it goes with the Templar myths of Scotland. Many legends about Scotland and the Templars exist, and certain folks believe every single one of them.

The legend goes that the Templar fleet set sail from La Rochelle and made its way around England and to the coast of Scotland, near Argyll, by some accounts. The Templars, now under threat of excommunication by the pope, needed asylum, and Scotland was the logical choice. King Robert I ("The Bruce") was at war with England and had himself been excommunicated by the pope for murdering a Scottish nobleman in 1306. England sought to absorb Scotland, while Robert the Bruce was determined it be an independent nation.

You say Sinclair, I say Saint-Clair

The common family name that runs throughout the Scottish Templar theories is Saint-Clair, or Sinclair, and it gets very confusing, mostly because so many of them are named William or Henry (showing an almost criminal lack of family imagination). Originally from Normandy, they have been a powerful and influential clan throughout Scottish history — even Shakespeare's *Macbeth* features the Earl of Caithness, a Saint-Clair, as a powerful Scottish laird. Here's the breakdown:

✔ **William "The Seemly" Saint-Clair** was granted the area around Roslin in 1057.

✔ **Henri de Saint-Clair, First Earl of Roslin,** fought in the first Crusade with Godfroi de Bouillon, and with Hughes de Payens, the founder of the Knights Templar. It is also claimed that Hughes visited Roslin, Scotland, in 1126, and was given the land to build the first Templar preceptory outside of the Holy Land at Ballontrodoch, known later as Temple.

✔ **Sir William Saint-Clair** (1260–1303) was the first Baron of Roslin.

✔ **Sir Henry Saint-Clair** (?–1330), was Sir William's eldest son, and a friend of Robert the Bruce.

✔ Another **Sir William Saint-Clair** (1300–1330) was Henry's son, who was slain by the Moors in Spain in 1330 as he tried to head for the Holy Land to bury the heart of Robert the Bruce. This Sir William was married to Isabel, daughter of Malise, Earl of Strathearn, Caithness, and Orkney. It is this William Saint-Clair who is alleged by some to have been the last Grand Master of the Templars. But if he had actually been a member of the order, why did he and his brother Henry both testify in a Scottish trial against the Templars that they had heard suspicious rumors about the order's "secret" initiations?

✔ William and Isabel's son was another **Henry Saint-Clair, First Earl of Orkney** (1345–1400). It was this Henry who has been claimed to have explored Greenland and North America with the Venetian Antonio Zeno (see "Henry Saint-Clair and the Zeno Narrative," later in this chapter). He is sometimes referred to as Prince Henry I of Orkney, and is actually believed to have died in 1400 fighting the English, and not in Greenland as has been suggested.

✔ His son, **Henry Saint-Clair, Second Earl of Orkney** (1375–1422), served as Lord High Admiral, and later, Lord Chancellor, of Scotland. For a time, he was protector of the young James Stuart, who would become King James I of Scotland. It is through this connection that a supposed Templar and Masonic link is made to the Stuart line of kings and pretenders.

✔ Henry's son, **William Saint-Clair, First Earl of Caithness, 3rd Earl of Orkney, and Baron of Roslin** (1404–1480), was the builder of Rosslyn Chapel, which began in 1440.

✔ A later **William Saint-Clair of Roslin** is claimed in 1602 as the "hereditary Grand Master Mason of Scotland" by several stonemason lodges. It turns out he wasn't the best role model — he seems to have almost immediately skipped off to Ireland over an alleged affair with a local milkmaid. His son, yet another **William Saint-Clair,** was claimed by the stonemasons again almost 30 years later as their hereditary Grand Master, in a bit of power politics. The Masons wanted a patron with royal favor, but King Charles I declined to officially name Saint-Clair as the protector of their guild.

✔ And, just to add to the confusion, in 1736 one more **William Saint-Clair of Roslin** (1700–1778) was named as the first Grand Master of the Freemasons' new Grand Lodge of Scotland. He accepted the honor, and then signed away any hereditary claim to the position in favor of elected officers. Nobody gets out of a job that easily. They turned around and elected him to the position for life. Interestingly, he wasn't a Freemason when he was contacted with the offer and had to be initiated as a Mason before he could accept the job. When he died, he was the last Saint-Clair to be buried in the subterranean vaults of the chapel — so far.

Battle of Bannockburn

The legendary tale of the Templars in Scotland always leads to the story of the Battle of Bannockburn in 1314. Robert the Bruce's troops met King Edward II's advancing English forces at a stream called Bannock Burn in what was the decisive victory for the Scots in their first war of independence. The Bruce's Scottish forces of less than 9,000 men, armed mostly with spears, were heavily outnumbered by Edward's 2,000 men on horse and 16,000 foot soldiers. The legend goes that at a crucial point in the battle, out of the woods rode a fierce contingent of mounted Knights Templar, dressed in white, who turned the battle in Robert the Bruce's favor and forced Edward and his troops to flee back to England. And there was much rejoicing.

It is a romantic tale, but a highly unlikely one. The Templars had not been on a major field of battle since the fall of Acre in the Holy Land in 1291; they had essentially lived quiet lives across Europe until their arrests in 1307.

Even if you believe that large numbers of Templars really were hiding out in Scotland, the battle-trained fighting men from the Holy Land were, frankly, a little long in the tooth after more than 20 years of inactivity to be donning their chainmail and riding into battle.

Of course, one variation on the tale includes the use of the Ark of the Covenant as a weapon of mass destruction. This particular legend claims that the aging knights used the secret, sacred, and divine powers contained in the Ark, which they had smuggled from Jerusalem to France, and then to Scotland, to defeat the overwhelming English army.

An account written shortly after the battle really identified these mysterious Scottish troops who came out of the woods as something of a rabble of untrained and unarmed scavengers, and not a highly trained and disciplined legendary army of warrior monks. Robert the Bruce was a master of guerilla tactics in the field and had told this motley collection of miscreants to assemble in a clearing behind the woods, hidden from the view of the English troops. They fashioned spears and made flagpoles and pennants to look like fresh troops. Then at the moment when the English were trapped between advancing Scots forces, the woods, and a creek, Robert called for this group to run screaming out of the woods to give the illusion of a flanking attack. The trick worked, and the English fled the battlefield.

Still, believers in the Templars' exploits at Bannockburn have their own explanation. The Templars were hiding in secret, fearing for their lives that unsympathetic Catholics would rat them out. Robert the Bruce was excommunicated and was a sharp enough leader to gratefully accept any military help he could get in his fight for Scottish independence. He was also sharp enough to know that, after the war, he would need to make nice with the Church again, so it would be pretty foolish to publicly acknowledge that he'd given safe haven to the dissolved Templars. Therefore, after the war was over, using the talents of his friend Sir William Saint-Clair (1300–1330), Freemasonry was created in Scotland as a society for the Templars to safely provide cover for their mutual protection. That's the legend, anyway.

Rosslyn Chapel

A little chapel just south of Edinburgh, Scotland in the little village of Roslin is ground zero in the legends of Templars in Scotland. The Collegiate Chapel of St. Matthew, better known as Rosslyn Chapel, was built as a private place of prayer and burial for wealthy families. Scotland has several of them, so from that perspective, it is not unique. It was conceived and started by William Saint-Clair (or Sinclair, depending on the source) in 1446, and was intended to be a small chapel attached to a larger structure. In fact, the old foundations to the unbuilt cathedral that was planned still lie buried in the grass outside. It took some 40 years to complete.

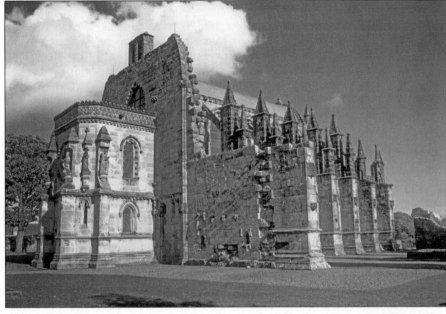

Figure 7-1:
Rosslyn
Chapel,
ground zero
of Templar
mythology.

Inside, the chapel is a wonder of the sculptor's art. Nearly every column, cornice and cranny of the building is carved in some decorative way. The Saint-Clairs were wealthy and spared little expense.

Over the years, literally reams of paper and ink have been spent on placing Rosslyn Chapel at the center of a dizzying array of theories about the Knights Templar and what they possessed, and perhaps buried, in its crypts. Many people are convinced that Rosslyn was built by the Templars and contains some kind of secret within its walls and carvings. And most of it starts with a burial stone in the chapel, marked "William Sinclair, Knight Templar."

William Sinclair's grave: A Knight Templar?

The problem is that there is precisely zero evidence that William Sinclair, Third Earl of Orkney and Baron of Roslin, was, in fact, a Knight Templar at all, or even that this is his stone. The burial marker is an old one, true, but the words *Knight Templar* were not added to it until the 1800s. And the burial marker itself, which depicts the carving of a knight's sword, is small and in keeping with other markers across Scotland that were used for children, not adults. The addition of a sword to it often meant that the grave was the child of a knight. There is no real way of knowing just which of the many William Sinclairs it referred to. Those trying to make the case for the chapel being a Templar building presume it was the William who built it, but he was a pretty important Scottish Lord and would have undoubtedly been placed in the crypt in the floor, instead of the smaller area where this marker appears — if he was buried in the chapel at all.

A pagan temple

Much is claimed about the literally thousands of carvings throughout the chapel as being "Templar," "Masonic," or "pagan." Researchers have stared at the carvings of Rosslyn for centuries and imprinted on them their own interpretations. Templar theorists always concentrate on the same handful of carvings, desperate to make a Templar connection. One in particular shows a knight on a horse, and it is often claimed that there is a second knight on the horse with him, proving it to be Templar. But the actual carving clearly shows that the second figure is walking *behind* the horse. Worse, it is pretty clear that the carving has been altered at some point. Many scholars believe it once showed St. George slaying a dragon, and that the dragon was chipped away to make it more "Templar-esque."

Another altered carving deals with the supposed Masonic connection to the chapel: a face, said to be the allegorical figure of the Masonic character Hiram Abiff, with a gash over his forehead, as is described in Masonic ritual. The problem is that the gash in the carving's forehead wasn't there until the 1800s. Prior to that, for a time, a slash was painted on in red, and before that, the figure had no "wound" at all.

Yes, there are demons and "green men" and many strange images to be found in Rosslyn Chapel, but it is by no means unique in Scotland or anywhere else in Christian countries, in terms of hundreds of carved, decorative, or allegorical figures.

The subterranean secrets

It has long been alleged that the real secrets of Rosslyn Chapel lay in its columns, crypts, or other subterranean caverns. The Apprentice Pillar, in particular, has been said to be hiding . . . something inside. The preserved head of Christ is one of the more common conjectures.

Rosslyn was built as a private chapel for the Saint-Clairs, and one of the principal uses of private chapels in the Middle Ages was for burying their dead. Anyone who has visited the larger cathedrals in Europe knows that the stone floors cover a minefield of luminary corpses. Churches, large and small, are built over a *crypt* (a basement used specifically for burying people). Rosslyn Chapel is no different. Periodically, the floor stones are lifted away to allow caskets to be lowered in and mourners to bid their last farewells. The last time this happened in Rosslyn Chapel was in 1778, for the burial of one of many the Saint-Clairs named William. Dozens of people descended into the vault below the floor, where they found caskets and bones from previous interments, not treasure. Of course, there are certainly other places under the floor that no one has seen for centuries.

Over the years, many claims have been made about doing deep-ground radar and ultrasound scans of Rosslyn's floors to search for the buried treasure of the Templars. Sometimes, they have been permitted, but mostly they are not. The chapel itself is under the protection of the Rosslyn Chapel Trust, and the crypt is protected by the common law *right of sepulchre,* which is the doctrine that says human remains should remain undisturbed, apart from the most unusual circumstances. Scottish law would certainly frown on widespread burrowing in the basement.

We still regard these claims with skepticism. Let's say for a moment that, buried in the vaults of Rosslyn Chapel, next to the moldering bones of the Clan Sinclair's loved ones, are the Holy Grail, the Ark of the Covenant, or the head of Christ. These are the most sought-after relics of faith the world has ever known, eluding millions of people for centuries. Unlike Dan Brown's Mary Magdalene/Jesus bloodline story, their discovery really *would* shake things up. If the Scottish authorities or the Saint-Clair/Sinclair family truly believed there was a chance of their being down there, wouldn't they have fired up the backhoe decades ago and gone digging?

So, why Rosslyn?

We come back to why Rosslyn Chapel is the center of attention to begin with. It is no mere coincidence that the tales of the Templars fleeing to Scotland after the arrests in France in 1307 were unheard of before the late 1700s, and the reason they began then is because of the growth of Freemasonry (see Chapter 8). The evidence is very compelling that much of the lore of the Templars in Scotland came from Freemasons in the late 1700s and early 1800s who were creating mythical origins for use in their lodges. The Scottish lodges were in a philosophical battle with their English counterparts over who had the first, most authentic Masonic rituals and practices. And if the Scots could prove they were the oldest, with the most impressive historical pedigree, they'd show those uppity English Masons who was who.

The English Masons claimed they were descended from stonemasons, so the Scots manufactured a Templar origin, and the large, old, and famous Saint-Clair family was easy to add legendary feats to. Yet, when the Saint-Clairs employed Father Richard Augustine Hay to research and write the family history in the early 1700s, there was no mention of any Templar or Masonic connection to them whatsoever. The whole Scottish Templar/ Freemason legend doesn't appear in full form until a book by a Scottish Freemason named James Burnes in 1830. The Templar claim for Rosslyn Chapel, and most of the Scottish legend, we are sorry to say, is most probably a Victorian Masonic myth.

Templars Part Deux: Return of the Living Knights

The most likely scenario as to the fate of the Templars is also the most commonly overlooked one. We were strolling through London's Inns of Court one afternoon, after having just left the Temple Church, when we struck up a conversation with an elderly barrister on his way to his office. The topic of the Templars and their treasure came up, and he started to chuckle, as though he'd had this same conversation with every starry-eyed tourist who wandered through his neck of the woods. "Come now," he said. "Anyone with a brain knows they went to Spain and Portugal."

The Iberian Peninsula, made up of Spain and Portugal, was a hotbed of Templar activity long before their arrests in France. The Muslim Moors had overrun both countries, and the Christians were being pushed north and east. Refer to the map in Chapter 2 and you can easily see why there was a panic. Muslim forces were all across North Africa, squeezing westward along the edge of Constantinople, and pushing across Gibraltar into Portugal and Spain. Christian Europe stared at infidel Muslims all around the shoreline of the Mediterranean, with no one but Italy and France able to hold out.

Portugal and the Order of Christ

Just a year after the Templars' official formation at the Council of Troyes in 1128, Portugal came to a sobering conclusion. If the rest of Europe wanted to go to the Holy Land to fight infidels, more power to them. But the Moors were streaming in through Europe's side porch in the west and no other countries seemed to be interested in helping. Portugal's Queen Teresa devised a cunning plan. She turned over a large tract of land, the town of Fonte Arcada, to the new Knights Templar, if they would come and defend Portugal from the Moors.

Throughout the 1100s, the Templars had stunning success against the Muslims in Portugal, and a grateful government kept handing over larger properties to them as payment. It was a good deal — no cash out of pocket, and if the Templars built commanderies on these properties, there would always be Templar Knights around to defend the country. Their castle at Tomar today still stands and is a magnificently preserved Templar fortress (see Chapter 16).

In 1307, King Dinis of Portugal got the arrest orders for the Templars living in his realm and ignored them, at first. The order did not come from the pope, but in the form of a letter from King Phillip of France. Only when Pope Clement finally issued the arrest order did Dinis comply. Instead of turning the knights over to the Church, he conducted his own investigation of the order, and found absolutely no merit to the charges against them (which was the same result in every other country in which they were tried). The king and the Portuguese knights, however, faced a dilemma. The pope subsequently dissolved the Templar Order, so they couldn't go on living as Templars. The king's answer was to create a new order, the Order of Christ. Castles, chapels, farms, and other property formerly belonging to the Templars, Dinis proclaimed, had only been *loaned* to them, and really belonged to the Portuguese crown. After he had told the pope to go pound sand, the king simply handed the properties over to the new order.

Their prowess on the sea became legendary. Portugal's greatest hero, Prince Henry the Navigator, in the 15th century, was a member of the order. And when the Italian Christopher Columbus got money from the Spanish king and queen to bankroll his voyage westward into uncharted waters in his search for a shortcut to the Orient, the crew he hired were Portuguese members of the Order of Christ. The sails of his ships were even decorated with what looks for all the world to be Templar crosses. (For more about the Order of Christ, see Chapter 9.)

Spain and the Order of Montesa

The Moors didn't let bothersome things like borders hinder them, and they had advanced well into Spain by the time of the formation of the Templars. The Spanish used the tern *Reconquista* for their campaigns to push the Muslims back across the Straits of Gibraltar, and the Templars assisted in Spain as they did in Portugal. In return, large land grants were given to them — principally, the kingdom of Aragon was turned over to the order. By the time of their fall, the Templars had massive holdings across Spain.

When the Templars were dissolved by Pope Clement V, their property was to be handed over to the Knights Hospitaller. As in other countries outside of France, the Templars in Spain had been found innocent of wrongdoing, and it seemed startlingly unjust for them to lose their holdings. So, as in Portugal, at the request of King James II of Aragon, a new order was created in 1312, the Order of Montesa, made up of Spanish Templars located primarily in Aragon and Valencia. It remained a largely autonomous order until it was combined with other chivalric orders in Spain in 1739.

The Hospitallers

The thousands of members of the Templar order who had not been arrested, or who had been found innocent of wrongdoing, were eventually given a place to go. When Pope Clement V dissolved the Order of the Temple, members of the order were given the option of joining the Knights Hospitaller. (For more about the Hospitallers, see Chapter 9.)

Switzerland

Authors Alan Butler and Stephen Dafoe's book *The Warriors and the Bankers* presents a different theory about the Templars, and perhaps even their treasure. They do not point to the Templar fleet, nor do they envision a mass exodus to Scotland. Anyone who's ever seen *The Great Escape* knows that the simplest way to hide 2,400 men is to put them in street clothes, and send them off walking in plain sight, preferably to Switzerland. Likewise, it makes far more sense that escaping Templars took what gold and silver that was easily transportable, divvied it up, and made their way not to the sea, where Phillip's men would be looking, but eastward to the mountains of Switzerland.

Fascinating and compelling bits of evidence support this theory.

- ✔ The time period roughly corresponds with the founding of the states, or *cantons,* in Switzerland. Even the official history of the country is hazy about its origins.

- ✔ Switzerland butts up against the eastern border of France, and was, therefore, convenient for fleeing Templars to stroll into.

- ✔ If the Templars were forewarned of the arrests, it makes that much more sense that they may very well have sent their treasury toward the forbidding mountains of the Alps, instead of coastal ports where every local official could see, and report, their activities. Such reports were never made.

- ✔ There are legends in Switzerland of knights dressed in white who assisted the Swiss in fighting off foreign invaders.

- ✔ The flag of Switzerland features a Templar cross in white on a red field, just the opposite of the order's white tunics with red crosses. Several cantons featured flags with the same motif.

- ✔ The Swiss have always been tolerant of different religions, in a way similar to the Templar behavior when dealing with the Muslims, Jews, and Cathars.

- ✔ The Templars were the bankers of Europe, inventing the concepts of international transfers of money, checking accounts, safe-deposit boxes, and other revolutionary concepts that would not appear again until Italian bankers later copied their methods. Likewise, Switzerland has been renowned for its banking prowess, combined with strict confidentiality.

A curious site to explore in Switzerland is the French-speaking village of Sion in the Valais canton. Named after the French word for Zion, the Holy Land, it seems almost tantalizingly ready-made as a Templar town.

The Greatest Templar Myths

The tales of the Templars in Scotland are just the tip of the iceberg when telling tall tales of the Templars. Here are some of the more popular ones.

Templars possessed the Ark of the Covenant

In the Book of Exodus, God tells Moses to build an ark — the sacred box that would hold the tablets of the Ten Commandments. Moses is told the exact measurements and materials to use, and after it was completed, the power it contained was so awesome that it had to be transported wrapped in a veil, animal skins, and blue cloth.

The Ark is a supremely dangerous artifact. Moses's sons Abuhu and Nadab are struck dead by simply looking into it. Its power parts the Jordan River and burns a path through thorns and fallen trees; sparks fly from it to kill scorpions and serpents. At the Battle of Jericho, Joshua has the Ark carried around the city seven times, and its power causes the walls of the fortress to collapse. (Of course, if you saw *Raiders of the Lost Ark,* you know all this stuff.)

According to 1 Kings 8:6–9, the Ark was placed in King Solomon's Temple, until Jerusalem was plundered by the Babylonians. It is at this point that the fate of the Ark gets lost in myth. Most historians believe it was carried off to Babylon and destroyed, but many legends abound as to its true hiding place. A longtime tradition in the Ethiopian Orthodox Church claims that Prince Menelik I, who was supposed to have been the son of King Solomon and the Queen of Sheba, carried it off to Ethiopia. (The Ethiopian Orthodox Church contends that it does, indeed, have the Ark, and that it's kept under constant guard in the Chapel of the Tablet at the Church of Our Lady Mary of Zion in Axum.)

A different variation on the tale is that the Templars found the Ark and took it to Ethiopia themselves. This one says that while white people were rarely seen in sub-Saharan Africa prior to the mid-1400s, the Ethiopians have a legend that a group of "fair-haired" men came to Axum and used the power of the Ark to magically raise a 78-foot-tall obelisk, the tallest solid granite object ever quarried. And, just maybe, those fair-haired men were the Templars. Unfortunately for those who believe this tale, the obelisk was carved in the fourth century, 800 years before the Templars appeared.

Another legend involving the Templars says that the original members of the order discovered the Ark while digging under the Temple Mount in the first few years of their formation, and that a carving on a column in Chartres Cathedral in France shows the knights moving it from Jerusalem to France on a cart. The column is in what is known as the North Porch, and the Latin inscription below it enigmatically reads, *"Hic Amititur Archa Cederis,"* meaning "Here things take their course: Through the Ark thou shall work." Most historians debunk this claim, saying that the carving merely shows another claimed fate of the Ark, being smuggled to Egypt during the reign of King Manasseh (2 Chronicles 33), where it was placed into the Well of Souls. Again, Indiana Jones fans take note.

And, of course, there is again the tale that it is, in reality, buried in Rosslyn Chapel's underground vaults, after being moved there from France when the Knights were tipped off about their pending arrests. Again, there is nothing but wishful thinking going on here. No one has conclusively seen the Ark of the Covenant since King Nebuchadnezzar's troops sacked Jerusalem in 587 B.C.

A Templar connection to the Shroud of Turin

In the Cathedral of St. John the Baptist in Turin, Italy, is an artifact that has excited the world for more than 600 years, the Shroud of Turin. It is a linen cloth that appears to have been used to wrap the body of a man who had been crucified, and ghostly images appear of a man with a bearded face. In spite of almost immediate pronouncements by the Catholic Church that it was a fake, the faithful believed that the image was of Jesus, and they continue to believe this today. Chemical analysis and carbon dating techniques used in 1988 provided results that the markings were paint and that the cloth dated from about the 14th century, but those results were almost immediately called into question. The Shroud is, today, the property of the Vatican, which has always refused to declare it to be the authentic image of Christ.

The Knights Templar are implicated in the Shroud's history in a couple of ways:

- ✔ The Shroud was in the possession of the family of Geoffroy de Charney, Templar Preceptor of Normandy, who was burned at the stake along with Grand Master Jacques de Molay in 1314.

- ✔ Geoffroy's nephew, Geoffri de Charney, apparently had the Shroud, and upon his death, his widow, Jeanne de Vergy, first displayed it in public in 1357.

- ✔ If the Templars had the Shroud in their possession, it is possible that it was part of the fabled treasure discovered under the Temple Mount.

It is also possible that it and the image found on it are connected to another artifact that has been said to have been in the hands of the order. Author Ian Wilson has claimed in *The Shroud of Turin: Burial Cloth of Jesus?* that the Templars may have found the preserved head of Jesus, and that the Shroud was used to wrap it. In which case the Shroud really would authentically reveal the face of Christ. But the Shroud depicts the whole body of a man, about 6 feet tall, and not just a head.

Robert Lomas and Christopher Knight, on the other hand, believe that the Shroud, in fact, displays the face and features of none other than Jacques de Molay. They make the argument in their book *The Second Messiah* that the last Grand Master of the Templars was tortured before his execution, that the Shroud displays the blood of his wounds, and that the long hair and beard fit his description. Further, using the carbon dating results from a 1988 test of fabric from the Shroud, which place its origin between 1260 and 1380, the time frame fits the period of de Molay's imprisonment and torture. They conclude that the Shroud was wrapped around de Molay after he had been brutally worked over but was still alive.

A completely different theory should interest fans of *The Da Vinci Code.* Clive Prince and Lynn Picknett's book, *Turin Shroud: In Whose Image?,* makes the claim that the image was actually a hoax created by none other than Leonardo da Vinci himself, possibly using an unknown, primitive photographic chemical process and a pinhole camera.

Templars discover America!

There is absolutely no evidence that the Templars had known about the Americas in the 13th and 14th centuries, but that hasn't stopped the speculation that they did. Various researchers have claimed that the Templars had based much of their wealth on Aztec gold and silver. Aztec tales abounded of a "great white god" from the East who had come to bring civilization to them. But there is no archeological evidence of any European presence in the region prior to the Spanish conquistadors. And that "great white god" stuff was ancient history to the Aztecs by then. That they meant "Templars" is highly unlikely.

Authors Tim Wallace-Murphy and Marilyn Hopkins (and several others) have advanced the notion that, while the order flourished, the Templars ventured across the North Atlantic, following a similar path as the Vikings, and traded with the Native American population of northeastern Canada. After the dissolution of the order, the Templars moved to Scotland, so the legend goes, and the Saint-Clair (or Sinclair) family became their protectors. And this is where the tale of the Templars discovering America really kicks in.

Henry Saint-Clair and the Zeno Narrative

In 1396, so the legend goes, the Earl of Orkney, Henry Saint-Clair, went into partnership with a Venetian merchant family known as the Zenos. Saint-Clair is said by some to have made two trips across the North Atlantic almost a full century before Columbus. Based on a document called the *Zeno Narrative,* the Sinclairs and the Zenos hoped to establish colonies in the Americas, away from the influence and reach of the Catholic Church.

The *Zeno Narrative* is derived from letters between real brothers from Venice — Antonio, Carlo, and Nicolo Zeno — and was published anonymously in 1558. In it, a voyage is described by Nicolo Zeno in 1385 from Venice to England and Flanders, in which he claimed to have been shipwrecked on a large island called Frislanda, a mythical place complete with a mythical prince. Referred to in the narrative as Prince Zichmni, Nicolo claims to have undertaken voyages to what is presumably Greenland for him over the space of two decades. At the end of the tale, after encountering strange and exotic people and places, Prince Zichmni remains in Greenland, starting a settlement called Trin.

True believers say that Prince Zichmni is in reality the Earl of Orkney, Henry Saint-Clair, and that the giant island nation of Frislanda is actually the smallish Orkney Island off the coast of Scotland — curious, because Nicolo described an island larger than Ireland. The *Zeno Narrative* comes complete with a map, but although portions of it and the narrative sort of match up with Iceland, Scotland, and other North Sea and North Atlantic geography, the glaring flaw is that the mythical Frislanda doesn't.

Beginning in the late 1700s, a series of authors began making convoluted attempts to explain how Zichmni and Saint-Clair are one and the same. In the 1870s, a geographer named Richard Henry Major took up the Sinclair cause and the *Zeno Narrative;* his fiddling is the principal source of the nonsense. There had never been any suggestion in any record of the family history that Henry was an explorer of any kind, nor that he had ventured far from Orkney or Scotland at any time in his life, but that never kept a good myth down. Major took huge leaps of imagination, not to mention outright fabrication, in his mistranslation and interpretation of the narrative, forcing it to fit the Henry Saint-Clair mold.

Saint-Clairs and Sinclairs around the world were ecstatic. Here was "proof" that the Saint-Clairs, descended from the Knights Templar, builders of Rosslyn Chapel, founders of Freemasonry in Scotland, had also been the "discoverers" of America, a hundred years before that upstart Columbus. New Zealand resident Roland Saint-Clair wrote a glowing "biography" of Henry, calling him an "Orcadian Argonaut." Thomas Sinclair in Chicago started a "Society of Sancto-Claro" and made announcements about Henry's fame as the "discoverer of America" as a counterpoint to the Columbian Exposition that was celebrating the 400th anniversary of Columbus. Never mind that, even if Henry really had sailed across the North Atlantic and established a colony at Tinn, it was Greenland, not America. Pesky details, we know. So, others have added further conjecture to the tale, claiming Saint-Clair explored into Nova Scotia, and as far south as what is now Rhode Island and Massachusetts.

The *Zeno Narrative* has been debunked as a hoax by scores of researchers, and it has been shown to have actually been copied from Columbus's own descriptions, and others, of Mexico and the Caribbean islands, with some artful name changes. And the accompanying map was apparently copied from a chart made in 1539. Finally, Nicolo Zeno has been conclusively placed in Italy during the period he was supposed to have been sailing and exploring. Court records show that he was less than heroic, being convicted of embezzlement in 1396 and imprisoned for five years.

Author Andrew Sinclair today continues to cling to the story and has claimed that the mythical expedition was a secret mission of Templars, Gnostics, and Freemasons to establish a religious and military empire in the New World, with Venetian cooperation. Most historians, geologists, and archeologists place little credence in the theory. Well, okay — none, really. But there are some curious items that have been linked to the tale: the Westford Knight and the Newport Tower. And, of course, Rosslyn Chapel.

The Westford Knight

Located near the town square in Westford, Massachusetts, is a slab of rock that is purported to have been carved with the image of a Knight Templar, holding a sword and a shield. Most who have examined the rock say that it appears to have been a combination of natural erosion lines with a "punch-carving" of a sword hilt, while the shield has been painted on recently. True believers say it was placed along a popular path for tribal traffic in the late 1300s by Henry Saint-Clair's expeditions. Archeologists say that's nonsense. It was more than likely buried under a hillside at that time, and the sword carving was made in the 1800s by a pair of boys. The Templars themselves had not existed as an order for almost 100 years at the time of Saint-Clair's alleged expedition, so the question is obvious: Why would anyone take the time to carve a 12th-century image of a knight on a rock when there was no real connection to them to begin with?

The Newport Tower

A little bigger and a lot more enigmatic is a round, stone tower in Newport, Rhode Island. At first glance, it certainly looks like the ruins of a medieval European tower. And without a great leap of imagination — if you believe that post-trial Templars were stomping around the New England coast three centuries before it became New England — it may even look like a round Templar church.

Of course, the Newport Tower has looked like other things to other researchers too, depending on their personal pet theory — everything from a Viking observatory, to a Portuguese or Irish signaling tower, to a 14th-century Scottish church, which would place it right up Henry Saint-Clair's bailiwick. Of course, like the Westford Knight, the Newport Tower is only "near" Saint-Clair's mythical settlement in Greenland, in the same way that Miami is "near" Las Vegas, but who cares when trying to shore up a good myth? Naturally, the fable has been altered to suit the "evidence," and enthusiastic Templar fans have claimed that Saint-Clair explored as far south as Nova Scotia and, just so he could build this tower, Rhode Island.

Unfortunately, what it looks most like is exactly what local folklore has claimed for centuries: a windmill, patterned after an almost identical structure in Chesterton, England, and built in 1675 by Rhode Island's first governor, Benedict Arnold (not the famous Revolutionary War turncoat of the same name). Arnold was originally from the area around Chesterton, and it has long been said that he patterned the Newport windmill after the one he saw back home in his youth. Some researchers have discounted this theory, saying the Chesterton windmill hadn't yet been constructed when Arnold was in the area, so controversy remains.

A-maize-ing Rosslyn Chapel "evidence"

It is hard to pick up a book that talks about Scotland's Rosslyn Chapel without encountering an almost breathless description of an archway decorated in carvings that "proves" the Sinclairs came to America and returned with knowledge that no one else could have had when the chapel was built in 1446. The "proof" is a decorative band of carvings that are usually described as "corn" or "maize" plants, and aloe vera — vegetation that existed at the time only in the Americas. There's only one way that the carvings could have gotten there: Henry Saint-Clair and his Templar explorers had to have gone to America and seen them!

In Greenland? Forgive us, logic returned for a second. But again, the question arises: If you believe the *Zeno Narrative,* what was corn or aloe vera doing in Greenland for Henry Saint-Clair to find it there — especially given that any backyard gardener can tell you that Greenland is a lousy place for a cornfield? Of course, no one can say when those particular carvings were made, apart from the certainty that they wouldn't have been put in until the building itself was completed. And there's also the possibility that they are just carvings of wheat, lilies, and strawberries, in which case all of this is just huffing and puffing.

Oak Island money pit

In 1795, three young men were exploring the miniscule Oak Island off the coast of Nova Scotia, when they noticed a block and tackle dangling from a tree over a low spot in the ground. To them, it had all the look of an arrangement used for burying something heavy underground. So they started digging. Thus began what remains one of the most frustrating and tantalizing mysteries of the last 200 years.

Two feet down, they came across a series of flat stones, of a variety not found on the island. At 10 feet, they hit wooden planks. Certain that they were onto something big, they continued digging, only to hit more log platforms at 20 and 30 feet. Frustrated and confronted with an excavation problem far beyond their means, they left the island. But the Tale of the Pit lived on.

Several years later, a group of investors financed a return to the island and began digging again. At 90 feet, they supposedly discovered something truly enigmatic: a stone, written in a simple code that said "Forty Feet Below Two Million Pounds Are Buried." Instead, what was found was a series of booby traps — horizontal shafts that flooded the pit with seawater, preventing further exploration until more sophisticated methods could be found.

Over the years, six men have been killed and millions of dollars have been spent attempting to excavate the Oak Island Money Pit, and the bottom has never been reached. A few tantalizing items have been retrieved — links from a gold chain, scissors, a sheet of iron, an unreadable piece of parchment. But the excavation is such a mess today from the many attempts to find the treasure that the original shaft location has been lost, and little about the accounts of what has really been found there can be believed.

Wild theories have been proposed over the years as to the source of the treasure (if there really is one down there), including the pirate Blackbeard or Captain Kidd's respective stashes, pre-Revolutionary French or English payroll trunks, Spanish treasure, and, of course, the requisite lineup of UFO theories. One particularly convoluted and hilarious claim says that bottles sealed in mercury are buried in the pit, containing the proof that Francis Bacon actually wrote the plays of William Shakespeare. Undoubtedly, Jimmy Hoffa is down there as well.

But the one theory that continues to resurface is that it is the location of the lost treasure of the Templar fleet. The pit was alluded to in the opening minutes of the film *National Treasure* (2004), as a temporary location of the loot hidden by the Templars and protected by the Freemasons.

Author Steven Sora's *Lost Treasure of the Knights Templar* postulates a two-fer theory — that the treasure was at one time buried in the crypt of Rosslyn Chapel, but the loyal Catholic Sinclair clan dug it up and brought it to Oak Island to keep it out of the hands of Protestant forces in 1545. (Here's another clue for you: *Nova Scotia* is Latin for "New Scotland"!)

The Wood's Hole Oceanographic Institute made a brief study of the pit in the 1990s, and made the pronouncement that the flooding was a natural phenomenon caused by hollow limestone cavities that permeate the island, and not from some carefully installed booby trap. But the team managed to discover little else. Enthusiasts said that an underwater video shot with a remote camera in 1971 revealed submerged trunks, tools, and human bones, but the Wood's Hole scientists, looking at the same tape, saw only mud.

Legends, claims, and counter-claims abound, and true believers contend that the pit could have been dug only by expert engineers, like the Templars. Many companies have been organized over the years to drill and explore the pit, including one with a famous investor, President Franklin Delano Roosevelt (whose membership in the Freemasons, linked with the Oak Island pit, has provided heaps of fodder for conspiracy theorists). But in more than 200 years, nothing of substance has ever been found. Still, just what *were* all those underground platforms doing down there? (We talk about the Oak Island money pit, along with many more possible Templar treasure spots in Chapter 17.)

The Templars Survived!

We discuss some of the more modern chivalric organizations that claim some kind of connection with the medieval Templars in Chapter 9. But for them to claim a connection, there has to be something to base it on. Again, legends of the order took on a life of their own, almost immediately after their execution.

Whether it is true or not, one tale says that, after the fire had consumed the bodies of Jacques de Molay and Geoffroy de Charney, someone quietly waded into the ashes and retrieved the bones of the Grand Master. They would, so the story goes, show up again almost 500 years later.

The Larmenius Charter

Certain branches of the Ordo Supremus Militaris Templi Hierosolymitani (OSMTH; see Chapter 9) contend that they are the direct descendents of the original Knights Templar, and the proof they use is a document called the Carta Transmissionis, or more commonly, the Larmenius Charter. It is said to have been written in the Knights Templar codex used to encode their secret documents and banking paperwork.

The story goes that the Templar's Grand Master, Jacques de Molay, prior to his execution in 1314, verbally handed over the succession of his office to Father Jean-Marc Larmenius, a Palestinian-born Christian who had joined the order in its final years. After the mass arrests of the Templars and their dissolution by Pope Clement V, Larmenius supposedly called together the remnants of the order at a secret meeting in 1324. At that meeting, he provided these brave, surreptitious knights with the Charter of Transmission, a document that provided a plan of succession for the survival of the order. The OSMTH has based their claim of succession on this document.

The charter (which is actually in the hands of the Freemasons and is available for inspection at Mark Masons Hall in London), is indeed written in a cipher code, and when translated, is in Latin, as one would expect a document from a 14th-century Catholic order of monks to be. But it is not in the ecclesiastical form of Latin typically found in religious documents of the period. Instead, it is polished, formal, and quite scholarly — a little too scholarly, in fact. Most serious researchers have concluded it is a forgery from the 17th or 18th century. It was written by someone with a good understanding of Templar and Masonic lore, but in the sort of Latin used in universities of the time, *not* medieval Latin.

The charter contains a list of signatures of the supposed successors to the position of Grand Master since Larmenius, written in their own blood. Critics have suggested that, because one in particular, Bertrand du Gueselin, was known to be illiterate, anything more than an *X* would have been suspicious, although he may have known how to sign his own name, or someone else may have signed it to cover the embarrassing shortcoming of illiteracy.

The document allegedly reemerged in 1804 in the hands of Dr. Bernard Raymond Fabré-Palaprat, the court doctor of Napoleon Bonaparte. In addition, Palaprat also came across a copper box that contained Templar documents with supposedly authentic seals, Jacques de Molay's sword, and best of all, the actual charred bones of the Old Grand Master himself.

Some researchers have suggested that it was actually forged by a colleague of Dr. Fabré-Palaprat, a certain Dr. Landru. Indeed, as time wore on, Palaprat continued to "find" more items. While rooting around in a Paris bookstall, he "stumbled upon" a Greek manuscript, called the *Leviticon*. (Lucky guy. All we ever stumble upon in Paris bookstalls are 1960s paperbacks about mad-eyed socialists and old copies of *Paris Match* with Marilyn Monroe on the cover.) This book described the beliefs of the Templars as being both Gnostic and Johannite (see the "Gnostics and Johannites" sidebar in this chapter). Palaprat began to introduce the Johannite teachings of the Leviticon into the "newly revived" Order of the Temple, but most members seemed disinterested in — or offended by — the philosophy, and the Order soon split apart over the controversy.

One interesting side note of the Larmenius Charter is a passage that specifically condemns "Scotch Templars" as "deserters of the order," and "despoilers of the dominions of the militia." If the Larmenius Charter is genuine, it seems to rebuke the Templars who supposedly fled France for Scotland. If it is a fake, it seems to be a trump card added to denounce the Masonic Templars in Scotland in order to make this newly "revived" order seem more authentic. You make the call.

Gnostics and Johannites

The term *Gnosticism* comes up a lot in modern-day speculation of the Knights Templar. Gnosticism was partly a pre-Christian concept that transformed into a full-fledged movement up through the Christian Church of the second century A.D. For the purpose of this brief explanation, we're very generic, but bear in mind that *Gnosticism* is a generic term that covers a wide variety of beliefs. There is no one, single Gnostic Church.

The core of Gnosticism teaches that God is infinite and incomprehensible to humans. God created the cosmos but left the smaller jobs, like the creation of Earth, to a lesser divinity, known as the *Demiurge.* Because God did not create Earth, but allowed a lesser and flawed divinity to do so, the world is likewise flawed. In addition, beings called *Archons* preside over the material world, and they are not always benevolent. In more recognizable Christian terms, the Demiurge is comparable to Satan, and the Archons are angels and demons. As a result, Gnosticism's overarching philosophy is one of dualism, that good and evil, right and wrong, light and darkness, are in constant battle for supremacy on Earth.

For Christian Gnostics, Christ is seen as an emissary from God, who possessed esoteric knowledge and passed it on to a select few. One of the most pervasive themes running through Gnosticism is that it's almost a kind of secret society itself — a very few, learned adepts have the inner knowledge of how to eventually escape the evil world of the Demiurge. It cannot be studied or learned. It is knowledge of true enlightenment that can only come from divine revelation to the individual — hardly the far more inclusive message of Christianity. For this reason — and others — Gnosticism came into conflict with the Catholic Church on many occasions. (We talk more about Gnosticism in Chapter 14.)

Johannites were a particular sect of Gnostics who rejected the belief that Christ was the Messiah. They believed that John the Baptist, not Jesus, was sent by God with esoteric knowledge of redemption, and they defended this belief by saying that John was performing baptisms before the beginning of Christ's ministry. Some claimed that Jesus could not (and, indeed, did not) perform any miracles until after John was killed, when he inherited John's special powers. Others simply regarded Jesus as a heretic and a pretender, while John was the true Son of God.

Because the biblical account of John's death concerns his beheading by King Herod, no shortage of relics attributed to John are floating around the Holy Land. No fewer than three heads around the world are venerated as John's, and a veritable bone pile of hands, arms, and skull pieces are in Egypt, Rome, Syria, Turkey, and England. It should not be surprising that the Templars were reputed to have been in possession of a head of John, and many have claimed that they were Johannites because of it. The south of France was a home for a large percentage of Templars, and they were sympathetic to this popular local heresy. Tales during the trials in France were told of the Templars worshiping a head, and by embellishing the charge to make it the head of John the Baptist, the accusation became just that much more believable. Such claims have never been substantiated.

In this same French hotbed of heresy, the most prominent sect of Gnostics was called the Cathars. They were very much in sympathy with the Johannites. The Cathars' principal stomping ground was the region of southwestern France, Toulouse and the Midi, smack-dab in Templar territory. The Catholic Church undertook a 20-year military campaign to wipe out the Cathars between 1209 and 1229, called the Albigensian

Crusade. Like the Templars, the Cathars came to their end by fire — the Inquisition burned them as heretics, with the last executions ending almost a century later. It should be noted that the Templars, although well represented in the Languedoc countryside, refused to take part in the persecution and destruction of the Cathars. Curiously, like the Templars, a legend has long circulated that the Cathars had a treasure that was secretly smuggled out of the area from their last stand at Montségur. Some versions of the story say it was the Holy Grail.

Several modern speculative books regard the document as legitimate, and use it to bolster some of their theories, as in Christopher Knight and Robert Lomas's *The Second Messiah* and Lynn Picknett and Clive Prince's *The Templar Revelation.* Other respected researchers in medieval history, and the Templars in particular, regard it as drivel and a forgery.

The Priory of Sion

We discuss the Priory of Sion in conjunction with the legend of Rennes le Château in Chapter 11, but we briefly mention it here as well.

The legend goes that the Prieuré de Sion was a secret society founded in 11th-century France to preserve the secret of Christ's alleged marriage to Mary Magdalene, as well as the bloodline of their descendants (see Part IV of this book for the various windings of this story). Where the Templars enter the tale is the theory that the order was created as a military arm of the Priory. Dan Brown alleges in *The Da Vinci Code* that the Priory of Sion was a real organization, but most researchers agree that it is a modern-day hoax, started in the 1950s.

Rex Deus

Latin for "King God," Rex Deus is purportedly a European branch of royalty descended from the biblical King David and High Priest Aaron of ancient Israel, who have somehow managed to trace and preserve their bloodline for almost three millennia. A variation on the Priory of Sion theme, Rex Deus members are supposedly the keepers of the true secret knowledge of Judaism and Christianity.

They're connected to the Templars by an allegation that Rex Deus directed the order to excavate the Temple Mount, where they discovered the treasure of Solomon's Temple. They knew where to tell them to look, of course, because their relatives buried it there to begin with.

Of course, famous international kook David Icke has a different variation on this ancient royal bloodline idea. He believes they are actually shape-shifting alien reptile-humanoids, and every powerful figure — from George W. Bush and Queen Elizabeth II to the Rothschild banking family — regularly feasts on rodents when no one is looking.

Templars spawn the modern-day conspiracy theory

The Templars were implicated in the beginning of the modern conspiracy-theory movement, and it happened at the end of the French Revolution. Whereas the American Revolution was essentially decided on the battlefield, the French Revolution limped to an end by running out of citizens to kill. The French had started by seeking to replace the notion of the divine rights of kings and popes with freedom and the rule of law. But within a very short period of time, the wholesale carnage inflicted on France by its successive waves of revolutionaries led more and more people to the guillotine. Legend tells us that they killed aristocrats. The fact is that they killed everybody — pathetic and dispossessed prisoners, priests and nuns, the middle class, opposition politicians, and anyone whose name began with the letter *d*. Eventually, of course, they ran out of victims and started killing one another.

When the blood stopped flowing and the dust settled, France was in ruins. The shame of the survivors over what had happened during the Terror sent them looking for someone left alive to blame, and they settled variously on the Freemasons, the Illuminati, and, somewhat inexplicably, the Templars.

In 1791, a man named Cadet de Gassicourt wrote a book called *The Tomb of Jacques Molay,* in which he described a secret plan by the surviving Grand Master to exact revenge against the French monarchy and the Catholic Church, and the Revolution was the culmination of the plot. De Gassicourt's theory was that the Templars had done just what the Scottish Masons were claiming in the late 1700s — they had gone underground and resurfaced as the Freemasons. He contended that a small core of just eight members of an inner circle of Templars/Masons sparked the Revolution.

In 1797, John Robison, a Scottish inventor (of, among other items, the siren) penned *Proofs of a Conspiracy Against All the Religions and Governments of Europe Carried on in the Secret Meetings of Freemasons, Illuminati and Reading Societies* in which he blamed the Freemasons of France and a small, long-defunct group called the Bavarian Illuminati for the Revolution. Strangely, Robison was a Freemason himself. He wrote the book specifically to point out the differences between what went on in sane and noble British lodges, versus the radical nutcase Jacobin Masonic lodges on the Continent. Unfortunately, Robison's motives were lost on a Frenchman seeking refuge in England named Abbé Augustin Barruel.

Barruel was a former Jesuit priest and an abbot, and between 1797 and 1798 he published a massive four-part tome called *Memoirs: Illustrating the History of Jacobinism.* The book was a raging success all across Europe, and was one of the most widely read books of the 19th century. In it, Barruel carefully laid out a massive conspiracy of Freemasons, the Illuminati, and the French *Philosophes* (a group of 18th-century French Enlightenment intellectuals). Of course, those he implicated were influenced by — you guessed it — a rogue's gallery of anti-Catholic Gnostics, Cathars, Martinists, and the Knights Templar.

No matter how methodical and detailed Barruel's memoirs may have been, he was factually incorrect when it came to pointing fingers at the men he believed were the Masons who caused the French Revolution. But facts never got in the way of a good conspiracy theory. Unfortunately, his book is still often quoted today as a reputable source by modern conspiracy theorists who believe that the Freemasons and the Illuminati *somehow* control the world, and that, *somehow,* it all started with the Templars.

Chapter 8

"Born in Blood": Freemasonry and the Templars

A hundred years ago, 1 out of every 4 American men was a member of some kind of fraternal organization, and 1 out of every 25 was a Freemason. Chances are pretty good that someone in your own family's recent past was a Mason.

No modern organization is more commonly tied to the Templars — by serious historians, conspiracy hucksters, and starry-eyed wishful thinkers — than the Masons. Freemasonry is the oldest and largest men's fraternity in the world. It may also be the least-secret "secret society" that has ever existed. The name comes from the group's own legendary origins — from the trade guilds in the Middle Ages that built the Gothic cathedrals and castles of Europe. The fraternity today uses stonemasons' tools and symbolism in its ceremonies (for example, the square and compasses that have become an identifying "logo" for the group).

For at least 270 years, it has been rumored that Freemasonry may have actually been a direct descendant of the original Knights Templar. The idea first popped up in the 1730s in France. Not long after that, a new group within the Masons began to appear, calling itself the Knights Templar. In 1919, a youth group for boys was started, sponsored by the Freemasons and named after Jacques de Molay, the last Grand Master of the Order, who was burned at the stake in 1314. There's no denying that the Freemasons don't mind being associated with the Templars.

Compasses: They always travel in pairs

If you took math in the United States, your teacher probably referred to that little device that helps you measure and draw circles as a "compass." We've got news for you: Your teacher was wrong. A *compass* is that little gadget you can use to figure out which direction you're going (if your car's overhead console doesn't already tell you). A *pair of compasses,* or just *compasses,* are what you use to measure circles (and what stonemasons use in their work). If you think of a pair of scissors, pants, or trousers, it'll make sense: You never say, "scissor," "pant" or "trouser" — it's always plural.

In 1989, a historian named John J. Robinson wrote a book called *Born in Blood: The Lost Secrets of Freemasonry,* which popularized the concept of the Templars being the source of Freemasonry's beginnings as a secret society. *Born in Blood* was a huge hit among Masons but also resulted in an influx of new members who were fascinated by Robinson's tales of the Templars, Solomon's Temple, symbolism, and secrecy — and their possible connection to Masonry. Robinson's book was followed by many others that expanded the premise.

In this chapter, we explain who the Freemasons are, how they developed, and what they do. We fill you in on what the modern Masonic Knights Templar are up to these days. And we reveal the Templar theories of the formation of Freemasonry as a secret society.

For much greater detail about the Freemasons, see *Freemasons For Dummies,* by Christopher Hodapp (Wiley).

The Masonic Fraternity: Who Freemasons Are and What They Believe

The generally accepted origin of modern Freemasonry is believed to have been from stonemason guilds formed during the Middle Ages in Scotland, England, and France. As early as the eighth century, French Masons were being organized and instructed by the Frankish king Charles Martel. The earliest English documents claim that a guild of masons was chartered in the city of York in A.D. 926 by Athelstan, the first king of a united England. The first written records of the stonemason guilds appear in the 1300s with a document known today as the *Regius Manuscript.*

The modern philosophical and fraternal organization that exists today evolved in the late 1600s in England during the Age of Enlightenment. The fraternity was officially established in its present form in London in 1717. It is nonsectarian and open to all men who profess a belief in a Supreme Being. In addition, it draws its members from virtually every faith and every class of society, with no religious, social, or economic barriers.

The most basic level of what is called Ancient Craft Freemasonry initiates and advances its members through three ritual ceremonies, called *degrees.* (The phrase, "Give him the third degree" is a somewhat cheesy reference to the Freemasons.) These three degrees are conferred in Masonic lodges that can be found in nearly every town across the United States and Canada, and in almost every country of the world. For symbolic purposes, these individual local lodges are referred to as craft lodges or, in the United States, *blue lodges,* probably emblematic of the "canopy of heaven" referred to in the rituals.

The term *lodge* can refer not just to the room in which the members meet, but more correctly, to the members themselves, as a group.

The fraternity teaches its members symbolic lessons about character building, using tools, language, and allegories based on the construction of King Solomon's Temple. The goal of Freemasonry is to make good men into better and more responsible ones. By improving individual men, Freemasonry hopes to improve society as a whole. Freemasonry's most visible accomplishments are the many charities supported by the fraternity, but that is only a small part of the fraternity's attraction for millions of men.

The principal thread that runs throughout the three degree rituals is the symbolism of Solomon's Temple, culminating in the Masonic legend of Hiram Abiff, a widow's son, who was the Grand Architect of the building of the temple. In the Masonic story, Hiram Abiff is attacked by three workmen who want the secrets of the master masons but have not earned them. Hiram chooses to die rather than break his word by revealing the secrets.

During the 1950s, there were around 7 million Freemasons worldwide, and more than 4 million in the United States alone, driven by unprecedented membership gains after World War II. By 2006, those numbers had dwindled to less than 3 million worldwide, with slightly fewer than 1.5 million Masons in the United States. Freemasonry is, by tradition, a male-only organization, although there are women's auxiliary organizations within mainstream Freemasonry, as well as female and mixed-gender Masonic lodges that operate outside of the accepted mainstream Masonic world.

It's unknown where the term *Freemason* comes from. Some historians say that it refers to the fact that the members of the stonemason guilds were not required to stay in a certain city or county, so were free to travel and look for work — thus, *free masons.* Another is that it may be a shortening of the term *freestone mason. Freestone* is a generic term for a soft, fine-grained stone that can be carved, like sandstone or limestone (as opposed to harder rock with heavy grain, like granite, that has to be split).

A quick tour of Masonic history

Bear with this section, because it's important to understand *who* the Masons are and *what* some of their beliefs and practices are before delving into *why* some researchers think they may have sprouted from the Templars.

Freemasons today use the terms *operative* and *speculative* to describe the "difference between the two distinct periods of Freemasonry. *Operative* Freemasonry refers to the time before 1700 — the period when Freemasons were really working with stones, chisels, and hammers. After the operative workers began to be replaced by "admitted" or "gentleman" masons, the order evolved into a philosophical, fraternal, and charitable organization, and became known as *speculative* Freemasonry.

Operative Freemasonry

The medieval Freemasons built Gothic cathedrals and castles from massive stones. They were masters of the science of geometry and could transform a small drawing into an enormous structure. They were skilled at architecture, physics, hydraulics, and art. Their techniques were jealously guarded trade secrets — secrets not even divulged to the clerics and kings who employed the masons. The guilds developed to train workers in these skills and enforce a code of high standards, along with setting a fair price for their work. They truly were the first labor unions.

Most important, the guilds were established to protect these highly prized trade secrets. A Mason in possession of the right knowledge could travel and work all over the country, wherever the guild was working. Master Masons were taught the Master's *word* and *grip,* secret methods these workmen used to recognize each other. It was a simple way to quickly identify oneself as a trained member of the guild, because the idea of business cards, diplomas, and dues cards hadn't been invented yet.

Masons established *lodges,* which were huts or cabins next to their job sites. This was where plans for the job were kept and consulted, training sessions were held, and meals were shared; sometimes they even slept there. Over the centuries, they developed ceremonies to initiate and instruct their new members, or to graduate their master craftsmen.

The Masons claimed a mythical origin dating back to the great building projects of the Bible — the Tower of Babel, Noah's Ark, and especially the Temple of Solomon. This is obviously where the inklings of a connection between Freemasonry and the Templars began, because both had a legendary connection to the Temple of Solomon.

The Masons held a unique position in society. True, they were peasants, but they were very skilled peasants. Kings and popes and lords and bishops all needed their services, and needed them in a big way. All over Europe, they were admired both for their expertise and their moral code. In addition, these were very religious times, and the Masons claimed that their practices and heritage dated back to events described in the Bible. The skills they possessed were considered to be both magical and divine, given to the biblical Masons by God himself, and passed down through the ages.

Understanding what Freemasonry became requires a brief understanding of the forces that shaped it. With the dawn of the Renaissance, the Catholic Church was faced with a noisy call for reform on the one side and open revolt on the other. Catholicism was losing its once total grip on the nations of the West, and the 1500s and 1600s were marked by a long, bloody series of religious wars that affected every country of Europe. Cooler heads knew religious wars were a messy way to change society.

The Age of Enlightenment, which began in the 1700's, is sometimes called the Age of Reason, and it's important because it ushered in revolutionary ideas about philosophy, thought, learning, and religion. Enlightenment scholars valued the process of acquiring new knowledge, instead of rooting around in dusty manuscripts looking for ancient wisdom, or looking to religion as the explanation for everything. It was during this time that the modern scientific method of experimentation, observation, and reason developed. A scientific conclusion had to be observable, measurable, and provable.

Meanwhile, a curious change began to happen to Freemasonry, beginning in Scotland in the 1600s. Noblemen began to express interest in becoming members of the Masons' lodges. They had no uncontrollable urge to crawl in the dirt with the peasants and learn to do something more useful than boss around their serfs. Yet, records began to appear showing lodges admitting these nonoperative, "accepted" members. The first recorded instance of such a member being admitted to an operative lodge was Sir Robert Moray in 1640. Moray would go on to help found the exclusive Royal Society in London after the civil wars ended in the 1660s, with a fellow accepted Mason, Elias Ashmole. Masonic lodges were suddenly becoming attractive for some *very* learned men.

Speculative Freemasonry

Gothic architecture died out as the favored style by clerics and kings by the end of the 1500s, and the stonemasons lost their primary source of work. The Great London Fire in 1666 had provided plenty of opportunities to construct grand, new buildings, but it was a different style. Bricks replaced massive stones as the major building material, and the operative Freemasons (see the preceding section) were out of a job. But as the members who actually worked with stone in the building trade began to drift away from the guilds, shopkeepers, other tradesmen, *gentlemen* (educated, upper-class men), and even members of the nobility were replacing them. Instead of meeting in lodges on job sites, they began to gather in more comfortable and convenient taverns and coffeehouses.

No one can make a definitive answer as to why stonemason guilds turned, virtually overnight, into dining and drinking clubs, basing their organization, symbolism, and initiatory ritual ceremonies on the old trade guilds. No one really knows how or why it happened, but it did.

A meeting was held in London in 1717 to forge a new governing body for this new kind of Freemasonry. There were four lodges left in the general vicinity of St. Paul's Cathedral, so the lodges all gathered at the Goose and Gridiron tavern to form what they called a *Grand Lodge.* The Grand Lodge's role would be to make up rules for the governing of the organization and issue charters for new lodges. While speculative Freemasonry had been growing across England, Scotland, and Ireland, this was the first time that a central authority had ever been established to unite the individual lodges under one collective roof.

Grand Lodges soon began appearing in Scotland, France, and other countries, and Freemasonry quickly spread around the world on the trading and military ships of the colonial nations of Europe. In less than a hundred years, speculative Freemasons were in every civilized nation of the world.

The brotherhood code of the lodge

Freemasons refer to each other as *brothers,* and one of the principal obligations of a Mason is to help other Masons and their families. In fact, Masons have what is called the Grand Hailing Sign of Distress, which is a phrase and a special gesture used to signal other Masons when they're in danger.

Freemasonry has long been tagged with the label of being a "secret society," usually accompanied by a reference to occult practices and funny handshakes. In North America, Masonic lodges are listed in the phone book and often have signs in their yards big enough to spot from low earth orbit. U.S. Masons themselves wear rings, jackets, hats, and ties with Masonic symbols on them, and their cars often have Masonic license plates or bumper stickers. This is hardly the behavior of a secret society.

In the United States, Freemasons proudly point to the participation of early Freemasons who were Founding Fathers and other notable figures, including: George Washington and 13 other presidents, Ben Franklin, Paul Revere, John Hancock, plus military heroes, business leaders, inventors, movie stars, and more.

Outside of North America, Freemasonry is a little quieter. Many societies have a deep suspicion of Masons, believing them to be part of a mysterious cabal of men who seek to control governments, businesses, criminal empires, or worse. As a result, Freemasons in many countries do not outwardly display Masonic symbols, and keep their membership very quiet. Masonic lodge buildings in other countries are often not identified as such, to avoid vandalism or outright attack.

Non-Masons, anti-Masons, and conspiracy theorists have inflated the notion of Masonic secrecy into something evil, unethical, and perhaps even illegal. The truth is that Masonic secrecy is actually confined to very few subjects:

- ✔ *Grips* **(those funny handshakes), passwords, signs, and steps:** These are known as *modes of recognition,* and they're used by Masons to identify each other and to verify their membership.

- ✔ **Certain portions of the rituals, especially the 3rd degree Master Mason ceremony:** What good is an initiation if you tell everyone about it ahead of time? Masons promise not to write, print, stamp, stain, cut, carve, hew, mark, or engrave any of their ritual secrets in a manner that non-Masons may read.

- ✔ **Information privately exchanged between individual members (known as** *on the square***), with the exception of murder, treason, or illegal activities that conflict with a person's duty to God, his country, his neighbor, or himself:** Masons are taught to be discreet, but they certainly don't protect criminals in their midst. Keeping a secret between Masonic brothers is more of a demonstration of a member's ability to honor his promise to his brethren. Although in their *obligations* (oaths), Masons agree to suffer dire and bloody penalties if they break the rules, the truth is, the worst punishment a Mason has to endure is having his membership revoked.

Identifying the Possible Templar Origins of Freemasonry

There is another version of the creation of Freemasonry (beyond the one we outline in "A quick tour of Masonic history," earlier in this chapter). Well, there are several, but one of the most popular, romantic versions is the formation of Freemasonry by a band of Knights Templar.

In 1989, the author John J. Robinson wrote a book entitled *Born in Blood: The Lost Secrets of Freemasonry,* which took the Masonic world by storm. In it, Robinson assembled a series of theories that traced the Knights Templar from their arrest and suppression in France to Scotland. Robinson did not claim to have come up with this connection on his own, but he was the first to make an attempt to prove it.

The Templars already had extensive holdings in Scotland before their suppression, and although there was a brief trial of just two Templars in Scotland, the order there was found innocent of any wrongdoing or heresy.

The story goes that Robert the Bruce, king of Scotland during this period, was already excommunicated by the pope in 1306, which meant that the rest of the country suffered the same fate with him. That meant no Catholic weddings, no Catholic christenings, no burial services, and no Communion on Sunday. The king was in the midst of a war with England at the time, and such saber rattling from faraway Rome didn't bother him nearly as much as real swordplay and a relentless series of invasions led by England's Edward I. So when the Templar fleet arrived off the coast of Scotland looking for a refuge from France, Bruce was grateful to have them.

Because Scotland was under an order of excommunication when Pope Clement V issued heresy charges against the Templars, Bruce had a spiritual loophole that allowed him to give them sanctuary. If Scotland was excommunicated, no member of the Catholic Church could read out the charges against the knights — and if no charges could be read out, then the knights were free to call Scotland home.

The biggest part of the legend has to do with the famous Battle of Bannockburn in 1314. Robert the Bruce was engaged in a battle with England's King Edward II, who ascended the throne in 1307, the year the Knights templar were arrested. The tale is told of a mysterious group of fierce knights on horseback, dressed in white tunics, who turned the battle decisively in Scotland's favor. No evidence or contemporary account of the battle exists, but these mysterious knights have often been rumored to be the Knights Templar.

Robinson lists several Masonic references that may have originated with the Knights Templar to bolster his theory:

- ✔ **Passwords:** The Templars were on the run and had to hide from loyal Catholics who might otherwise betray them, so they needed to establish secret passwords and other modes of recognition.

- ✔ **Aprons:** According to some claims, the Templars wore a sheepskin "girdle" around their waists as a symbol of chastity, and it's possible this developed into the aprons that Freemasons wear during their meetings. However, there is no historical record that the Templars did any such thing. They wore a cord around their waists, not a girdle or apron.

- ✔ **Nonsectarian discussions:** The Templars considered themselves to be devout Catholics whom the Church had betrayed, so discussion of Catholicism would have been a social faux pas, as well as potentially deadly if a devoted parishioner discovered the Templars' secret identity. Members of their new inner circle would only have to profess a belief in God, not align themselves with the Church.

✔ **Unprecedented religious tolerance:** This goes hand in glove with the nonsectarian discussions. The notion has long been that the Templars had come to a new kind of religious tolerance after their years in the Holy Land (a sort of "When in Rome, do as the Romans do" theory of survival), and that they were amenable to allowing Jews and Muslims to worship as they wished, even inside of Templar chapels. The theory is that this laid the groundwork for Masonic tolerance of all monotheistic religions.

✔ **Possible French origins of Masonic words and phrases:** Because the Templars were a French order that spoke French in their daily activities, Robinson gives possible French origins to many unusual words associated with Freemasonry. Of course, the French-speaking Normans had conquered England in 1066, and there were constant friendly contacts between Scotland and France in subsequent years, so similarity of words is hardly surprising.

✔ **The similarity between the square and compasses and the Seal of Solomon:** The symbol for Freemasonry and the symbol attributed to King Solomon and the Temple are similar, and it can be argued that the Masonic "logo" is a thinly veiled copy (see the nearby sidebar, "The square and compasses and the Seal of Solomon").

Most historians, Masonic and otherwise, discount Robinson's theories, and even the present-day Knights Templar order of Freemasons does not claim a direct link to the original knights. Nevertheless, Robinson brings up interesting possibilities and more than a few unanswered coincidences. There are similarities and plausible arguments to be made that may, indeed, connect Freemasons with the Templars, and there is no denying that operative Freemasonry first began to change into speculative Freemasonry in Scotland.

Rosslyn Chapel and the Masons

Templar enthusiasts and Freemasons have long claimed that Rosslyn Chapel, near Edinburgh, Scotland, is chock-full of symbolism for both the Templars and the Freemasons. The writing teams of Robert Lomas and Christopher Knight, Michael Baigent and Richard Leigh, and Tim Wallace-Murphy and Marilyn Hopkins were among the first authors to publicize and explore the chapel's potential connections to the Templars, the Freemasons, and a host of other speculative theories. Many more researchers have followed in their footsteps. We talk about Rosslyn Chapel throughout this book but for the sake of this part of the story, you just need to know a little bit about the chapel made world-famous by the end scenes of *The Da Vinci Code*.

The square and compasses and the Seal of Solomon

The symbol of the square and compasses (shown on the left in the nearby figure) has become synonymous with Freemasonry. They are tools of the building trades, which use them in the everyday application of geometry.

In North America, the letter *G* commonly appears in the center. Because the earliest stonemasons believed that the secret knowledge of geometry was a gift to them by God, and that God himself was believed to the Grand Architect of the Universe, the *G* stands for both *God* and *geometry*. Elsewhere in the world, the *G* rarely appears in the square-and-compasses symbol.

Some scholars have pointed out the similarity of the symbol's basic outline with the Seal of Solomon, or Star of David (shown on the right in the figure). Today, the Seal of Solomon is most commonly associated with the Jewish faith and the flag of the State of Israel. Jewish legends claim that King David had a shield with the symbol that protected him from evil. His son, King Solomon, had the symbol on a signet ring that came from heaven, which he used to perform magic and control demons.

The symbol, made of two triangles, has had many interpretations to Jews, Christians, Muslims, and alchemists. In *The Da Vinci Code,* Dan Brown declared the symbol to be a representation of the masculine and the divine feminine, and many believe it represent good and evil, heaven and earth, and other similar yin-yang themes.

Although the symbol of two inverted triangles appears in some Egyptian archeological locations, the actual symbol itself didn't become identified with the Jews or King Solomon until the 1300s in Prague, and didn't become widespread until the 1600s. It actually appeared more commonly in Islamic art during the time of the Crusades.

When, in the 1400s, Sultan Suleiman the Magnificent undertook major renovations of the Temple Mount in Jerusalem where Solomon's Temple once stood, he built new city walls and decorated them with the Seal of Solomon as a talisman to protect the city. Because of the Seal of Solomon's connection to the Holy City of Jerusalem and King Solomon, some have claimed that its blatant similarity to the Masonic square and compasses shows a direct progression from the Knights Templar to the Freemasons.

Meanwhile, the square and compasses appear in Christian art and alchemical books all throughout the Middle Ages as symbols of geometry and knowledge, and often are depicted in the hands of God.

The chapel was built in the 1400s by Sir William St. Clair (or Sinclair, depending on the source). The St. Clairs were a noble family descended from Norman knights from France. Historians don't know when the chapel became associated with either the Templars or Freemasonry, but the connection doesn't seem to have been discussed prior to the late 1700s, in spite of outlandish claims to the contrary. The chapel was built as a private church for the St. Clair family, and its construction wasn't started until more than 130 years after the Templars were dissolved. Nevertheless, what makes the chapel unique are the unusual carvings and artwork that are packed into every conceivable crevice.

Masonic carvings?

Among the carvings in Rosslyn Chapel are images supposedly of the Templars. One such carving is said to show the classic image of the Order — two knights on horseback, although it looks to most people more like a mounted knight with a squire, a monk, or perhaps his wife walking behind him.

Another carving is said to depict a Masonic Entered Apprentice prepared as modern initiates are today, with a blindfold (called a *hoodwink*) and a noose (referred to as a *cable tow*) around his neck. He appears to be situated between two pillars, perhaps with an open Bible in his hand. Of course, it could also be a figure of a man about to be executed — that's the funny thing about symbolism. If it is, indeed, a Masonic reference, it should be pointed out that the introduction of the hoodwink and cable tow into Freemasonry's rituals did not occur until the late 1600s. The chapel was built two centuries before that.

As Robert Cooper has pointed out in his 2006 book *The Rosslyn Hoax,* the chapel itself was dedicated to St. Matthew. Matthew 15:12–14 may be a clue to the carving's real origin: *"Let them alone: they be blind leaders of the blind. And if the blind lead the blind, both shall fall into the ditch."*

Freemasonry is *loaded* with symbolism. Squares, compasses, plumbs, levels, anchors, arks, gavels, trowels, aprons, and a hundred other images play a part in the ritual ceremonies of the Masonic fraternity. In spite of the many claims that Rosslyn is "loaded" with Masonic symbolism, it is not. In fact, it is fair to say that there are *no* images that are *specific* to Freemasonry anywhere in the tiny chapel's thousands of intricate carvings. No matter how many books and experts claim to see Masonic imagery in Rosslyn Chapel, it is wishful thinking.

The Apprentice Pillar

Central to the chapel's Masonic folklore is the Apprentice Pillar, a magnificently detailed marble column (shown in Figure 8-1). The tale goes that the Master Carver was afraid of starting work on it without first traveling to Rome to see the original in person. While he was off gallivanting in Italy, his apprentice got both impatient and cocky and carved the pillar himself. When the Master returned, so the story goes, he became so enraged at the perfection of his apprentice's work that he killed the young man by striking him in the head with a mallet, just as in the Masonic legend of Hiram Abiff (see "The Masonic Fraternity: Who Freemasons Are and What They Believe," earlier in this chapter). A gash on the pillar today is where the Master's mallet allegedly whacked the column after clobbering his apprentice. Of course, before the late 1700's, this was called the Prince's Pillar, and there was no tale of an angry Masonic Master.

Figure 8-1:
The dazzlingly intricate Apprentice Pillar in Rosslyn Chapel.

HIP / Art Resource, NY

Masonic Knights Templar should know that the chapel contains an inscription that appears in the ritual of their Chivalric degrees: *Forte est vinum fortior est rex fortiores sunt mulieres super omnia vincit veritas,* or "Wine is strong, a king is stronger, women are stronger still, but truth conquers all." This quote is from the First Book of Esdras, a part of the Eastern Orthodox Church's Old Testament, but rejected by Jewish, Catholic, and Protestant biblical scholars as apocryphal.

The Templars' sacred subcontractors

French author Paul Naudon has proposed a different take on the Templar origin of Freemasonry theory, and it's somewhere between the stonemason theory on one side, and the secret-society-of-renegade-Templars theory on the other. Naudon's notion is that the Templars had literally hundreds of castles, preceptories, chapels, and outposts, which contained myriads of inner buildings, plus fortifications, docks, and a fistful of other structures, all constructed in a very brief period of time. There is absolutely no record that the warrior monks themselves actually hauled, carved, and stacked the stones to build these massive structures, and there is nothing to suggest that they used prisoners or slave workers. The structures are constructed with precision and skill, and many have survived over the centuries. The Templars had to hire *somebody* to build them, and those somebodies were the stonemasons.

Naudon postulates that these stonemasons in the employ of the Templars were influenced by Templar philosophy and practices. Moreover, the Templars employed Armenian, Syrian, and Byzantine masons for their projects in the Holy Land and surrounding areas. These other influences certainly rubbed off on the European stonemasons, who made sudden and massive changes to forms of architecture in a very brief time.

The Templars first learned their building practices from the Cistercians, but they quickly adopted designs and practices that they found after entering Muslim cities and strongholds like Tyre. Templars were ingenious military engineers, and became skilled in the building of siege engines — battering rams, mobile platforms, catapults, and other designs that had peacetime uses as well. With little modification, such machines could be used as scaffolding and methods to transport and lift massive stones.

When the Knights built their temples and preceptories in Paris and London in the 1100s, they brought their own builders with them from the Middle East. They weren't going to trust such projects to just any group of scruffy rock stackers. Simply put, Naudon's theory is that these Templar contractors introduced much of the symbolism, philosophy, and customs that grew into modern Freemasonry, including an unusually strong sense of religious toleration.

The Masonic Knights Templar and Where They Came From

The most basic degrees of the Freemasons are the first three: the Entered Apprentice, the Fellow Craft, and the Master Mason. You may have heard of men who claim to be 32nd- or even 33rd-degree Masons. They didn't make it up. The confusion comes from what are called *appendant bodies,* groups that formed over the last three centuries that confer additional degrees and require their members to already be 3rd-degree Master Masons before "advancing." These additional degrees developed in a somewhat chaotic manner all across Europe. In North America, these many different individual degrees settled into two different general groups known as the York Rite and the Ancient Accepted Scottish Rite, and it is in these two different groups of additional degrees that the Templars most blatantly appear.

The best way to think of these two appendant bodies is as two different types of continuing Masonic education. Some Masons join them both, some only join one or the other, and most don't join either one of them. They are not required, and Masons who have achieved the 32nd degree of the Scottish Rite are of no higher "rank" than a 3rd-degree Mason.

The many degrees found in the Scottish Rite and the York Rite developed in Europe beginning in the mid-1700s. They grew for a variety of reasons. Some tell prequels and sequels of the Hiram Abiff legend (see "The Masonic Fraternity: Who Freemasons Are and What They Believe," earlier in this chapter). Others use stories from the Bible and describe the building of the second Temple by Zerubbabel in 515 B.C. and its expansion by King Herod in 19 B.C.

The tale of the Knights Templar fleeing to Scotland after the mass arrests in France is not new. The legend of Robert the Bruce and the Templar army riding out of the mists to save the day at the Battle of Bannockburn in 1314 has been around almost since the battle happened. The modern Royal Order of Scotland claims that Scotland's King James II created a chivalric order in 1440 called the Order of the Knights of St. Andrew or the Thistle, based on the same Templar legend.

As more aristocratic members joined Freemasonry, especially in France, a series of appendant degrees began to pop up. Plump landowners who hobnobbed with royalty enjoyed the ritual ceremonies and the fun aspects of being initiated into a growing number of impressive sounding groups, but they didn't much care for the idea that they were joining something that had sprung from a labor union of peasant stonecutters. So they began to invent new degrees. These new degrees were based on chivalric stories — tales of knights and heroic deeds.

The effect of the new degrees went in both directions: It made the nobility more comfortable by inventing a new pedigree for them, and it suddenly gave low-born shopkeepers and laborers an opportunity to have honors and titles bestowed upon them far beyond anything they could hope for in the world outside of the lodge.

Chevalier Ramsay begins a knightly legend

The Chevalier Andrew Michael Ramsay was born in Scotland in 1686, but he spent most of his life in France. This was a pretty common occurrence during this period. After the English Civil War, Charles II was brought to London and became king. He knew that one of the little personality quirks that had resulted in his father's head being lopped off was the appearance that he might have been a Catholic. Charles II had no intention of making that kind of mistake, so he kept his religious opinions to himself all through his reign. Unfortunately, his successor wasn't that shrewd.

Charles II died with no legitimate heirs, so his brother, King James VII of Scotland, rolled into London to be crowned as James II of England. James was a staunch Catholic and proceeded to so enrage most of the country over his choice of religion that he was expelled from the country and replaced by his Protestant daughter, Mary, and her husband, William. Parliament finally put a stop to the Catholic/Protestant fight by passing laws forbidding any more Catholic kings. The result was a huge wave of English and Scottish Catholic expatriates who moved to France.

France was a very sympathetic Catholic country, and there was a certain adolescent glee over playing host to the enemies of England. Annoying the English was a longstanding French pastime. The supporters of James became known as *Jacobites,* and there was a sizeable number of them. It is believed that modern Freemasonry came to France from Scotland with the Jacobites, and that it was these disaffected Scots and English who began to develop many of the appendant degrees. In spite of its name, the Scottish Rite of Freemasonry actually began in France.

Chevalier Ramsay briefly was employed as a tutor to the exiled King James II's two sons, and his many travels were turned into popular books. But he is most important to Freemasons for one document, known as *Ramsay's Oration.* Whether Ramsay actually gave it as a speech in public is unknown, but his 1737 paper told a story about how Freemasonry began in the Holy Land and how its secrets were actually brought back to Europe by the crusading knights. He never said that the knights were the Templars — in fact, he actually credited the Knights of St. John. And he never suggested creating new degrees or introducing chivalric orders into the fraternity, but it didn't matter. Creative Freemasons, mostly in France, took Ramsay's ideas and ran with them. You can see the scale to which the new degrees can be attributed to these expatriate Scots in the term the French used to describe them — they were called the *Ecossais* degrees, French for "Scottish."

Freemasonry's mysterious "Unknown Superiors"

Freemasons traveled across Britain and Europe, and they took their local customs and innovations with them. Certain of these new degrees became popular and were adopted in more and more lodges.

In the 1740s, Baron Karl Gotthelf Hund claimed to have been initiated into a Templar Masonic Order by a mysterious *Eques a Penna Rubra* (Knight of the Red Feather). He believed this disguised knight was none other than Charles Edward Stuart, the son of the deposed (and now deceased) King James III. The descendants of James III lived on in France and were something of an ongoing boogeyman for England over the years, which regarded them all as a line of pretenders to the throne. And it was no secret that the exiled Stuart family wanted desperately to return to England and take back the crown.

The Baron claimed that he had received a mission from "Unknown Superiors" to reform Freemasonry, and he formed a group called the Rite of Strict Observance, which contained a Knights Templar degree. The Rite of Strict Observance became hugely popular across France, Germany, Austria, Sweden, and Holland for a brief period, before dying out. Members became tired of waiting for new instructions from the "Unknown Superiors," and Hund seemed to be too honest to have made the whole thing up. By the 1780s, the Rite had disappeared. But the Templar notion lived on.

Templarism in the American colonies

The Green Dragon Tavern in Boston became famous in U.S. history by being the hotbed of pre–Revolutionary War groups like the Sons of Liberty. Paul Revere, and John Hancock were among the tavern's regular patrons. It was also the home of an upstart Masonic lodge called St. Andrews. The lodge had not been officially chartered by the Grand Lodge of England or any other legal governing group, so its formation was just as revolutionary as its members (who quietly took credit for the Boston Tea party in 1775). What makes it important for this discussion is that it was also the first lodge in America to have officially conferred a Masonic Knights Templar degree in 1769. In fact, Paul Revere was among the first Knights Templar in America.

In those days in the American colonies, Freemasonry often spread by way of military lodges made up of soldiers who held meetings in tents, in caves, in private homes, in taverns, onboard ships, or anywhere else they could find some privacy. The Grand Lodges of Ireland and Scotland generally chartered the military lodges, while stationary lodges in the colonial cities were usually chartered by the Grand Lodge of England. The soldiers picked up new ceremonies and customs as they traveled, and they conferred degrees on civilians as well. This is most probably how the Templar degree came ashore in America.

Templar drill teams: The origins of Masonic Knights Templar military costumes

After the end of the U.S. Civil War, fraternal groups were all the rage. Literally hundreds of different varieties of lodges, orders, chapters, councils, dens, encampments, grottos, shrines, and temples, all claimed to be grand, ancient, noble, majestic, or otherwise really impressive. It is not an exaggeration to say that most of them patterned their ceremonies and hierarchy on the Freemasons.

One curious development grew out of the desire of Civil War veterans to recapture the camaraderie they had felt with fellow soldiers during the war, combined with a large number of military supply companies that suddenly found themselves without customers. Thus were born the fraternal military orders. The Masonic Knights Templar, along with similar military-themed orders like the Knights of Pythias, the Knights of Columbus, the Grand Army of the Republic, and many other fraternal groups started drill teams to march in parades, wearing slightly altered Civil War uniforms and swords. This custom survives today.

Skulls and crossbones!

For a long time, one of the common symbols of the Masonic Templars was a skull and crossbones, which appeared on their aprons worn during ritual ceremonies and meetings (see Figure 8-2). They also appear on gravestones of Masonic Templars throughout the 19th and early 20th centuries. The skull and crossbones were associated with the real Knights Templar, and the skull plays a part in the modern Knights Templar Order's ceremonies.

Figure 8-2:
The skull-and-crossbones style Templar apron has been prohibited for use since the 1920s.

You can find the gruesome-looking Templar aprons in antiques stores and on eBay, but they have been officially prohibited for use by the Order since the 1920s, because of the public perception that they were somehow evil. In spite of its more recent connotation as a symbol of malevolence, during the 18th and 19th centuries, the skull and crossbones was a symbol of mortality and was often used to caution the living to prepare for their own end. This is the way it is represented in the Templar ritual today.

Order of DeMolay

Before World War I, the phenomenon of scouting for children took the world by storm. Starting in 1907, the Boy Scouts, Girl Scouts, and other similarly styled groups spread across Europe and North America, largely based on the writings of Robert Baden-Powell and his experiences with young men trained as scouts for the British Army in India and North Africa. As scouting grew in popularity, so did other types of youth groups, and it wasn't long before many of the popular fraternal groups started their own.

In 1919, a Freemason named Frank S. Land started a youth group in Kansas City, Missouri, for nine young men. Land was especially concerned for boys who had lost their fathers during World War I. The boys were meeting in the local Masonic hall, and they were intrigued by the Masonic traditions of ritual ceremonies and degrees. Land was also a Knights Templar, and he told the boys the story of the fall of the original Templar Order; their last Grand Master, Jacques de Molay; and his tragic martyrdom (see Chapter 5). Excited by the tale, the boys adopted de Molay as their namesake, and a ritual was designed around his story.

The Order of DeMolay (officially known today as DeMolay International, to reflect its growth beyond the U.S. borders) confers two degrees:

- **The Initiatory degree:** The Initiatory degree teaches its members seven precepts or cardinal virtues: love of parents, reverence for all things sacred, courtesy, comradeship, fidelity, cleanliness, and patriotism.

- **The DeMolay degree:** The DeMolay degree portrays the suffering and martyrdom of the Grand Master, stressing his love and loyalty for his brother knights.

Today, there are about 20,000 members of DeMolay, and it's open to young men between the ages of 12 and 21 who, as in Freemasonry, profess a belief in a Supreme Being. It is nondenominational. Many of DeMolay's members go on to become Freemasons, but although the Masonic fraternity supports DeMolay, there is no direct connection between the two organizations.

There is, by the way, no relationship between the Freemasons or the Order of Knights Templar and the Skull and Bones fraternity at Yale University, made famous most recently by the membership of both 2004 presidential candidates George W. Bush and John Kerry, other than the use of the same images of mortality. *Bonesmen,* as the Yale guys are called, are neither Knights Templar nor Freemasons.

The Templars' place within Freemasonry

The Knights Templar Order is part of the York Rite system of additional Masonic degrees, which, in the United States, also include four degrees of the Royal Arch, three of the Cryptic Council, and three Chivalric Orders (the Illustrious Order of the Red Cross, the Order of the Knights of Malta, and the Order of the Knights Templar). Outside of the U.S. there are organizational differences.

Masonic Knights Templar meet in commanderies or preceptories. Their state-wide governing bodies are known as Grand Commanderies, and the national organization is called the Grand Encampment (or Grand Priory in Canada).

The Templars are unique in Freemasonry because, unlike most other degrees and appendant bodies, it is one of the few groups that requires a belief in — or at least a willingness to defend — Christianity. The rest of the Masonic fraternity is nondenominational, requiring only a belief in a Supreme Being. In most jurisdictions, men who want to become Knights Templar must also have been through the Royal Arch degrees. Apart from its ritual ceremonies and its drill teams, the Knights Templar is also a philanthropic organization that endows medical-research programs, as well as sponsoring trips to the Holy Land for ministers of all Christian denominations.

Several symbols are identified with the Masonic Knights Templar. The most common is a crown and cross, a cross pattée surrounded by swords, and the motto: *In hoc signo vinces*, Latin for "In this sign, conquer!"(see Figure 8-3). The motto comes from the story of the Roman Emperor Constantine in A.D. 312, who converted to Christianity after seeing a vision of a chi rho cross in the sun, along with the Latin phrase. Constantine didn't have a clue what the vision meant, but Jesus appeared to him in a dream and explained that he should use the sign of the cross to conquer his enemies.

Figure 8-3: Typical symbol of the Masonic Knights Templar: the cross pattée, a crown and cross, swords, and the motto *In hoc signo vinces* (Latin for "In this sign, conquer!")

Earlier in this chapter, we mention the Scottish Rite as being the other branch of appendant bodies in Freemasonry. The Scottish Rite does not confer Templar degrees, per se. However, it does present a series of degrees (the Rose Croix and Knight Kadosh degrees) that are a veiled retelling of the betrayal of knights based in Jerusalem at the hands of a king and an unjust church, and the burning at the stake of their members. That should sound familiar.

The Templar degrees also exist in Freemasonry outside of the United States and Canada, although the York Rite under which they are categorized in North America is different in many countries, and may not exist at all in others. Every country has its own customs. There is no international governing body for Freemasonry in the world. Each country — or in the case of the United States and Canada, each state or province — has its own Grand Lodge, as well as its own governing groups for the appendant bodies.

Nevertheless, one thing all Masonic Knights Templar groups agree upon is that they are definitely *not* directly descended from the original order of warrior monks. They have based their rules, ceremonies, and governing bodies on the original Templars, but none of them claim to be heirs of the crusading Templar Order.

Chapter 9

Modern-Day Templars

In This Chapter

▶ Tracking the Templars today

▶ Reviving their chivalric and religious ideals

▶ Making tenuous Templar connections

▶ Trading in Templar trademarks

*A*lmost immediately after the excommunication of the Knights Templar, whispers of new organizations began to appear that either claimed a direct descent of the order, or became a haven for the fleeing knights. But as the centuries passed, the Templars occupied a unique place in mythology.

Their popularity was something of an enigma. On the one hand, they were admired for their skill in warfare, their devotion to Christ, their ingenuity in the creation of international banking, and their artistry in building. On the other hand, they had been excommunicated for heresy, distrusted for their secrecy, and damned for their less-than-Christian activities. And — go get a friend, as this will require a another hand — on the third hand, they gradually became the source of endless speculation over their supernatural connection to the occult, the unknown mysteries that they may have discovered within Solomon's Temple, and no shortage of mind-blowing mystical manifestations heaped on them ever since.

The result over the centuries has been a gaggle of groups, from pseudo-military orders at one end, to secret societies on the other, all claiming some kind of kinship with the Templars of old. And because of the wide range of activities and myths attributed to the Templars, that kinship can cover a lot of unusual ground.

During the 1800s in particular, the Templars became the subject of an incredibly far-flung romance with the chivalric qualities of protection, honor, faith, and decency. In addition, the 1800s was a period of widespread fascination with legends connected with the Templars — Solomon's Temple, the Ark of the Covenant, and the Holy Grail.

In Chapter 8, we discuss the principal group most often identified with the Knights Templar — the Freemasons. In this chapter, we cover the less famous groups around the world that claim to be descended or derived from, inspired or spawned by, or otherwise related to the Templars, as well as a few that sound similar but aren't. We also look at some of the ways that advertisers cashed in on Templar mania. And we finish up with a look at the huge popularity of the Templars in the 21st century and their appearance in games, books, comics, and movies.

Modern Templar Orders

During the 1800s, Freemasonry was just one of the literally hundreds of fraternal organizations that sprung up across the United States and around the world. Most of the "secret societies" that followed its success patterned themselves after Masonic lodges and ceremonies. They initiated candidates using solemn ceremonies that conferred different grades or *degrees,* and required their members to take oaths promising never to divulge their secrets. It wasn't just eating-and-drinking clubs that were doing this stuff. Benevolent assistance groups that mostly existed to provide cheap insurance policies for their members, and even labor unions soon began dressing up their officers in fancy costumes, creating lavish and ever more convoluted rituals, and bestowing bilious and bloated titles of rank and honor upon each other.

The most common thread that ran though these groups was the title of *knight.* Chivalry was something that a railroad worker, coal miner, or plumber was unlikely to encounter in his daily life, and knights only existed in storybooks. But in their lodges, knighthood flourished. Swords tapped them on the shoulders and titles of rank and honor were bestowed left and right. And there were literally dozens of these groups, from the Knights of the Mystic Circle, the Knights of Pythias, and the Knights of Columbus, to the Knights of the Golden Circle and even the Knights of the Invisible Colored Kingdom.

Apart from the Masonic Knights Templar (see Chapter 8), several fraternal and esoteric groups aligned themselves with the Knights Templar, many of which survive today. They run the gamut from serious religious or chivalric organizations to temperance leagues and even doomsday cults. It is a testament to the power of the Templar mystique that so many groups have sought to identify in one way or another with them. More astonishing is why many religious, and especially Catholic, groups would align themselves with the memory of an order that was excommunicated for heresy.

Order Militia Crucifera Evangelica

Claiming origin in 1586 in Germany, the modern international organization known as the Order Militia Curcifera Evangelica (OMCE) was started in 1990, and has a strong esoteric element to its mission. It's a nondenominational order and has strong ties to Rosicrucianism (see the nearby sidebar). This should be no surprise — it was founded by Gary L. Spenser, who was at one time the Grand Imperator of the Ancient Mystical Order Rosae Crucis, one of the largest Rosicrucian orders in the world. Open to both men and women, the OMCE has priories in the United States, Canada, Australia, Brazil, the Caribbean, the United Kingdom, Sweden, Norway, Greece, and Singapore. (Go to www.omcesite.org for more information.)

Rosicrucians

Any time you stick your toe in the water of fraternal and esoteric groups, the two that appear over and over again are the Freemasons and the Rosicrucians. We discuss the Freemasons in Chapter 8, but it's worth knowing about the Rosicrucians as well.

Esoteric comes from the Greek word *esôterikos,* meaning "inner," and Rosicrucianism is a legendary order dedicated to the study of the esoteric, or inner knowledge. The term itself comes from the symbol of a rose and cross, a longtime symbol of Christ.

The legend of the first Rosicrucians first appeared in three books published in the early 1600s in Germany: *Fama_Fraternitatis* (1614), *Confessio Fraternitatis* (1615), and *Chymical Wedding of Christian Rosenkreutz* (1616). Without trying to get an argument started among true believers, we can tell you that the probable author of at least the last work — and probably all of them — was a German theologian named Johann Valentin Andreae. In it, the story of the order's mythical founder, Christian Rosenkreutz, is recounted. According to the legend, Rosenkreutz traveled the Middle East during the 1400s and studied esoteric knowledge under the tutelage of the greatest sages and mystics. He returned to Europe and founded the Rosicrucian Order to bring about the reformation of the world. The order was supposed to

be limited to just eight members, who traveled the globe in search of knowledge and were supposed to return every year to share what they had found. According to the legend, the order disappeared, but it was reborn in the 1600s, not coincidentally with the publication of the three important books about them.

Rosicrucianism in its various incarnations incorporates alchemy, hermeticism, astrology, and spiritual healing, with a special fondness for ancient Egyptian teachings. The modern Rosicrucians use alchemy as a symbolic lesson for taking the baser aspects of man and, through spiritual alchemy, perfecting the soul, just as the ancient alchemists labored to turn base metals into gold.

It's a strange thing about esoteric societies: The vast majority of them have been riddled with breaks, schisms, lawsuits among the leaders, fights among the faithful, and a general clash of largish egos. The story of the Rosicrucians since about 1700 has been no exception. Over the years, there have been a wide variety of Rosicrucian groups, but the largest and best known is the Ancient Mystical Order Rosae Crucis (AMORC), founded in 1915 by Harvey Spencer Lewis. Its headquarters today are in Rosicrucian Park in San Jose, California, which is noted for its Egyptian Museum and planetarium.

Ordo Supremus Militaris Templi Hierosolymitani

This order's name is taken from the Latin, and it means "Sovereign Military Order of the Temple of Jerusalem." The particular group was founded in 1804 in Paris, and today is a nondenominational, Christian chivalric organization.

Ordo Supremus Militaris Templi Hierosolymitani (OSMTH) is one of the few modern Templar groups that, at least until recently, claimed a direct descent from the medieval knights, by way of the Larmenius Charter (see Chapter 7).

OSMTH long alleged that a continuous line of Grand Masters continued to meet in secret for four centuries. In 1705, in France, a group of noblemen elected Phillip duc d'Orleans as the new Grand Master of the order; he revived it publicly as a "secular order of chivalry." Having Phillip as the head of the order lent it great prestige; he became the Regent of France and held this position until his death in 1723. During the French Revolution, the order's then Grand Master, the Duke de Cosse Brissac, was executed, but the group reemerged in the 1800s and expanded between 1818 and 1841across France and into Great Britain, Germany, Belgium, Switzerland, Sweden, Brazil, India, and the United States.

In 1940, during World War II (WWII), the control of the order was centered in Belgium. When the Nazis occupied the country, the order's records were secretly sent to politically neutral Portugal. They were placed in the care of a Portuguese nobleman, Count Antonio Campello Pinto de Sousa Fontes. You can't have a secret society very long before egos, schisms, and lawsuits get in the way, and this order is no exception. After the war, Fontes believed that the position of Grand Master had been transferred to him, but the surviving Belgian group disagreed. It wasn't long before suits and countersuits started flying, especially when Fontes died. Normal protocol would have demanded an election of a new Grand Master, but Fontes simply willed the position to his son. That seems to have been the final straw for the various pre-WWII priories around the world.

The result has been a half-century of arguments and court decisions. In the United States, a flurry of incorporating and trademarking ensued, and the order is known as the Sovereign Military Order of the Temple of Jerusalem, Inc. (You can find out more about the order at http://us.osmth.org.)

A competing, pro-Fontes organization in the United States is the Ordo Pauperum Commilitum Christi et Templi Solomonis, Equis Templi (www.knighttemplar.org).

The problem is in the rest of the world, where the groups each call themselves the exact same name. The pro-Fontes group — known informally as the Loyalists or OSMTH-Regency — is on one side. On the other side is a larger group that officially reformed in 1995; the new OSMTH (www.osmth.org) is actually an umbrella organization of approximately 5,000 members, with associations located in Austria, Canada, England and Wales, Finland, France, Germany, Italy, Norway, Scotland, Serbia, and the United States.

Ordo Novi Templi

In the years leading up to World War I (WWI), there was a fascination in Germany and Austria with Viking paganism, as anyone who has sat through all 16 hours of Richard Wagner's *Der Ring des Nibelungen* four-part opera trilogy can attest. Heroic tales of Germanic gods, dwarves, mythical creatures, cryptic *runes* (symbols), and magic rings didn't start with Peter Jackson and the *Lord of the Rings* (or with J. R. R. Tolkien, for that matter) — Wagner is where Tolkien got the idea in the first place. And in turn, Wagner got it from the writings of Guido von List.

Between about 1890 and 1935, two Austrians garnered a huge interest in these Nordic legends with their writings: Guido von List and Jörg Lanz von Liebenfels. List himself was a follower of a Russian-born mystic, magician, and esoteric author, Madame Helena Petrovna Blavatsky, and her theories of *theosophy,* which blended a whole raft of Eastern philosophy, Hinduism, Buddhism, spiritualism, and mystical parlor tricks together with her own arrogant ideas about racial superiority.

List salted in his own mix of worship of the old Norse god Wotan, along with tales of the magical effects of 1st-century German and Scandinavian inscriptions called *runes* (the swastika and the dual lightning-bolt symbol adopted by the Nazi SS are both examples of runes). List believed that a secret ancient Aryan priesthood had developed this esoteric knowledge.

He eventually amassed a large following of fans, and a Guido von List Society actually formed before WWI, with a fairly impressive membership list of prestigious and famous people. One of those fans was Adolf Josef Lanz, another Vienna student of the occult. Like List, Lanz had been born a Catholic, and he had even become a Cistercian monk for a while as a young man. In truth, Lanz remained captivated by the ritual and history of the Catholic Church, especially in its medieval days.

Lanz didn't have much use for List's Wotan worship and his fanciful mythology of Germany's glorious past, but he was very interested in List's theories about ancient, secret knowledge of runes, magic, racial purity, and esotericism. The difference was, Lanz didn't need some silly nonsense about Viking gods. He knew exactly who those secret Aryan priests were: They were Knights Templar.

In 1907, Lanz founded the *Ordo Novi Templi* (Order of the New Temple), in the Castle Werfenstein, overlooking the Danube, flying a flag that included both the fleur-de-lis and the swastika, a rune symbolic of power, many years before it was adopted as the symbol of the Nazi Party. Lanz tinkered with List's ideas and developed what he termed *Ariosophy,* which he applied to his new form of chivalric knighthood. This Aryan philosophy was a variation on Darwin's survival of the fittest, applied to human beings; Lanz was especially contemptuous of Christian compassion for what he termed the "weak and inferior." Lanz believed that a race could only wind up at the top of the heap of civilization if it dispensed with its underprivileged citizens and unsatisfactory racial types through arrest, abortion, sterilization, or starvation, while encouraging the breeding of an ever-improving "master race." He promoted his theory in a magazine called *Ostara,* and it became popular throughout Germany and Austria.

The Ordo Novi Templi seemed to be more overtly directed to political ambitions than engaging in racial purity experiments. It supported the Serbian secret society, the Black Hand, a group made up of military officers who assassinated, among others, Archduke Ferdinand in 1914, the action that set off WWI. And it was a key supporter of the Austrian National Socialist Party in the 1930s. Curiously, when Adolph Hitler came to power, the Ordo Novi Templi was one of the first groups to be outlawed by the Nazis, in spite of its founder's clearly like-minded theories and the order's support of fascism. Even so, the Nazi Party didn't mind heroic depictions of Hitler himself as a heroic crusading knight (see Figure 9-1). And Hitler's head of the SS, Heinrich Himmler, had visions of the SS as an elite knightly order, like the Templars and the Teutonic Knights (see Chapter 15).

Figure 9-1: Hitler as a crusading knight. *The Standard Bearer (Der Bannertrager),* 1938, by Hubert Lanzinger.

Erich Lessing / Art Resource, NY

Ordo Militia Templi

Formed in 1979, this order is headquartered in Siena, Italy, in a small complex of 12th-century Templar buildings collectively known as the Castle of the Magione. Originally, it was started as a program for Catholic Scouts, but it has developed into an adult organization, made up of several hundred members around the world. Ordo Militia Templi is a Roman Catholic lay order, whose purpose is to promote the Catholic faith by taking strict vows and following the spirit of Templar monastic knighthood.

They appear to be part of a "traditionalist" movement within the Catholic Church, and they celebrate the mass using the pre–Vatican II Latin liturgy. This order is open to both men and women, but be aware that their regimen is very demanding — in 2005, there were just four members in the United States. (The U.S. Web site of Ordo Militia Templi is at `www.militiatempli.org`.)

Chivalric Martinist Order

The Chivalric Martinist Order (`http://interfaithinstitute.cqhost.net/ChivalricMartinistOrder.html`) is a relatively new order, but its origins touch on a group of Gnostic (see Chapter 5) and esoteric studies collectively known as Martinism (see the "Martinism" sidebar in this chapter). This order initiates its candidates into a Christian knighthood whose philosophy comprises Christian, Gnostic, hermetic, and Rosicrucian beliefs. It is open to both men and women.

Order of the Solar Temple

The name of this group may ring a bell with you, and not a pleasant one. The modern group seems to have come from a 1984 schism (there's that word again) from an earlier order formed in 1952 in France. Its principal founders were a jeweler and clockmaker named Joseph Di Mambro, and a homeopathic doctor named Luc Jouret.

Di Mambro and Jouret were living in Geneva, Switzerland, and both were students of esotericism. They convinced the members of the new order of the Solar Temple that they were both reincarnations of 14th-century Knights Templar. (Why does everyone who claims to be reincarnated say they're former nobility? Don't fifth-century shoe cobblers or 19th-century chimney sweeps ever get reincarnated?) Even better, they claimed that Di Mambro's daughter Emmanuelle was the product of a virgin birth.

Martinism

Louis-Claude de Saint-Martin was an 18th-century French mystic. Though in the United States his influences are largely unknown to anyone but the most dedicated student of obscure knowledge, Martinism pervades many esoteric societies across Europe, and is beginning to make inroads in the United States. It's important to our discussion here because several organizations claim both Templar and Martinist influences.

Born in 1743, Louis-Claude de Saint-Martin was a French nobleman. He was briefly imprisoned during the French Revolution but was released because local authorities wanted him to become a schoolteacher. This was during the period of the Age of Enlightenment, when the application of the scientific method was applied to virtually everything in the world, including religion. The Enlightenment philosophers turned away from the superstitions of the past, along with notions of astrology, alchemy, and mysticism. Saint-Martin disagreed with this approach, as most of his contemporary students of esotericism did. In many ways, the wave of interest in spiritualism, magic, and similar "mystic arts" that swept across the Western world in the 1800s and early 1900s was a reaction against the Enlightenment, with the implied message that not everything in the world could be explained scientifically.

Louis-Claude became a student of an 18th-century kabbalist named Joachim Martinez Pasquales, and later translated several obscure 17th-century works by a German mystic, Jacob Böhme, into French. Using them as inspiration, Saint-Martin developed his own philosophy about Life, the Universe, and Everything, called the Way of the Heart. Essentially, Böhme had theorized that in order to achieve a state of grace, man had to fall away from God and do

battle with the demons and evil angels who caused the sins of the world. Only after spiritual victory over these evils could man again return to God's good graces. There is nothing new under the sun — the Gnostics and the Cathars got slaughtered by the Inquisition for these kinds of "heresies." The only difference was that the Protestant Reformation of the ensuing years had blunted the Catholic Church's monopoly on judging who was a heretic and who wasn't.

Saint-Martin's discussion circles became popular, and eventually more formalized as an organization called the Society of Friends. His writings were signed by the enigmatic name of the Unknown Philosopher. Saint-Martin objected to the prevailing custom of most esoteric societies of the period that prohibited women from joining, and he allowed female members to have equal membership status. After his death in 1803, similar societies began to spread, largely through the efforts of an enthusiastic supporter named Gerard Encausse (who went by the name of Papus), and there was much crossover between the usual suspects of esotericism: Rosicrucians, Freemasons, Gnostics, and these new Martinists. In 1888, Encausse formed a mystery school called the Ordere Martinist, and by 1900, there were chapters in a dozen countries, with hundreds of members.

WWI killed off the principal leaders of the order, and its central organization dissolved. Several splinter groups supported an attempt to restore the kings of France. Others became enamored with a strange movement called *Synarchy*, an attempt to rule European countries by means of secret societies. Sounding a lot like the modern kooky conspiracy theories of Lyndon LaRouche, Synarchie was promoted by an occult mystic named Alexandre Saint-Yves d'Alveydre, who

(continued)

(continued)

claimed to get telepathic messages from Shangri-La, directing his actions for world takeover. A small clot of enthusiastic Martinists got excited at the prospects of taking over the governments of Europe, and formed the *Ordre Martiniste Synarchie*. Obviously, it didn't work, and Saint-Martin himself would have been somewhat appalled. In response, three of the surviving old guard from the late 1800s got together and formed the *Ordre Martiniste Traditionale* (Traditional Martinist Order), in an effort to restore the group to Saint-Martin's "Way of the Heart."

WWII all but destroyed Martinist societies in Europe, as the Nazis imprisoned or executed most members of so-called "secret societies" that they hadn't created themselves. The Traditional Martinist Order had made its way to the United States through Rosicrucian groups in the 1930s, and it survives today. The Internet has done much to spread Saint-Martin's philosophies, and new groups have appeared recently along with the traditional ones. They cover a broad range of philosophies and disciplines, with some incorporating Rosicrucian influences, some borrowing from the largely Memphis-Mizraim branch of Freemasonry that has been deemed irregular by the majority of the mainstream Masonic world, and some simply adhering strictly to Saint-Martin's philosophies.

The story was that Emmanuelle was, in fact, a "cosmic child," who would lead the members of the Solar Temple to a secret planet in orbit around the star Sirius (better known as the "Dog Star"). But in order to get there, there was one small step that Solar Temple members would have to undergo: a cataclysmic death by fire at the end of the world.

The Solar Temple was a strange mélange of Protestantism, Rosicrucianism, plagiarized Masonic rituals, UFO-ology, New Age silliness, and even a little homeopathic medicine tossed in for good measure. They ultimately aimed a little high for their goals — the ultimate reunification of Christianity, Judaism, and Islam to prepare for the second coming of Christ.

Unfortunately, the real goal seemed to be to lavishly line the pockets of Di Mambro and Jouret, who charged gobs of cash for initiation fees, regalia, robes, swords, medals, and of course, advancement to the higher levels of secret knowledge. The group moved to Quebec, Canada, and Di Mambro started investing in real estate around the world, amassing new "temples" to conduct services in luxurious vacation hotspots. Meanwhile back in Quebec, construction began on a massive, concrete-lined bunker to prepare for the coming End of the World festivities. Jouret began amassing a stockpile of weapons, just in case, insisting that, in The End, only Quebec would be saved from total destruction.

The trouble with doomsday cults is that, sooner or later, you have to put up or shut up. Humans are, by nature, impatient. And if you don't produce an apocalyptic cataclysm that consumes the Earth's vast majority of sinners and saves the small clot of the faithful in a timely manner, your members quickly get restless. Likewise, Solar Temple members began to walk away when the global ball of fire and the plans for their trip to Sirius both failed to materialize. The founders had to do something. And they did.

In October of 1994, Di Mambro announced that an infant born in the group's Quebec compound was, in fact, the antichrist, and ordered it killed. The baby was stabbed repeatedly with a wooden stake. A few days later, Di Mambro and 12 followers reenacted the Last Supper, and what followed made headlines around the world. Solar Temple followers in Switzerland and Canada were found dead, victims of ritualistic mass murder-suicides. Fifteen inner-circle members (referred to as the "Awakened") committed suicide with poison, 30 (the "Immortals") were shot in the head or smothered, and another 8 (the "Traitors") died in other various ways. Electronic timing devices set fire to the temple, so the members would undergo the much-promised cataclysmic death by fire. Shortly afterward, another 48 members were discovered in an underground Swiss Solar Temple and a French mountain chalet, dressed in ceremonial robes, and drugged or shot. Many had placed plastic garbage bags over their heads as a symbol of the ecological disaster that the Earth would find itself in once the virtuous Solar Temple members had departed for Sirius. In the coming years, several similar murder/suicide attempts by Solar Temple members were thwarted, all around the solar solstices and equinoxes. In all, 78 deaths were attributed to the cult between 1994 and 1997.

Step right up and be a Templar!

Templar Knighthood is now on sale — and easily purchased on your Visa or MasterCard — in the Hereditary Knights Templar of Britannia, a division of Charter Gallant & Company! Based in England, prices range from $150 to $10,000 to purchase titles like Sir, Knight, Lord, Baron, Viscount, Count, Marquis, or Earl, along with a wide assortment of rings, swords, and robes!

This group is run by a character named Gary Martin Beaver, who has become notorious in Britain for selling fake titles of nobility. It is only one of several companies that Beaver has started over the years, and he has a wide variety of impressive sounding titles: Lord Beaver of Newport; His Serene Excellency, the Magistral Prior of Notre Dame St. Mary of Magdalene; the Chevalier Baron de Richecourt, KGCNS, KtJ; the Marquis of Aulnois; and the Most Reverend Archbishop Gary, Hugues II.

The purchase of European titles has been a scam for centuries, and the Internet makes it that much simpler to perpetrate. The British Embassy in Washington, D.C., has become so weary with questions about bogus nobility titles that it has placed a warning on its Web site, stating: "The sale of British titles is prohibited by the Honours (Prevention of Abuses) Act, 1925," and that such titles are, in fact, meaningless. With very few exceptions, titles must be inherited or earned. And while plunking some lordly prefix or suffix to your name on a business card can certainly look spiffy, it won't snag you a special table in a restaurant, early boarding on a plane, or a Get Out of Jail Free card if you get caught driving like a jerk. True knights, lords, dukes, viscounts, and the rest do have a place in British and European society, but the establishments and institutions that deal with them on a daily basis are hip to the bogus nobility racket and are unimpressed by rubes with store-bought baronage. Bottom line: They're expensive and of little use, apart from trying to pick up gullible dates in Monte Carlo bars.

The group is believed to survive today with somewhere between 140 and 500 members. Its purported leader, a Swiss musician and conductor named Michael Tabachnik, has been arrested and tried several times for connections to a criminal organization. He was most recently acquitted in December 2006.

Ordo Templi Orientis

The Ordo Templi Orientis (translated as both "Order of the Oriental Templars" and "Order of the Temple of the East") is another organization with its roots in pre-WWI Germany. The OTO exists today but has gone through several phases. Today it claims approximately 3,000 members in almost 60 countries, although the bulk of its membership is in the United States.

The OTO's connection to the Knights Templars is tenuous at best — a few of its degrees are based on Masonic tales of the Templars, but the OTO is most definitely not associated with Freemasonry at all, and barely with the Templars. Nevertheless, the OTO is an enthusiastic group, and its founders were among some of the most influential promoters of esoteric, spiritualistic, and mystical movements beginning in the late 1800s. (You can find more information on the modern OTO at their Web site, www.oto-usa.org.)

Knights But Not Templars

Organizations that espouse chivalric ideals, or that claim descent from medieval chivalric orders, are not all derived from the Knights Templars. Many such groups exist around the world, and listing them all here would be impossible. We include a few just to differentiate between those that are Templar and those that sound or seem similar.

Equestrian Order of the Holy Sepulchre of Jerusalem

This Catholic order traces its origins to knights who kept constant vigil and protected the Church of the Holy Sepulchre in Jerusalem during the Crusades. First chartered in A.D. 1122, they are authorized by the Vatican, and they sponsor pilgrimages to the Holy Land, Rome, and other sacred sites.

The present order was resurrected in 1847 by Pope Pius IX, who authored the oath taken by its members to "reject modernism" and accept unconditionally all teachings of the Church. The order owns the Hotel Columbus (the former palace of Pope Julius II, the Palazzo dei Penitenzieri) in Rome, both as their headquarters and as a source of income. (You can find more information about them on their Web site, www.holysepulchre.net.)

Order of the Grail

This organization has undergone several name changes over the years. Known variously as the Rosicrucian and Military Order of the Sacred Grail and its French name, Les Chevaliers de la Rose et de La Croix, the Order of the Grail is a Rosicrucian/Martinist order (see the "Martinism" sidebar, earlier in this chapter). Open to both men and women, the order promotes the study of esoteric Christian teachings, and promotes the traditional chivalric values of integrity, morality, and courage. Although its religious leanings are more to Gnostic and hermetic traditions, knights and dames of the order can be Roman Catholic, Orthodox, or Protestant. (For more information on the Order of the Grail, check out their Web site at www.orderofthegrail.org.)

Sovereign Military Order of Malta

The Knights Hospitaller (see Chapter 3) survived long after the Templars were disbanded. In fact, they exist today and can trace a direct line of descent back to their formation in A.D. 1087. Like the Templars, they were an order of warrior monks, charged with the duty of protecting pilgrims. And like the rest of the Christian forces during the Crusades, the Hospitallers were forced to withdraw from the Holy Land in the face of defeat. The Hospitallers were granted the property of the Templars after their excommunication and dissolution in 1312.

Retreat to Rhodes

When the Hospitallers retreated, they took up residence on the Greek island of Rhodes, after a brief stop at Cyprus, in 1309. Their first mission in Jerusalem had been the administration of a hospital, hence their name. After they moved to Cyprus, and then to Rhodes, their mission changed, along with their name. They became the Knights of Rhodes and turned far more militaristic. They were sovereign over the island and, thus, were something of a constant target for Barbary pirates and Islamic forces, who attacked them repeatedly over the next centuries.

Move to Malta

In 1522, the Sultan Suleiman (Arabic for Solomon) led an invasion of 200,000 troops against 7,000 defending Knights of Rhodes. The knights held off the siege in their walled city for six months, before finally surrendering. The few suvivors were allowed to retreat to Sicily, and in 1530, they were given the island of Malta by King Charles V of Spain. He hadn't done them any big favor — Malta was a sitting duck between Libya and Sicily in the middle of the Mediterranean

Sea, alone, isolated, and nowhere near any helpful neighbors. Again the order changed its name, to the Knights of Malta.

The Ottoman Turks weren't noted for their hospitality as far as Christian warrior monks were concerned. Sulieman in particular wasn't exactly pleased that the Knights had simply changed their address. So he attacked the island and its new landlords in 1565. This time the Knights prevailed in the face of another huge force, in what was a humiliating defeat for the Ottomans. The Knights' fortifications still stand today, and they ruled the island until Napoleon came along in 1798. Stopping off on his way to Egypt, Napoleon asked to make a pit stop at the island. When his ships were in the harbor, in a show of supremely bad manners, he blasted away at his astonished hosts. Worse, Napoleon looted the treasure of the Knights before sailing on to go plunder Egypt. The French occupied the island until a revolt in 1880, backed by England. It was an English protectorate until achieving independence in 1964.

The Hospitallers had vast holdings across Europe and into Russia, partially because the Church gave them so much Templar property. As a result, they were a force to be reckoned with. Unfortunately for the order, Protestantism began to chip away at their assets. King Henry VIII dissolved the order in England and confiscated their substantial property. As German and Scandinavian states converted to Protestantism, the Knights in those areas reconstituted themselves as a Protestant order. And the Knights briefly found a staunch ally in Russia in the late 1700s.

The order today

The Sovereign Military Order of Malta (or their proper name, the Sovereign Military Hospitaller Order of St. John of Jerusalem of Rhodes and of Malta) survives today as a modern Catholic order of knighthood. All officers of the order must be of noble birth. What makes them unusual is that, even though they no longer hold territory in Malta or anywhere else, the order considers itself to be *sovereign,* a legal term that sort of makes them a kingdom with no kingdom. The Knights own two buildings in Rome, and they are exempt from local laws, much like a foreign embassy. If you're standing in either the Palazzo Malta or the Villa Malta, you're technically on foreign soil. Today, the Knights largely engage in humanitarian and charitable work, and have "permanent observer status" within the United Nations, along with diplomatic relations with 93 countries. They maintain a close relationship with the Vatican, and the pope appoints representatives and clergy to the order. Priories in the United States are located in New York; Washington, D.C.; and San Francisco. There are more than 25 U.S. chapters with approximately 1,700 knights and dames of the order. There are more than 11,000 members worldwide. (You can find more information at their Web site, www.orderofmalta.org.)

Most Venerable Order of St. John of Jerusalem

The Order of Malta was dissolved in England by King Henry VIII when he pitched the Catholics out of the country in a fit of pique over the Church's objection to divorce. The Knights of Malta survived elsewhere, but they disappeared in England.

In 1826, a group of French noblemen were seeking mercenaries to fight for Greek independence from the Ottoman Empire. They were actually a branch of the surviving Order of Malta, and their motives for helping Greece was to seek a new homeland for the order in Rhodes, because Napoleon had pitched them off of Malta 30 years before. They formed an English branch of their order to raise money and men for the cause. But the Greeks managed to win their revolution without help from these new Knights. The English priory survived as little more than a club in London, with its headquarters in the Old Jerusalem Tavern in Clerkenwell, the area that had been the original London headquarters of the Knights Hospitaller in the 1100s.

Over the years, several attempts were made to jumpstart a new order based on the Knights of Malta, but without the Catholic connection. In keeping with the Knights Hospitallers' original mission from the Holy Land, in 1877 they formed the St. John Ambulance Association. This was the period of the Industrial Revolution, and accidents were fast outpacing disease as the principal cause of death. The association took on the job of training the public in techniques of first aid and issuing certification to graduates of their classes. They published manuals on the subject and provided first-aid supplies, becoming successful enough in a short time to be able to build a new headquarters and storehouse at St. John's Gate.

In 1882, the order established an eye hospital in Jerusalem, which still operates today. Five years later, they organized the St. John's Ambulance Brigade in London. In 1888, the order was declared a Royal Order of Chivalry by Queen Victoria, and the reigning king or queen of England is considered to be the official head of the order.

The Catholic Order of Malta refused to recognize the Protestant English order until 1963, and they became part of an alliance that jointly recognized five Orders of St. John from around the world as the legitimate heirs to the traditions and titles of the original Knights Hospitaller born in the days of the Crusades. (You can find more information on the Most Venerable Order of St. John of Jerusalem at their Web site, www.orderofstjohn.org.)

Deutscher Orden (Teutonic Knights)

The Teutonic Knights (see Chapter 3) remained a strong military force long after the Crusades slipped into history. Until the 1500s, they held lands along the Baltic Sea in Prussia, Estonia, Latvia, and Poland. Eventually, the Teutonic States became the Duchy of Prussia, and Teutonic Knights were a force to be reckoned with up through the 1700s in wars between German states and the Ottoman Empire. Teutonic Knights were often called upon to serve as commanders for mercenary forces by Habsburg kings in Austria. The order was officially ordered dissolved by Napoleon Bonaparte in 1809, although the order continued to survive in Austria until 1923.

In 1929, the order was reorganized as a strictly religious group, but when the Nazis took control of Austria in 1938, the Knights again disappeared. That didn't stop Hitler and his propaganda ministers from using images and legends of the old Teutonic Knights as inspiration for their new army of greater Germany, but the Nazis had no use for secret societies or any other sort of order that harkened back to an earlier time that they did not control — which meant that the Teutonic Knights were a terrific group to emulate, as long as no one really *was* one.

Nevertheless, the order once again remade itself after WWII ended, and, like the Knights of Malta, became a charitable, international organization, with a special concentration on clinics for German communities in foreign countries. After a financial crisis in 1990, the order was reduced to just 1,000 or so members, which includes 100 priests and 200 nuns. They are known today simply as the Deutscher Orden (German Order). (You can find more on them at their Web site, www.deutscher-orden.at.)

Order of Christ

The Order of Christ occupies a curious position in Templar lore and history; we discuss its origins in Chapter 5. Its origin in Portugal as the Templars with a different name on the door after their excommunication and dissolution is well known. Portugal's King Denis had simply informed the pope that the Templar property in his kingdom had merely been on loan and that it really belonged to him. The Templars changed their name and went on, business as usual.

In the 1700s, the Order of Christ seemed to pass out of the control of the Portuguese monarchy and into the hands of the Vatican. The argument went that the Portuguese were given the right to bestow the order in the 1300s by papal decree, and what the pope giveth, he mayeth also taketh awayeth. Even today, the Portuguese dispute Rome's control of the order; they went to far as to arrest anyone caught wearing the medals of the order who had not received them from the king.

Nevertheless, the Order of Christ is considered the supreme order of chivalry bestowed by the Catholic Church. It is seldom awarded (the last known instance was in 1987) and is reserved only for European heads of state who are Catholics. The last holder of the order died in 1997, and it is unclear whether the award will survive in the future.

Teetotaling Templars of Temperance

America's great experiment with the prohibition of alcohol was not a rousing success, but it was a long time in the making. The temperance movement in the United States stretches back into the early 1800s, and for some reason, a few organizers believed the Templars were just the group to emulate. At the height of the original Templars' power, there was an expression making the rounds concerning someone who was a slave to the grape as "drinking like a Templar." So it is with no little irony that at least two teetotaling Templar groups popped up in the 19th century to carry the banner of temperance.

Templars of Honor and Temperance

A group was formed in 1845 that would eventually be come to known as the Templars of Honor and Temperance to fight the scourge of alcohol. Actually created as a more ritually elaborate branch of an earlier group called the Sons of Temperance, they were organized in a manner similar to Freemason lodges, They initiated new candidates into the order using a ceremonial ritual, conferred a series of six degrees, wore Masonic-like collars and aprons, and had secret passwords and handshakes. They have not survived in modern times.

International Order of Good Templars

In 1851, an unrelated group was formed in Castor Hollow, New York, calling itself the Order of Good Templars. Like the Templars of Honor and Temperance (see the preceding section), they had a similar mission to battle the sale, use, and abuse of booze. Their name would seem to imply that they were distancing themselves from "bad Templars," and they may very well have been reacting to post-meeting drinking parties of the Masonic Knights Templar. They also fashioned themselves after the Masonic lodges, required collars and aprons, and conferred three degrees on their members.

The Templar "Superfine Small Car"

It's a fair bet to say that when you think of the Knights Templar, you probably envision fearsome guys with swords and lances riding on powerful, snorting, majestic steeds, and not tooting around in 4-cylinder, wooden-spoked, open roadsters. But in 1917, that's just what appeared on the market in America.

Born in Lakewood, Ohio, just outside of Cleveland, the Templar Motors Company came into being. For reasons known only to its founders, they chose to name their upstart company after the order, and adopted the Maltese Cross (see Chapter 4) as their logo. WWI was raging in Europe, and the new car factory was almost immediately pressed into service manufacturing war munitions. Nevertheless, a few of the company's first cars rolled off the assembly line, and they were unlike other cars on the road at that time.

From the start, the Templars used an innovative 4-cylinder engine design that was more fuel-efficient than most cars of the day, and for the size of the engine, its 43-horsepower output was impressive (by comparison, the 1911 Model T Ford was rated at 22 horsepower. A modern-day Ford Escort manages about 110 horsepower, while a new Corvette cranks out almost 350 horsepower). It's overhead valve design inspired its name, the Templar Vitalic Top-Valve Motor.

Templar Motors offered a two-passenger roadster and four- and five-passenger touring cars, priced between $1,985 and $2,255, ($33,000 to $39,000 in 2007 dollars), at almost four times the price that Henry Ford was hawking Model Ts for.

The Templars were truly luxury cars, sporting 27 coats of paint, wooden-spoked wheels, an electric horn, an onboard tire pump, a searchlight, a clock, a locking ignition switch, a windshield wiper, a dashboard light, a complete set of tools, and a unique "neverleak" convertible top. The car also had a special outside compartment that housed a compass and Kodak camera. The company's advertising called it "The Superfine Small Car."

In 1920, a Templar Sportette driven by Erwin "Cannonball" Baker (who went on to be the first commissioner of NASCAR) set a series of speed records, including driving from New York to Los Angeles in 4 days, 5 hours, and 43 minutes.

The Templar cars were successful and became the #15 car company out of more than 40 operating in the United States at the time. Between 1917 and 1924, 6,000 Templars were sold by more than 160 dealers. Unfortunately, their history would be similar to the Knights who were their namesake. After a brief period of notable success, they ended — literally — in flames. Financial mismanagement and a catastrophic fire at their Lakewood plant finally killed off the company by 1924.

Templar Motors is not the only company to use the symbolism of the order. More than 1,900 businesses in the United States alone have the word *Templar* as part of their name. And the next time you're in the grocery, look for King Arthur Flour. Founded in 1790, it's the oldest flour company in the United States. Its label depicts a Templar knight, carrying a banner with a red cross.

Good Templars took a lifelong pledge to abstain from consuming or selling alcohol. Members were prohibited from any kind of activity that promoted the alcoholic-beverage business, including renting their property to purveyors of hooch, selling apples to anyone who might use them to make hard cider, or even delivering coal to a distillery.

The order quickly grew in popularity and was dedicated to the swelling temperance movement that was sweeping the United States. By 1865, there were 60,000 members. Just four years later, with the end of the Civil War, the membership swelled to more than 400,000, and they helped to form the independent Prohibition Party.

In the 1860s, the order spread to Britain, and by 1900, it had expanded worldwide. In the United States, they became especially popular within Scandinavian immigrant communities, and the order's lodges became social centers for Swedes and Norwegians fresh off the boat.

The organization still exists today as the International Organization of Good Templars, and describes itself as the largest international nongovernmental organization working in the field of temperance. It dropped the Masonic-like ceremonies and regalia in the 1970s, apart from initiating new candidates. In spite of its American origin, it is headquartered today in Sweden, and has expanded its mission in more than 40 countries to fight substance abuse of all kinds. (You can find more information on the order at its Web site, www.iogt.org.)

Part IV
Templars and the Grail

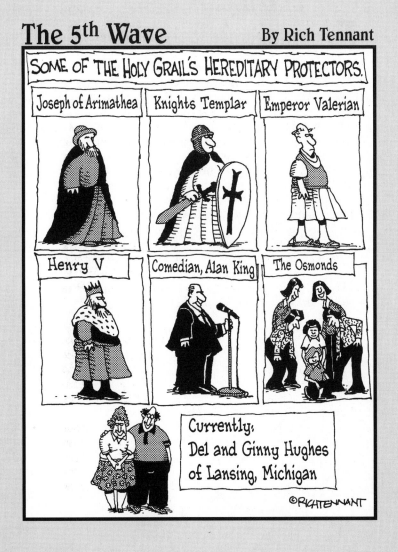

SOME OF THE HOLY GRAIL'S HEREDITARY PROTECTORS.

Joseph of Arimathea | Knights Templar | Emperor Valerian

Henry V | Comedian, Alan King | The Osmonds

Currently:
Del and Ginny Hughes
of Lansing, Michigan

©RICHTENNANT

In this part . . .

The Knights Templar, both in myth and reality, are tied fast to the core myth of knighthood — the Holy Grail. This part explores the Grail myths of the West, the tales of knights and their ladies fair, and their connection to the Templars. Chapter 10 looks at the origins of the Grail tales and the myths of King Arthur, and how the Templars became intertwined with them. From there Chapter 11 leaps back to the 21st century, into the brand-new saga of the Templars that has taken the world by storm, in the wake of the feverish Grail-mania brought on by *The Da Vinci Code*. It lays out the evidence for this new Grail legend in a bloodline of Christ, beginning in the 1st century B.D.B. (Before Dan Brown) with the brave few who carefully and cautiously put forward the notion that Jesus might have been married. From there, we hit the open road for the South of France, to the mysterious hill town of Rennes-le-Château, in order to blow away a little of the pixie dust and examine the possible truths behind the many mysteries of the land that the Templars called home.

Chapter 10

The Templars and the Quest for the Holy Grail

Ask anyone on the street today what the Holy Grail is, and most will tell you it was the cup used by Jesus at the Last Supper. Readers of *The Da Vinci Code* may have a different answer for you, but most people would agree that the Last Supper reference is probably the right one.

The many Grail legends over the centuries have always told the story of a quest by a hero who must prove his worthiness before he can possess the Grail's powers or secrets. But, curiously, the Grail hasn't always been seen as a cup — or even as holy, for that matter.

The Grail legend first appeared in the 12th century as part of a larger collection of heroic tales about a young, inexperienced knight named Percival, one of the knights of King Arthur's mythical kingdom of Camelot. Although they came from French sources, the stories were set in Wales or Britain. Though the fables of King Arthur and the Holy Grail are well known today, they took a long, circuitous route throughout history, and the Grail itself has represented many things other than the cup used at the Last Supper.

This chapter is a whirlwind exploration of the different theories and metaphors that have made up the many myths of the quest for the Holy Grail.

The Holy Grail: A Ten-Century Quest

It is in Luke 22:14–20, at the Last Supper with Jesus and his apostles, that the cup is first mentioned. It appears not only in the Gospel of Luke, but in Matthew and Mark as well. In these three gospels lie the only biblical references to what became the legendary Grail — either the cup that held the wine or, perhaps, the dish that held the Passover lamb.

No further reference to either of these famous pieces of dinnerware appears anywhere outside of the biblical record until an eighth-century hermit had a vision and wrote it down in a book called *Gradale* in A.D. 717. Even that book has not survived the centuries, and we only know about it because it was described by a Cistercian monk named Helinandus in the 13th century.

The medieval Latin term *gradale* meant "shallow dish," and it was translated into medieval French as *greal, graal,* or *greel* (spelling and pronunciation was a more fleeting, transitive, and mushy concept in those days). Authors Michael Bagient, Richard Leigh, and Henry Lincoln played a word game with the medieval French terms *San Greal* (Holy Grail) and *Sang Real* (Royal Blood) in their book, *Holy Blood, Holy Grail,* and the same ball was picked up and run with by Dan Brown in *The Da Vinci Code* (see Chapter 11).

The Grail itself took on a variety of guises over the centuries, and not all of them were necessarily Christian in nature. In fact, not all of them have been a physical object. Here are some of the different versions of the Grail itself:

- **The cup or serving dish used by Jesus at the Last Supper prior to his arrest.**

- **A bowl or dish — possibly the same one from the Last Supper — used by Joseph of Arimathea to collect the blood of Jesus as he hung on the cross (or afterward in Jesus's tomb).** This Grail was said to have been taken by Joseph to Britain, where the Christian conversion of England began.

- **The *lapsit exillis*.** Wolfram von Eschenbach's popular epic, *Parzival,* describes the Grail as a stone or crystal that heals the sick, provides limitless food, and confers immortality. The Latin term is translated as "the stone from the heavens." Some have described it as a legendary jewel that fell from the crown of Satan while he battled the angels of heaven. Others have suggested that it was part of the stone that covered Jesus's tomb after the crucifixion.

- **The Philospher's Stone.** Since the *lapsit exillis* was a stone, some believe the Grail may be the "Philosopher's Stone," the illusive secret ingredient of alchemy during the Middle Ages. The Philosopher's Stone, if it were ever found, was supposed to allow the alchemist to transmute base metal into gold and allow the body to retard aging and prevent death.

✔ **The alabaster jar of ointment used by Mary of Bethany to anoint Jesus in the house of Simon the Leper in Matthew 26, Mark 14, and John 12.**

✔ **A different alabaster jar (or box) of scented oil that an unnamed women uses to anoint Jesus in the house of the Pharisee in Luke 7.**

✔ **The Virgin Mary.** For some, the Grail may not have been an object at all. Because the Virgin Mary, Jesus's mother, was the sacred "vessel" that had contained Christ before his birth, some hypothesize that the Grail was a metaphor for Mary.

✔ **Mary Magdalene.** The theory that Jesus may have been married to Mary Magdalene, that she came to France after the resurrection, and that she bore Christ's daughter has led some to speculate that the Grail refers to both Mary Magdalene and the long line of descendants from that marriage. Again, this is the concept of Jesus's alleged wife as a sacred vessel, or simply their bloodline, as the Grail. This is the central thesis to *The Da Vinci Code,* and we discuss it in detail in Chapter 13.

✔ **Secret knowledge.** In some versions of the story, the Grail becomes a metaphor for hidden, esoteric knowledge, and the knights who search for it are initiates who must purify themselves and become worthy enough to receive these secrets.

The Quest Begins

Most histories of the Grail myths begin with Chrétien de Troyes, a French troubadour in the 12th century. He was a storyteller who entertained courts in France and Flanders, and although his tales of the Grail are widely considered to have come from Celtic and other sources, Chrétien was the first to get them down in writing.

At the time of Chrétien de Troyes, some parallel concepts developed. The Crusades had started nearly a century before, so stories of crusading knights on a quest had become pretty common currency in the storytelling business. An important influence on him was his benefactress, Marie, Countess of Champagne, the daughter of French King Louis VII and Eleanor of Aquitaine. Eleanor's grandfather William IX, Duke of Aquitaine, was France's first troubadour. She is often credited with almost single-handedly creating the notion of "courtly love" and carrying it to France and then to England with her second marriage to King Henry II (see the "Courtly love" sidebar in this chapter).

Chrétien de Troyes

Chrétien de Troyes's story, *LeConte du Graal* (Story of the Grail), or *Perceval,* is where·the first tales of a knight in search of the Grail appear. He wrote, or dictated it, between 1181 and 1190, but he died before it was completed.

Courtly love

Courtly love (and we're not talking about the widow of Kurt Cobain and lead singer of Hole) was a concept that appeared in Europe in the 11th century. It was at the French court of the powerful Eleanor of Aquitaine that the concept of courtly love was born and reached its full flower, a tradition enthusiastically continued by her daughter, Marie. *Romance* in French means "song" or "ballad," and *roman* means "novel." Chrétian de Troyes may have been writing poetry, but in writing it down instead of singing or speaking it, he was really writing the first novel.

It is the stuff that fairy tales and epic poems were filled with. "Courtly love" generally occurred between a queen, princess, or other noble lady, and an admiring knight or troubadour. In its loftiest form, it was a chaste love affair from afar that was almost never consummated by a proper knight — although that wasn't *always* true, as in the tale of Sir Lancelot and King Arthur's wife, Queen Guinevere, a love that started as the courtly variety but ended in the bedroom and the destruction of a kingdom. But in the perfect situation, the knight gifted his lady with adoration, even if he knew he could never have her sexually. She was the symbol of all that was pure and noble in femininity. He performed heroic deeds,

engaged in tournaments, and embarked on quests in the hope of being found worthy by her. Whether she was married was immaterial, because the goal was rarely adultery.

The arranged marriages of the period were often loveless couplings, and everybody needs a little romance in their lives. Interestingly, others have speculated that courtly love was actually a Cathar-like concept — adoring women for a spiritual purpose, while shunning sexual gratification.

Courtliness became a synonym for *etiquette.* The point of all of this was that a knight attempted to improve himself morally, physically, and even spiritually, by suffering for this love unfulfilled. So in a sense, courtly love was a civilizing force on rough, boorish, and decidedly unsophisticated fighting men.

Unfortunately, the Church didn't much care for the idea. Faith was supposed to be the civilizing force in the world, and certainly not the unhealthy, hot-blooded hedonism of moping around over a married woman. Church fathers didn't see anything spiritually uplifting about it at all, and by the 13th century, they began to spread the word that courtly love was heretical. Killjoys.

Perceval and the Graal

Perceval is the son of a widow, raised by his mother in the forests of Wales, cut off from civilization. He is a complete innocent when the tale begins. Over the years, knights pass through the forest, and Perceval longs to be one of them. At last, he decides to leave home and join the court of King Arthur, over the protests of his mother. There, he is knighted and a young girl at the court foresees that he will achieve great deeds. He is mentored by Gornemant, and the young knight is a quick learner in combat skills. Unfortunately, he is not so quick at learning the other things required of a knight. Because Perceval was raised alone and isolated from the world, he is naive and a little dimwitted. Gornemant suggests that he not ask so many questions, in an effort to keep him from looking foolish.

Perceval sets out one day and discovers a wide, impassable stream, and a fisherman in a boat, who is known as the Fisher King. He invites Perceval to rest at a nearby castle that seems to appear out of nowhere. There, Perceval sees a curious ceremony. An old, crippled man is brought into the Great Hall in a bed. After speaking with Perceval for a while, a young woman enters with a sword in a lavishly decorated scabbard, which the old man presents as a gift to the young knight. A procession begins, and a servant enters the hall with a spear that drips blood from its tip. He is followed by a young girl with beautiful golden cup — a *graal.* In the cup is a single Eucharist. Perceval wants to ask about what he sees, but he recalls Gornemant's warnings to not make a fool of himself and decides to keep his mouth shut.

Perceval awakens the next morning to discover the castle deserted. As he rides away, a little miffed that he's been abandoned, the drawbridge slams shut behind him, and the castle disappears. Meanwhile, King Arthur has become concerned over his absence, and all the knights go in search of the young knight. When they find him, Arthur tells Perceval that his mother has died, stricken with grief over his departure. Perceval decides that he'll spend the rest of his life in search of battle and never stay more than one night in any place, until he can find the mysterious castle again. He vows to find out the secret of the bleeding lance and who it was that the Grail served.

Five years later, Perceval is a broken man who has lost his faith. He is confronted by a creepy old hag, who tells him that the old man in the castle was none other than his own uncle, and that he died. The reason he died and the castle disappeared is because he failed to ask his question, "Whom does the Grail serve?" If he had asked, he would have discovered that the old man was the father of the Fisher King, the castle's lord, and that the Grail served the Eucharist to him to sustain both him and the land around it.

From here, the story takes a "meanwhile back at the ranch" approach and follows the tale of Sir Gawain, Arthur's nephew. It briefly returns to Perceval, but Chrétien de Troyes died before it was completed, having created just 9,000 lines of his tale.

The Continuations

During this period, the overwhelming majority of people were illiterate. Chrétien de Troyes's story was probably dictated by him (there's a question as to whether he could read himself) and it was intended to be read aloud. Finished or not, his *Story of the Grail,* along with an earlier work, *Lancelot, the Knight of the Cart,* became incredibly popular.

Almost immediately after his death, four different authors came forward and added to the tale of Perceval, extending the storyline of Arthur's knights, the mysterious Fisher King, and, of course, Perceval himself. Known as the *Continuations,* these additions fleshed out the background of the Grail. One of these, *Manessier's Continuation,* has Perceval at last returning to the castle of the Fisher King, where he asks his questions and becomes the new king him-self, who possesses both the Grail and the Bleeding Lance. After seven years as king, Perceval wanders into the woods one day with the Grail and dies, taking it up to heaven.

Robert de Boron: The Grail becomes holy

In Chrétien de Troyes's version and its *Continuations,* the Grail isn't fully explained, and it isn't yet connected with the Last Supper or Jesus in any way. All that changed with a new author, Robert de Boron. His version is called *The History of the Grail,* and the holy relic really is the centerpiece of the story.

De Boron had previously written a tale of Joseph of Arimathea who has pos-session of the serving bowl or chalice from the Last Supper. *Remember:* It was Joseph who provided his own private tomb for the burial of Jesus after the crucifixion. In de Boron's story, Joseph helps prepare Jesus's body for interment by wiping the blood from his body and collecting it in the Grail. De Boron's inspiration came from an Apocryphal gospel, the *Acts of Pilate,* also known during the medieval period as the *Gospel of Nicodemus.*

In the Gospel of Nicodemus, Joseph is locked up for 40 days after Christ's ascension, and Jesus appears to him. In de Boron's version of the Grail tale, Joseph is thrown into prison, where Jesus appears to him and explains the powers and mystery of the Grail. He transports both Joseph and the jail cell itself out of the prison, and Joseph escapes with his followers to France. The Grail is passed by Joseph of Arimathea to the first Grail king, and eventually Perceval receives it.

Perlesvaus

Also in the 13th century, an anonymous version of the Grail legend called *Perlesvaus* appeared. This tale is unusual because it departs radically from what came before, and the Grail takes on different qualities.

Percival arrives at the mysterious castle, but there is no Grail there. Instead, it is a place inhabited by a knightly order. Two teachers meet the young knight and bring in 33 men, dressed in white with red crosses on their tunics — very Knights Templar–esque. The castle is not a Grail castle, but the teachers there know of the Grail's powers.

What makes this version so different from the others is that the Grail seems to represent secret knowledge. At different times it appears as a king with a crown; a child; an image of Jesus with a crown of thorns and blood flowing from his forehead, hands, breast, and feet; and finally, a wine glass. In this decidedly esoteric telling, the Grail is more of an experience or an idea than a thing. As a result, many people have attached Cathar or Gnostic interpretations to this version.

Wolfram von Eschenbach's Parzival

In the early part of the 1200s, a German poet named Wolfram von Eschenbach took up Cretian de Troyes's *Perceval* and decided it needed an overhaul. The result was *Parzival,* a complete retelling of the legend, in which he takes a swipe at his French predecessors as not knowing the real story. The basic storyline of *Perceval* is intact, but von Eschenbach adds the soap-opera touches of long-lost relatives and unknown identities. The work is considered the greatest of early German epic poems, and it became the basis for Richard Wagner's 1882 opera, *Parsifal* (why can't anyone agree on how to spell this kid's name?).

In this version, the Grail was kept at the Castle Monsalvaesche (or Monsalvat), and more than one 20th-century Grail-seeker has believed that this was actually the Cathar village of Montségur in France or the monastery at Montserrat in Spain (see Chapter 11).

A big difference in von Eschenbach's version is that the Grail is not a dish or bowl, as in Chrétien de Troyes's version or the *Continuations.* This time, it is a clear stone or crystal. It heals the sick or injured, and it provides an endless food supply when it gets trotted out for dinner.

The rest of the story

The myths that took shape in the 1100s with Chrétien de Troyes caught fire in the imagination of Europe, and the Grail legend mixed with the tales of King Arthur, Merlin, Camelot, and the Knights of the Round Table. Celtic influences from Wales, England, and elsewhere crept into the legends. Different versions of the stories filled out the canon over the centuries, even though many contradicted each other. These are the most important:

- ✔ **Thomas Malory's** *Le Morte d'Arthur (The Death of Arthur)* appeared in 1470, and it seemed to set the storyline and characters on a more linear path. Malory combined the previous French versions of the story with English variations. It has become the basis for most of the Arthurian legends told ever since. Malory introduced the *Seige Perilous* to the legend — a chair that is to remain vacant at the Round Table by the order of Merlin the magician. Only the purest and most worthy knight may sit in it, and he will be the one to seek the Grail. It is fatal to all others. Sir Galahad is the only knight who can sit in it and survive.

- ✔ **Alfred, Lord Tennyson's *Idyls of the King*** (1856–1885) are a series of 12 poems, revolving around King Arthur. The Grail appears in a tale told as a flashback by Sir Percivale, who is now a monk.

- ✔ **T. H. White's *Once and Future King*** leaned heavily on Malory's version and is perhaps the most easily accessible of the bunch. Written between 1938 and 1950, it progresses from a lighthearted, almost childlike book in the beginning, to a dark, pessimistic parable about World War II. It was the basis of the 1960s musical *Camelot*.

The Templars and the Grail

The legends of the Holy Grail just so happened to start taking shape at the same time in history that the Knights Templar were getting organized, and the Templars themselves were the inspiration for many legendary stories spun by the troubadours, poets, bards, and jesters of the 12th and 13th centuries. In early versions of the stories, Sir Gawain was identified as having a shield of white with a red cross, much like the shields wielded by the Templars.

There is a modern allegation that the anonymous 13th-century *Perlesvaus* was written by a Templar, but no serious researcher believes it. Likewise, modern attempts to claim that the Grail was part of the secret treasure excavated from under the Temple Mount in Jerusalem are not credible. The Grail legends were nonexistent until the late 1100s, so even if the order had discovered a chalice, there would have been little to connect it to the legend of the Holy Grail at that point in history.

As we discuss in Chapter 11 and throughout Part IV of this book, the version of the Grail legend told in the novel *The Da Vinci Code* is based on the suggestion that the Grail is not a cup used by Christ at the Last Supper. Instead, it is the notion that Jesus and Mary Magdalene were married, and that *she* is the sacred vessel that contained the holy bloodline of Christ, in the form of their child, a baby girl named Sarah.

The Templars enter this theory by way of the suggestion made in Dan Brown's source material, the pseudo-historical book, *Holy Blood, Holy Grail*, by Michael Baigent, Richard Leigh, and Henry Lincoln. It introduced a shadowy, heretofore unknown, secret society called the Priory of Sion, and it further speculated that the Templars were formed as their military arm. And, so this version of the story goes, the priory's mission was — and is — to protect the surviving descendants of Jesus and Mary. (We examine this part of the story in detail in Chapter 11.)

The other alleged connection between the Templars and the Grail concerns — what else? — Rosslyn Chapel! Some speculative authors believe that the Holy Grail is hidden in the hollow Apprentice Pillar of Rosslyn. There is absolutely nothing to indicate that the Templars had the Grail, that they took it to Scotland, that they buried it in Rosslyn Chapel, or that the Apprentice Pillar is hollow, but that doesn't seem to matter where legends are concerned. (We talk more about Rosslyn Chapel all over this book, but especially in Chapter 7.)

The Real Grail?

It is curious that an obscure item from Jesus's dinner table is never mentioned for ten centuries, then suddenly becomes the subject of so many authors and captures the imagination of so many people. It goes hand in hand with the fascination in the Middle Ages with the trade in holy relics. Pieces of the True Cross were scattered from one end of Christendom to the other. By the time of the Templars, there were at least four claimants to the Holy Lance, the Roman lance that was thrust into Jesus's side by the soldier Longinus, who was mentioned in the apocryphal Gospel of Nicodemus (Acts of Pilate). Likewise, by 1300, there were no less than 20 "Holy Grails" claimed around the Christian world. Several survive today (see Chapter 15).

Chapter 11

The 21st Century Dawns with a New Grail Myth

The legends of the Templars are inextricably tied to faith, power, treasure, mystery, and secrecy. Historians, archeologists, theologians, Freemasons, and barking-mad nutcases have all had their various takes on what the Knights Templar may have known and possessed, where they hid it, and whether it still exists, whatever it is. Or was. Or might have been.

For centuries, the myth was simply that the Templars had a vast treasure, and that they managed to get it out of France before their mass arrests in 1307 and hide it somewhere. (We discuss most of these theories in Chapter 7.) But throughout the last half of the 20th century, a new notion began to appear in some corners of speculative research. For hundreds of years, the Templars had been linked with, among other revered, mythical objects, the Holy Grail. This new theory came at the Grail legend with a different take: that maybe the Grail wasn't a cup, a goblet, or a "thing" after all. Perhaps the Grail was an idea. Perhaps the Grail itself was something that had to be hidden away, not because it was a priceless relic, but because it was a truth that would shock Christians and Christianity. And perhaps it had to be hidden during the volatile times of the Templars because it amounted to heresy, and people got burned to a crispy crunch for such things.

These various disparate theories of the Templar and Holy Grail myths, a strange secret society, all collided in the obscure and mysterious French village of Rennes-le-Château before they became the basis of Dan Brown's novel *The Da Vinci Code*.

Holy Couple: The Search for the Bloodline of Christ

If you are part of the tiny handful of folks who hasn't read *The Da Vinci Code,* allow us to spoil the ending for you. The "shocking" revelation of the book is that Jesus was married to Mary Magdalene, that they had a daughter together, and that, after the death of Christ, his wife and child were secretly taken out of Jerusalem for their protection to the south of France. Further, for their own motives, early leaders of the Catholic Church eliminated any scriptural mention of such a marriage, and worse, to hide their tracks, spread the propaganda that Mary Magdalene was, in fact, a prostitute. In Chapter 13, we look in detail at this part of the legend in particular, but we give you the short version here.

The biblical account of Mary Magdalene

Mary Magdalene has had a troubled past in Christian interpretation of the Bible over the centuries. Unfortunately for the sake of clarity, there were too many Marys populating the New Testament. Apart from Christ's mother, Mary, there is Mary of Bethany (the sister of Lazarus and Martha, who appears in Luke 10:38–42 and John 11:1–2), and Mary Magdalene who is described in Luke 8:2 and even several lesser Marys, such as Mary the mother of James and Joseph and an early follower of Jesus. Jesus casts out demons from Mary Magdalene, healing her "evil spirits and infirmities," and she goes with him and the disciples to Jerusalem. She has also been identified by various scholars as the "woman with the alabaster box" who anoints Jesus's head with oil just before his arrest.

Mary Magdalene is present at the crucifixion, and she is the one who discovers the empty tomb, where Christ appears to her. She's also present at the resurrection. Many have claimed that the wedding at Cana, when Jesus turned water into wine, was, in fact, the marriage of Jesus and Mary Magdalene. Some have also claimed that, in Christ's time, it would have been almost unheard of for a Jewish man of his age to have been unmarried (unlike today, when at 33, millions of men of every faith are just starting to think about moving out of their parents' basement).

In the end, the theory comes down to the supposition that Mary Magdalene would not have been present at so many important points in the story of Jesus unless they *had* been married. The problem has always been, and will always be, that such a theory can't be proved. There is no biblical passage, no Gnostic document, no Dead Sea Scroll, no chiseled inscription, no nothing that even remotely hints that Jesus and Mary were married. However, for some who use a peculiar brand of circular logic, lack of proof is enough "proof" that the evidence has been destroyed.

The legend

This notion of a marriage between Mary and Jesus is not a new one. In spite of the frenzy of *The Da Vinci Code,* it has been around for centuries. The story goes that, because Jesus had been arrested by the Romans, Jerusalem was too dangerous for Mary, his wife, which admittedly makes sense. Joseph of Arimathea, a wealthy friend of the family who had provided his own tomb for Jesus's body after the crucifixion, took Mary, who was pregnant, and fled to the south of France, possibly stopping first in the Jewish community of the Egyptian port city of Alexandria. There, she had the child of Christ. (As we discuss in Chapter 10, Joseph of Arimathea got around. The English think he went to Glastonbury, too.)

Eventually, so the tale continues, Jesus and Mary's daughter Sarah married into the family that would eventually become the Merovingian line of French kings, who ruled between the fifth and eighth centuries. These "divinely descended" kings, included the great Clovis I, who is considered to be the founder of France, the first king to successfully unite the nation of Gaul.

Further "proof" of a connection to Mary Magdalene cited by some authors is the very name Merovingian itself. It has long been established that the origin of the name comes from *Merovech,* the father of Childeric I, founder of the legendary dynasty of Frankish kings in the fifth century. Margaret Starbird contends that it is derived from the roots *mer* (Mary) and *vin* (vine, as in the dynastic vine of the line of David, a metaphor used a few times in the Bible). We both speak French, and to our ears, *mer* has always meant "sea," and *vin* has always meant "wine," two things that go great together. But we digress. Because centuries of dynastic families, from the Seljuq Turks to the Tudors and Plantagenets and the Capetians of France, have almost uniformly followed the grand old tradition of taking their dynastic name from their founding father, we tend to side with the Encyclopedia Britannica on this one.

Holy Blood, Holy Grail: The Legend Rediscovered

In 1982, three authors co-wrote a book that brought the Mary Magdalene story to a modern audience, with a few twists. Michael Baigent, Richard Leigh, and Henry Lincoln published *The Holy Blood and the Holy Grail* (or its simpler U.S. title, *Holy Blood, Holy Grail*), based on a documentary film made by Lincoln. In the book, they told the tale of Mary Magdalene's flight from Jerusalem to the south of France, and the fate of her supposed offspring.

Here are some of the claims they make:

- ✔ The term *Holy Grail* in French is *San Greal*. But by moving the space between the words by one character, it spells *Sang Real,* meaning "Royal Blood" in medieval French.

  As interesting a word game as that may be, it is just that: a word game, like attaching a solemn, historical, ecclesiastical significance to the fact that *god* is *dog* spelled backwards. There is no instance, before Baigent et al that anyone else ever spelled *San Greal* as *Sang Real.*

- ✔ Jesus and his followers staged the crucifixion and the resurrection, and Christ lived to a ripe old age outside of the Holy Land — a recycling of the worn (and discredited) theory of the 1965 Hugh Schonfield book, *The Passover Plot.*

- ✔ A secret society, known as the Priory of Sion, was created in A.D. 1099 to protect the secret of the bloodline of Christ and Mary Magdalene, a royal lineage that leads all the way back to the Old Testament's King David.

- ✔ The Priory of Sion formed the Knights Templar as a military and financial wing.

- ✔ The Catholic Church killed off the Knights Templar and other groups like the Cathars to thwart the Priory's plan to restore Christ and Mary Magdalene's bloodline as the *hereditary* head of the Church, as opposed to the *apostolic* succession of Peter, through whom the popes claimed their authority.

- ✔ The Priory's ultimate aim was to restore the Merovingian dynasty to the throne of France, and eventually to place them on the thrones of all the kingdoms of Europe. Finally, they would make a Merovingian the King of Israel.

- ✔ The modern-day mystery of the Priory was centered around a small town in southwestern France called Rennes-le-Château, and the strange activities of a certain Catholic priest in the late 1800s. Father Bérenger Saunière had inexplicably become very wealthy, and the book alleged that he had found documents in the little town's church that led to a treasure, as well as a secret he used to blackmail the Vatican.

- ✔ A 1640 painting, *The Arcadian Shepherds,* by Nicolas Poussin, was said to contain a Latin phrase that was an anagram for "Begone! I keep God's secrets." It was further speculated that a tomb depicted in the painting was located in the hills near Rennes-le-Château, that it contained the bones of Jesus or some other important religious figure, or perhaps buried treasure, and that this was the secret that Father Saunière discovered, the secret of the Priory of Sion.

- ✔ Saunière made extensive alterations to the church in Rennes-le-Château, along with several suspiciously expensive construction projects that contained strange details that referenced Mary Magdalene.

The "married Messiah" part of the tale was not new. It was a common legend in France for centuries, and William E. Phipps had recently (in 1970) published a book called *Was Jesus Married? The Distortion of Sexuality in the Christian Tradition*. It was the Priory of Sion wrinkle that charted new territory. The authors claimed their hypothesis was based on new evidence. But that evidence had come from none other than a member of the Priory of Sion. In the following section, we examine the many claims made in *Holy Blood, Holy Grail*.

The Priory of Sion

Baigent, Leigh, and Lincoln based their theories principally on a book published in France in the 1960s, *L'Or de Rennes* (The Gold of Rennes, later republished under the title *Le Tresur Maudit de Rennes-le-Chateau*) by Gérard de Sède, along with a tale told to them by a Frenchman named Pierre Plantard.

As we discuss in Chapter 7, there is a long tradition among so-called secret societies of inventing mythical and ancient pedigrees for themselves. The Priory of Sion was no different. While certain documents claimed that the Priory was a thousand years old, it was actually started in 1956, in the French town of Annemasse, to promote the cause of cheap government housing. Really.

French law required that all clubs and associations had to be registered with the government, so the Priory sent in the appropriate forms listing Pierre Plantard, Andre Bonhomme, Jean Delaval, and Armand Defago as officers. Its purported purpose was for the "education and mutual aid" of its members, with its headquarters in Plantard's apartment. But Plantard had bigger dreams for the Priory, hoping it would become an influential association of men dedicated to reviving chivalric virtues and restoring the monarchy. Oh, and there was one other trifling item on his agenda: He wanted to become the King of France.

Plantard claimed that he was a descendant of the Merovingian kings, and therefore, according to *Holy Blood, Holy Grail,* that made him related to Jesus, Mary Magdalene, and even the Old Testament's King David. Of course, it should be noted here that, according to Jewish history and tradition, Zerubbabel, who led the Jews back to Jerusalem after the Babylonian captivity, was the end of the Davidic line, regardless of the claims of Jesus being of the House of David in the New Testament.

The "Secret Parchments"

The proof of the existence of the Priory of Sion initially came from a series of documents "discovered" in 1975 in the Bibliotheque Nationale, the national archives of France, located in Paris. Of course, "discovered" is a strong word, since Plantard had planted the documents there himself in the 1960s.

Four documents were said to have been found by Father Sauniere inside of a hollow column in the church, sealed in wooden tubes. One document was a small parchment, written in medieval Latin, that contained a secret code. When deciphered, the message read, *"A Dagobert II Roi et a Sion est ce tresor, et il est la mort"* (To King Dagobert II and to Sion does this treasure belong, and he is there dead). The first clue that the message was, perhaps, a modern one is that the decoded message was in modern French, deciphered from a supposedly medieval Latin source.

Les Dossiers Secret

Another document was described as the "Secret Dossiers," which listed a continuous lineup of "Grand Masters" of the Priory of Sion going back to A.D. 1188. Along with a sprinkling of templar Grand Masters, it included some stellar names:

- Leonardo Da Vinci (Italian painter, sculptor, scientist, inventor; the original Renaissance man)
- Victor Hugo (French author of *The Hunchback of Notre Dame* and *Les Misérables*)
- Isaac Newton (renowned English scientist of the Enlightenment)
- Claude Debussy (French classical composer)
- Jean Cocteau (20th-century French artist, surrealist, poet, and filmmaker)

Another of the documents contained a list of the descendants of the Merovingian line since King Dagobert II's assassination in 679. History says his son Sigebert IV died at the same time, but the parchment claims he actually fled to Rennes-le-Château, and became known as the "Plant-Ard," from whence Pierre Plantard's family name descended. It further alleged that this bloodline produced the Blancheford family, of which a Grand Master of the Templars, Bertrand de Blancheford, was a member, along with none other than Pope Clement V. Godfroi de Bouillon, first Christian protector of Jerusalem, was also said to be a descendant.

Rennes-le-Château

The picturesque village of Renne-le-Château is in a beautiful location, albeit off the beaten path. It sits in the Pyrenees, right in the middle of Templar territory, along with a region once populated by Cathars. It's surrounded by castle ruins and other evidence of long-forgotten battles and the horrors of the Albigensian Crusade. In the 1950s, getting to Rennes-le-Château was difficult, and not many tourists came to wander its charming, medieval streets. A local hotel owner, Noël Corbu, wanted to change that. What the town needed to beef up its economy was a surefire tourist trap. So he invented one.

Corbu spread the rumor that a 19th-century priest in the village, Father Bérenger Saunière, had discovered certain parchments during a remodeling of the church in 1892. The parchments apparently detailed the secret location of a buried treasure. According to Corbu's rumor, Saunière had found a secret cache of cash, or at least a vast store of some kind of treasure. And thus, the first mystery of Rennes-le-Château was born. Of course, Corbu had an inside track on the story, or so he said — he had bought Saunière's home, the Villa Béthanie, and opened it as the Hotel de la Tour in May of 1955. His tall tale first appeared in a series of articles in the regional newspaper *La Dépêche Du Midi* in 1956.

Father Saunière and the treasure of Rennes-le-Château

In 1897, the little parish priest really did suddenly embark on a major redecoration of the church, seemingly — at first — with no visible source of income. Then, between 1901 and 1905, the truth was that Saunière did go on a building spree, constructing an estate, a gothic-styled tower with a breathtaking view that served as his private library (the *Tour Magdala*), as well as gardens and terraces. So where did he get the money? Did he find buried treasure?

The rumor that he had excavated under the church altar and found skeletons and gold was just that — a rumor, made up as the tales of the priest were further embellished over the years. The truth was far duller. It seems that the late 1800s were volatile politically in France, and there was a growing conflict between the Catholic Church and the government. Saunière was a reluctant priest, but a rabid, pro-monarchial, anti-republican firebrand, and there was a strong desire among Catholics at the time for France to shuck off its republic and return to having a king. Saunière found a way to capitalize on that sentiment. He began to "sell" masses, meaning, for a donation, he would offer up the Sunday Mass for God to wipe out the republic and bring back a monarchy. These days, it may be difficult to imagine that such a scheme would make much more than pocket change. *Au contraire.*

Saunière took out ads in religious magazines and journals all over France, like *Semaine Religieuse, La Croix, L'éclair, L'Express du Midi, L'Univers,* and *Le Télégramme.* His moneymaking scheme actually created an embarrassing problem for him. Priests were allowed to say no more than three masses a day, and Saunière received literally thousands of paid requests, far more than he could ever honor. He was literally "trafficking" in masses.

Over the years, the priest made lots of money with this method, as well as having what appeared to have been an affair with a wealthy lady in town. These were the real sources of income he used to redecorate the church and build a house and the Magdalene Tower. There has never been any proof that Saunière found a treasure, and the "millions of francs" that he was said to have had in his possession have never been substantiated.

It took 25 years, but the Church finally caught on to (or got fed up with) Saunière's side business. He was dismissed as a priest in 1911 and died in 1917. By every bit of evidence that exists, including his failed attempts to borrow against his house in 1913, along with his will, he died in poverty — scarcely the life of a man who amassed millions.

Blackmail?

Another rumor was that part of what Saunière discovered were documents that "proved" Jesus was not divine, and that he and his followers had staged the crucifixion and resurrection. Indeed, *Holy Blood, Holy Grail* speculates that Jesus was crucified on "private property" where it would have been simple to stage a phony crucifixion, and that perhaps even Pontius Pilate was a willing accomplice. Saunière supposedly used this blockbuster information to blackmail the Vatican into paying him millions in hush money.

What makes this contention curious is that the same people who trot out this concept adhere to the notion that the Jesus/Mary bloodline was "divine," without seeing any contradiction.

The strange church in Rennes-le-Château

The village church was consecrated in A.D. 1059 and is dedicated to Mary Magdalene. In spite of the provable hoaxes involved in this story, the church really does have some oddities installed by Saunière.

The inscription over the church door reads, *"Terribilis Est Locus Iste,"* which generally gets translated by tourists, tour guides, and authors of sensational books as "How terrible is this place!" But it is actually taken from a line in Genesis 28:17, after Jacob awakens from his dream in which he saw a ladder rising to heaven: *"How awesome is this place! This is the house of God, and the gate of heaven, and it will be called the palace of God."* Awesome, not terrible.

Gérard de Sède claimed in his writings that Saunière made alterations to the church worth "millions of francs." Other researchers have studied the work and come up with a figure one-fiftieth of de Sede's estimation. Several of the "mysterious" statues and decorations that are supposedly one of a kind and bizarre were actually manufactured of plaster; some of them match others provided to several churches in the region. Saunière ordered them plain and painted them himself.

Outlandish claims have been made concerning some of the statuary, especially the Stations of the Cross, including that the priest added details that point to Freemasonry, Mary Magdalene worship, and other curiosities. Upon actually examining them, some of these suggestions seem to be figments of the imagination. For instance, a child is seen watching as Christ passes by with the Cross. The blanket wrapped around the child's backside is clearly a Hebrew-style cloth pattern, but some have said it is "plaid" and, therefore, alludes to Scottish Freemasonry!

Nevertheless, the strangest addition Saunière made was a large statue of a demon that greets visitors as they enter the church. It is supposedly Asmodeus, a demon who appears in several non-biblical Jewish stories of the Book of Tobit. Some legends claim that he was a demon who was tricked by King Solomon into helping to build the Temple in Jerusalem. That's what tourists are told. But the Asmodeus association was first made by none other than Pierre Plantard, and not before, in order to make the tenuous link to Solomon's Temple, the Templars, and maybe even the Freemasons. Others have interpreted the image of the Devil as Saunière's swipe at the French Republic, while the baptismal font opposite showing Christ's baptism symbolized the French Monarchy.

Another whopper is the supposed tomb of Sigebert IV within the church. There is no evidence whatsoever that the son of King Dagobert II survived his documented death in 679, and "secretly" fled to Rennes-le-Château. No evidence except the word of Pierre Plantard. No one had ever heard such a legend until he came along.

There are also several references to Mary Magdalene in Saunière's new décor. A Latin inscription had been painted under the altar that has since been defaced by vandals. It read *JESU MEDELA VULNERUM SPES UNA POENITEN-TIUM PER MAGDALENAE LACRYMAS PECCATA NOSTRA DILUAS* (JESUS, YOU REMEDY AGAINST OUR PAINS AND ONLY HOPE FOR OUR REPENTANCE, IT IS THANKS TO MAGDALENE'S TEARS THAT YOU WASH OUR SINS AWAY). Some researchers have said that the Latin is poorly constructed and contains deliberate errors that a Catholic priest like Saunière would not have made. Perhaps. But there is nothing especially odd about the church being decorated with paintings and quotations dealing with Mary Magdalene — it has been dedicated to her for 1,000 years. She's a popular saint throughout the entire region.

The peculiar Pierre Plantard

Pierre Plantard had a mighty unusual methodology for an aspiring king. Between 1937 and 1945, during World War II, he engaged in a series of schemes that caught the attention of Paris police. He was accused on several occasions of inventing phony anit-Semitic and anti-Masonic organizations, dedicated to the "purification" of France. They seem to have existed largely to scam money from their members. A police report issued on May 9, 1941, by Paris police while under the occupation of Nazi troops stated:

> La Renovation Nationale Française seems to be a "phantom" group whose existence is purely a figment of the imagination of M. Plantard. Plantard claims 3,245 members, whereas this organization currently only has four members (the executive committee).

It was the sort of outlandish claim that he would use again and again. Plantard couldn't stay out of trouble, doing jail time in 1953 for "abuse of trust," and again between 1956 and 1957 for the "corruption of minors." In the 1960s, he met up with French author Gérard de Sède, and began feeding him outrageous claims about the Priory — that it was connected to the Knights Templar, that it was protecting the bloodline of Christ and Mary, and that he was, himself, descended from France's King Dagobert II, the last of the Merovingian kings.

The perfect marriage of a man and a myth

Plantard came to Rennes-le-Château like hundreds of others did in the 1950s — in search of hidden treasure. Treasure hunters, drawn by Corbu's phony story about Father Saunière's buried gold, came from all over Europe with shovels and metal detectors and started to dig in the hills around the village. The garden on the old estate of Saunière was dug up, rocks from his terrace were chipped out and stolen, the church was ransacked, and even the occasional dynamite explosion rocked the countryside as the searchers blew up possible hiding places.

The town archives of Rennes-le-Château burned to the ground in 1961, and suddenly the Priory of Sion hoaxers had a fortuitous opportunity. If no documents could be accessed about the early history of the village, they could simply make it up.

Philippe de Chérisey

Plantard and his friends began to design an elaborate hoax, centered around Corbu's phony rumors about Saunière, and tying it to the tale of the Priory of Sion. Plantard constructed an increasingly complex story. He made the acquaintance of an odd character named Philippe de Chérisey, who was a part-time actor with a fascination for surrealism and esoteric puzzles.

They deposited a series of phony documents in Paris' Bibliothèque Nationale in the mid-1960s, and sent author Gérard de Sède to go look for them in 1975. These became the basis for de Sède's original book about the mysteries of Rennes-le-Château, which led to Baigent, Leigh, and Lincoln's subsequent, *Holy Blood, Holy Grail,* and an avalanche of others, including Picknett and Prince's more skeptical *The Templar Revelation.* The documents were purported to be copies of parchments that Saunière had supposedly found in his church. The peculiarity that they were mere photocopies instead of the real thing was easy to explain — the archives of their village had burned down, but, so the tale went, the Mayor had made copies of the documents Father Saunière had supposedly found in his church. It is important to understand that *no* original documents have *ever* been produced, only copies and transcriptions. So, the entire "proof" of the existence of the Priory of Sion has been based on two Xerox copies.

De Chérisey is believed to have been the source of the coded Latin parchment. Investigations revealed that the document was a modern forgery, and had been poorly copied from a Latin text of Luke 6 known as the *Codex Bezae*. De Chérisey had no knowledge of Latin, which explains the errors in the text. The larger document was copied from a modern Latin Vulgate text of John 12 from 1889, and not from a medieval source.

The most important part of the Rennes-le-Château tale centers around these so-called parchments that Father Saunière found while renovating his church. The truth is that Nöel Corbu invented the story of the parchments to begin with, and Philippe de Chérisey drew them. In 1974, de Chérisey admitted it in writing when he was embroiled in a dispute with Gérard de Sède over being paid for his artwork he had created — the parchments!

The priory exposed

Over the years, every piece of so-called evidence of the existence of the Priory of Sion has been debunked, and many through the admission of the original pranksters. In the 1990s, both Plantard and de Chérisey went on the warpath against the original author who told their story, Gérard de Sède. They both fessed up and gave their original phony documents and written confessions to French author Jean-Luc Chaumeil.

The funniest aspect of this long, complex hoax is that Pierre Plantard himself, source of the Priory of Sion information, ridiculed the Jesus/Mary-bloodline aspect of *The Holy Blood and the Holy Grail*. He made no such claim himself that he was descended from Christ's bloodline, only that he was related to King Dagobert II, the last of the Merovingian kings. Of course, given his anti-Semitic writings during World War II, it's probable that Plantard would have rejected the notion that he was descended from a Jew, no matter how divine the Jew may have been. Over the years, Plantard insisted on several name changes. Pierre of France had a noble, kingly feel to it. His later *nom de hoax*, Pierre Plantard de Saint-Clair, was a transparently silly attempt to tie in with the Scottish Templars and Freemasons (see Chapter 7 for a discussion of the many Saint Clairs and the myths that surround them).

In 1993, Pierre Plantard inserted himself into an unrelated, sensational case involving financial fraud. It was a notorious investigation in France that had nothing to do with the Priory of Sion, involving French millionaire Roger Patrice Pelat and his influential friends in the government. Plantard voluntarily came forward and testified that Pelat was, in reality, a Grand Master of the Priory of Sion. The suspicious judge, Thierry Jean Pierre, had Plantard investigated, discovering his loopy contention that he was the rightful King of France. Eventually, he confessed under oath that the entire story of the

Priory of Sion had been an elaborate hoax that he had spent almost 40 years fueling. Plantard was rebuked by the judge for playing games with France's judicial system, and he vanished into obscurity. He died in 2000 without ever getting the chance to place his backside on the purple cushion of the throne of France.

Was any of it real?

There actually was an Abbey of St. Mary of Mount Zion in the 12th century in Jerusalem. It was a small monastery of Augustinean monks (known as *canons*), whose order was created in 1143 by papal decree of Pope Celestine II. It was built over the ruins of an earlier Byzantine church, the Hagia Zion, but was destroyed by Muslims in 1219. But there is absolutely no connection between the abbey and the Priory of Sion.

Alas, the Priory of Sion in *Holy Blood, Holy Grail* was nothing but a figment of Plantard's imagination. Many other books have been published basing their "research" on the accounts related by Baigent, Leigh, and Lincoln, including *The Da Vinci Code*. In fact, an entire industry has grown up around the mystery of Saunière, Mary Magdalene, and this enigmatic little village in the Pyrenees. But they're constructing their premise on what has been proved to be the sandy foundation of an elaborate hoax.

Meanwhile, the tale is told and retold to the tourists. More than 100,000 came to the village in 2006 alone, and frankly, the villagers are sick to death of it. But the truth is, there were no Saunière parchments, and there is no mystery in Rennes-le-Château.

Part V

Squaring Off: The Church versus the Gospel According to Dan Brown

In this part . . .

This part of the book is a little different from the other four. Literally millions of people first heard of the Knights Templar in Dan Brown's *The Da Vinci Code,* where the order was fictionally wrapped up with lots of, well, fiction. Unfortunately, it was presented as factual information, and lots of Brown's readers have been left confused over what's true and what isn't.

This part takes a careful, nonfiction look at the historical claims put forth in *The Da Vinci Code*'s take on the superstructure of the Christian faith that didn't exactly thrill the Catholic Church.

Chapter 12 explores the tale of the Templars and other "secret societies" in *The Da Vinci Code* universe. Chapter 13 explores Brown's many assertions about the "sacred feminine," and it delivers up some surprising facts about women in the history of the Church, as well as in Celtic and other pre-Christian cultures. Chapter 14 presents the amazing behind-the-scenes politics in the creation of the Bible as we know it today. We fearlessly tread on the thin ice of the topic of celibacy, and its improbable survival into the age of pole-dancing and pay-per-view porn. We cut through the PhD-speak and look at the Dead Sea Scrolls, the Apocryphal books that didn't make it into the Bible, and the rediscovered Gnostic Gospels that have caused many to reexamine the foundations of their faith. This part closes with the place of the Knights Templar in the postmodern world, and the latest theories of Templar influence on the survival of these alternative gospels and the secrets they contain.

Chapter 12

Templars and *The Da Vinci Code*

*A*s a result of Dan Brown's novel *The Da Vinci Code*, a large chunk of society will go through life believing that Jesus was married, that women were officially despised by the Church throughout Western history, and that the entire foundation of Christianity is built on a series of poorly crafted lies thrust upon them by pointy-hatted fascists at the Council of Nicaea. Unfortunately, using Brown as your source is like getting your history from watching an Oliver Stone movie — entertaining, but deranged.

Because of Brown's book, the next generation may believe that the Templars were not devout, independent warrior monks, but were controlled by a dark and formidable inner secret society called the Priory of Sion, a society for which there is not one, single, solitary shred of historical evidence, not even a phone number scribbled on a matchbook. The Templars really are shrouded in mysteries that are never even mentioned in the novel, fascinating enigmas and shocking possibilities that never play a part in the secret-society-drenched plotline of *The Da Vinci Code*.

Dan Brown's own Web site proudly touted a *New York Daily News* review that proclaimed, "His research is impeccable." Actually, it's as peccable as a duck's backside. (There's a reason the newspapers in New York are dying.)

In this chapter, we examine some of that "impeccable" research, dig up his sources and see whether the "facts" he presents about the Templars have any facts in them at all.

The Secret Societies of Dan Brown

So why all the hubbub over a piece of fictional beach-reading material? As writers, we two have agreed to disagree on the subject of *The Da Vinci Code*–as-novel. One thinks it's a smooth and clever thriller, with a wonderful sense of playfulness about cryptography; the other thinks it's a purloined piece from beginning to end. Yet, we both agree on one thing: Dan Brown's irresponsible misuse of history is downright criminal. When it suits Mr. Brown, *The Da Vinci Code* is merely a novel, not to be examined as if it were the Dead Sea Scrolls. And when it suits Mr. Brown, *The Da Vinci Code* is the real scoop on history and the powerful secret societies that control it, and he merely chose to deliver it up as fiction in order to make it more exciting, and less threatening to the sinister powers that be.

But any book that opens with the provocative and now notorious statement that "All descriptions of artwork, architecture, documents, and secret rituals in this novel are accurate," is really just asking for it, in terms of the dreck it dishes up as history. Brown is particularly asking for it in terms of the many and various secret societies he tosses around with paranoid regularity, for both good guys and bad guys. In Dan Brown's universe, you come into this world with a birth certificate, a Social Security number, and a dues card.

Not a single theory, no matter how wide-eyed, that gets trotted out in *The Da Vinci Code,* didn't originate somewhere else first. What made the novel so successful was something else entirely: a human hunger for mystery, conspiracy, and hidden truths beneath the surface of obvious ones. It's been rearing its head in the literary world for some time now.

Every generation has its *Da Vinci Code. Chariots of the Gods* put forward evidence of alien visitation in the ancient world, and it spawned a film and two sequels, becoming a full-fledged phenomenon. Before that, *The Passover Plot* was in every dorm room, which purported to prove that a cabal of radical, anti-Roman Jews had faked the crucifixion so that a living Jesus could reappear, just like the magician David Copperfield, for his jaw-dropping "resurrection." *The Late Great Planet Earth,* in print since 1970, spun a web of biblical prophesy from Isaiah to Jesus to hint that the end of the world and the rapture was just around the corner, in 1988. (Witness the success of the *Left Behind* series of novels inspired by it.) All these books were like *The Da Vinci Code,* the topic de jour of radio talk shows, classrooms, and parties.

The difference is that each of these books had the courage to present themselves openly as history — *speculative* history, of course, but still history. Each of these authors was willing to stand up like a man and take the critical brickbats that were thrown at them from both the academic and the clerical community. Dan Brown, on the other hand, cowers behind the skirts of the novel form, as the world's biblical and secular historians take apart his research.

However, there is one place where Dan Brown deserves sympathy (or brownie points, if you will) — and maybe a fruitcake for Christmas with a nice card. He certainly didn't deserve the continuing harassment of lawsuits from the two authors of *Holy Blood, Holy Grail.* (Henry Lincoln, the third author, refused to have any part of it.) Why sympathy? Because, with a great deal of courtesy and generosity, he lays out the names of the books from which these theories were drawn — they're mentioned prominently within the dialog. This kind of a mention is free advertising that an author can only dream about. It's not unheard of, but it's certainly unusual in a novel, and Dan Brown deserves to be praised for setting a terrific precedent. It was the gentlemanly thing to do.

The Da Vinci Code's "facts" of the Priory of Sion

In *The Da Vinci Code,* Robert Langdon explains to Sophie Neuvu the meaning of a key with a *PS* symbol on it that has been given to her by her grandfather. Langdon recognizes it as the logo of the Priory of Sion, as if it were as common a bit of currency as a Star of David or a stop sign. He describes a brief outline of this "oldest surviving secret society on earth," with the facts pulled directly from the *Holy Blood* playbook listed in the preceding section.

We discuss the Priory of Sion and the origin of the hoax that perpetrated it at length in Chapter 11, but here, we need to spell out some of the claims made about it as they relate specifically to the Dan Brown universe, because it is on this foundation that *The Da Vinci Code* is partially built.

The tale goes that, in A.D. 1090, Frankish knights of the Merovingian bloodline founded an organization called the Prieuré de Sion, igniting the Crusades to take their rightful place on the throne of Jerusalem. After this was accomplished, the order was restructured in 1099, establishing a military arm called the Poor Knights of Christ and the Temple of Solomon, and the same officer served as Grand Master for both brotherhoods — until 1188, that is, when the Grand Master of the Knights Templar and the Priory of Sion broke up, a divorce that was precipitated by some sort of spat over the fact that the Templars had bungled the Battle of Hattin and lost the city of Jerusalem. The Priory, the parent organization, went its own way, to cause more mischief all over Europe in its attempts to restore the Merovingian dynasty of French kings (A.D. 476–A.D. 750) to their rightful place on the throne of France. The arrogance of the Merovingians is perfectly understandable in light of the fact that they're the direct descendants of Jesus Christ.

These are the "authoritative facts," right from the book *Holy Blood, Holy Grail* upon which Dan Brown built *The Da Vinci Code.* Mr. Brown apparently did (and does) accept these as indisputable facts. But in truth, they're pretty disputable.

The "sacred" bloodline

The Merovingians were the first of what could be called a dynasty of French kings, though they were more properly called "Franks" or "Gauls," and *not* "the kings of France." The Dagobert II discussed so often in *Holy Blood, Holy Grail* was the king of a nation called Austrasia, divided from its Merovingian-ruled neighbor, Neustria, because of a war between two of King Clovis's sons. Neustria ran roughly to the north and west, Austrasia to the south and east. Dagobert II was the rightful king of Austrasia, but as a young man, he was dethroned, shoved into an Irish monastery and usurped by an adopted son of his father's, the son of the evil mayor (a high palace official) of the Austrasian palace, Grimoald. It caused a war and, eventually, Dagobert was called out of the monastery in Ireland to take back the half a throne of Austrasia.

Many of these events are subject to historical debate, particularly the ones we were merciful enough to leave out. Myth records at least one marriage for Dagobert, which produced only daughters, but history has its doubts even about that. However, it's true that Dagobert II was assassinated while out hunting, on December 23, A.D. 679. Once more, according to myth and not history, he did indeed fall asleep under a tree and was speared through the eye by an unknown assassin. According to the *Holy Blood* playbook, he was done in by operatives of the pope, who were frightened by his "sacred" lineage and its potential threat to the papal throne.

But boring old history books actually say Dagobert II was probably ordered to be killed by his mortal enemy at the Neustrian court, a man named Ebroin, the ambitious mayor of the palace. (These "mayor" guys were nothing but trouble — for heaven's sake, hire a butler!) These books say that Dagobert II had no son, hardly a serious dynastic threat to anyone, and that he spent the greater part of his time on the throne founding monasteries and churches. He was soon afterward made a saint by the Church that supposedly assassinated him. His childless state led to the end of the dynasty. Of course, for the Dan Brown/*Holy Blood* team, the boring history books are all lying anyway.

At the end of Part One of *Holy Blood, Holy Grail*, in Chapter 4, the following statements are presented not as speculations, or even likelihoods, but as facts:

✔ **There was a secret order behind the Knights Templar founded in 1099, which created the Templars as its military and administrative arm.** This order, which has functioned under a variety of names, is most frequently known as the Prieuré de Sion (Priory of Sion).

✔ **The Priory of Sion has been directed by a sequence of Grand Masters whose names are among the most illustrious in Western history and culture.**

✔ **Although the Knights Templar were destroyed and dissolved between 1307 and 1314, the Priory of Sion remained unscathed.** Although itself periodically torn by internecine and fratricidal strife (in other words, civil wars) it has continued to function throughout the centuries. Acting in the shadows, behind the scenes, it has orchestrated certain of the critical events in Western history.

✔ **The Priory of Sion exists today and is still operative. It is influential and plays a role in high-level international affairs as well as in the domestic affairs of certain European countries.** To some significant extent, it is responsible for information leaked to the public about itself since 1956. What they mean is that's when the Priory apparently came out of the closet.

✔ **The avowed and declared objective of the Priory of Sion is the restoration of the Merovingian dynasty and bloodline — not only to the throne of France, but to the thrones of other European nations.** We think someone needs to tell these guys that there hasn't *been* a throne of France since 1876. Not to pick nits, but the Merovingians were kings *in* France, not kings *of* France. And while we're at it, there aren't many thrones left in Europe, apart from countries small enough to be fully carpeted, like Monaco or Luxembourg. It doesn't seem likely that any of them would step down in favor of the son of Pierre Plantard.

✔ **The restoration of the Merovingian dynasty is sanctioned and justifiable, both legally and morally. Although it was deposed in the eighth century, the Merovingian bloodline is not extinct.** On the contrary, it perpetuated itself in a direct line from Dagobert II and his son, Sigisbert IV.

The weakest link in the bloodline

And just who is Sigisbert IV? Why, he's the infant son of Dagobert II, born in the authors' favorite hallowed ground, Rennes-le-Château, whose very name is never mentioned in any other historical reference books. When the confused reader peers at the footnote for this information, he finds that — *surprise!* — the existence of Sigisbert IV is taken from the Priory of Sion's own documents! 'Round and 'round we go. And where does this direct line eventually lead? Why, it leads right to the doorstep of the man who fed these three authors this information to begin with — Gérard de Sède, the pet author of one Pierre Plantard (a.k.a. Pierre Plantard de Saint-Clair), a French huckster and compulsive founder of secret societies who had a really interesting record with the French police. They used to lock guys up in a padded room for claiming to be Napoleon. Now those guys get a book deal.

The "Da Vinci" Templars

The Knights Templar are almost as fictional in *The Da Vinci Code* as the Priory of Sion. Although hero Robert Langdon at first hesitates to bring up the Templars in his lectures because very mention of them brings out the conspiracy lovers, Brown has no problem making them part of his own conspiracy theory. Here are some of the Templar references in *The Da Vinci Code,* along with our comments:

- ✔ **The true goal of the Templars in the Holy Land was to retrieve the secret documents of the Priory of Sion from beneath the ruins of the temple. The documents prove the sacred bloodline of Christ and Mary Magdalene.** The *true* goal of the Templars was to protect pilgrims to the Holy Land. Although fanciful claims have been made that the Templars were digging for treasure, there has never been any record or proof of it.

- ✔ **The Templars did not grow beyond nine men until Hughes de Payens returned from a trip to France (where he went to secure funds and papal support). His trip was to deliver up the damning documents that the nine knights had unearthed in nine years of digging.** Actually, there is ample documentary evidence of the job the Templar knights (who were growing in number from the first year) were doing patrolling the roads of Jerusalem.

- ✔ **The secret documents were used to blackmail the pope into issuing the papal bull that gave them the various rights they enjoyed as the holy monks and warriors of God. De Payens supposedly returned with bullion stuffed everywhere but his BVDs. Overnight, they were wealthy beyond the mere dreams of mortal men.** The boring truth is that, even though the central records hall of the Templars was destroyed on Cyprus after the fall of Acre, records exist all over Europe of the gifts of money, and principally of lands and manors, that were given over to the Templars by the faithful. The King of Aragon in Spain was so grateful for the work the Templars had done in helping to hold off the Moors from his kingdom that, when he died childless in 1131, he willed one third of his entire *kingdom* to the Knights Templar. The idea that they blackmailed the pope to gain their wealth is just plain stupid.

- ✔ **The Templars invented modern banking; traveling crusaders deposited gold and silver into their local Temple Church, and could then withdraw**

it from any other Temple Church along the way to the Holy land. Sort of true, but not really accurate. Yes, the Templars did indeed invent international banking. But deposits were not made or withdrawn from Templar churches. The Templars were among the most devout Christians who ever lived, and they did not turn God's temple into a bank. They knew the story of Christ driving the moneylenders from the temple. Templar commanderies and preceptories across Europe and the East, as has been explained in other chapters, ran the gamut in size and wealth, but they were in effect small villages or small, fortified cities. The bank was usually a centrally located *donjon* or *keep,* because the chapel or church was also centrally located, for the same reason (safety from attack). But the bank was the bank, the vaults were the vaults, and the church was the church. The vaults below the Templar churches were for burying the dead knights and others of the faithful, as were the church graveyards.

✔ **The Templar Grand Master was more powerful than kings.** The Grand Master was frequently an advisor to kings, not their overlord. On paper, the Templars were exempt from the laws and edicts of kings, and could only be tried or disciplined by the pope. But remember that it was a king, Phillip IV of France, and not even a pope, who brought down the Templars.

✔ **The Knights Templar were killed by the pope, "unceremoniously burned at the stake and tossed into the Tiber."** The Tiber River flows through Rome. But all the Templar knights who were burned at the stake were torched in France by King Phillip IV, not Pope Clement V. The pope wasn't even *in* Rome during the suppression of the Templars; he was in Avignon. Rome never had anything to do with it.

✔ **Rosslyn Chapel south of Edinburgh was built by the Knights Templar in 1446.** The Templars were arrested and disbanded in 1314. The chapel was built by William Sinclair, and there is no evidence whatsoever that he was a Templar, even a 132-year-old Templar. The book further describes an enormous five-pointed star engraved by centuries of footsteps into the floor. There is nothing of the kind there, despite the hands-and-knees efforts of hordes of tourists to find it.

✔ **There are two direct bloodlines from Jesus, and that these two families, Plantard and Saint-Clair, are in hiding, protected by the Priory of Sion.** They weren't in hiding then, and they aren't now. But oh, how we wish they were.

Brown's misunderstanding of who and what the Templars were comes shining through near the very end of the book. Robert Langdon states that he has explained to Sophie the fact that the Knights Templar were the principal influence on modern Freemasonry, "whose primary degrees — Apprentice Freemason, Fellowcraft Freemason, and Master Mason — harked back to early Templar days." The Templars did not wear aprons and use the three degrees; this aspect of Freemasonry is drawn from the medieval guilds of the stonemasons. There are some tenuous and unproved ties between the Templars and the Freemasons, all of them strictly theoretical (see Chapter 8) Unfortunately, the Templars of *The Da Vinci Code* have little to do with their historical counterparts.

Opus Dei

The controversial Catholic sect called Opus Dei is the only secret society mentioned in *The Da Vinci Code* that may well have some of the smear coming. This is not to say that Silas, the mad and murderous Albino monk, is even remotely a fair depiction of the organization. It does seem fair to say that part of the philosophy behind the organization could easily become twisted, delivered up in just the right way to just the right suspicious mind.

Not everyone in Opus Dei is expected to remain celibate. In fact, home and family are both emphasized deeply, as you may expect of a Catholic organization. Yet, parallels with the Knights Templars exist, in that both are organizations "attached" to the Church, quasi-independent, in the case of Opus Dei with something called a "personal prelature," a status that has only existed since Vatican II. And both require a far higher degree of sacrifice from their members than attending Mass on Sunday.

Opus Dei was founded in 1927 by St. Josemaria Escrivá, a parish priest in rural Spain. In later years, in Rome, he became a member of the Pontifical Academy of Theology and a prelate of honor to the pope. At his death in 1975, thousands of lay Catholics and a third of the world's bishops asked the Holy See to open a case for canonization. Pope John Paul II beatified Escrivá in 1992 (which is a sort of pre-saint status) and then canonized him ten years later on October 6, 2002.

The organization is in 61 countries worldwide, with around 87,000 members, and it's involved with education and relief work. At its spiritual core, Opus Dei is founded on the belief that God should be a part of daily life. The phrase *Opus Dei* means "Work of God" in Latin, and the group is sometimes referred to by its members as "the Work." The overwhelming majority, 98 percent, are lay Catholics (not priests or nuns), governed by an apostolic convention headed by a bishop.

There are four types of membership:

✔ **Supernumeraries:** Supernumeraries make up over 70 percent of members. They lead traditional lives, work, raise families, and so on, and they rarely practice such rigorous habits as celibacy or "corporal mortification."

- ✔ **Numeraries:** Numeraries, about 20 percent of the membership, are men and women who live in the Opus Dei centers, celibately, in segregated quarters. They are encouraged to be college graduates, and to work outside of the center, donating most of their money back to it, a very cultish practice.

- ✔ **Numerary Assistants:** Numerary Assistants are celibate women who live in the Opus Dei houses. They do not have outside jobs, and they take care of the cooking, cleaning, and other domestic matters of the center. The accusation of gross discrimination against women is generally aimed at the treatment of the members of this rank.

- ✔ **Associates:** The last small category of membership, Associates, have a high level of devotion but have obligations that require them to live outside the homes.

Numeraries, Numerary Assistants, and Associates live in celibate group homes, and so are far more likely to be considered by outsiders as members of a religious cult. Of course, to others, they might look more like monks in a monastery.

Despite this section's heading, Opus Dei is not a secret society. If it's anything negative at all, it may be a religious cult. Whether it's a harmless one is a matter of debate. They do incorporate a lot of medieval belief into their Catholicism, and that can make modern people nervous.

Part of their tradition is a monastic practice called *corporal mortification,* the idea that inflicting pain on yourself (or deprivation, as in a fast) is a way to "scourge yourself," to help achieve a state of grace. This practice was common in medieval Catholicism, though extremely rare today. It has also been practiced by other faiths besides Christianity. Members believe that this self-punishment, which is supposed to be inflicted in various mild forms, is their way of "taking up the cross," or in other words, sharing in Christ's pain in order to reach oneness with him.

Corporal mortification is only recommended in its mildest forms by the powers that be, who sometimes can't be held responsible when some nutcase decides to carry it over the edge. Members are encouraged to make small sacrifices here and there of the creature comforts we've become so used to; take a cold shower, sleep without a pillow, fast, or remain silent for a certain number of hours each day.

But some in the group houses let it get out of hand. Sometimes members flail themselves regularly with a small rope whip they call a *discipline,* while others go even farther, using a device called a *celise* mentioned in *The Da Vinci Code* that would make any sane man's flesh crawl — it looks like a cross between a Slinky and a piece of barbed wire, and it is to be worn beneath the clothing for a specified time, usually two hours, wrapped around the upper thigh, spikes pointing inward. According to Opus Dei, members are told *not* to draw blood with it. Terrific.

To be fair, corporal mortification isn't quite as loony as it sounds. In fact, aspects of it survive in our own culture in some very unlikely places. Its fans in Opus Dei describe it as a way of tuning in to a deeper level of awareness, a philosophy seen in many guises. Have you ever been driving home in the pouring rain, and you glance off to the side and notice a runner on the sidewalk, going for all he's worth, his face wearing a really unsettling grimace, but with sort of glassy eyes? Runners sometimes call this "being in the zone," a place where the pain is no longer felt, and the mind is at peace. As the body toils, even painfully, the mind clears, and a zone of inner serenity is reached that allows them to face their problems later with clarity and calm.

Now, do we recommend corporal mortification? No. In fact, we think it's a little nuts. On the other hand, we think the guy jogging 5 miles in the freezing rain is nuts, too.

A nonprofit organization called Opus Dei Awareness Network exists to reach out to people who have experienced a "negative impact on their lives" at the hands of the organization. According to the network, although Opus Dei isn't exactly a cult, they certainly do use many cult practices and, in general, exercise a high degree of control over their members — particularly, of course, the ones who live in Opus Dei houses.

Leonardo da Vinci and His Last Supper

Leonardo da Vinci was a unique artist, engineer, mathematician, inventor, musician, and writer. He was the embodiment of the true Renaissance Man, and every bit the eccentric genius he was reputed to have been. The question that undoubtedly comes up in any discussion about the Knights Templar and *The Da Vinci Code* is obvious: What does a Florentine artist from the 15th century have to do with a defunct order of medieval knights?

Da Vinci was definitely an esoteric character and a man of contrasts; a bastard son who rose to prominence; an early Deist who worshipped the perfect machine of nature to such a degree that he wouldn't eat meat, but who made his first big splash designing weapons of war; a renowned painter who didn't much like painting, and often didn't finish them, infuriating his clients; and a born engineer who loved nothing more than hours spent imagining new contraptions of every variety.

Da Vinci is listed in the Priory of Sion documents as a past Grand Master, a logical choice. Because he was an enigmatic man of eccentric genius, but little is known of his private side, people can impress on him any ideology they like.

Holy Blood, Holy Grail is not the only book that *The Da Vinci Code*'s hero, Robert Langdon, mentions. Another is *The Templar Revelation: Secret Guardians of the True Identity of Christ* (1997), by Lynn Picknett and Clive Prince. And it is here that the da Vinci connection to this whole story really begins, in their chapter "The Secret Code of Leonardo da Vinci." They specifically examine the two paintings that become central to *The Da Vinci Code: Madonna of the Rocks* and *The Last Supper*.

Da Vinci's famous *Last Supper* is actually an enormous painting that covers an entire wall of the Convent of Santa Maria delle Grazie in Milan, Italy. Although it was painted on a plaster wall, it is not, as it is sometimes described, a fresco. A fresco, for those of us who really care about such trivia, is painted on a *wet* plaster wall, so the paint actually is embedded into the plaster when it dries. Frescos last a long time. *The Last Supper,* alas, was simply painted on the dried surface of a plaster wall that constantly crumbles and is susceptible to temperature and humidity damage. Originally painted between 1493 and 1498, over the last five centuries it has been painted over, altered, and "restored" several times, with startlingly different results. The most recent, a process that took almost 20 years, painstakingly re-created what da Vinci painted, filling in with light watercolors where the original work was irreparable.

John or Mary?

One of the central themes of both the *Templar Revelation* and *The Da Vinci Code* is that the figure seated at Jesus's right hand is not a young St. John, but Mary Magdalene. "She" is alleged to be wearing feminine clothes, showing a hint of bosom, with a feminine face, and sitting in the place where a wife of Christ would normally be sitting, if he had one.

But if you actually *look* at the painting, *none* of it is true. "Her" clothes match the other apostles at the table — same look, same colors, even the same metal pin holding the neckline together. Anybody looking for a bosom here is hallucinating. And there is nothing else to indicate that the figure is anything other than the image of the very young male disciple that "Jesus loved," John. If he looks effeminate and needs a haircut, so does James, the second figure on the left, the one with the sort of Bette Midler look about him. And if we play along with this fantasy and say, okay, it *is* Mary Magdalene, then we have a math problem, because we'd be short one apostle in the room.

Another claim is that the cluster of apostles around Jesus's figure, along with the angles of Christ's shoulders and robe, form an *M,* and therefore create what amounts to a Renaissance billboard for Mary Magdalene. But again, if you actually look at the painting instead of taking Brown's — or our — opinion as fact, it could also be argued that da Vinci composed the space around Jesus as a *V,* as though you could expect rays of holy light to emanate from him at any second. Or a *V* for Vinci. Or maybe it was an *M* after all, and it stood for Milan. Or the Virgin Mary, which would mean it was *both* a *V* and an *M.* Or maybe it isn't there at all.

Writing about art is like knitting about music.

Sometimes a painting is just a painting, and sometimes what's in the painting is just what the painter put there. How do we *really* know that it's John sitting next to Jesus — or, for that matter, just exactly who each figure in the painting is supposed to be? After all, they aren't wearing name badges. Because da Vinci made preliminary sketches of the painting before he started, called *cartoons,* and in them, he wrote the name of every apostle next to everyone in the painting. The cartoons were for his own use as he worked out the design of the massive work. And da Vinci clearly identified the apostle next to Jesus. It wasn't Mary Magdalene. It was John.

The "missing" Grail found

> Sophie paused, realizing it was the trick question. And after dinner, Jesus took the cup of wine, sharing it with His disciples. "One cup," she said. "The chalice." The Cup of Christ. The Holy Grail. "Jesus passed a single chalice of wine, just as modern Christians do at communion."
>
> Teabing sighed. "Open your eyes."
>
> She did. Teabing was grinning smugly. Sophie looked down at the painting, seeing to her astonishment that everyone at the table had a glass of wine, including Christ. Thirteen cups. Moreover, the cups were tiny, stemless, and made of glass. There was no chalice in the painting. No Holy Grail.
>
> —Dan Brown, *The Da Vinci Code*

Oh, but there is, just not where it is *supposed* to be. Look at the painting. In reality, da Vinci's *Last Supper* (see Figure 12-1) is huge. If you stand up close, you'd never see it, because the Grail is not on the table in front of Christ, just as Teabing says. But as in all da Vinci paintings, it pays to look around, and then look again. It's part of his charm. Look at the last apostle on the left. Over his head is a window or doorframe. Up close, the lines just look like details of the alcove, even though such details don't appear in the other two similar ones behind it, or on the other side of the painting. But step back and look again, and the image of a chalice does indeed appear, floating right over the head of St. Bartholomew. When you see it, you'll look at it every time. (We're not the only ones to spot this in the painting. After we did, we went digging for allies. Have a look at code-breaker Gary Phillips's Web site at `http://realmoftwelve.fateback.com/about/grail.html`.)

Figure 12-1:
In spite of what Dan Brown claims, the Holy Grail is indeed in Leonardo da Vinci's *Last Supper,* over the head of the last apostle on the left, St. Bartholomew.

Erich Lessing / Art Resource, NY

But why him? Bartholomew barely appears in the New Testament accounts of the apostles — only as part of the lists of the followers of Christ that appear in Matthew, Mark, Luke, and Acts — and most biblical scholars believe he is also referred to as Nathanael in the Gospel of John. Curiously, according to Syrian tradition, his original name was Jesus. So there's lots of confusion among theologians about Bartholomew.

There is no Gospel of Bartholomew in the Bible. But there is an *apocryphal* Gospel of Bartholomew. It's a fascinating document that describes Jesus appearing to his disciples after the resurrection and, among other things, showing them the pit of hell, with a long interview between Bartholomew and Satan. But what may very well connect St. Bartholomew, the Grail, da Vinci's painting, and *The Da Vinci Code* is an episode in the gospel in which Jesus's mother, Mary, reluctantly tells the apostles about the circumstances surrounding her virgin conception of Christ. Here's a passage from the Gospel (Questions) of Bartholomew (4:5–6):

> Mary saith: Thou art the image of Adam: was not he first formed and then Eve? Look upon the sun, that according to the likeness of Adam it is bright. And upon the moon, that because of the transgression of Eve it is full of

clay. For God did place Adam in the east and Eve in the west, and appointed the lights that the sun should shine on the earth unto Adam in the east in his fiery chariots, and the moon in the west should give light unto Eve with a countenance like milk. And she defiled the commandment of the Lord. Therefore was the moon stained with clay and her light is not bright. Thou therefore, since thou art the likeness of Adam, oughtest to ask him: but in me was he contained that I might recover the strength of the female.

Now when they came up to the top of the mount, and the Master was withdrawn from them a little space, Peter saith unto Mary: Thou art she that hast brought to nought the transgression of Eve, changing it from shame into joy; it is lawful, therefore, for thee to ask.

In this little-known gospel, Mary says that by giving birth to Jesus, she has wiped away the original sin of Eve. If ever there a clear conflict with Church doctrine, it would have been this very contention! So, did da Vinci paint the Grail over Bartholomew because he wanted us to look at the gospel of this saint again for what was kept out of the Bible? Did he do it as an inside joke because Bartholomew's name was also Jesus? Or is there no significance to it being over Bartholomew at all, and the ghostly presence of the Grail in the background where we'd least expect it is just a visual prank? One thing is certain: *The Last Supper* took four years for da Vinci to complete. There is nothing there by accident. Teabing is right. There's no Grail in front of Jesus. But it *is* in the painting, and it's over Bartholomew.

Chapter 13

The Suppression of the "Feminine Divine": Truth or Feminist Fiction?

● ●

In This Chapter

▶ Scoping out the female side of God and finding it was there all along

▶ Refereeing the debate over Jesus and his "wife"

▶ Meeting some really divine fems

● ●

*F*eminine Divine. It sounds like a drag queen, doesn't it? Actually, it's the hottest thing to hit the university circuit since Women's Studies. The *feminine divine* is the hip new concept sweeping the nation, a term that was coined when some warmed-over scholarly theories about Neolithic goddess worship collided with modern feminist sensibilities to create a whole new angle on comparative religion.

But the feminine divine (or the *divine feminine* or *sacred feminine*) really hit its stride with the publication of a speculative history called *Holy Blood, Holy Grail,* which served up — along with a long menu of theories on everything from treasures to Templars — the notion that Jesus Christ may have been married. This idea wasn't a new one; actually, it had been hanging around for some time. But when combined with a little feminism and a great deal of speculation, it rushed onward to the peak of the craze, with the publication of Dan Brown's *The Da Vinci Code,* and its plotline about the descendants of Christ that turned it into the mega-blockbuster of all time.

The earth cooled, the mountains rose from the sea, mankind crawled out of the slime to build a civilization, God saw this and pronounced it good. And then Dan Brown wrote a novel, and everything changed.

That's really about the size of it. Like Thomas Paine's *Common Sense* or Harriet Beecher Stowe's *Uncle Tom's Cabin, The Da Vinci Code* was more than a book; it was a cultural earthquake. We now live in a post–*Da Vinci Code* age, a time when the mania for the book has finally died down, but a time in which most of the assertions of the book are accepted by the general public as holy writ.

Chapters 11 and 12 focus on the book as history, discussing the many and various aspects of *The Da Vinci Code* as they tie in to the Templars and other related subjects. This chapter focuses on an assertion that permeates the novel from beginning to end — the notion of the lost and abused feminine divine, and the theory that Judeo-Christian civilization, and the people who live in it, have been deeply wounded by this loss.

Defining Divine Femininity

So, what is the *sacred feminine* or the *feminine divine,* anyway? It's actually a pretty simple concept, particularly in *The Da Vinci Code.* Scholars and anthropologists discussing this subject can pile it on pretty high and deep. But remember, these guys have to prove to their fathers that the money they spent sending them to an Ivy League college wasn't wasted.

Dan Brown goes in the opposite direction, making his theme of the sacred feminine in *The Da Vinci Code* as simple, and supposedly as obvious, as A, B, C. He presents it as a war between two forces:

- ✔ The Old Way, the suppressed way of goddess worship and the "sacred feminine"
- ✔ The New Way, the Catholic Church, dominated by men, poisoned by celibacy, and determined to stamp out any power or prestige for women in order to keep men in charge

The pivot point of the novel is the theme of a marriage between Jesus and Mary Magdalene, a truth that the powers-that-be have spent 2,000 years hiding. This marriage, the bloodline stemming from it, and the Church's determination to destroy the evidence of it at any cost, becomes the central metaphor of Dan Brown's endlessly restated argument, that the Church has subjugated and tyrannized, not to mention demonized, women throughout history.

Dan Brown claims that over the course of three centuries, the Catholic Church burned over 5 million women at the stake. Nobody on this bus is defending the Inquisition or the "Witch's Hammer," the 15th-century do-it-yourself guide to exposing witches. But to portray the Inquisition as a genocidal attack on women is absurd. Both men and women went to the stake — Inquisitors were equal opportunity burners. As for the numbers, no one can say for certain, but it was far closer to 50,000, a tragic number to be sure, but a far cry from 5 million. The Inquisition was hardly a genocidal plot against women. It was a genocidal plot against *everybody.*

Dan Brown mentions three books prominently in the text of *The Da Vinci Code,* and states openly and honestly that they are the principal sources for the themes we outline here:

- ✔ The speculative history *Holy Blood, Holy Grail,* by Michael Baigent, Richard Lee, and Henry Lincoln
- ✔ *The Templar Revelation,* by Lynn Picknett and Clive Prince, which covers much of the same territory as *Holy Blood, Holy Grail*
- ✔ *The Woman With the Alabaster Jar,* by Margaret Starbird

These books are his main escape hatches, really, because Brown makes it crystal clear to the reader, through the mouths of his characters Robert Langdon and Sir Leigh Teabing, that he pulled 90 percent of the material from them. An honest rogue. All three books tie in to the Templars, the Grail, and the rest of the subjects in this section. We discuss the first two in greater depth in Chapter 12. We lay bare Margaret Starbird's book here.

The "lost bride"

To tell the truth, Margaret Starbird's groundbreaking book *The Woman with the Alabaster Jar* is not really that earth-shattering a set of ideas. We admit that it's the first time we've seen them gathered together in one easily accessible place. Starbird seems to know her stuff, and seeing all her knowledge of the Bible, of general history, and of myth, carefully laid out in a gigantic pointer toward one fact (that Jesus was married and that Mary Magdalene was his wife) makes for a very compelling argument. For Starbird, the denial of the Feminine Divine in the culture of the West has blinded people to the fact that Jesus obviously had a wife. She also believes that most of the violence, hatred and injustice of society is caused by the fact that our culture is skewed to the masculine while having lost the feminine, like a 2,000-year-old carburetor badly in need of an adjustment.

In the opening pages of her book, Starbird speaks eloquently of her spiritual crisis on reading *Holy Blood, Holy Grail.* She had been a devout Catholic, and the idea of Christ being married shook her up so badly that she became obsessed with it, determined to find out if there were any possibility of its being true. Afterward, she spends the rest of the book searching for the "lost bride," the bride of Christ, Mary Magdalene, in the firm belief that if this "lost bride" can be restored to her rightful place, society will be the better for it.

The thing is, this idea of Jesus having a wife isn't exactly new. People have been talking about it for years — one of us (Chris) heard about it when he was a kid, 30 years ago; the other (Alice), hadn't heard about it until reading *Holy Blood, Holy Grail.* (In the interest of full disclosure, we're both Catholic, but Alice's dad was a Presbyterian — a mixed marriage in those days. We're both open to the idea, if the evidence is there.)

The theory goes back even farther than Chris's childhood, and not much that's still alive and kicking can do that. For example, in 1946, Robert Graves of *I, Claudius* fame wrote a book called *King Jesus,* a novel that trotted out many of these same theories. But this earth-shattering and consciousness-altering contention remained mostly in the land of academia for many years. Before the astonishing find at Nag Hammâdi in 1945 (see the nearby sidebar, "Christian Gnostics") there were only a very few Gnostic texts available to researchers, as well as some fragments of larger works, tantalizing glimpses into a different kind of Christianity with a different belief system. Graves, as a professional scholar, would have had access to these, and he used his fertile imagination to fill in the rest.

TECHNICAL STUFF

Christian Gnostics

The Gnostic Gospels get mentioned a lot in *The Da Vinci Code* in relation to whether Jesus was married. The following is a criminally brief description, but both Chapters 7 and 14 discuss Gnostic beliefs in more detail.

For the most part, the Gnostic Gospels that Dan Brown is talking about were part of an incredible archeological find in Egypt in 1945. It was an entire Gnostic library that had been buried in a clay jar, probably to protect it from Byzantine church authorities who were hounding "heretics" back in the fourth century. These were gospels, stories of Christ by his followers, that were left out of the biblical canon, mostly because they reflected the Gnostic Christian viewpoint. Gnostics weren't just Christians — just about every religion on the planet has had a sect with a Gnostic point of view at one time or another. Gnostics believed, basically, in a duality in the universe, with good and evil in constant opposition.

What got the Christian Gnostics in trouble with the Church was some of the ideas that came out of this belief – for example, that Christ as well as all the material world had come out of the "evil" side of creation, or that God was evil as well as good. You've probably heard the terms for many of these famous heresies — Manichaeism, Arianism, Catharism, and Zoroastrianism. Lots of them are mentioned in this book, especially concerning the accusations of heresy against the Templars, who were accused of being Gnostics. In its first ten centuries of existence, the chief conflict in the Catholic Church was its attempt to stamp out these various heresies, despite many of them being very popular.

Robert Graves's imagination wasn't taken too seriously. That's because, even though these famous Gnostic Gospels of Nag Hammâdi were discovered in 1945, they floated around the Near East for years, sold in pieces by the Egyptian family who found them and had no idea of their worth. These leather-bound volumes called *codices* (a *codex* is an early form of book made by binding old-fashioned scrolls into an easier to read and carry format, the precursor to books as we know them) suffered heartbreaking damage during this period. The mother of the Arabic family who found them even burned some of them to light the family stove, thinking them worthless. Her sons sold them in pieces, while some came into the hands of a Coptic priest who was a family friend, and they finally ended up scattered here and there, to this university or that rare-book dealer. It took the scholarly world time to put it all together, time to translate it and correlate it all, to really understand the enormity of the find. You couldn't just walk into a bookstore in 1962 and buy a copy of the Gnostic Gospels the way you can today.

Of course, this isn't to say that the theory of a married Jesus wasn't causing the occasional flap long before Dan Brown. Slowly but surely, the Gnostic Gospels, with their indication of a Mary Magdalene of vital importance to early Christians, were making their way into the larger culture. For example, in 1970, the publication of a book with the straightforward title *Was Jesus Married?: The Distortion of Sexuality in the Christian Tradition,* by William E. Phipps, set off quite a firestorm in England, when a bishop of the Anglican Church read it, left the Church, and got married. But we're sorry to say that Mr. Phipps didn't have a whole lot to hang his hat on, factually speaking.

So what did the Vatican have to say about all this? They didn't try to suppress the theory, and they didn't secretly hire albino hit men to go out and kill anyone. They just smiled serenely and rode out the entire little flap. It's what Holy Mother Church has always done best.

The mysterious Magdalene

Before heading into the subject of the *speculation* concerning Mary Magdalene, it's important to start off with what we know *for certain* about her. It isn't much. For centuries, Biblical scholars haven't even been able to decide how many biblical passages are about Mary Magdalene, or how many references to a woman named Mary, as in Mary of Bethany, may really be talking about *the Magdalene.*

Too many Marys

The New Testament can be very confusing, insofar as who this or that person is, and the gospels as they exist aren't always careful about explaining. The authors weren't historians, and they probably didn't think it was that important.

Myths and legends got told and retold, with an overarching feel to them of a Borsch-belt comedian ("You see, there was this guy . . ."). For the authors of the gospels, the story being told, and its spiritual point, was the important thing.

It doesn't help that there was already a great deal of confusion about names, which is also nothing new. In Tudor England, for example, it's estimated that roughly 70 percent of the women were named Mary, Catharine, or Elizabeth. Just like the first generation of the second millennium A.D. will doubtless be overrun with Britneys, Anna Nicoles, and J. Los. It was the same in biblical days. Certain popular names, Mary or Sarah, John or Joseph, were used again and again. There were six separate Marys in the New Testament. Often, in the struggle for a little clarity, these people were referred to by the added name of where they lived — Mary of Bethany, for example, or Joseph of Arimathea, or even something odder, like Simon the leper. The confusion comes in trying to figure out whether Simon the leper was also Simon the fisherman as well as Simon the moneylender.

Are you a hooker, or am I just doing great with you?

Somehow along the way, mostly in the folklore and oral tradition, Mary Magdalene became Mary the prostitute, redeemed by her love and faith. Back in the sixth century, Pope Gregory I preached an influential sermon in which he stated that the Mary Magdalene, who had seven demons cast out of her by Jesus, was the same unnamed woman "sinner" that Jesus forgives in the story just before it. Of course, in the sixth century, people also believed that the sun revolved around the Earth. We don't believe that anymore. For centuries biblical scholars have known that there's no evidence to support this popular legend whatsoever. So why won't the image of Mary Magdalene as a prostitute finally be laid to rest?

The sun still revolves around the Earth in the world of cinema. In 1977, famed Italian director Franco Zeffirelli made a popular miniseries called *Jesus of Nazareth* (a film that sticks pretty close to the gospels in general), and, in 1988, director Martin Scorsese made the film *The Last Temptation of Christ* (a film that's a bit of a mess). In both movies, the Magdalene is a prostitute. Both directors are Catholic, both intelligent and well-read, yet neither would let this particular myth go. As for the Protestants, as far back as 1909, the Scofield Reference Bible, arguably the most detailed and referenced study Bible every produced, with its modern system of translation notes and cross-references, went to great lengths to point out that the Magdalene was not a prostitute or a sinner. Yet, so many years later, Zeffirelli and Scorsese still have her streetwalking for a living.

There is one certain thing, one image of Mary Magdalene that emerges from all four gospels: her very special place among Jesus's followers. When the so-called Gnostic Gospel of Phillip an apocryphal gospel that had not been included in the canon of the New Testament, was discovered at Nag Hammâdi, much was made of the fact that a particular passage says that Jesus had kissed Mary "upon the [blank]." Yes, it's that cruel a joke. The one little word upon which the work of so many speculative historians hinges appears where there is now a hole in the battered text. However, we don't see where it matters that much, despite all the brouhaha over it. Based on the context of the sentence, the word was doubtless either *face* or *mouth,* and either way it doesn't make much difference. No one who has read the New Testament in its accepted form needed this additional information to find out about the very special status of Mary in the entourage of Jesus; it has been a subject of speculation for centuries. But from papal bulls to the *Encyclopedia Britannica,* she is called not "St. Mary," but rather "the female disciple," perhaps a term of even more respect. In early Catholic tradition, she was sometimes called the *Apostola Apostolorum*, the "Apostle of Apostles," certainly implying her importance, not just to Jesus, but to the early preaching of the gospel. She was conceded a very high place within the Church if only for the fact that she was, without doubt, the first person to see Jesus after his resurrection, surely a sign of divine preference. All four gospels place her at the foot of the cross with Christ's family during the crucifixion.

As they would in spreading the new faith, women played a very important part in Jesus' ministry, and many women, of high and low rank, followed him. But chief among them was the Magdalene. That's the reason some people tend to get very huffy about the fact that Mary Magdalene was often cast as a prostitute. But it was merely confusion, not character assassination.

The Q Document

Often, when you're reading material about the Magdalene, a big deal will be made out of the fact that something appears in all four gospels. You may also hear the term *synoptic gospels.* The synoptic gospels are the first three: Matthew, Mark, and Luke. They're called that because they tell pretty much the same stories in the same order, often using similar phrases, while John is different.

Dan Brown makes hay in *The Da Vinci Code* out of something with the ominous, 007-esque moniker "The Q Document," which he says even the Vatican "admits" probably exists. But it's not the mysterious key to hidden gospels that he makes it out to be. The so-called "Q Document" is a gospel that scholars believe may have been written before the other three, and that's why the synoptic gospels are similar, because they raided things from the same source. It's only a theory — there is no actual document of this kind — but because some of the gospels were written as early as A.D. 70, it's very exciting for Bible scholars to think there may be something out there even older, perhaps written in Christ's lifetime.

But that's why it's so important if something appears in all four gospels. This fact alone definitely adds weight to the truth and or importance of the story.

In studying the four gospels of the New Testament, we believe it's pretty easy to figure out how the urban legends about Mary Magdalene got started. In the Book of Luke, Chapter 7, there is a story of an unnamed woman that could be one key to the mix-up. In this chapter, Jesus is invited to dinner in the home of a prominent local Pharisee, the *Pharisees* being the more conservative of the two main Jewish sects of the period. (The others were the *Sadducees*.) The apostles aren't thrilled that Jesus has accepted this invitation; they know very well that the man is Jesus's enemy.

During the dinner, an unnamed woman enters, carrying an alabaster box of ointment. Ointments and perfumes of all sorts were very prized in Judea in this period, and were often more valuable than silver or gold. The woman is referred to only as "a sinner." She kneels weeping at Jesus's feet, "washing them with her tears" according to the Bible, then drying them with her hair. She then anoints his head with the ointment. This anointing of the feet and head was a common act of courtesy extended to an honored guest, but, of course, scholars have spent volumes on it insofar as its obvious metaphorical message of anointing a sacred man. *This* is the unnamed "sinner," the woman with the alabaster box. Jesus forgives this woman her sins, sins that are never named or cataloged, and she leaves. Almost immediately afterwards, in the opening of the next chapter, Jesus meets the Magdalene for the first time. According to Luke he healed her, "casting out seven demons from her," a common ancient explanation for all sorts of illnesses. These lines about the Magdalene occur only a few lines after the story of the unnamed "sinner."

Now, remember two things:

- ✔ Those little separation notes in italics that break up Biblical chapters are modern conventions added much later. Early Bibles were done like one long, run on sentence. Within separate biblical books, chapters were not used to divide material until the 1200s, and verses didn't arrive until the 1500s.

- ✔ Being "possessed by demons," a state spoken of often in the gospels, was interpreted in many and various ways in the Middle Ages. Being in the grip of sin, as a prostitute or a violent murderer was, could be the same as being "possessed by demons" to the medieval mind, just as it could have meant something like being subject to epileptic seizures. They didn't make the fine distinctions we do today.

Okay, now look at Chapter 7 in Luke again. The two stories are very, very close to one another. It wouldn't have been hard to pick up the mistaken impression that the woman who is later cured of seven demons by Jesus, Mary Magdalene, was the prostitute of the story that has just been told, even though that woman wasn't specifically named as a prostitute; again, she has no name at all.

When someone thought of a woman as a "sinner" in those days, a prostitute tended to come to mind, or an adulteress. Maybe it's sloppy, but it wasn't deliberately spiteful. Some of the more paranoid feminist types writing about this have said that Mary Magdalene was quite purposely labeled a prostitute in order to demean her, because the early Church fathers were frightened and unnerved by a woman in a position of such prominence and grace. Nonsense. The Magdalene was cast as a prostitute because it made for such a great *story*. Despite Margaret Starbird's contention in *The Woman with the Alabaster Jar* that the temple prostitutes of pagan faiths were respected women (and we'd love to debate that one), the fact is that in all cultures, there was no one looked down on more than a prostitute. What a great tool to use to reach out to sinful people and show them God's love. It made a better story that way. If it didn't, Zeffirelli and Scorsese, storytellers both, wouldn't have been so determined to keep her the proverbial "hooker with a heart of gold." The cult of the Magdalene was a very popular one in the Church, from the beginning. The story of a prostitute who loved God really hit a nerve with everyday people.

This is how the entirety of the gospels is structured — stories *about* Jesus, and stories told *by* Jesus, to illuminate timeless lessons of brotherhood, tolerance, and faith. When Jesus tells the parable of the Prodigal Son, the subject of the story doesn't have a name and address; he's an archetype, a foolish young man eager for the good things in life that everyone can identify with. And when the Roman soldier comes to Christ and asks that his servant be healed, and then says that Jesus needn't bother actually coming with him, thereby showing his absolute faith, no book of the New Testament refers to him as anything apart from "the centurion." He had no name, and he didn't need one. It was a great story.

So, when one lone little monk, armed with nothing but a Bible, headed out for the pagan wilds of Ireland or Germany, he had one thing more — those great stories. Sitting around the fire at night with the locals, who ran the gamut from suspicious to hostile, he could pull up a log, take a deep breath, and then say, "You see, there was this guy. . . ."

Where people don't know, they tend to fill in for themselves. That's what folklore is all about. The very special place of Mary Magdalene in the gospels, combined with how little is actually known about her, has always made her a figure absolutely ripe for myth, too many of them to count. Now, with her new importance in the Gnostic Gospels and her "wedding" in *The Da Vinci Code*, the legends and myths of the Magdalene will be more numerous than ever before.

The woman with the alabaster box

So, it would seem that that little confusion over Mary has been tucked up nicely and put to bed. Unfortunately, there's more. There is *another* Mary in the New Testament, Mary of Bethany, who is also a "woman with the alabaster box." She is the younger sister of Martha and of Lazarus, the man Jesus raised from the dead. Bethany is near Jerusalem, and they are depicted as family friends in the Bible, who play host to Jesus whenever he travels there. In three biblical books, Matthew 26, Mark 14, and John 12, Mary of Bethany comes into the room where Jesus and the apostles are dining, carrying an alabaster box, and anoints him with oil, fragrant amber spikenard oil, which was very expensive. When Judas says it's a waste, and that the oil could have been sold and the money given to the poor, Jesus gives the ominous reply that the poor will be with them always, while he will not. He then blesses Mary for this act, and says she will be remembered for it.

Margaret Starbird makes much of this Mary of Bethany thing. She seems to think that if she can prove Mary of Bethany and the Magdalene are one in the same, it will prove Mary and Jesus were married. Maybe we're dim, but we just don't see it. In all three biblical chapters, Mary of Bethany anoints Jesus soon before his arrest and execution, and Christ even makes reference to this as a ceremony symbolic of his burial. (In Judea at that time, dead bodies were anointed in the same way.) It seems obvious from the story that the young Mary of Bethany has picked up on Jesus' references to his impending death, while his own disciples have not. But to say that this sort of closeness is something that would be felt by a wife is pretty much of a stretch, and not much in the way of proof.

The Starbird contention

Okay, here's the scoop on the facts laid out in Starbird's controversial book, *The Woman with the Alabaster Jar*. It begins with Starbird's perfectly logical contention that within a culture's myths and legends are to be found "fossils," the archeological remnants of the events that gave the stories birth. Many of the fossils she digs up are quite intriguing; others seem like a real stretch. But she uses them to structure this alternative account of Christ's life.

Jesus Christ was married, and his wife was Mary Magdalene. Mary of Bethany and Mary Magdalene were one and the same. The confusion over names is simple enough to explain: Mary of Bethany would have been of the place called Bethany, which sat at the foot of the Mount of Olives, just to the east of Jerusalem. Remember in the story of the Templars, for example, that sometimes the same man was referred to as Raymond de Saint-Gilles, Raymond of Toulouse, or the Count of Toulouse. They were all the same man. Starbird claims that the additional name of "Magdalene" was more of a title, "Magdala," meaning "tower," as in Micah the prophet's reference to the Daughter of Zion as a "tower over the flock." In effect, it could be like calling her "Mary the Great."

This business about "Magdalene" being a courtesy title is important to Starbird's theory. Mary Magdalene was probably at least a minor heiress of lands surrounding Jerusalem (as the lands of Bethany do), and that she may well have come out of the tribe of Benjamin. No proof, however is offered for this — it is mere speculation. There were 12 tribes of Israel, each with its own subtle shadings of character and special history. Benjamin was the tribe of Israel's first anointed king, Saul, and had Mary come out of Benjamin, with Jesus claiming descent from the line of David, it would definitely have been a dynastic marriage and would have been seen that way by people at the time.

Redeeming women

Margaret Starbird's book, *The Woman with the Alabaster Jar* puts forward two ideas:

✔ That rituals grow out of myths, and those myths can give us undiscovered truths

✔ That many of our culture's rituals and myths tell us that divinity was once feminine rather than masculine

Most historians would agree with the first part, at least. But she doesn't cite many examples to back this up, and we think she missed some whoppers on her own side of the debate. Here's one of them.

In Ancient Israel, a custom dating back to the mists of prehistory dictated that, at roughly 30 days after the birth of a child (which gave a woman time to complete her period of withdrawal after a birth, so that she would be considered ritually purified), Jewish parents took their newborn to the Temple or the local holy sanctuary to be "redeemed," quite literally; they paid the priest five shekels of silver.

Pagan Semitic peoples often believed that the firstborn, not just of women but of all creatures, should be sacrificed, in order to assure continuing fertility. Every mother knows that the first birth is always rough going. These Neolithic peoples believed that this first difficult delivery opened up the birth canal, making it — and there's just no delicate way to put this — a well-oiled machine that could now easily deliver up many more offspring.

But the desert God of the Hebrews was just and merciful, and abhorred more than anything else the sacrifice of children, as witnessed by the hatred of the Jews for Ruth, the Moabite, because she came of a people that practiced ritual child sacrifice. And so, it's probable that this idea of sacrificing the firstborn evolved over time into the ritual of a paid redemption, literally buying the child back from the hands of God. What's key here to the discussion is the sex of the child. Initially, all children were "redeemed" from God, but eventually, somewhere in the post-Exodus era, that changed, and only sons were redeemed. The implication being, of course, that only sons were worth redeeming. Quite a change of attitude.

Jesus's controversial life and violent death, along with the continuing danger from the authorities for his followers, would have put a wife in a very perilous situation. Jesus may have turned to the richest and most powerful of his followers, Joseph of Arimathea, to protect his wife and to spirit her out of the country. The south of France would have been ideal — there was civilization, with a small Jewish community and a half-hearted Roman presence, but it was off the beaten track, and filled with foreigners among whom she could disappear. Many of the legends of the Magdalene in the south of France tie her to the figure of Joseph. They may first have gone to Alexandria in Egypt, where there was a large Jewish population, so that Mary could deliver her child there before continuing on her journey. This would explain the "Cult of the Black Madonnas" so popular in the south of France. The Gauls in the south of France perceived Mary and her child Sarah in their myths as having come out of Egypt, and so gave statues and paintings of them dark skin.

After the Magdalene was spirited away, Christ's marriage became a dangerous secret of his inner circle, and in order to protect the woman they considered to be their rightful queen, not to mention the royal child she carried, they would have gotten her as far from Israel as possible. And it was there, the book contends, that she was lost to history. This aspect of the theory has a very respectable ring of logic — far more logic than a massive effort on the part of the Church to confiscate or burn anything that mentioned the marriage.

At this point the new narrative of Jesus's life picks up the *Holy Blood, Holy Grail* doctrine (discussed in Chapters 11 and 12) and runs with it. Mary and Jesus's daughter Sarah's descendants married into the Merovingian line of French kings (A.D. 476–A.D. 750), eventually setting off a struggle between the Merovingians and the forces of orthodoxy that lasts through their descendants into the present day.

Mary's Marriage: Pros and Cons

In his novel, Dan Brown makes much of Napoleon's quip, "What is history but a fable agreed upon?" Napoleon was the master of such quips, cranking out about 20 a day. But is Brown's contention really true, that history is "written by the winners"? If it is, then why do we know so much about the Nazis, or Stalin, or the Plantagenets, for that matter? Historians struggle to learn more every day about even the ancient losers, like the Etruscans who were wiped out by the Romans.

As with so much in the novel, there's truth in the statement, a surface truth anyway, but a surface that's far too slick to really build such an important historical argument upon. The true historian never blinds himself with preconceived notions about a subject, but does his best to free his mind of the shackles of convention and look only at the evidence at hand. This we'll do, with the evidence of a marriage between Jesus and Mary Magdalene.

The following sections lay out the intriguing pieces of evidence we possess that point to a marriage, or at least a sexual relationship, between Mary Magdalene and Jesus, and the equally intriguing arguments of the people who say this is a lot of baloney. Historians of the future will probably be armed with more information than this, from exciting discoveries of documents and archeological evidence that have yet to be made. In the meantime, look over the facts we have, and make a judgment call for yourself.

Pros

In the following sections we cover the major, and most respectable, arguments for a marriage between Jesus and Mary Magdalene. We may be prejudiced, but we just don't think that having a medieval Bible printer use a unicorn (a popular myth at the time) as his watermark symbol means he was trying to tell us that the horn symbolized the sexual potency of Jesus. We don't think much of looking for *M*'s in tarot cards as proof, either. Some of the facts in the following sections, however, strike us as compelling evidence.

A painting is just a painting

There's one annoying little foible that the Brownites share: their obsession with looking for hidden messages in medieval and Renaissance artwork. They don't seem to realize that this is all strictly interpretive; you see in it what you *want* to see in it. Stare at a dishtowel long enough and you'll see the Holy Grail. This obsession often blinds them to more powerful evidence for their own argument that's right under their noses. For example, only one of Dan Brown's admitted research books, *The Templar Revelation,* points out a compelling piece of pro-marriage evidence — the fact of just how far back this belief goes in the south of France. Documentary evidence of Cistercian monks going back to the 12th century discusses the "disgusting heresy" of the locals that Mary Magdalene was the concubine of Jesus.

Any historian will tell you that the older a piece of evidence is, meaning the closer it is to the event itself, the more likely it is to be at least partially true. It is a deeply-held belief in the south of France that the Magdalene preached the gospel there — many sites, all along the Mediterranean coast of France, are considered holy because she ministered and converted there. Myths, particularly of this age, don't appear out of thin air. The image of Mary Magdalene in France is different from any other place on Earth. It doesn't require an enormous leap away from logic to suppose that this difference grows out of the fact that they walked with her, knew her, and received a great deal of their Christian faith from her. And if they knew her, they knew what her relationship to Jesus was.

No unescorted ladies in the bar, please

Many passages in the New Testament seem strange to a historian who knows anything about the conservative nature of first-century Judea. In a time and place where women were not free to roam about following a desert prophet, Mary Magdalene did so. Combine this with the fact that several passages make it clear that she supported the new faith, passages implying financial support; they state that she "ministered to him" of her "substance" (Mark 15:40, Luke 8:3). Therefore, she was obviously a woman of at least some rank and wealth, hardly the poor prostitute of legend. Had she been a prostitute, nothing would have been said. But in those days, a single woman of rank and wealth traveling in the entourage of a single man, constantly in his company, would have caused more than raised eyebrows. This was a time when adulteresses were stoned (and by this they included "fallen women"). Yet, there's nothing in any of the gospels to imply that a single word was ever spoken against her, or that a single ugly incident occurred. Of course, nothing would have been said, if she had been Jesus's wife.

New gospels, new perspectives

The Gnostic Gospels present an entirely different Mary Magdalene, one at the very center of the young Christian movement. She is the first person to see Jesus after his resurrection, and she is, again, constantly by his side, although this time, unlike in the New Testament canon, she's actually allowed to talk. In several of the Gnostic Gospels, Jesus states that he has symbolically raised her to the position of a man, when the apostles question why a mere woman has been given such power. We don't believe this was intended as an insult, but as a reference to the union of sexes, because there is no sex in paradise, as Paul later states.

The Gnostics had a general tendency to treat women with equality. In the Gnostic Gospel of Thomas, the apostle Simon Peter, who is always presented as a thorn in Mary's side, says that she should leave the room for the conversation, for "women are not worthy of life." Jesus chides Simon Peter that he will then "make her male." In the Gnostic Gospel of Thomas, when Thomas asks Jesus what must be done to enter the kingdom of heaven, part of his reply is that "When you make the two one . . . and the above like the below, and when you make the male and the female one and the same," then you will enter heaven. The Gnostic Gospel of Phillip speaks openly of the close personal and touchy-feely relationship between Mary and Jesus. And in the Pistis Sophia, a Gnostic Gospel discovered much earlier than Nag Hammâdi, when Mary Magdalene asks to speak, Jesus replies, "Mary, thou blessed one, whom I will perfect in all mysteries of those of the height, discourse in openness, thou whose heart is raised to the kingdom of heaven more than all they brethren." Taken together, these new gospels really do suggest something far more for Mary than her simple New Testament status as a "follower."

Are you married? Then you're a bum!

When Dan Brown alleges that all Jewish men were married during the time of Jesus, there is an element of truth in what he's saying. We just wish he'd found a more tasteful way to say it. It leaves you with a Neil Simonesque image of the Jewish father in *Come Blow Your Horn* shouting at his bachelor son, "Are you married? Then you're a *bum!*" It's true that if Jesus was a rabbi, in particular, then he naturally would have married — it would simply have been expected of him. Yet, there were celibate Jews, sects of monastic, and often apocalyptic Jews like the Essenes, who believed that the Romans were one more sign that doom was just around the corner.

But all this is sort of dancing around the point. The real point is that if Jesus came with a message of celibacy, and a belief that all holy men should remain celibate, then why isn't it mentioned in the New Testament? His silence on this subject, and that of his followers, is deafening.

Cons

There is, of course, plenty of evidence for the other side, equally compelling.

New gospels aren't always better ones

Although the Gnostic Gospels paint a very different portrait of Mary Magdalene, an image of a woman with much more power and influence in the movement, the fact remains that none of them comes right out and says anything about a marriage or even a sexual relationship. These Gnostic Gospels were heretical, and they wouldn't have shrunk from pointing out a marriage if the writers (most of whom are very early, just after the turn of the first century A.D.) had known of such a marriage. The closest any comes is in the oft-quoted Gospel of Phillip, which probably said that Jesus kissed Mary Magdalene often on the mouth, which made the other apostles very jealous of her special status. (There's actually a hole in the document under the word *mouth* that Dan Brown fills in so freely. But any open-minded reading of the text will show that it had to be either *face* or *mouth* because of the structure of the sentence.) The problem is, that's all it takes to be married, a kiss on the mouth? If so, Britney Spears and Madonna need to go register for a china pattern. To the opposition, this isn't much of a proof.

What's in a name?

As far as most scholars are concerned, Mary Magdalene was called "Magdalene" because she was from the fishing village of Magdala on the shore of the Sea of Galilee, not because it was any sort of title. Incidentally, the rabbi we consulted couldn't come up with a Hebrew word similar to "Magdal" that meant "tower," which is Starbird's contention (that Magdalene could be a sloppy translation of "tower over the flock").

Humanity versus divinity

Unfortunately for Dan Brown, despite his contention that the Gnostic Gospels present a far more human Christ, if you sit down and read them, you'll find just the opposite to be true. In fact, many Gnostics were burned at the stake simply for believing that Christ *was* God, and if he was, then he couldn't really have been in a human body, because human bodies and all matter on Earth was evil, while all good was invisible and spiritual. Some thought that what the apostles saw wasn't a person, but just a projection, like a hologram, just something for them to see because they wouldn't have understood Jesus otherwise. Therefore, the Gnostic Gospels, taken as a whole, don't present a more "human" Christ that it's easier to believe would have had a wife.

Rome's lecherous gods and goddesses

The overwhelming majority of religions surrounding these new Christians were Hellenized religions, and no one would have thought twice about a god with a wife and child. *All* gods had wives and children — and lots of them. If we accept Brown's claim that *all* Jewish men were married, that means the Jews would also have had no problem with a married Messiah. And everyone else was a Gentile, all of them Hellenized, who would have accepted the deity-as-parent notion without a second thought. In fact, it was the very concept of Christ as a *celibate* that struck potential converts as being so strange, and so had to be overcome by the early evangelists to the Gentiles, like Paul.

But my wife is my best friend

Probably the worst place where Dan Brown dropped the ball is in his contention that, when Mary is referred to in the Gospel of Phillip as Christ's "companion," everyone knew that, in ancient Aramaic, *companion* meant "spouse." Brown assures his readers that "any Aramaic scholar" will tell you this. Well, we consulted several Aramaic scholars, and they confirmed nothing of the kind. Not one agreed that this statement was in any way correct.

Aramaic is an offshoot of Hebrew mixed with other Near Eastern dialects, such as Phoenician. It was the everyday language of Jerusalem in the time of the gospels, while Hebrew was the holy language of the Temple. A few of the gospels were originally written in Aramaic. In that language, as in many Romance languages, *wife* and *woman* are the same word, and neither is in any way related to the term *companion* or *friend*.

Rabbi Arnold Bienstock of Congregation Shaarey Tefilla, fluent in both Hebrew and Aramaic, conceded the merest shred of possibility that in Ancient Aramaic, the term *companion* may have been used in certain instances in the same way that the French use the term *petite amie* (my little friend), which is old-fashioned slang for a girlfriend or mistress. We have no way of knowing. That's about as far as anyone would go in Aramaic.

But the really funny moment came when we dug a little deeper. According to biblical scholar and translator Bart Ehrman, the entire Gospel of Phillip was written in Coptic, not Aramaic. Coptic was another Semitic language altogether, spoken mostly in Egypt, where this version of the gospel was found, at Nag Hammâdi. Moreover, the word as it appears in the original gospel was a word Coptic had borrowed from the Greek, so we now have *two* languages that aren't Aramaic. The word used for *companion* was *koinonos,* and even in Greek there is no confusion as to its meaning. It means either companion or friend, with no lingering wisp of lover or spouse. Therefore, this word game on which Dan Brown has hung so much of his argument is wrong in *three* languages.

This gospel is out, end discussion

The Brownites contend that the Church did its best to suppress gospels that were not "canonical." There is some truth in this, although many of these gospels were read through the centuries, right up until the Renaissance, while others fell into oral tradition. But they also contend that the monks doing the copying were diddling with the text, cutting out what didn't conform to the orthodox. Did they diddle with the text? Yes, all the time, for a variety of reasons. Did they cut out the little fact that Christ was married? It seems unlikely. This is because archeological finds of ancient documents don't just poke holes in the Church — sometimes they back it up. Codices of gospels in the New Testament canon that have been found from the very early second century, long before the Council of Nicaea, have proven remarkable in their own way. Yes, they're different from the ones in your local bookstore, but not that different. In many respects, considering the number of times they've been copied and the number of monks doing the copying, the similarities are powerful evidence in favor of the argument that the post-Nicaea Church did not run around rewriting gospels, or burning gospels they didn't like.

Why bother with celibate followers?

If the Brownites are right, and the Templars were the guardians of the Grail, and that Grail was the secret of the holy bloodline, then why were they celibate? And they weren't just celibate; they were *celibate.* Other orders of monks had had their sexual scandals, but not the Templars. Their image was squeaky clean insofar as sexual shenanigans are concerned. If the secret they guarded was that Christ was married, being obsessively celibate doesn't seem like the way they would honor their savior.

The Gospel of Mary, the only gospel written by a woman

We find it strange that Margaret Starbird doesn't hit on the Gnostic Gospel of Mary in her book more often. For our money, it's the most powerful clue we have that Jesus might — we say *might* — have been married to the Magdalene. It's the only gospel we have that is the words of a woman — the words, in fact, of Mary Magdalene to the disciples, after Jesus's death. Huge chunks of it are missing — only 52 lines of it have survived — and we can only hope that someday archeologists find it in its entirety. But what we have is incredibly compelling.

In the Gnostic Gospel of Mary, Mary tells the disciples of a vision in which Christ appeared to her, explaining the mysteries of the nature of the soul. The vision ends with a warning not to create too many laws or rules beyond the word of God, because they might be constraining, which sounds very much like Jesus's criticism of the tangle of laws governing the lives of the Pharisees and the Sadducees. When the apostle Peter, always hot tempered, challenges her version of the nature of the soul, saying that he never heard Christ say any such thing, Levi (the apostle Matthew's name before Jesus rechristened him) steps in and says that no one was more beloved of Jesus than Mary, and what she says goes. Peter and the rest of the apostles agree, and the gospel comes to a close. A powerful argument for Mary's high place among them.

If you'd like to read the Gospel of Mary for yourself, you can find it for free on various Web sites, including `http://www.gnosis.org/library/marygosp.htm`. If, as we hope, you decide you want to know more, we recommend two books:

- *The Gospel of Mary of Magdala*, by Karen L. King: There is an extremely intelligent examination of this gospel in this book.

- *Lost Scriptures*, by Bart D. Ehrman: If you want to read the other fascinating Gnostic Gospels, we recommend this book. Many other books on this topic exist, but for an introduction, Ehrman's is the easiest to understand.

Sacred sex

This business about *hieros gamos* really doesn't play well for the Brown team. The term *hieros gamos* comes from the Greek, and it translates to "holy wedding" or, if you will, "holy sexual union." It's a later term for the Neolithic and pagan practice of ritualized sex in reverence to the gods of fertility. It was often acted out in temples of the Near East as part of goddess worship, where the high priestess (standing in for the goddess) and the selected god/king (standing in for the god) have sex in the temple, either to rouse the gods to similar fertility, or to pay homage to them. In many pagan cults, "sacred prostitutes" were installed in the temples, so that, for a few shekels, any guy could take part in the fun, turning houses of worship into brothels, a thing often mentioned none too kindly by early Hebrew prophets.

In the famous "parable of the mustard seed" that's related in several gospels, Jesus, in the version in Mark 4, makes the relatively innocuous statement that he speaks in parables (stories) for the masses, but that, alone with his disciples, he will "expound all things." The Brownites claim this as a sign that the disciples were receiving secret teachings from Jesus that were too shocking for the masses. Through some similarly convoluted proofs, they try to assert that Jesus preached the *hieros gamos* as part of his doctrine of peace and love.

We have to say that this contention is not only criminally stupid, it's insulting. In roughly 168 B.C., the Hellenized Syrian emperor Antiochus IV, overlord of Palestine, attempted to install "sacred prostitution" on the Temple Mount. It set off the bloody revolt of the Maccabees that would eventually throw Antiochus out and establish the Hasmonean line of Jewish kings, a guerrilla war still celebrated in the holiday of Hanukkah. The victorious Maccabees went to great lengths to ritually cleanse the Temple afterward. These are not the actions of men who have any belief whatsoever in the "sacred" act of *hieros gamos*. It seems unlikely that Jesus, raised a devout Jew, would have had an attitude that was any different.

Goddess Worship and the Sacred Feminine: Do We Really Want It Back Again?

Dan Brown bought hook, line, and sinker into one of the more annoying foibles of Margaret Starbird and her imitators. They speak wistfully of that long ago Neolithic period of goddess worship, a time in which women were the respected equals of men, sex was not shameful but was openly performed in temples as part of religious ritual, and all God's children were happy and free, living in deep and joyful union with Mother Earth. If the French philosopher Voltaire was right, and Christianity is nothing but a myth, then this stuff amounts to a fairy tale.

The women who worshipped goddesses

Just because the High Priestess of a particular Neolithic cult was a woman doesn't mean the women of that time and place were more respected. The power players, the rulers and the generals of the armies, were almost invariably men. Sexual roles, as far as we can tell in a society without the written word, were about the same in Neolithic times as they were right up until the 20th century, and the same was true in the Far East.

The Neolithic period

Most of these assumptions about goddess or mother-earth goddess worship come to us from anthropologists, who often disagree on all sorts of things about this age. That's because the Neolithic period is two maddening things:

- The 15,000 years or so before the dawn of civilization in the Nile and Mesopotamia

- A period without the written word

Consequently, everything we know about it is based on anthropological field work, archeological digging, and scholarly surmise. *Surmise* is the word scholars use when they don't want to say "guessing."

But a bit of reading on the subject of the rituals of these prehistoric goddess worshippers gives more than a little pause. Fertility was everything, and whatever you had to do to get it was okay. Very often this included killing something, or *someone,* as a ritual sacrifice, their blood soaking the earth a symbol of renewal of the soil. *The Woman with the Alabaster Jar* in particular speaks of this worship in vague generalities, as does Dan Brown. To be more specific could prove occasionally inconvenient — it's hard to sound longingly melancholy about many of these cults, which practiced such delightful ceremonies as ritual sacrifice, particularly of virgins and children, but also sometimes of the god-king who "marries" the temple high priestess in the *hieros gamos* ceremony.

The "god-king" was not a real power but a paper king, merely a symbol, and as such, he could not be allowed to sicken or age. This god-king myth lived on for some time; it's clearly reflected in the stories of King Arthur and the belief in his eventual return from the Isle of Avalon, because Arthur and the land were one, and if Arthur actually had "died" (in the myths he is merely carried off) then the land, too, would perish. These Neolithic stand-in "god-kings" were often killed before they could age, then buried (literally "planted," in an obvious metaphor for enriching the soil).

But this was certainly not the only ritual sacrifice these believers in the "sacred feminine" practiced; archeologists cite the "conspicuous frequency" of skeletal remains of women and children in the burial places for the victims of these rituals. As for celibacy, the high priests of Greece and the Near East who served these goddesses often castrated themselves, thereby saving everyone the problem. On other holy days, such as the "Day of Blood" in the popular Neolithic Near Eastern "Cult of the Great Mother," the high priests sliced themselves and then spun around in an orgiastic frenzy, splashing the blood onto the statue of the goddess.

This same fairy-tale "Brownite" approach gets impressed upon Celtic and Druidic culture, often by the same people. But the same annoying facts hold true for the Celts: The power players were men. There are a few exceptions, such as the Celtic warrior queen Boudicca, but even in Celtic society, warrior queens were a rarity outside of the popular characters they made for in 19th-century operas. In the Age of Romance (which reached its peak roughly from 1820 to 1840), the Druid High Priestess was a staple of many a dramatic tale, often the story of a Druid queen or priestess falling in love with a Roman soldier. It usually ended with lots of sword fights, suicides, and stage blood all over everything. But in reality, the high priests of the Druid faith were men, period. Druids also practiced human sacrifice, though generally on captured prisoners of war, and the occasional male victim of the tribe, rather than women and children. It seems to have been a complex religion, from what we know about it, with many layers of belief about the sacred forces of the earth, the afterlife, etc. But it was definitely polytheistic, worshipping both male and female gods.

Female status was a bit different for Celts than for the Neolithic women before them. Women were perceived as being very close to the divine forces of the earth, partially because of their mystical ability to bear children. Celts often drew their family trees in a matrilineal fashion, which means simply that they followed the line of their mother, particularly if they didn't know who their father was. If the stories the stuffy Romans told of Celtic free love and wife-swapping are true, the reason for this is obvious – it was the only line you could be sure was yours. Also, it meant that women could inherit, and in many tribes, if the king had no son, his daughter could become queen, although it was common practice for the king to chose a son-in-law, adopt him, and marry him to the eldest daughter. Some powerful Druidic women were seers, and in this capacity advised important men. But the all-powerful priesthood was definitely a boy's club. Besides, Celtic warriors were the most aggressive and feared on earth — even the great Julius Caesar dreaded taking them on. It was a very macho culture. Which means that, just because a Celtic warrior listened in awe that very night to a prophetess reading the tribe's future in a copper bowl of water, that doesn't mean he didn't go home and beat his wife. Celtic warriors also were famous for collecting heads, but it didn't make them any smarter.

As for the preliterate societies of the early Neolithic and late Paleolithic periods, the Neolithic goddess worship that Brownites speak of is strictly a matter of speculation, particularly the farther back in history you go. A lot of interest is centered on the discovery, all over Europe and the Near East, of these really oddball little talismans that scientists named Venuses, after the goddess of love. These little clay statues are bizarre. They are undoubtedly female; in fact, they're a little *too* female. The breasts, hips and buttocks of these figures are grossly oversized, while there is usually no face and very often no head, as if to imply that it represents, not a single woman, but all the attributes of woman writ large. Very large.

The Venuses are remarkably similar, from France to the steppes of Russia, and they've always led anthropologists to believe these people were worshipping a mother-earth fertility goddess. On the other hand, the Venuses could have been the *Playboy* centerfolds of Neolithic Mesopotamia, and the guys who carved them just thought they looked cool. After all, in a society where it was constantly difficult to get enough to eat, women with a great deal of cellulite were probably looked upon as the absolute apex of feminine beauty.

This, then, is the essential problem with Starbird's thesis where the marriage of Jesus is concerned. In *The Woman with the Alabaster Jar,* she states that because certain phrases and rituals (such as Mary of Bethany anointing Jesus) recall the high-priestess/sacred-bridegroom marriages of pagan goddess worship, we can sort of slide into the illogical conclusion that this proves that Jesus and the Magdalene were married, and that these references constitute hints and fossils in the text for the culturally aware.

But if you look at the society around you, you'll see that hundreds of things we do are invested with all sorts of mythological baggage. Judges wear black robes and sit on high benches, and they have since time immemorial, while brides wear white gowns, virgin or not. But none of this changes who and what we are, what we think, and what we believe. We're perfectly willing to concede that ancient goddess worship, and certain mythological motifs of death, sex, and sacrifice, ran throughout many of the words and actions in the New Testament, including the mysterious anointing of Jesus by Mary of Bethany. We're also willing to concede that many of those unconscious motifs were in the minds of Christ and his disciples when the event occurred. Our question here is: So what? It doesn't change anything and, what's more, it doesn't prove anything. Both of us are absolute Halloween fanatics, but that doesn't make us Satan worshippers, despite the incessant "motifs" of devil worship that surround the holiday.

The women who worshipped the male God of Israel

So, it seems there may be a flaw in the Dan Brown's logic. The worship of the "sacred feminine" in a culture's temples didn't necessarily mean the women who lived in those cultures had it so great. This could be a flaw in our own logic, of course, but it seems obvious to examine the other side of the coin. If women in pre-Christian cultures might not have had absolute equality, then maybe women in Christian culture haven't been a bunch of cringing little milksops. Because the Brownite argument stems from the oppression imposed on women by the Christian religion, then the Bible seems the place to start. And because Christianity didn't magically appear out a mystical mudhole, it also makes sense to start with the Old Testament that gave birth to the New.

Powerful women in the Old Testament

In the Old Testament, some of the powerful women who are still deeply revered in the Jewish faith might surprise you. Deborah, for example, was a great warrior/queen in the mold of David and Joshua. You will find her story in *Judges*. The men who ruled Israel in the period between the death of Joshua, who'd been the successor of Moses, and the arrival of King Saul, were called "judges," and Deborah was one of them. There were 13 in all. Deborah, wife of Lapidoth, and a prophetess, was the fourth judge of Israel. Canaanite raids were making life very dangerous — this would be around the 11th century B.C. Deborah called a warrior named Barak out of Kedesh to be her general (he would later be the fifth judge), and the two of them, fighting side by side, utterly routed the Canaanites in a heated battle at Mount Tabor.

The strange thing is, you might at least expect some word in the biblical account about Deborah being a woman, but there isn't one. Obviously, they didn't think it was a big deal. She'd been chosen by God, and that was that. They must have had some concept of the sacred feminine. Incidentally, after the battle, the Canaanite general named Sisera was on the run, having lost just about his entire force. He stumbled to the tent of an old woman named Jael, who offered him a mantle for his shoulders, then food and drink, putting him at ease. And when he fell asleep, she picked up a tent nail and a hammer and drove the nail through his head. The Bible succinctly states, "So he died." We would imagine so, and it was probably for the best. Once again, not a peep out of anyone over the fact that this savage act of war was committed by a woman. You just didn't mess with these ladies of the Old Testament.

Other Jewish heroines of the Old Testament, who were also revered by Christians, may not have been quite so militant (or so bloodthirsty), but they still used their courage and their brains to save their people. Esther, one of the greatest heroines of the Jewish people, gave herself in marriage to the king of the Persians, then later stood against his evil minister Haman when that man wanted to annihilate her people. The king was on Haman's side, but Esther openly opposed him, risking not only her place as queen, but her life, and in the end saved her people. Haman was later hanged.

Then there's Ruth, the Moabite, mother of the Davidic line of kings. Ruth was a beautiful young widow, and she brazenly went to lie in the fields one night with Boaz, a kinsman of her husband, to escape an unwanted marriage to another kinsman that attempted to claim her. Ruth and Boaz married and gave birth to a dynasty. Ruth, after being widowed, famously refused to leave her mother-in-law, Naomi, who was also a widow, despite the danger of hunger in a foreign land. Her words, "Whither thou goest, I will go, and whither thou lodgest, I will lodge; thy people shall be my people, and thy God, my God," are some of the loveliest in the Old Testament. For many Christian societies, from the Templars to the Eastern Star, an appendent body of Freemasonry, Ruth was the symbol for faithfulness.

There was only one stand-alone queen in the short history of the Hasmonean dynasty, the last dynasty of Jewish kings. But she was really something. Salome Alexandra became Queen of Judea in 76 B.C. and, like Elizabeth I in England, she brought a period of peace and prosperity in a time of civil strife. She was a master of diplomacy, doing a graceful balancing act with the powerful empires around Judea, including Rome, that wanted to swallow up the Jewish nation. She stipulated that all children must be educated in public schools, and despite being a Hellenized queen, she made a union with the conservative Pharisees to bring this about. After her death, the land was plunged once more into civil war, and many would look back with nostalgic affection on the halcyon days of Queen Salome.

Women in the new faith

Women played an incredibly important role in launching Christianity. They took the faith as their own from the very beginning, and stood by it through three centuries of on-again/off-again Roman oppression. Paul was perhaps the most important apostle, for he was the apostle to the Gentiles, traveling the world to make converts, not caring whether they were Jews. He sought out and won over many women of the aristocracy to the cause; he knew that if he converted them, the rest was in the bag. His attitude about marriage and fidelity didn't hurt his cause. Divorce had grown increasingly common in Ancient Rome, and many a matron found herself cast aside for a trophy wife. Christianity said one wife for life, period. The element of charity in the new faith also had great appeal to these ladies of Rome, as well as the other countries of the Mediterranean where Paul preached the word. The gospels all present a list of the "women who followed Jesus," and Paul made the women of Rome aware of this, making them feel a part of the Church from the beginning.

When Paul preached against marriage, it was always in connection with the coming apocalypse. He believed that when Jesus said he would return, he meant *now,* maybe next week, maybe this very minute. Families, of course, should stick together. But taking on new obligations wasn't such a hot idea. In I Corinthians 7:26 he comes right out and says that single people like him should stay single because of the impending crisis that will be brought about with the return of the Lord. Later biblical letters of Paul, many of which scholars believe were written by later theologians, softened this apocalyptic view. It had been a century by that time, Jesus had not returned, and it didn't look like he was coming anytime soon. So, of course, their stance on celibacy softened; for everyone except the clergy, that is.

Paul was definitely no sexist. The real Paul, the one who had the women of Rome and Antioch eating out of his hand, comes shining through in passages such as the famous Galatians 3:28, in which he states that all are now baptized in Christ. "There is no longer Jew or Greek, there is no longer slave or free, there is no longer male or female; for all of you are one in Christ Jesus." Along with his anti-divorce stand, Paul is reported to have said repeatedly that "In Christ, there is no male and female." Of the 13 letters listed in the New Testament under Paul's name, scholars doubt highly that he wrote even half of them. And the later ones, such as the epistles of Timothy and Titus, that speak of the natural submission of women in church, were of a certainty not written by Paul. If he'd been alive, he probably would have sued.

The remarkable fems of the West

An incessant theme of *The Da Vinci Code* is that the Catholic Church pretty much stomped women into the dust, grinding them under the Church's booted heel. It is stated so often, in such a variety of ways, that you really do begin to believe it.

The problem is, there's an awful lot of evidence to the contrary. No one is saying that women haven't been considered second-class citizens in many respects. This was an attitude that had greater currency in some cultures, less in others. An amazing number of even ancient philosophies and movements preached the equality of women, from the Greek Epicurean and Cynic philosophers, right on through to the feminist giants of the Age of Enlightenment. Yet, it was an idea that ran like a constant thread through the history of the West (and the East, as well), that Woman was Man's helpmate, the keeper of hearth and home, and by implication, someone whose pretty little head was not to be bothered with weighty matters.

But to hear Dan Brown tell it, men have called *all* the shots, and women were deliberately and maliciously persecuted by Christian patriarchy for 2,000 years. Yet, taking a long hard look at the history of that 2,000 years could easily lead to the label of its being a "proto-feminist period" — meaning a time when women were too busy handling things to stop and think that they were inferior. These dreary and oppressed little drudges of the Christian West have made a whole lot of noise in the last two millenniums.

As we discuss in this chapter, women had an enormous impact on the spread of Christianity. The Romans often referred to the "priestesses" of this new faith, emphasizing their feeling that women were running the show. A good later example of women as power players involves the period of the Crusades and the Templars. Women, particularly of the nobility, played a vital central role in the warfare of the Middle Ages. The feudal system in Europe gave each noble a "fief," and that property was his to

(continued)

(continued)

control and to defend as a vital link in the feudal chain. The lady of the fief was incredibly important to its daily life, and she was equally important to its defense. For a feudal warlord, his most important officer was his "marshal." The marshal was second-in-command, the lord's right hand in battle and his chief military advisor. It was as common as dandelions for a feudal lord to make his wife his marshal, especially his marshal in charge of castle defenses, so that his marshal/knight could accompany him to a battle.

For example, one of the worst defeats suffered by the Knights Templar was the Battle of Hattin in 1187. Raymond of Tripoli, overlord of the feudal Crusader state the County of Tripoli, was in the city of Acre having a council of war when news reached him that Saladin's army was on the march, and that they had laid siege to the city of Tiberius, where his wife, the Countess Eschiva, was in residence. The countess took charge of the defense, rallying the few knights she had for a long and bitter siege. Raymond must have trusted her a great deal. When King Guy of Jerusalem began to push for an immediate response in order to relieve Tiberias, Raymond instead wisely counseled waiting until the troops were ready, an argument he eventually lost. We know that he loved his wife very much, so obviously this attitude didn't grow from an uncaring indifference. Clearly, Raymond felt comfortable that Eschiva had things under control.

We also know of an even more famous example, in Spain in 1100. With the death of El Cid, the great knight who was the hero of Christian Spain in its struggle against the Moors, it fell to his wife, the legendary beauty Princess Jimena, to hold the city of Valencia for the king. She reorganized the army, and held back the Moors for over three years before she even asked for any help, which is clearly more than most of the knights of the period could manage, since the Moors had overrun three-quarters of Spain. El Cid had always sought her wisdom and counsel, and doubtless would not have been surprised by her skill as a warrior.

But apart from these famous stories, we know of hundreds of examples of wives acting as their husband's war marshals. In the documents that tell these stories, they are generally related in a very dry tone, as if nothing at all unusual is going on. So much for the Second Sex. As for the rest of the Church's position on the status of women in society, it's extremely telling that, when Pope Urban II preached the First Crusade at the Council of Clermont in 1095, every version we have of what he said contains a particularly interesting admonition. As a fever swept the crowd, catching the pope off-guard, and the knights began to swell forward to take the Cross, he said that he would only accept this offer of service from *single* men. Married men were told to go home and talk this serious decision over with their wives. If their wives agreed that they should go, then they could return and take the Cross. And if their wives wanted to go too, then they should be allowed to do so, for the sake of their own souls. According to Dan Brown, the Church believed that women *had* no souls. So, we ask the question: Does this sound like a Church that held women in contempt?

As for the Renaissance, Enlightenment, and even the Victorian Age, women were no slouchers, there, either. This Church that supposedly hated women sure crowned a lot of them queen. In the 16th century, Europe was dominated by three of the most powerful and cussedly stubborn women who ever lived: Queen Elizabeth I of England, Queen Mary Stuart of Scotland, and Catherine de Medici, the don't-mess-with-this-lady Queen of France. Russia had its greatest age of glory in the 18th century under three remarkable women: Catherine I, the widow of Peter the Great; Elizabeth I, her daughter; and the immortal Catherine the Great, Elizabeth's daughter-in-law, a German princess who became more Russian than her Cossack guards. The two Tsars who reigned for blessedly brief periods in this century, Peter II and Peter III, were complete screw-ups, the worst of them being Catherine the Great's husband Peter III, who was mad as the proverbial hatter. Incapable of watching Russia go down the tubes, Catherine staged a palace coup and overthrew her ineffectual husband, just as her mother-in-law had done, ruling alone from 1762 to 1796. After her death, it took a great deal of time and a couple of assassinations for the Russian people to find a man who could fill her dainty shoes.

No, all the influential women of the Christian world were queens. Historians could, and have, filled library shelves with books about shrewd, powerful, and influential women, from Venetian poet Veronica Franco to chief presidential advisor Abigail Adams, who didn't sit on purple cushions. And, although *The Da Vinci Code* contends that losing the feminine in the divinity of the Church caused our society to be more violent than it would otherwise have been, women are fairly well represented in the criminal classes as well. The Countess Elizabeth Báthory, "the Bloody Lady of Cachtice," in Hungary, tortured and murdered hundreds of young girls before her arrest in 1611. And in a footnote of history relevant to our own age, it was a woman named Sophia Perovskaya, who invented the suicide bomber. The product of a normal and pious middle-class upbringing, she nonetheless founded one of the most violent terrorist organizations in history, called the People's Will. They shot and bombed hundreds of innocent people, until at last they got their target, the most liberal tsar in Russia's history, Alexander II. Sophia was caught and hanged with the rest. She neither asked for nor received any mercy on account of her sex.

A historian could easily go on all night about the highborn, rich, and important women who aided Christianity, from Helena, the mother of the Emperor Constantine, to Anna Comnena, the daughter of the Byzantine Emperor Alexius who had called for the First Crusade; she was one of the greatest scholars of the age. Paul even had a female apostle, St. Thecla. But it was the everyday saints who propelled the faith forward. Julian the Apostate, the fourth-century emperor who tried to bring back the pagan faith, griped endlessly about his disgust with these hordes of Christian women, who gave their charity, not just to other Christians, but to pagans, as well, turning them to a faith that he despised in the process.

Flip open a roll call on the lives of the saints, and you'll find it about evenly matched between men and women, not to mention representatives of every race, color, and creed on earth. Although some of these saints are invoked for some really dippy stuff, everything from mice infestations to eczema, you'll also find that some of the most courageous saints of the early Church were women. From Geneviève to Joan of Arc, women fought and died for their faith, even to the present day: In 1980, four Maryknoll nuns were brutally assassinated in El Salvador during that nation's bloody civil war.

The Catholic Church's Relationship with Women

Nowadays, Catholics must feel that they just can't win for losing. In the wake of *The Da Vinci Code,* Catholics are accused of strangling the feminine side of divinity, choking it in a male-dominated tyranny. But for centuries, they've been taking it on the chin for something that's about as opposite as you can get — the accusation that the Church was far *too* wrapped up in the feminine divine, obsessed with devotional figures from the Magdalene to St. Teresa, and most particularly *Our Lady,* the mother of Christ. In countless books, Protestant devotional tracts, and general histories, Catholic worship of the Virgin Mary has been compared to a pagan mother-earth cult. This negative attitude was worsened by the strange intricacies of the Catholic doctrine on the Immaculate Conception, something that confuses even some Catholics. They think it means the virgin birth of Christ through a miracle of God, and to some degree, it does. But it also means that Mary *herself* was free of any stain of sin, from the moment of her conception. This was a doctrine that smacked to Protestants of putting Mary on a par with Christ, and perhaps it does. So where's the beef now with a supposed lack of respect for divinity in women?

There's no question that the Church has stumbled in one regard — or at least, they had a hand in the debacle: This was the growing ideology that sexuality was lust, lust was a sin, and that sin had to be fought at any cost, up to and including self-castration. This idea took hold in the Middle Ages, long after the establishment of the faith, and it became part of the mindset of medieval times. Medieval or not, it's difficult for a lot of modern women to forgive a Church that cooked up ideas like *original sin* (Eve ate the apple and disobeyed God, so all of us are forever suspect) and celibacy, which these same modern women, we believe, somewhat mistakenly, can be interpreted as a hatred of women.

Ideas of celibacy were hardly embraced by everyone in the Church; in fact, it took several centuries of struggle for the medieval Church to force priests, particularly in the countryside, to give up the wives they'd taken when they thought it was all right to do so. Paul speaks at length in Corinthians on the subject of the sanctity of marriage, and the importance of a just and fair relationship between husbands and wives. And as for original sin, many a Christian scholar spoke against it, on the doctrinal basis that Mary's immaculate conception had wiped the slate clean, or that this sin was borne by Adam and Eve equally, since both disobeyed God.

Of course, anyone who thinks that celibacy was an invention of the Catholic Church would be sadly mistaken. In fact, most of the world's major faiths, either in the mainstream or in offshoot sects, have practiced religious celibacy. It seems to be something of a universal in logic: The most wonderful things in life are love, sex, family, wine, good food, and luxuries of all sorts, all of which are things of the senses, and should therefore be given up by anyone seeking a higher plane of contact with the spirit. Consequently, celibacy has been practiced by the clergy in various sects of just about every major faith except Islam. As a concept, it does not automatically imply a hatred of women. (We talk a lot more about the concept of celibacy and who stuck us with it in Chapter 14.)

The real burr in the saddle

We think that a lot of the anger of women that Dan Brown tapped into so effortlessly grew not out of the way women have been treated for the last 20 centuries, but the way they've been treated in the last two. A whole lot of the harshness toward Christianity that runs through feminist doctrine, which lists it as one of the chief oppressors, grew out of this two-century period far more than it did ancient Rome or 14th-century Italy.

During the Age of Enlightenment particularly between about 1750 and 1820, women were getting hot as a pistol in England and America. Painters like Marie-Louise Vigée-LeBrun, and Angelica Kauffman, founding member of the British Royal Academy of the Arts, writers like George Sand and Jane Austen, philosophers like Madame De Staël, politicians like Madame Roland, even political assassins like Charlotte Corday, had their hands all over the cultural steering wheel. It was an eruption of liberty, not just political, but social and even sexual. Language, always a barometer of a culture's openness, was free and easy, and remarkably vulgar, so much so that many a "father of our country" type returned to his journals in the 1830's and 1840's in order to clean up all that "coarse" language. Women moved more freely in society than they ever had before — they drank and they danced, they gambled and attended horse races, they played cards and flirted and read books on all subjects. This wasn't only happening in New York, but in parlors and parties in Richmond and Charleston, Baltimore and Providence, all over the brand-new 13 states. Always eager to imitate Europeans, Americans were holding their own intellectual salons to discuss the great issues of the day, and they were very often hosted by women. Most important of all, women were *interacting* with men, and with the world around them. Even the clothing of women at the turn of the 19th century reflected this new freedom; easy, flowing and sometimes shockingly revealing garments that were extremely naturalistic, incorporating motifs of the newly unearthed societies of ancient Greece and Egypt.

Victorianism

Then, somehow, though she could hardly be held completely to blame, Alexandrina Victoria Hanover came to the English throne at the age of 18 in 1837, and everything began to change. Chastened language became the order of the day, and one little "damn" could get you sent to bed without any supper. Young English girls increasingly became prisoners of the nursery, held from any knowledge of life or men, until they were unleashed on the world at the age of 17 or 18, utterly unprepared to be sacrificed on the altar of marriage. In America, the predominant religion, a comfortable Christmas-and-Easter sort of Anglicanism (with a large number of Congregationalists and Presbyterians), was being challenged by a massive wave of tent-revival style evangelism. Uneducated but fiery preachers were sweeping the country-side by the 1820s, winning souls in droves to the new religions, especially the Baptist and Methodist churches. Women had been the movers and shakers behind the family religion for centuries, and evangelists openly went after them in particular. In the journals of the early Victorian period, many of the most devout men, from senators and congressmen to millers and black-smiths, make it perfectly clear that their wives had become converts to the new fundamentalism first, and that they had been drawn into it by their wives and mothers afterwards. It's sad to think, because it's like a slave fastening on her own shackles every morning after she brushes her teeth.

Facing the future

Of course, there were some good things about this new religious fervor. The Abolitionist movement to free slaves the world over was given an enormous boost by it, and as for sexual equality, Methodists in particular were known for the equal status they gave women, so long as it was expressed in preaching the Word. But overall, the toxic blend of religious fundamentalism and the new Victorianism turned into one of the heaviest weights of oppression women would ever bear. This is the oppression that modern feminists have battled for the last century, but it has little to do with the status of women 10 or 20 centuries ago, or of Neolithic women, for that matter.

Chapter 14

Getting Our Acts Together: Constantine and the Council of Nicaea

. . . .

In This Chapter

▶ Getting the scoop on the real Council of Nicaea

▶ Not knocking Gnosticism

▶ Discovering why priests are bachelors, and meeting some who aren't

▶ Going to the source on celibacy

. . . .

*I*f you picked up this book because of your interest in the Knights Templar, this chapter won't hold much interest for you. But if you came to this book because of what you read in Dan Brown's *The Da Vinci Code,* this chapter goes right to the core of his story: namely, that the direction of the Catholic Church and Christianity was decided by the Roman Emperor Constantine I and the Council of Nicaea.

Brown's book presents a view that has very little to do with the historical record. Like the Templars (see Chapter 12) and the legend of Mary Magdalene (see Chapter 13), *The Da Vinci Code* version of the Council of Nicaea and the early days of Christianity is *almost* completely fictional. Almost. The names are spelled right.

In this chapter, we discuss two pivotal turning points in both Christianity and the Roman Catholic Church: the conversion to the faith by Constantine, and the activities of the Council of Nicaea. We explain some of those supposedly missing "gospels" commonly known as the Apocrypha. We examine the horrible destruction of the Cathars during the Albigensian Crusade. And, in case the only place you've ever read about this stuff was in *The Da Vinci Code,* we set the record straight on some of Dan Brown's other historical howlers.

Fiction, History, and the Early Church

Go ahead and say it. "What part of the word *fiction* do you guys not understand?" The problem is not simply that much of what is presented as historical fact in *The Da Vinci Code* is wrong. It's that it is so *incredibly* wrong, and that Brown carefully binds it all together with the patina of truth. Sure, that makes Dan Brown a talented author of fiction. The problem is that a substantial portion of his more than 60 million readers believe him when he says his fictional books are factual.

According to *The Da Vinci Code,* much of what we know about Jesus is wrong because of Emperor Constantine I and the first Council of Nicaea that met in A.D. 325. The book alleges that the Christian conversion of Roman Emperor Constantine I was political rather than spiritual, that Jesus was considered merely a mortal man for four centuries up until the Council of Nicaea, and that the Church burned and suppressed gospels that did not conform to their vision of a patriarchal, male-dominated, sexually repressed version of Christianity. To understand the controversy, you need to take a closer look at the real Council, what it really did, and the evidence as to whether it tinkered with the word of God. And you need to understand the place of Christianity in Roman society after the death of Jesus up until Constantine and the Council.

Early Christianity: A secret society

When discussing the early Christians, the words of the ancient Roman nobility usually dripped with arrogance, if not venom. The Emperor Nero famously accused Christians of setting the Great Fire of Rome in A.D. 64. In telling Nero's story, the Roman historian Suetonius really fries the mad emperor (who famously "fiddled while Rome burned"). But in an effort to be fair and balanced, Suetonius does present a list of some of the *good* things Nero did, including "punishments inflicted on the Christians, a sect professing a new and mischievous religious belief."

Tacitus, the noble Roman historian, called Christians "a dangerous cult," hated because of their "shameless activities," which had come out of Judea, "the origin of the evil." He accused them of everything from cannibalism to using the blood of babies in their obscene ritual of the Mass. And the Emperor Trajan had Christians executed for breaking two laws: his edict against "secret societies," and his law requiring the worship of the state gods and sacrifices to the god/emperor.

On top of being a religion for the plebs and the mob, Christianity was also perceived as being a faith run by women more than men, and that it was women who were doing the bulk of the converting. Julian the Apostate, the fourth-century emperor who tried to return Rome to its former religion of gods and goddesses, grouses endlessly and bitterly about hordes of Christian women, who converted the lowest scum of the street by feeding them and giving them a place to sleep. Those bloody do-gooders.

Christianity underground

A visit to the catacombs of Rome is a unique glimpse at the very different culture the new religion created in the center of the Roman Empire. The bodies of the first Christian martyrs were buried in the Roman-style necropolises. Wealthy Roman Christians offered up their own private aboveground cemeteries for the burial of some members of the Christian community, but with the persecutions that started under the Emperor Claudius in A.D. 41, they were soon defaced and destroyed. The solution was to go underground, out of sight and out of the easy reach of troublemakers.

In A.D. 150, the Cecili family gave their private burial ground on the Appian Way outside of the city walls to the Christian community, and the digging began in earnest. In time, more than 60 different sites of catacombs were dug all around the city's walls, through the fourth century.

Romans referred to a necropolis as a "city of the dead," but Christians called theirs a dormitory *(coemeterium)*, which was a place of rest until the physical resurrection of the body. Burial niches were carved into the volcanic rock walls, like endless rows of four-story-high bunk beds, and bodies were interred as Jesus was — wrapped in linen, anointed with scented oil, and sealed behind a slab of stone. And this kind of burial was not only for the rich. The astonishing size of the catacombs is a testament to the desire for the rich and the poor to

have a proper burial. Even criminals and abandoned babies had their places in these subterranean vaults. More important, there was a curious sense of community in being buried together in these massive places. And digging down to almost 70 feet allowed them to bury thousands of bodies under a relatively small piece of topside real estate.

Larger areas were excavated for subterranean chapels, often attached to the tomb of a saint or martyr. Families would dig out family-size crypts so they could all be buried together. Some were decorated with fresco paintings as well. However, the longstanding myth that these were underground hiding places where Christians concealed themselves from Roman search parties are largely untrue. The Romans knew exactly where these places were all around the city, and the stench of hundreds of rotting corpses would have been unbearable for any length of time.

The catacombs declined in popularity after Christianity was declared a state religion and bodies were allowed to be buried in church cemeteries. The catacombs were largely forgotten until large-scale exploration of them began in the 1800s. The largest that can be seen today are the catacombs of St. Calixtus, near the St. Sebastian Gate. There are 12 miles of tunnels that actually interconnected four different burial sites; they're estimated to contain as many as 500,000 graves.

In the early 300s, Christianity was not popular (making up no more than about 8 percent of the Roman population), lower class, pretty much illegal, and not exactly the sort of religion that would attract an emperor (after all, emperors were being *worshipped*). The period immediately before Constantine took the throne was, for the Christians, called the era of the Great Persecution. They had suffered oppressions off and on since their inception, the worst being under Nero. But the two co-emperors just before Constantine — Diocletian and Maximian — passed some of the most oppressive laws against Christians yet, burning their churches, outlawing their Mass, burning their sacred books, and putting them to death. As far as we know, Constantine, as well as his father, the Emperor Constantius, fully approved these laws.

Dan Brown's version: Teabing does the talking

Some of the biggest historical whoppers in *The Da Vinci Code* begin in Chapter 52, in a key sequence between Sir Leigh Teabing, Robert Langdon, and Sophie Neveu. Most of this scene consists of pronouncements on Brownian history from Teabing, described as one of Britain's foremost historians, who has devoted his life to the study of the Holy Grail and its "real meaning." Here are some of Teabing's claims about the Council of Nicaea and Constantine:

- ✔ **The Emperor Constantine made the important decisions at the Council of Nicaea in A.D. 325.** According to Teabing, Constantine was not, as history tells us, a Christian, but a lifelong pagan, converted on his deathbed when he was "too weak to protest."

- ✔ **Constantine's conversion was a strictly political move to bring peace to the two warring factions of Christians and pagans in the city of Rome.**

- ✔ **Jesus was not considered divine before the Council of Nicaea.** Constantine pushed through the idea of Jesus's divinity so that he could follow through with his dark plan to invest absolute power in the Vatican, in order to consolidate his own.

- ✔ **Church leaders voted at Nicaea on Christ's divinity, and that it was "a relatively close vote at that."**

- ✔ **Over 80 "gospels" were considered for the New Testament, but only 4 were chosen, only the ones that showed Jesus as divine, with no human traits.** The rest were burned.

- ✔ **Mary Magdalene was Jesus's wife; she carried his child; the Holy Grail was in reality Mary Magdalene; and the "blood in the cup" was the holy bloodline.**

What Boring Old History Books Say

Back in the days of the very first *Star Trek* series, it was a common event in almost every episode for the U.S.S. *Enterprise* to get whacked with a photon torpedo from some alien ship, and when they did, the camera shook and everybody on the bridge fell out of their chairs. When a fan asked the series creator, Gene Roddenberry, why there weren't seat belts in the seats, he answered, "If there were, they couldn't fall out of their chairs!" People falling out of chairs is more dramatic than people just getting shaken around. The same is true with *The Da Vinci Code*. We know that if Dan Brown had stuck to the facts of history, he wouldn't have sold 60 million copies and set the world talking about Jesus, Mary, and the Bible. And people wouldn't have fallen out of their chairs.

The problem comes in when Brown claims that people and events were facts when they weren't — and the readers don't know the difference. So, here we crack open some moldy old history books and see what they say about the claims of Brown's characters about the early days of Christianity.

The Christian conversion of Constantine

The Roman Emperor Constantine I was converted to Christianity on October 28 in the year A.D. 312, just before a battle at Milvian Bridge. Constantine saw a vision of a cross in the sky, one he later had cast in gold — it was a *chi-rho cross,* the cross with two Greek letters at the top, the first letters of Christ's name in Greek (see Chapter 1).

When Constantine had his vision of a cross in the sky he was already an emperor and an extremely successful general — hardly someone who could be called a wannabe looking for some new followers. At that time, Rome was ruled by two emperors — one in the East and one in the West — because of the cumbersome size of the empire. Constantine was engaged in a civil war with the emperor of the West, with whom he was about to do battle at the aforementioned Milvian Bridge.

According to Constantine, his vision occurred at dawn just before the battle. He also said that Christ came to him in a dream that same night and revealed the same sign to him, promising him protection from his enemies. Constantine's vision, accompanied by a voice that told him, "In this sign, conquer," can't be dismissed out of hand; its effect on the course of history was too great. So, he was a liar, he was a lunatic, or he got a message from God. Constantine's nimble handling of the reins of power in the coming years made one thing clear: The man was no nutbag in need of a jacket that laced up the back. And a reason for lying doesn't come quickly to mind. But modern, secular people don't put much stock in visions, spiritual or otherwise.

Rome ≠ Vatican ≠ Church

Throughout *The Da Vinci Code,* Dan Brown's characters persistently, *constantly,* refer to "the Vatican" as being in cahoots with Constantine, as suppressing fourth-century Gnostic Gospels, as being the dark force behind the Crusades, and other evil deeds. The Vatican wasn't even built until the 14th century, and it was quite some time after that before it came to be an interchangeable term with *Catholic hierarchy.*

Even if Constantine's religious experience is explained away in modern terms — like a narcoleptic seizure, a psychoneurotic episode, or, another popular theory, that what he saw was a comet — one question still rises above all others: How likely is it that a man of the highest rank would convert to the religion of this oppressed and despised minority of vagrants and derelicts because it was "politically expedient" or a "smart business move"?

Dan Brown's fictional character of Sir Leigh Teabing asserts in *The Da Vinci Code* that Constantine was never *really* a Christian. Many in the Brown/ Teabing camp have implied that Constantine's contemporary, friend, and biographer, the early Church father Eusebius, exaggerated the stories of his conversion for his own dark purposes. Yet, shortly after his victory at the Milvian Bridge, Constantine issued the Edict of Milan, which proclaimed that all Romans were free to worship whatever divinity they chose, without fear. When he presented the edict to his legions and explained that he had become a Christian but that they in no way had to follow his example, the legionaries began to come forward in droves to be baptized by the bishop who was present — he was overwhelmed by the crowd.

Constantine's conversion to Christianity involved nothing shady — he didn't "back the winning horse." The Christians were an oppressed minority in the Roman Empire and had been since their beginning. It was quite simply against the law to be a Christian. They were despised by the upper classes, of which Constantine represented the cream at the top. They represented 5 percent to 8 percent of the population. There was no rioting between Christians and pagans — pagans ruled the city, and Christians spent a lot of time hiding from them, especially during the reigns of Nero, Diocletian (Constantine's predecessor), and several other deeply anti-Christian emperors. This is the "winning horse" that the conquering hero Constantine is so eager to have on his side that he abandons his own faith?

The Da Vinci Code also makes the astonishing statement that Constantine was "a lifelong pagan who was baptized on his deathbed, too weak to protest." Constantine was a Christian from the time of his conversion, in A.D. 312. He was baptized on his deathbed in 337 by Eusebius in a ceremony that was quite common at that time. It was practiced by other heretical sects, and even later by the Cathars. The belief was that, after baptism, the soul is cleansed of all sin and heads straight for paradise. The ritual of the Last Rites, called *Extreme Unction,* was only beginning to be used in the late second century and took much longer to become a regular practice. The seven sacraments of the Catholic faith — Baptism, Confirmation, Holy Eucharist, Penance, Extreme Unction, Orders, and Matrimony — weren't even finalized as doctrine until the Council of Trent, the 19th ecumenical council of the Church, in the 16th century. In Constantine's day, a man could remain a practicing Christian, called a *neophyte,* and then be baptized on his deathbed as a sort of Last Rites ritual by another name. (The Cathars in the south of France did precisely the same thing, having their final ritual of swearing to the ascetic life, called the *consolamentum,* put off until they were aged or dying. If a Frenchman's going to give up wine, women, and rich food, he'd rather do it when he can barely make it from the bed to the chamber pot!)

The real Council of Nicaea and what happened there

The Ecclesiastical Council at Nicaea in A.D. 325 was not the first of its kind. The first "general council" of Christian leaders, the Council of Jerusalem, was called in A.D. 49, only 16 years after Christ's crucifixion, in an attempt to settle differences between Jewish and Gentile practices within the two types of followers of Christ's teachings. And there would be many more to follow Nicaea, as important as it was. Dozens of councils over the centuries would decide important issues of the Catholic faith, right up to the 20th century's Vatican II, between 1962 and 1965.

The Council of Nicaea is usually listed as the first ecumenical council, but there have been at least 21 of them over the centuries. They are called *general councils,* because cardinals and other officials may attend. These 21 councils have decided an incredibly wide variety of issues over the years, from Nicaea in 325, right up to Vatican II from 1962 to 1965.

From the beginning, Christians viewed Jesus Christ as divine. The more than 300 bishops, along with 1,300 other deacons, priests, and interested bystanders who attended the Council of Nicaea, viewed Christ as divine. The argument wasn't over his divinity, but over the *nature* of his divinity, a question that would plague the Church for centuries (if not to the present day) and would spawn major heretical sects with a different opinion. At Nicaea, the biggest bone was being picked by the Arians, who believed that Jesus was *like* God, but not *actually* God, per se.

The Council of Nicaea had other fish to fry as well, like deciding the proper day to celebrate Easter (in order to separate it from the Jewish Passover). But the most important thing the Council did, after 300 years of arguing, was to achieve consensus on one set of principles, one calendar, and one set of definitions that would, at last, achieve common ground from which Christianity could proceed. Consensus wouldn't last long, but the Council of Nicaea did achieve it for a time. And it took a 900-pound gorilla like the Emperor Constantine to get everybody to do it.

Keep in mind that Constantine was a neophyte Christian. We're certain that, like any new convert, he came in excited and full of questions. When he was confronted by priests and bishops who couldn't answer them, his solution was to get the movers and shakers of the faith together and force them to make the rules and decisions that needed to be made to put an end to the organizational chaos.

The arguments that led to the Council of Nicaea

The main reason that the Council of Nicaea was called was to deal with the growing problem of the *Arian Heresy*, which was a fundamental argument over the exact nature of the divinity of Christ. Was he a god or a man? Was he part of God, of the same substance? Was he a human being, touched by the divine? Was he just some kind of ghost or vision who didn't actually have a physical body? And what makes it worse for the non-historian is that every philosophy, creed, sect, and point of view had a name. Here's a brief rundown of the major players in this debate:

- **Docetists** believed that Jesus was not human at all but strictly divine, and his humanity was only a façade. Cathars and many other Gnostics believed this as well.

- **Adoptionists** believed that Jesus was human in every way, but that he was the best and most righteous human on the planet, so God chose him, adopting him, to be his son.

- **Patripassianists** believed that Jesus actually was the Father and that they were one, an idea pretty roundly rejected by most people. (After all, how could God suffer and die?)

- **Dualists** believed that there were two forces in the universe — good and evil — and that the world was created by the evil side. Dualism was the foundation of most Gnostic faiths.

Early Church fathers were trying to avoid anything in the faith that might smack of more than one god — they left belief in more than one god for the pagans. But how do you explain an overarching God on high, one whom Jesus spoke to, but Jesus is down here on Earth, and he's God, too?

The unspeakable name of God

In *The Da Vinci Code,* supposed professional symbologist and super genius Robert Langdon blithely explains that the "tetragrammaton," which is four Hebrew letters that are sort of analogous to *YHWH,* comes from the name Jehovah, which he claims is a union of the masculine *Jah* and the pre-Hebraic name for Eve, *havah.* Try this one on a rabbi. It's wrong in so many places, it's tough to choose where to start. The word *Jehovah* is English. It wasn't even invented until the late Middle Ages. It came into use because it was an attempt, in English, to come up with a pronunciation of those four letters. The letters of the tetragrammaton, YHWH, are sacred to Jews. They are four letters of the Hebrew alphabet: *yodh, heh, vav,* and *heh.* At the burning bush, when Moses asked for God's name, he got the reply, "I am that I am. Tell them 'I am' has sent you" (Exodus 3:14). In Biblical Hebrew, YHWH is a form of the words *to be,* as if they were calling him "I am." For Jews, it was blasphemy to even attempt to speak the name of God. We say "Yahweh," the Hebrew word, but by the third century B.C., this word was forbidden to Jews. They have many acceptable names for God, the most common being *Adonai,* which simply means "My Lord," or *Elohim,* meaning "god," a generic word for a god of any religion.

During the period of Constantine, there were two large sects of Christians causing the biggest headache for the more mainstream or orthodox church leaders:

- **Manichaeism,** based on the dualist beliefs of the Persian prophet Mani. Even St. Augustine had once been a Manichaean.

- **Arianism,** a rather complex brand of dualism that said there was only one God the Father. His first creation had been Christ the Son, who then went on to create all things, but who was subordinate to God the Father. Christ the Son then became human in order to bring his message and to die for our sins, before he died to rejoin his Father in heaven.

Arianism was a far worse betrayal to the Church than Manichaeism because it was founded closer to home, by a highly respected teacher of religion in Alexandria named Arius. Arianism became very popular all over Europe, and would remain so with the newly converted Goths, Franks, and especially Germanic peoples.

Arius's chief critic was another Alexandrian, a church deacon and eventual bishop named Athanasius. Athanasius believed that Christ was divine, had always been divine, and was not a created entity. Christ and God shared the same essence.

The Nicaean Creed defines Christ's divinity

The Council of Nicaea discussed and voted upon many issues, but the most important thing to come out of the council was a final statement of position from the Church on the nature of Christ, known as the Nicaean Creed. This statement not only remains the Church's position on the nature of Christ's divinity, but it is also accepted, with minor differences, by virtually every Christian denomination. The Nicaean Creed spelled out the concept of the *Holy Trinity*: one God, but with three natures (three faces), all equal: God the *Father*, God the *Son* and God the *Holy Spirit*.

"Closing the Canon": Determining the books of the Bible

In *The Da Vinci Code,* the character Leigh Teabing claims that over 80 "gospels" were considered for the New Testament, but only four were chosen, only the ones that showed Jesus as divine, with no human traits. He goes on to say that the rest of these discarded books were burned or otherwise destroyed.

No one has any idea how many gospels were considered for inclusion in the canon that became the new Testament. Jesus's life was not recorded by "thousands of followers," as Teabing says in *The Da Vinci Code.* Not only were these people illiterate for the most part, but he makes it sound as if, before the Council of Nicaea, everyone had a gospel of his own, until some evil jack-booted goons in the Church came along and confiscated them.

Constantine and the Council of Nicaea had absolutely nothing to do with deciding which texts would be in the Bible, and which texts would be omitted. Here's the straight dope on Dan Brown's claims:

- ✔ **The 4 gospels and 27 books of the New Testament were not decided upon at Nicaea.** The four main gospels were a bedrock of the Christian faith long before then. The inclusion or exclusion of the others is the process called *closing the canon.* It was the product of a long, drawn-out debate in all corners of the Christian world that went on for about five centuries — long before Constantine's birth, and longer after his death.

- ✔ **The contention that any books not included in the New Testament canon were rounded up and destroyed is nonsense.** Not only is there no historical evidence to prove it, but there is ample historical evidence that such a roundup and destruction never occurred. These alternative gospels remained popular all over the world, whether they were actually in the Bible or not. Some weren't even written down, but they became part of myth and folklore all over the Christian world. And some of them were included in the Catholic Bible that were not included in the King James Version.

> ✔ The Latin Vulgate Bible did not come about until A.D. 380, when the books in common use by the church were translated by St. Jerome.
>
> ✔ The contents of the Bible were officially hammered out and agreed upon at the Synod of Hippo in A.D. 393 and the Synod of Carthage four years later in 397.

Pre-Vulgate copies of New Testament gospels are remarkably similar to the ones we have now. As for the books left out, there's no question this was a subjective judgment call.

The Apocrypha and the Bible

The term *apocryphal* appears through this book, and it has a couple of meanings. *Apocrypha* is derived from a Greek word that means "to hide away." If you're the sort of person who tends to believe in conspiracies, this alone should raise your hackles. And when the term gets applied to certain books that are or aren't in the Bible, you're definitely venturing into Dan Brown territory.

There seem to have always been two views of the term *Apocrypha.* The first is applied to a particular group of Old Testament books that were first included in the original Latin Vulgate versions of the Bible, and then removed from the King James Version editions published after 1640. Most Protestants have never seen the deleted books called the Apocrypha, while Catholic Bibles have always included them.

The other use of the term *Apocrypha* is in the case of books such as those found at Nag Hammâdi that were not included in any official bible after the Synod of Carthage. Some speculative authors have claimed that the books were "hidden" because they contained esoteric knowledge that was too mysterious, subversive, or dangerous to become common knowledge. Others argued that they were hidden because they contained ideas that were heretical to current Church doctrine.

Early Christians largely decided the makeup of their Old Testament based on the books accepted by Jewish scholars, but there were *additional* books that were of perhaps equal antiquity, rejected by most Jewish traditions. First-century Christians argued for their inclusion in their biblical canon, which may very well have led to the final split between the Jews of Jesus' era and the Christians who incorporated gentile practices (who didn't follow Jewish dietary and circumcision laws, for example).

The Old Testament Apocrypha

The earliest Christian Bible came from first-century Greek sources of the Old Testament, known as the *Septuagint,* and not the Hebrew texts. Seventy-two Jewish scholars had translated the Septuagint into Greek in the third century B.C. for King Ptolemy II, but there were many differences between it and the first-century Tanakh. The version of the Septuagint that the Christians in

Alexandria were working with after the death of Christ included the books of the Apochrypha, or as they are known in Roman Catholic writings, the Deuterocanonical books.

The Deuterocanonical books include: Wisdom; Sirach; Tobit; Judith; 103 additional verses of Esther; 1st and 2nd Macabees; Baruch; an expanded Book of Daniel that includes the Prayer of Azariah, Song of the Three Holy Children (or the Three Jews), Susanna, and Bel and the Dragon.

The early Christians argued for the inclusion of these books because they seemed divinely inspired, and because their original source material had included them. Later scholars, including St. Jerome between A.D. 380 and A.D. 405, believed the Greek Septuagint was extremely flawed, and preferred to go back to Hebrew sources.

Why most Protestants have never heard of the Apocrypha

The Apocrypha became part of Martin Luther's list of complaints against the Roman Catholic Church. The growing 16th-century Protestant movement in Europe finally argued strongly against the inclusion of the Apocrypha. In particular, heated arguments erupted during the Protestant Reformation over items that are discussed only in these books that became Roman Catholic rules or traditions (in particular, the concept of Purgatory, as well as the practice of offering Masses for the dead, which are contained in 2 Maccabees). The King James Version of the Bible included them for three decades, but editions published after 1640 eliminated them.

In 1592, the Roman Catholic Church responded to the Protestant furor by reaffirming most of the books of the Apocrypha as being part of their official canon. This remains the position of the Church today.

But wait, there's more! The Gnostic Gospels

The discovery of the Nag Hammâdi Library in Egypt in 1945 and the Dead Sea Scrolls in the West Bank between 1947 and 1956 turned up more biblical era documents that some scholars believe should be considered as part of the New Testament. These additional books include the Gospel of James; the Gospel of Phillip; the Acts of Peter and the Twelve; and many more. (The Gnostic Gospel of Mary Magdalene was discovered in Egypt in 1896, but it was not contained in the Nag Hammâdi texts.)

Gnosticism itself can be a very difficult term to understand, because it encompasses many different sorts of beliefs. Also, in the last couple of decades, people have been tossing around the term *Gnostic* with unbelievable irresponsibility, using it as an adjective to describe almost anything that's either esoteric, occult, or not an orthodox belief. ***Remember:*** *Gnosticism* is a generic term that covers a wide variety of beliefs. There is no one, single Gnostic Church. Gnosticism was partly a pre-Christian concept that teaches that God is infinite and incomprehensible to humans. Gnosticism's essential belief is dualism, the idea that good and evil are in a constant struggle for supremacy in the Universe. Christian Gnosticism became a popular movement up in the Christian Church of the second century A.D.

Dan Brown's characters in *The Da Vinci Code* argue that the Gnostic Gospels are every bit as valid as what's in the commonly accepted New Testament, but biblical scholars almost completely disagree with that viewpoint. The Gnostic Gospels were not excluded from the biblical canon simply because they contradicted what Church fathers wanted to hear. The Gnostic Gospels were written, in most cases, 150 to 200 years after Christ, with a few notable exceptions (the Gospel of Thomas, possibly written in A.D. 50, being the most famous of these exceptions, though its date of origin is disputed). In the case of the almost purely Gnostic writings discovered in Nag Hammâdi, they were most certainly hidden in about A.D. 390 by the monks of the monastery of St. Pachomius after the rulings of St. Athanasius that Gnostic texts were heretical.

Conflict over celibacy

One of often-repeated themes of *The Da Vinci Code* is that so-called Gnostic Gospels have a more open attitude about sex, and that is one of the reasons why the Gnostic Gospels were "suppressed " by the Church (even though reading them doesn't supply any evidence to back this up). Because of *The Da Vinci Code*'s overarching theme that Jesus was married, and that a Church terrified of that fact has been willing to kill to cover the secret up, it does seem important to say a few words on the subjects of sex and celibacy.

Celibacy in the ancient world

The Catholic Church didn't invent celibacy. The concept of *shamanism,* the wise ascetic living alone in the desert, is nearly as old as man, and usually included celibacy. The most famous Roman celibates were the Vestal Virgins, a community of priestesses who took a solemn vow to abstain from sex for 30 years. (After that, if someone wanted you, go for it.)

Although Robert Langdon and other characters in *The Da Vinci Code* speak wistfully of some peaceful, all-natural, bygone era of goddess worship, those religions could be pretty brutal, and celibacy was a cruel part of it. High priests and priestesses of pagan goddesses were often expected to remain celibate. In one particularly gruesome example, "The Great Mother of the Gods," a popular figure in Eastern and Greco-Roman paganism required priests to castrate themselves in order to enter the order. Then, every March at the goddess's annual festival, the "Day of Blood," the priests lacerated what little was left of themselves and swirled madly, sending blood flying onto the altar. It's a bit difficult to accept Dan Brown's assertion that the reason our society is so violent is that we've lost goddess worship as part of Western culture.

Cathars, heresy, and the Albigensian Crusade

The Cathars appear throughout this book, and they touch on Gnosticism, heretical philosophy, and the Knights Templar. They also illustrate, along with the Inquisition, the darkest page of Catholic history.

Catharism was a Gnostic belief that arose in the years leading up to the 11th century, and it grew throughout southern France and into Spain. What put the Cathars into conflict with the Roman Catholic Church was their view that the world was created by a lesser, imperfect "god," who was analogous to Satan, and not the *true* God. Catholicism taught that resurrection — both in the case of Jesus, as well as the resurrection of the faithful on the Judgment Day — was a physical resurrection of the body out of the grave, into the Kingdom of Heaven. Cathars, on the other hand, taught that resurrection was simply a *spiritual* rebirth. In addition, they were *anti-sacerdotal,* meaning they did not believe that bishops, priests, or any other mortal human could perform the works of the "true God" on Earth. Cathars were very critical of the corruption they saw among the hierarchy of the Roman Church, and they weren't shy about it.

Cathars, like other Gnostic sects, had the appearance of almost being a "secret society" — not just in keeping their beliefs low-key to outsiders, but within the organization itself. There was the general population of the faithful and there was an inner core of ascetic elders; the latter group practiced extreme self-sacrifice and deprivation in their efforts to attain the most supreme inner knowledge of the true God. The sacrifice of worldly goods and pleasures were meant to keep the evil things of the physical world that were created by the lesser god, or *demiurge,* from corrupting the spirit and the body. They did believe in Jesus, but not in the form that the Church had at last settled on. To the Cathars, Jesus was like a divine hologram — a projection of spiritual energy who appeared to be a man, but was more of a ghost. The God of the Old Testament was an evil imposter, but Jesus was sent by the true God as His messenger.

All this may seem harmless enough, but the Roman Catholic Church didn't see it that way. Catharism was clearly heresy, and it was quickly growing in popularity. The first known Cathars popped up in Limousin in central France in the early 1000s; they were promptly put to death by the Church as heretics.

As the movement grew and came to be centered in the Languedoc region of France, the Church attempted to send missions to the Cathars to change their ways, including Templar patron Bernard of Clairvaux, all of them ultimately unsuccessful. Worse, local noblemen and regional royalty seemed to be protecting Cathar strongholds. The largest concentration of Cathars coincided with Knights Templar outposts in the south of France and northeast Spain, but the order did not seem to take any interest in assisting the Church in rooting out the heretics.

After a little more than 200 years, the Church finally was at its wits' end. In 1208, the pope sent his personal legate, Pierre de Castelnau, to excommunicate Count Raymond VI of Toulouse for supporting the heretics. Raymond reacted a little disproportionately and had the pope's representative murdered.

Pope Innocent III retaliated by calling for a new Crusade (known as the Albigensian Crusade) against these heretics living in the very midst of Europe. In 1209, the town of Béziers was attacked by the crusading army. When the pope's commander, Cistercian abbot Arnaud-Amaury, was asked how to tell Catholic from

Cathar, his famous reply was, "Kill them all. God will know his own." Arnaud had spent years trying to convert the Cathars and had been humiliated at their reception of his attempts. At Béziers, he got his revenge. He had 20,000 men, women, and children burned alive.

The crusaders then turned to attack Carcassonne. Its Viscount, Roger-Raymond, was taken prisoner during truce discussions and murdered, but unlike Béziers, Carcassonne's population was allowed to surrender.

Arnaud-Amaury needed a true military commander to finish the big job ahead. He pressed Simon IV de Montfort into service, with the promise of new land possessions as a reward. De Montfort reluctantly took the job, but when he got started, killing Cathars was like eating potato chips, and there was no stopping him. He burned 140 Cathars at Minerve, and at least 50 at Cassès. Between 1210 and 1218, he took Lastours-Cabaret, Bram, Termes, Lavaur, and Castel. In 1213, he defeated King Peter II of Aragon in Spain, and then turned back for sieges and battles that ended for him at the endlessly troublesome Toulouse in 1218. Simon was killed by a rock dropped on his head by several women in the village.

The crusade began to suffer setbacks, largely as a result of the rebellious Raymond of Toulouse, followed by his son, Raymond VII. France's new 18-year-old King Louis VIII was eager to expand his realm and entered the crusade with great ferocity in 1224. By 1229, the fighting was ended by a treaty, and the Inquisition officially began to exterminate the last of the Cathars. In 1233, mass burnings of them took place, and the Inquisition went so far as to dig up dead Cathar bodies and burn them as well. Further uprisings occurred, and a brief holdout at the French village of Montségur has been the topic of wild speculation for centuries about a secret Cathar treasure or secret being smuggled out — perhaps even the Holy Grail (see Chapter 10). The last known Cathar burning by the Inquisition in the Languedoc happened in 1321. An estimated 1 million Cathars and their neighbors, nearly half of the population of the Languedoc, were killed in the first true genocide of Europe.

Finding celibacy in just about every major world religion leads inevitably to the conclusion that there's just something in the human mind that wants to separate the spiritual from the physical, and that a denial of the physical pleasures of life will help in focusing on the divine.

The Da Vinci Code contends that Judaism "condemned" celibacy, and that all Jewish men were married, but this is clearly not true. Few of the apostles mention wives. And the most prominent sect of Jewish celibates was the apocalyptic Essenes. It is believed by many researchers that the Essenes were the men who wrote the Dead Sea Scrolls. Jesus may well have studied with them, and John the Baptist was probably an Essene. But as far as we know, no one has claimed to have found any evidence of a lost wife of John the Baptist.

Christian celibacy, and why Paul stuck us with it

Actually, if you cruise through the New Testament, you'll find that Jesus didn't have much to say on celibacy. So, as for who's to blame, we'll come right out and say it. St. Paul did it in I Corinthians 7:

> I would that all men were even as myself; but every one hath his proper gift from God. . . . But I say to the unmarried and to the widows, it is good for them if they so continue, even as I.

Paul was a great believer in purity for Christians. Even so, in his defense, he stood by the words that "the two shall be of one flesh" regarding marriage, and spoke of its blessed state. It's just that celibacy was better, a higher calling, as far as Paul was concerned.

To be fair, many scholars have theorized that the emphasis on celibacy in Paul's time grew out of the apocalyptic bent of mind a lot of early Christians had. When Christ said he was coming back, and the judgment was at hand, they thought he meant next week. And if that were true, then keeping yourself ritually pure was more important than the directive to "be fruitful and multiply." But as a couple of centuries passed, and the Church began to realize that they may have been over-anticipating a bit on this apocalypse thing, then the attitudes in the last books of the Bible toward marriage warm up, including some of Paul's later letters. By that time, the Church was building a system, with a bureaucracy and with a congregation. And you don't get a congregation by telling people to remain celibate.

The Catholic tradition

The Roman Catholic Church based its rules about celibacy for the clergy around the concept of imitating the life of Jesus. Priests are considered to be acting *in persona Christi,* literally "in the person of Christ," when performing the sacraments, and with no evidence to the contrary, Jesus was assumed to be celibate. Moreover, Jesus does have a few words to say on the subject. In Matthew 19, Jesus mentions men who do not marry living as "eunuchs for the sake of the Kingdom of Heaven." In Luke 18, he says that anyone who gives up marriage, children, and possessions for the sake of the Kingdom of God, he shall be repaid many times over. And Paul speaks of chastity in I Corinthians. But there is absolutely no *scriptural* doctrine against marriage. Roman Catholic rules of celibacy among priests are a part of Church tradition, which is subject to rulings by the pope or ecumenical councils. As recently as 1965, Pope Paul VI stated, "man cannot fully find himself except through a sincere gift of himself."

Earlier Church practices seemed to reflect the view that priests may marry, but that higher ecclesiastical positions could not be entered if a man had a wife. (The Eastern and Oriental Orthodox Churches do this today. Both allow priests to marry, but bishops must be unmarried, or their wives must enter a monastery). Priests were required to abstain from sex prior to performing the miracle of the Mass, the transubstantiation of bread and wine into Christ's body and blood. It didn't take long for the Church leadership to figure out that this rule was pretty flagrantly ignored. The simple solution was to disallow married priests altogether and to require complete celibacy.

The Synod of Elvira in the early 300s met in Spain to hammer out a series of ecclesiastical issues, and one of them was clerical celibacy. Its Canon 33 prohibited marriage for bishops, priests, and deacons. If they were already married, they weren't forced to leave their wives, but having children was out. Throughout the next century, St. Augustine, St. Ambrose, St. Jerome, St. Hilary, and others all wrote in favor of celibacy among the clergy.

Pope Siricius in A.D. 385 declared that the apostles had abstained from sex, and therefore, so should the clergy. Subsequent popes reaffirmed the opinion. The decrees were apparently being ignored on a wholesale basis, because in 1074, Pope Gregory VII finally decreed that married priests would not be allowed to say Mass or "serve the altar in any way."

Between the fifth and ninth centuries, the Church really began to put the pressure on about married priests. Early on, many had married in all innocence, thinking it was all right. Later, when asked to put away their wives, it was a crushing blow. Afterward, for many centuries, in the countryside it was common enough for a priest to have a woman about the house, someone the villagers called a "housekeeper" but knew to be a wife. Cardinals may have lived in luxury, but parish priests were poor, humble, and generally loved. So, that tension between what the hierarchy of the Church in their scarlet robes said your parish priest *should* do, and what he really did, was just a normal, accepted part of life. Man lived in sin and did the best he could to earn forgiveness. Then came the shrug. The average villager loved his priest, and didn't see why the poor man should have to live without the comfort of a wife. After all, it was Augustine, the most passionate of celibates later in life, who famously said when he was young, "Oh God, give me chastity and continence, but not yet!

Bear in mind that the early Christians had many other examples of celibacy among priests in earlier religions, from the ancient Egyptians' cult of Isis, to the earliest Gnostic Christian sects and various Hermetic movements that practiced sexual abstinence among their priests. Curiously, Islam went the opposite direction. It was *against* Islamic law to be a celibate; the whole concept was derided as "monkery."

Married to the Church

The one thing that the New Testament did seem to have plenty of references to was that a man should only have one wife, and that he shouldn't remarry if he was widowed. And I Timothy 3 clearly said that a man who wanted to be a bishop should only have one wife. So, a new explanation arose in the 400s that seemed to paper over this subject. Clergy were considered to be "married" to the Church. Thus, if a priest took the Church as his "bride," he had to be faithful to her, and therefore, celibate. Likewise, nuns are considered to be the "brides of Christ." This is the terminology applied within Roman Catholicism today.

You may be surprised to hear that there are, indeed, married Roman Catholic priests today. The catch: Since Pope Pius XII in the mid-20th century, the rule is that any Protestant minister who is already married and wants to become a Catholic priest may do so and remain married. Defrocked or laicized priests who still want to remain Catholic may get married by special dispensation of the Church. (For more about celibacy and the Catholic clergy, see *Catholicism For Dummies,* by Rev. John Trigilio Jr., PhD, ThD, and Rev. Kenneth Brighenti, PhD [Wiley].)

Part VI
The Part of Tens

"In conference with some Past Masters and a Grand Master, it was decided that this year you deserve to become a Master and wear the apron, too."

In this part . . .

It can't be a Dummies book without these fun chapters of ten tantalizing topics. Chapter 15 points you toward ten possible candidates for the location of the Holy Grail. Check the expiration date on your passport before venturing into Chapter 16, because we plan your itinerary with ten must-see Templar sites. And break out your whip and fedora and channel your inner Indiana Jones — Chapter 17 gives you ten starting points to start hunting the famous long-lost Templar treasures such as the Ark of the Covenant, the Holy Grail, the Spear of Destiny, or even secret parchments that might change the world. Holy cow.

Chapter 15

Ten Candidates for the Site of the Holy Grail

- -

In This Chapter

▶ Seeking the hiding places of the Grail

▶ Examining grails that survive today

▶ Discovering surviving grail castles

- -

*T*he earliest reference to a claim as being the actual cup used by Jesus at the Last Supper came from a seventh-century Anglo-Saxon pilgrim to Jerusalem named Arculf, who wrote that he saw a two-handled silver chalice in a Jerusalem chapel between Golgotha and the Martyrium. It disappeared long before the Crusaders got there.

The period of the Crusades was a bull market for the trade in sacred relics coming out of the Holy Land. During the Middle Ages, there were no less than 20 candidates for the Holy Grail floating around Europe and the Middle East in various locations.

We discount Dan Brown's contention that Mary Magdalene is the real Holy Grail, the sacred vessel that contained Jesus's offspring, and that her bones are buried under I. M. Pei's glass pyramid at the Louvre in Paris. In this chapter, we list ten possible locations where the Holy Grail may have been over the years, or may still be today.

For more on the origin of the Holy Grail legends, turn to Chapter 10.

Glastonbury Tor, England

Sticking up out of the English countryside like a big geological lump stands Glastonbury Tor, a high, oblong hill that can be seen for miles. At one time, it was an island, but the sea has receded, leaving this strange geographical sight. It has been identified over the centuries as the mythical Isle of Avalon of King Arthur's time. What makes Glastonbury such a startling sight today is the ruined entryway of the abbey's tower that sits at the top of the knoll.

The source of the belief that that Glastonbury could be the location of the Holy Grail is in the legend of Joseph of Arimathea. Christians in Britain have long told the legend that Joseph came to the island shortly after Christ's ascension, and that he and his fellow travelers founded the monastery at Glastonbury. The tale goes that he was accompanied by the Bethany sisters (Mary and Martha), Lazarus, Mary Magdalene, and others followers. A variation of the tale is that Joseph even brought the teenaged Jesus to Britain before Jesus began his ministry! Of course, much of this legend may have had more to do with claiming that Christianity was alive in Britain long before the Roman Catholic Church was established, as part of the British feud between Catholics and Protestants, than it did with history.

In A.D. 1190, after a fire that consumed the abbey, two massive oak coffins were discovered buried below the ruins, with the inscription *Hic jacet sepultus inclitus rex Arthurus in insula Avalonia* (Here lies King Arthur in the island of Avalon). Since that time, many have believed that the remains really were King Arthur and his wife, Guinevere.

As you may expect, there is a Holy Grail associated with Glastonbury. Known as the Nanteos Cup, it is a bowl said to have been made of olive wood. For many years, it was in the care of the Nanteos family, but it's now in a museum in the Welsh village of Aberystwyth. True believers have drunk healing water from the cup over the centuries, some going so far as to nibble bits of wood from its edge. As a result, little is left of it today.

The Welsh Commissioner of Monuments has said that the artifact is, in actuality, made of Witch Elm wood, and is actually a bowl from the 1400s. Others believe it to be the genuine grail brought to Britain by Joseph of Arimathea.

Hawkstone Park (Shropshire, England)

When the term *Holy Grail* gets mentioned, most take it to mean the cup or chalice used by Christ at the Last Supper before his arrest. But others have a different view. Some have said that the Grail is a jar used by Joseph of Arimathea or Mary Magdalene to collect blood, sweat, or tears from Christ as he hung on the cross. And it is from this notion that a tiny alabaster or onyx jar in England enters the picture.

In Hodnet Church in Shropshire, England, there is a stained-glass window that depicts, among other saints, St. John the Evangelist. Unlike the others in the panel who are older, with beards (Sts. Matthew, Mark, and Luke), this is a young, almost feminine John, shown holding a chalice. Some have suggested that this person is, in fact, Mary Magdalene, and not St. John.

As we discuss in Chapter 13, Mary Magdalene is often misconstrued as the "woman with the alabaster jar," who anointed Christ with oil before his arrest. Curiously, in 1920, a small alabaster cup, the size of a shot glass or an eggcup, was found in a hidden recess of a statue's base, deep within a grotto in Hawkstone Park, Shropshire. Author Graham Phillips is a believer that this cup is, in fact, the Holy Grail.

Hawkstone has long been in the running as a possible location for the final resting place of King Arthur, and it's through him that the legend of the little cup first came to be associated with the Grail legend.

The statue was commissioned in the 1850s by Thomas Wright, who had long claimed that he possessed the Holy Grail. The statue was part of a set of four in the grotto — of a lion, an angel, a bull, and an eagle. These were early Christian symbols of the four gospels, and they do, in fact, appear over the heads of Matthew, Mark, Luke, and John in the stained-glass window in Hodnet Church. The eagle appears over the head of John, and it was the eagle statue that contained the cup.

Through a complex story, Phillips suggests that the image in the stained-glass window is Mary Magdalene, not John, and that the little alabaster cup that is attributed to the "woman with the alabaster jar" was hidden in the eagle statue, with the window as a clue. Others must have believed it, too — in 2006, vandals were caught trying to remove the John/Mary panel from the church with a crowbar.

Takt-i-Taqdis, Iran

The Holy Mountain of Shiz in Iran has long been believed to be the origin of the ancient religion of Zoroastrianism, in what was once the eastern part of Persia. There, a curious ruin still exists today of a temple erected in A.D. 660, the Temple for the Throne of Arches. The Temple itself only lasted 30 short years before being destroyed and looted by the Byzantine Emperor Heraclius. And yet, it has been rumored to be the resting place of the Holy Grail.

The tale goes that the builders of the Temple captured Jerusalem in A.D. 614 and discovered the *True Cross* (of Jesus's crucifixion) and the Holy Grail. The relics were promptly hauled off to the Throne of Arches, where they remained until the invasion by the Byzantine forces. Contemporary accounts speak of the cross being taken back to Byzantium, but not the Holy Grail — which means it could still be there.

The temple itself was lost for centuries. In the 1200s, a German poet named Albrecht von Sharfenberg found it after reading about it in a manuscript he had translated. He simply went right where the legend said it was and found it. Until its second rediscovery in 1937, it was still believed to have been a mythical place. Its location and setting closely match a medieval description of the location of the grail castle setting in paradise, surrounded by a lake, a meadow, a stream, and a mountain.

The Santo Caliz (Valencia, Spain)

In the Our Lady of the Forsaken Basilica in Valencia, Spain, there is a chalice that has long been thought to be the Holy Grail. The chalice as it exists today is a simple, brown, stone cup, set into a larger, more ornate, gold base.

Researchers believe the stone cup really is a Middle Eastern artifact that dates back to the first century, while the gold base was added during medieval times. It is inset with pearls, gemstones, and alabaster. A curious part of the more modern base is that it is partially composed of an inverted bowl that also dates to the first century.

The legend of the Santo Caliz is that it was taken to Rome after Jesus's resurrection by St. Peter, for safekeeping. It was believed to have been given to St. Laurence in A.D. 258 by Pope Sixtus II to Valencia by Emperor Valerian in the third century. Both Laurence and Sixtus became martyrs, murdered by the Romans for practicing Christianity and for refusing to turn over the chalice to them. Documents exist verifying its Spanish history since the 11th century.

The chalice was endangered during the period of Moorish occupation of Spain in the eighth century, and again during the 20th-century Spanish Civil War. That it has survived with a provable pedigree so many centuries is miraculous in and of itself. In 1982, Pope John Paul II became the first pope since Sixtus II to celebrate a mass with the chalice, and Pope Benedict XVI used it at a mass in July 2006.

Sacro Catino (Genoa, Italy)

The Sacro Catino (Holy Basin) in Genoa, Italy, is another longtime contender for being the Holy Grail. According to the medieval author William of Tyre, it was discovered in a mosque in Caesarea in 1101. Long thought to have been a bowl cut from a giant emerald, it's actually made of green Egyptian glass (discovered by accident when it was broken by Napoleon's butterfingered henchmen in the early 1800s). This came as a rude surprise to the Genoese, who had accepted it as payment for a large debt, thinking it was really made of emerald.

Over the years, some embroidery has been added to the tale of this particular cup. Not only is it claimed to have been used by Jesus at the last supper. It is also purported to have been given to King Solomon by the Queen of Sheba, some 3,000 years ago.

Rosslyn Chapel (Roslin, Scotland)

Somehow, Rosslyn Chapel (www.rosslynchapel.org.uk) in Scotland manages to make every list when it comes to the Templars, the Freemasons, or the Holy Grail. We talk about the many legends associated with Rosslyn all throughout this book, but here's its Grail connection:

The legend goes that the Templars fled France when their arrests were imminent, and fled to Scotland, hauling the Temple treasure from their Paris vaults. The treasure may have included the Holy Grail and other sacred relics. When the Saint-Clair family built Rosslyn Chapel in the mid-1400s, it was constructed with hidden crypts and other hiding places to tuck the treasure into. Some researchers believe that the Grail is hidden within the presumably hollow Apprentice Pillar in the church.

Wewelsburg Castle (Buren, Germany)

In the western part of Germany, known as Westphalia, is a town whose skyline is dominated by a massive Renaissance-era castle. And during the period of Nazism between the 1930s and 1940s, it was a very curious place indeed.

Heinrich Himmler, Reichsfürer of Hitler's *Schutzstaffel* (better known as the SS, Adolf Hitler's feared internal secret police and engineers of the Holocaust), came to Buren in 1934 and took over the imposing castle. On the surface, the plan was to make Wewelsburg Castle a school for new SS officers. But Himmler had other plans for it as well. He had visions of the SS as an elite Knightly Order, like the Templars and the Teutonic Knights, and Wewelsburg Castle would become the place of initiation of this new order. It would become the new spiritual center of the Nazi paganism that was based on Germanic legends.

The Reichsfürer's plans were grandiose, and he eventually wanted to take over the entire village, making it a community inhabited only by members of the SS and their families. But such plans were never realized. Refurbishing the castle was a large enough task to accomplish. In 1939, a small concentration camp was established in the nearby Niederhagen forest to provide prison labor for the project. Of the 3,900 prisoners brought to the village, more than 1,200 died — literally worked or starved to death as they labored on Himmler's building project.

In the imposing North Tower, a round chamber known as the Obergruppenführersaal was constructed, with a sunken area in the floor and a round, oak table. Wewelsburg was Himmler's private Camelot, and this was the chamber for his round table. There were just 12 seats around it, for the top dozen officers of the SS. In the domed ceiling there remains today a stylized swastika set in stone, modified with the symbol of the SS at each corner. Meanwhile, the round chamber immediately below this room was a crypt with a well set into the floor. This was to be where the ashes of all dead SS members were to be interred, adorned with an eternal flame.

The Holy Grail enters into this lurid tale via two paths. The first is through the work of a dedicated Grail seeker named Otto Rahn. Rahn was inspired by Wolfram von Eschenbach's epic poem *Parzival,* in which it is said that the Grail was kept in the "marvelous castle at Montsalvat in the Pyrenees." Rahn's research led him to Montsegur in France, a former stronghold of Cathars near Rennes-le-Château. There he explored caves, grottos, and castles in search of the Grail. Rahn was seduced into joining the SS by Himmler, who wanted his expertise in Cathar and Grail studies.

The second legend was that Himmler himself secretly visited the Spanish abbey of Montserrat near Barcelona in 1940. He, too, was inspired by *Parzival,* but he believed the Montsalvat in the opera was Spain's Montserrat, where a supposed grail castle stood during the Middle Ages. It is said that Himmler went there in search of the Grail, but came back empty-handed. That's not a big surprise — the monks at the abbey were well aware of Himmler's (and Nazi Germany's) anti-Catholic positions and sent him packing.

The curious aspect of associations between the Nazis and Christian relics like the Spear of Destiny (that stabbed Christ's body as he hung on the cross) and the Holy Grail is that these were sacred items that belonged to a Jew, which would seem to be contradictory with Nazi doctrine. But the Nazis went to great lengths to engineer an elaborate explanation that Jesus was descended from Jacob, who, they said, was not Jewish at all, but an Aryan. The *Ahnenerbe Forschungs-und Lehrgemeinschaft* (Ancestral Heritage Research and Teaching Society) was created to use the methods of science to bend history and archaeology enough to suit the Nazis' racial and cultural policies. Ahnenerbe's headquarters were based in Wewelsburg Castle. One of Himmler's goals was to find the Holy Grail, and he put Ahnenerbe to work on it. There was even a special room in Wewelsburg set aside for the Grail when it was found.

As for Otto Rahn, rumors abounded for decades that he discovered a crystal believed to be the Grail, and that it was, in fact, placed in the special room at Wewelsburg. This is likely a myth, given that Rahn once wrote that he believed that the Grail had perished with the end of the Templars in 1307. The truth of what Rahn may have found in the south of France may never be known, but it was rumored that a large quartz crystal stone was placed in the castle that was reputed to be the Grail — interesting because the Grail described in the *Parzival* poem is not a cup, but a stone.

After an altercation with Himmler, Rahn was consigned briefly as a guard at Dachau Concentration Camp. In 1939, he requested dismissal from the SS, but shortly after his request was made, he died while mountain climbing. Whether he fell, was murdered, or committed suicide, no one can say.

Rahn is curious for other reasons. His works were not translated from German until recently, but his influence on research into the Cathar and Templar regions in the Languedoc are everywhere in the speculative books written since the 1970s. In addition, Rahn has long been believed to have been an inspiration for the fictional character of Indiana Jones.

Montségur, France

The heart of the Languedoc in France was once Cathar territory, until their destruction at the hands of the Catholic Church in the Albigensian Crusade. One of their last strongholds was the village of Montségur, in the Pyrenees Mountains. In 1243, approximately 10,000 Catholic troops surrounded and laid siege to the village. The Cathars held out until May of 1244. When they finally surrendered, more than 200 of them were burned as heretics for refusing to renounce there faith.

The legend goes that two dozen Cathars escaped before the fall of their fortress and smuggled out a treasure of some kind. Some have speculated that part of it may have been the Holy Grail.

As we mention in the preceding section, the German researcher Otto Rahn believed that Montségur was the legendary grail castle referred to as Monsalvat in Wolfram von Eschenbach's tale of *Parzival,* because both words mean "safe mountain." In addition there are other connections between Montségur and the Parsifal legend: Raymond de Péreille, commander and builder of Montségur's Cathar fortress in 1210, had similarities to Parsifal. And a later telling of the Grail tale, Albrecht von Scharfenberg's *Jüngerer Titurel* (1272), identified the first Grail King as Perilla. That was close enough for Rahn to start looking in Montségur.

If Rahn did, indeed, find the Grail in Montségur while he was working for the Nazis, he never said so and neither did they. The fortress walls that stand around the village today are not those built by Raymond de Péreille and the Cathars, no matter what the tour books and local guides may tell you. Their fortifications were torn down and completely reduced to rubble after the Cathars surrendered in 1244. The walls there today were built by royal French troops in the 1600s.

The Metropolitan Museum of Art (New York City)

In 1910, Syrian workers digging a well near the ancient city of Antioch discovered a curious artifact: a silver cup or chalice that held a simpler, inner cup. The exterior depicted images of Christ and ten others, along with vines, scrolls, a rabbit, a lamb, and an eagle. The belief for many years was that the inner cup was the cup of the Last Supper, and the exterior was a later, more ornate and ceremonial addition. This artifact became known as the *Antioch Chalice* and is believed by some to be the Holy Grail. But what was it doing in Antioch?

The legend goes that the Grail had indeed been found in England, centuries after Joseph of Arimathea brought it from Jerusalem. Then, when the Crusaders conquered the Holy Land in the 1100s, the desire was to return it to its rightful place of honor in the Holy City of Jerusalem. Unfortunately, the people delivering it to Jerusalem were attacked outside of Antioch by Muslim forces and knew they faced certain defeat — so they buried the Grail so the infidels couldn't possess it.

Today, the cup is in the Cloisters section of New York's Metropolitan Museum of Art. Experts have dated the exterior silver chalice to be from the fourth to sixth century A.D., and they do not believe the inner cup is from the time of Christ. But who is to really say? Have a look for yourself at www.metmuseum.org/toah/ho/06/waa/hod_50.4.htm.

Castle Stalker (Argyll, Scotland)

A tall narrow castle, built on an impossibly tiny island scarcely larger than the castle itself, Castle Stalker (www.castlestalker.com) is isolated — and the perfect location for the Grail. Built in 1320 by the MacDougall clan, the Lords of Lorn, it passed to the Stuarts in 1388. The long history of the castle is filled with murder, intrigue, sieges, and the occasional loss in a drunken bet.

The ruined castle became a labor of love for Lt. Col. D. R. Stewart Allward and his family beginning in 1965. They spent decades restoring it to its present condition. Allward died in 1991, but the family continues to own and operate the castle as a tourist site. Owing to its lonely, forbidding location near Port Appin, it can only be reached by a rowboat at high tide, and a wet, sloppy walk at low tide.

What makes this a candidate for the Holy Grail? Come on, everybody knows it's there. At one point, occupying French forces in the castle even admitted to King Arthur they had it: "We've already got one, you see?"

Besides, it's the castle at the end of *Monty Python and the Holy Grail,* the "Castle Aaaaaagggh."

Chapter 16

Ten Absolutely Must-See Templar Sites

*T*he Templars were the "Bob the Builders" of the crusading period. If your job was to protect pilgrims, hold the Holy Land, and conceal cash, you needed someplace to do it from. Or in the case of the wide reach of the Templars, you needed a couple of *hundred* places to do it from.

A few surviving Templar sites are in the on-again/off-again war zones of the Middle East, and depending on the day of the week and the prevailing winds of international politics, places like Syria aren't really tourist-friendly for Westerners. But in spite of the daily reports of suicide bombings, air strikes, and ongoing battles between Palestinians and Israelis, pilgrims still flock to the holiest sites of Judaism, Christianity, and Islam, literally by the millions.

It adds an extra touch of swashbuckling adventure to risk your life for a great photo of you standing in front of a 12th-century Crusader castle in the middle of a war zone, but there are plenty of places *outside* the Middle East where Templar castles still stand. You can walk the battlements and imagine life in a very different time and place, without risking being the subject of potential hostage negotiations. When the Templars were dissolved, their castles across Europe didn't just fall down; in many cases, the Knights Hospitaller got handed the deed and the keys to the drawbridge, made improvements, and kept the old commanderies functioning for several hundred more years.

Despite the devastations of eight centuries of war, neglect, adaptive reuse, natural disasters, and urban development, some dazzling Templar buildings have survived, either intact or relatively so. Here are ten of the best.

Where It All Began: Temple Mount (Jerusalem, Israel)

The Temple Mount in Jerusalem (shown in Figure 16-1) is where the order was born. King Baldwin II turned over much of the Temple Mount to the Poor Knights of Christ in 1119, including the Al-Aqsa Mosque, which became their headquarters, along with the subterranean area that came to be known as Solomon's Stables.

Figure 16-1:
The Temple
Mount in
Jerusalem.

The Crusaders who came to Jerusalem and found the Al-Aqsa Mosque and the Dome of the Rock, both standing on the Temple Mount, assumed that they were seeing the King Solomon's Palace and the Solomon's Temple described in the Bible, and not more-recent buildings constructed by the Muslims. Whether the Templars believed this or not, no one can say.

The place called Solomon's Stables is actually below the upper level of the mount, and is a large area made up of arched passageways that acted as sort of a supporting sub-basement for the area of the temple above, probably constructed when King Herod rebuilt the temple. The mount itself is a wild combination of natural rock, monumental stonework, and clever engineering, and the stables were part of an extensive attempt to make the top of the plateau level. During the period of the Crusades, they were actually used as stables, with room, it was said, for 2,000 horses or 1,500 camels. (Humps take up more space.)

Today there is little visible evidence of the Templars' presence on the mount — and some Muslims today deny that the Temple of Solomon was ever on the mount to begin with. This the official position of Adnan Husseini, director of the Islamic *waqf*, the trust that oversees the Dome of the Rock. It is also the official position of the Palestine Liberation Organization (PLO), stated by Yasser Arafat, that, "historically, the Temple was not in Palestine at all." Such is the battle between politics and archeology. If the Muslims admit that the temple existed before the arrival of Islam, then it would mean that Jews could claim first dibs on the mount, yank down the mosques, rebuild the temple, and trigger Armageddon, as prophesied in Revelation 16. And, politically, whoever controls the top of the mount has psychological and spiritual control over Jerusalem, regardless of what the United Nations may say. It's sort of an ecclesiastical game of King of the Hill, and they all take it *very* seriously.

The Islamic *waqf* absolutely forbids any messing about in the foundation of the site, while engaging in a feverish building program themselves up top. In 1996, Israeli archeologists opened a subterranean tunnel's entrance, which erupted into riots by enraged Muslims. Eighty-five Palestinians and 16 Israelis were killed, and more than 1,200 Palestinians and 87 Israelis were wounded. The Palestinian press frequently reports that the Israelis are attempting to weaken the structure of the mount, in order to cause the collapse of the mosques and the Dome of the Rock and, therefore, start a new war.

As for Solomon's Stables, in 1996 they were converted into a mosque capable of holding 7,000 people. Ham-fisted excavation was carried out hastily by the *waqf,* and many archeological critics say that much archeological material was destroyed by the Arabs, further obscuring evidence of the original temple. The Arab authorities say this isn't the case.

Temple Church (London, England)

When walking through the old capitols of Europe, you come across the word *Temple* in the names of streets and neighborhoods, even subway stations. In almost every case, it's a pretty safe bet that you've come across property held at one time by the Knights Templar. Not every Templar commandery or preceptory was enormous, but two of the biggest chunks of the Order's real estate were in Paris and in London.

Hidden behind the walls of the Inns of Court in London, just off Fleet Street at Chancery Lane, stands the Temple Church, with its distinctive circular design and stone effigies of buried Templar knights. The oldest portion of the church is the round end at the west, said to be patterned after the Church of the Holy Sepulchre, the place of Christ's burial, in Jerusalem.

The Templars' original home in London had been up the hill at the north end of Chancery Lane near High Holborn Street, but they quickly outgrew it. Templar holdings in London covered a massive area, from the Thames River north to High Holborn Street. The Temple Bar, where Fleet Street turns into the Strand, was the western boundary of the City of London (literally marked by a gate or bar) and the beginning of the Templar property.

The church was completed and consecrated in 1185, and such was the prestige of the Templars that Heraclius, the Patriarch of Jerusalem, came all the way to London for the ceremony.

Well, not exactly. Heraclius had a lousy reputation as being ignorant, degenerate, and something of a crook, and he was really in town looking to give his blessing to anyone who would be willing to come back and be king of Jerusalem (and his willing stooge). As protection, Heraclius brought with him the Grand Masters of both the Knights Templar and the Knights Hospitaller. While in London, he offered the job to King Henry II, who wasn't impressed. Phillip II Augustus of France had been offered the job before him and had turned it down, and Henry didn't much like being second on anyone's list, but *especially* any list that started with the king of France — not a big surprise given that Henry owned more of France than Philip did. He, too, refused the job.

Nevertheless, the consecration of the new headquarters of the Knights Templar in England was a momentous event. The interior of the church looked different than it does today. Stretching east of the round portion was a rectangular chancel, much like what is there today, but considerably shorter. The stone walls and carvings seen these days were lavishly painted in bright colors.

The church has been altered and rebuilt many times since the Templars were dissolved and the property handed over to their rivals, the Knights Hospitallers. Eventually, the Templar holdings were rented out to two different colleges of lawyers, and the area is known today as the Inns of Court. The church is jointly used and maintained by the colleges, known as the Inner Temple and the Middle Temple. When the area became home to the legal profession and the Inns of Court, the term *passing the bar* literally meant crossing the old city boundary at the Temple Bar into the judicial section of town.

World War II was not kind to the church. Nazi bombings of London destroyed the roof and gutted the interior. The architect Christopher Wren had constructed a detailed choir, pulpit, and other pieces after the Great Fire of London in 1666, but these had been removed during a remodeling in the 1840s. Wren's old pieces had been displayed in a museum for a full century, and were reinstalled in the 1950s to replace what the German bombing had destroyed.

The Temple Church is a key player in *The Da Vinci Code* by Dan Brown, and scenes from the 2006 film were shot on location.

The marble effigies of knights in the floor are the clearest reminder of the Knights Templar themselves. The Temple Church remains a working church, and concerts are often performed there.

The church can be a devil of a place to find, and its hours are very haphazard; it's *usually* open Wednesdays through Sundays. Even worse, the Temple and Chancery Lane Tube (London Underground, or subway) stations are generally closed on Sundays, so plan your visit carefully, and still expect the occasional disappointment. Consult the church's Web site (www.templechurch.com) for the latest schedule — it can change at the drop of a hat.

After you visit the church, walk a few blocks up Chancery Lane and have lunch at the Knights Templar Pub, built in a former bank.

Royston Cave (Hertfordshire, England)

We talk about the many unique underground tunnels that crisscross under Hertfordshire in Chapter 17, but the Royston Cave in particular has been well explored and contains no gold or silver. It does, however, contain another kind of enigmatic treasure of the Templars.

In 1742, a mysterious underground shaft was discovered underneath a large, flat stone in the marketplace in Hertfordshire. Excited discoverers did what they usually do any time this sort of thing gets found — they sent a kid down to see what was there. What he found was a man-made cave, a few human bones, and walls covered with religious drawings.

Researchers believe the circular design, combined with certain construction techniques and the nature of the drawings, are the work of Knights Templar in the 13th century. The carvings are extensive and detailed, and include the signature symbol of two knights sharing a horse, the seal of the Templars. It may have been a chapel used in secret after the suppression of the Order, or even a hiding place. No one knows.

For more information on the Royston Cave, check out its Web site at www.roystoncave.co.uk.

Rosslyn Chapel (Roslin, Scotland)

We discuss Rosslyn Chapel in many places throughout this book (see especially Chapters 8 and 12), so it seems almost superfluous to reiterate it here. The legends wrapped up with this place are so numerous that it's hard to separate sense from silliness, but we try to keep the qualifying statements to a minimum.

Its full and proper name is the Collegiate Chapel of St. Mary, and it's located just south of Edinburgh in the little village of Roslin. The chapel was built by William Sinclair (or St. Clair, depending on who's doing the spelling), Third Earl of Orkney, Baron of Roslin, and First Earl of Caithness. Started in 1446, it took 40 years to complete. Some have suggested that the small chapel was intended to be part of a larger cathedral to be built later, while others claim it was intentionally small, for use as a family chapel, or even a Gothic representation of the Inner Chamber of King Solomon's Temple.

Although an inscription in the church identifies William Sinclair as a Knight Templar, even that has never been proved conclusively — the inscription is a fairly recent addition. His descendant, also named William, became the first Grand Master of the Grand Lodge of Scotland, and it's entirely possible that the inscription was added to strengthen the theoretical story of a Templar origin of Freemasonry (see Chapter 8).

The principal points of fascination within the chapel for most people are the many carvings that detail every nook and cranny: pre-Christian, pagan, leaf-covered, Green Men faces; knights on horseback; men in postures that resemble Freemasonic rituals; American plant life carved before Columbus ever got there — the list goes on. Many of these descriptions seem far-fetched when you see the actual carvings in person, but go and judge for yourself.

Present-day visitors to the chapel may be startled to discover a supremely ugly temporary roof erected over the building. Previous attempts to preserve the delicate carvings and stone walls with sealant resulted in more harm than good, sealing water within the stone, and causing hairline cracks to develop. The goal is to dry out the entire building — difficult in Scotland's soggy natural state.

Since the publication of Dan Brown's *The Da Vinci Code,* the little chapel that is the location of the book's finale has been choked with visitors. *Code* fans are a little disappointed to discover that the chapel does not have a six-pointed Star of David (or Seal of Solomon) in the floor, that the Knights Templar didn't build the place, and that Rosslyn is *not* the Scottish form of *Rose Line.* (*Ross* means "cliff," and *lyn* means "running water" in the language of the Scots.)

Kilmartin Church (Argyll, Scotland)

In their book *The Temple and the Lodge* (1989), Michael Baigent and Richard Leigh traveled to the Scottish village of Kilmartin and closely examined some unusual headstones in the churchyard there. In amidst the many family gravestones are 80 curious ones, unmarked and anonymous, except for the carving of a sword. The authors believe that these graves are solid evidence that the Knights Templar really did escape from France and come to Scotland to seek safe haven from arrest, and that the namelessness of the slabs reveals their origin. Templars fleeing arrest could not use their real names and might very well have been buried in this manner.

Some people scoff at this theory. They claim that Templar headstones were never designed in such a way. Of course, this presupposes that Templars in Scotland escaping the dark days of excommunication and arrest would want to be identified in their graves. Go, visit, and decide for yourself.

Chinon Castle (Chinon, France)

Chinon Castle (shown in Figure 16-2) in France's Vienne River Valley is an important place at several stages in French history. A fortified pile of some sort has existed on this plateau overlooking the river ever since the Romans wandered through (and back when "all Gaul was divided into three parts"). In the fourth century, it was a monastery, but it was expanded into an extensively fortified castle. Over the centuries, it has been held by both English and French kings, as those who get their history from movies like *The Lion In Winter* will quickly attest. England's King Henry II, Eleanor of Aquitaine, and their son King Richard the Lionheart were buried nearby. And followers of the Joan of Arc story know it as the place where the young Joan recognized the dauphin as the heir to the throne, Charles VII, and implored him to declare himself King of France and pitch the English out on their collective arses. The English burned her at the stake for her trouble.

Figure 16-2: Chinon Castle overlooking the Vienne River.

Robert Fried / Alamy

What makes Chinon important to Templar mavens is that its dungeon, known as the Coudray Tower (or *keep*), was where King Phillip IV tossed many members of the order — including Grand Master Jacques de Molay — when they were arrested in 1307. The cylindrical structure still stands today, and graffiti attributed to the knights can barely be made out among the modern defacement of centuries of tourists.

In 1308, Pope Clement V ordered a team to travel to Chinon and interrogate the Templars. The results of their questioning and subsequent absolution of their confessed sins were revealed in a document referred to as the Chinon Parchment, which remained hidden from researchers until the 1700s. Templars were kept at Chinon for seven years, as King Phillip slowly meted out torture and death sentences, and Clement did nothing to stop him. (We discuss the Chinon Parchment in more detail in Chapter 6.)

The castle later became a state prison for more than 200 years. Today it is a fascinating complex to explore, in case you needed an excuse to go visit the Loire region of France — apart from beautiful scenery, magnificent chateaux, great food, and fine wine.

Templar Villages (Aveyron, France)

The Templars didn't just build castles and churches. A Templar preceptory or commandery was often a self-contained village, with homes, farms, and other services for the many people who lived and worked there. These areas have not survived undisturbed over the last 800 years, but there are still places to catch a glimpse of what life in a medieval European Templar community was like.

Probably the best can be found in the Aveyron region in south-central France — the villages of La Couvertoirade and Sainte-Eulalie-de-Cernon. The area was part of the busy pilgrimage trail that led from Paris to the Mediterranean, and on to the Holy Land, so it made sense for the Templars to establish settlements there. The farmland was perfect for raising crops and grazing horses and sheep — all essential goods needed to support the long journey to Jerusalem. The villages developed in the classic style of the period — a castle was built for defense, and the supporting community grew up around it.

Like most of the Templar property in France, the villages were turned over to the Knights Hospitaller when the Templars were dissolved. The new landlords added to them, but the general feel and flavor remain much as they were when the Templars built them.

Nearby, the village of La Cavalerie was also a Templar town, although little remains of the Templars' influence apart from the ruins of a Templar church. Its fortifications largely came from the Hospitallers. The other major ruins of the period are in Viala du Pas de Joux, where a tall tower built by the Hospitallers still stands. And in the village of Sainte-Eulalie-de-Cernon, on every other Sunday in July, a procession passes through the tenth-century village carrying relics from the Crusades, including one of the sacred thorns from Christ's crucifixion crown.

The Aveyron region is famous for Roquefort cheese, in case your traveling companion has no interest in Templar stuff. And try not to get completely white-knuckle terrified while driving over the world's highest bridge, the Millau Viaduct, on your way there.

For more information on the Templar villages in the Aveyron region, check out www.aveyron.com/english/travelinfrance.html.

Tomar Castle (Tomar, Portugal)

The mother of all Templar sites in Europe is Tomar Castle in central Portugal, about 85 miles northeast of Lisbon. The Templars came to the aid of the Spanish and Portuguese Christians in an effort to push the Moors off the Iberian Peninsula. Muslims made other attempts to reoccupy the area, but the Templars' defense succeeded.

Muslims continued to occupy the southern portion of Spain and Portugal from 711 until 1492, but the defensive line drawn in the sand by the Templars prevented the Moors from mounting any more serious incursions north. The infamous Spanish Inquisition was actually started to root out both Muslims and Jews who may have falsely converted to Christianity in order to stay in the country. The eight centuries of battling the Moors for control of the Iberian Peninsula is known as the *Reconquista*.

As a reward for their victories against the Moors, the Templars were given a large fiefdom surrounding the area of Tomar in 1159, which became the Portuguese headquarters of the Order, as well as the first Templar province established outside of Jerusalem. Tomar was in a largely unpopulated part of the frontier, and the Templars had their hands full while they both defended against the Moors and encouraged new Christian settlers to move in. Continuous victories extended the Templars' holdings in Portugal.

The castle at Tomar, known as the *Convento de Cristo* (Convent of the Order of Christ), was built by Gualdim Pais, the provincial Grand Master of the Templars, in about 1160. Using designs learned the hard way under battle conditions, it features round turrets at the corners — trickier to build, but simpler to defend than square ones. Central to the commandery is the large octagonal church, or *charola* (see Figure 16-3). Like the Templar church in London, its design is said to have been inspired by the Church of the Holy Sepulchre, but more likely, the Dome of the Rock, in Jerusalem. The church was used in Templar initiations of new members, who were brought in on horseback. (A similarly magnificent example of this design can be found in Veracruz, Spain.)

The nearby Church of Santa Maria do Olival was the first Templar church in Tomar and became the burial place of more than 20 knights of the order. In and around this church, as well as on several Templar gravestones, can be found the image of the five-pointed star, or *pentagram*. Though associations between the pentagram and witchcraft and Satanic worship are common today, such a connection is largely a modern invention, in spite of hysterical claims otherwise. The Templars may very well have brought the symbol to Tomar from Jerusalem, where early Christians attributed the symbol to the five wounds of Christ's crucifixion.

Figure 16-3:
The octagonal church at Tomar, Portugal.

B.A.E. Inc. / Alamy

Tomar is the largest European Templar settlement still standing today. It is also unique because of Portugal's treatment of the order after their suppression in 1312. Unlike many other European nations, Portugal did not arrest the knights. Instead, the new Order of the Knights of Christ was created in Portugal, with the express encouragement of King Dinis, and the Templars simply changed their name (see Chapter 7). Tomar never fell into the hands of the Hospitallers, so it has retained its original Templar structure and character.

Domus Templi — The Spanish Route of the Templars (Aragon, Spain)

In the Aragon region of Spain, about 200 miles south of the border with France, where the Iber River flows into the Mediterranean Sea, the Templars assembled a string of Commanderies, known as the *Domus Templi* (Dominion of the Templars). The stream of Spanish pilgrims traveled the path down the Iber toward the sea for passage across the Mediterranean. The seaport at

Peñiscola became a strategic point from which the Templar fleet could ferry knights, pilgrims, and supplies.

For Templar fans, the Spanish *Domus Templi* is a gold mine of medieval castles, towers, houses, churches, and more. Commanderies of the order were clustered in Gardeny (known in Templar days as Lleida), Monzón, Miravet, Tortosa, and Peñiscola; all are worth visiting today. The tenth-century castle at Tortosa is especially impressive, while Peñiscola's castle on a peninsula overlooking the ocean is the best preserved (see Figure 16-4). It was the location used in the film *El Cid* (1960) starring beefy Charlton Heston.

Figure 16-4:
Peñiscola
Castle.

Jon Arnold Images / Alamy

For more information on the *Domus Templi,* check out www.domustempli.com.

Where It Ended: Île de la Cité (Paris, France)

Paris is a place where only ghosts of the Templars can be found. The vast portion of the city — nearly one-third of it — once belonged to the order, no doubt a contributing factor to King Philip IV's jealousy of them. The mighty Templar Preceptory with its tall, fortified citadel, is long gone. It survived as a dungeon until after the French Revolution, when Napoleon had it destroyed. (The royal family had been imprisoned there during the Revolution before meeting Madame Guillotine, and Bonaparte didn't want it to become a shrine for royalists.) Today, there is a quiet park on the site, and the Temple Métro station is on nearby Rue du Temple.

The order's last Grand Master, Jacques de Molay, died on a tiny isolated island adjacent to the Île de la Cité, called the Île-des-Juifs (Island of the Jews) in the middle of the Seine River west of where the magnificent Notre Dame Cathedral stands. The island itself, now part of the Île-de-la-Cité, is shaped almost like the prow of a ship, and there is a park there now, the Square du Vert Galant. It was there that de Molay and his friend Geoffroy de Charnay were tied to a stake on March 18, 1314. (The plaques on the island say the 19th, but historians agree that it was the 18th.) The old Grand Master, weary after seven long years of imprisonment, asked to be faced toward the cathedral and his hands tied such that he could fold them in prayer. As the fire was lit, he called out for both King Philip and Pope Clement V to join him before God's tribunal within the year. The pope obliged and died a month later, followed by King Philip on November 29th.

There is a legend that, when the fires died and the ashes settled, the bones of the Grand Master were taken away and kept. Believers in the tale of the Larmenius Charter (see Chapter 9), a secret document that passed control of the order onward to the present day, say that when the document was rediscovered in the 1700s, the charred bones of Jacques de Molay were still contained in the box with it, wrapped in white cloth.

Chapter 17

Ten Places That May Be Hiding the Templar Treasure

In This Chapter

▶ Digging for Templar treasure

▶ Discovering medieval hiding places

▶ Looking for secrets in plain sight

*L*et's cut to the chase.

This chapter is the real reason you picked up this book. You aren't buying for a second that the Templars only had some lofty spiritual treasure, or that the bloodline of Christ was the most valuable thing they were hiding. You *know* the Templars fled France with a whopping wad of swag, lucre, and pelf. There's just *gotta* be a buried treasure somewhere — there's just *gotta!* And all you need is a map and a shovel. So, in this chapter, we list ten places that the Templars are alleged by various sources to have stuffed their loot.

Please obey all No Trespassing signs, and remember that if you're caught packing explosives, we're not bailing you out of some foreign jug.

Rosslyn Chapel (Roslin, Scotland)

This is it. This is the Mother of All Hiding Places. We discuss Rosslyn Chapel throughout this book, and it's the location of the big finish of Dan Brown's *The Da Vinci Code.* The Chapel is the focus of a huge spectrum of speculative scrutiny, and every year brings a new theory — or five — about what its thousands of peculiar carvings really mean, what's hidden in its columns, and what's buried in its crypt. Never mind that, so far, all that's been found in its floors are dead Scotsmen.

There's an old legend rattling around that if you stand on a special spot in the chapel and blow a particular note on a special horn, the secret passage will open and the treasure will be revealed. It hasn't happened yet.

If you're a careful reader, you'll notice that we also include Rosslyn Chapel in the list of possible locations of the Holy Grail in Chapter 16. It's all there.

Oak Island Money Pit (Nova Scotia, Canada)

This tiny island off the coast of Nova Scotia has been the subject of speculation since the discovery of a mysterious hole in the ground in 1795. So far, no one has reached the bottom, and manmade barriers have been struck regularly enough during the troublesome excavation that those involved have been convinced a massive treasure is just beyond the next layer. Although speculation has raged for more than two centuries about what's at the bottom, nothing of serious value has ever been found. Still, enthusiasts have claimed that the pit hides pirate treasure, lost Spanish gold, bizarre otherworldly deposits from UFOs, or, most important for our discussion, Templar treasure.

Author Steven Sora has speculated that the pit is the hiding place of Templar treasure, moved to Nova Scotia by the Catholic Sinclair family from its underground vaults in Rosslyn Chapel in 1545 to keep it out of Protestant hands. Seems like a lot of effort and expense, but who are we to argue with a zealous fascination with treasure?

So much of the area has been churned under by major excavations in the last 100 years that the original opening to the pit has been bulldozed and lost. Since its first discovery, at least six people have been killed while digging for the treasure that always seems to be just beyond the next scoop of mud. In spite of recent hopes that the Canadian government would turn it into a tourist destination, the pit portion of the island was sold recently to a U.S. drilling company for $7 million. In 2006, a group of Michigan investors said a new expedition would begin soon.

We discuss the Oak Island Money Pit extensively in Chapter 7.

Temple Bruer (Lincolnshire, England)

About 200 miles due north of London is the village of Lincolnshire. Nearby stands Temple Bruer, built by the Templars between A.D. 1150 and A.D. 1160. It was reputed to be the second richest preceptory in England, second only to

London's. Temple Bruer was passed to the Knights Hospitallers in 1312 when the Templars were suppressed, and was dissolved as a Hospitaller preceptory in 1540.

Like many Templar preceptories, Temple Bruer featured a circular church, patterned after the Church of the Holy Sepulchre in Jerusalem. The church itself no longer stands, nor do most of the other buildings of the compound, apart from a tall tower that has been rebuilt several times. But an excavation from the 1800s revealed some lurid and tantalizing finds.

The Reverend George Oliver, Doctor in Divinity, Vicar of Scopwick, and Fellow of the Society of Antiquaries in Edinburgh, was a respected historian of the Victorian era. In 1837, he made an excavation of the Temple ruins and was shocked by what he found. Dungeons were uncovered, with the remains of corpses that had been beaten, tortured, and burned. Labyrinths of tunnels and vaults were everywhere, and there were more that hadn't been excavated.

Recent speculation has placed Temple Bruer at the center of a five-pointed star (or *pentagram*) made up of intersecting lines drawn from other significant churches. If this design is truly based on an intelligent design of sacred geometry and not just wishful thinking, the significance could be that there is something far more important than old bones buried in undiscovered vaults hidden under the Bruer heath. Could it be the Templar treasure?

Hertfordshire, England

While we're still in England, there's another location that has stirred up controversy in the last few years. The Templars had another preceptory in Hertford, at Temple Chelsin in nearby Bengeo, and recent discoveries of tunnels beneath the town have drawn international attention. Tunnels connect the dungeons of Hertford Castle with the County Hall, and other locations.

The story goes that the Templars literally went underground in Hertford after their suppression, and that they continued to meet secretly beneath the town for centuries. Even today, rumors fly of secret, mystical Templar groups meeting in these subterranean passages, including a short-lived group from the 1940s and 1950s called the Knights Templar of Aquarius.

The tunnel network is extensive, and many of the vaults seem to have been sealed up in the 1800s. Rumors abound of secret, booby-trapped vaults that may be hiding the Holy Grail, or, you guessed it, the vast Templar treasure. King Edward II imprisoned many of the local knights, and was desperate to find their hoard of gold and silver. He never did. Maybe it's still there, waiting for you.

Bornholm Island, Denmark

Buried treasure is almost always on islands, so here's another one to weigh anchor at. Located in the Baltic Sea, this Danish island lies smack-dab between Denmark, Sweden, Germany, and Poland. Its obviously strategic position has made it the object of military tug of war for centuries, and it played a vital tactical role to the Nazis in World War II.

For a little place, Bornholm Island has a large number of medieval churches — 15 in all, and 4 of them are of a distinctive round shape, a favorite design of the Knights Templar.

Speculative authors Erling Haagensen and Henry Lincoln have postulated that the churches on Bornholm Island were, in fact, built by the Knights Templar. And more important, when they are aligned with other important archeological sites — Rennes-le-Château in France, in particular — it becomes clear (to them, anyway) that what the Templars built was a colossal network of astronomical observatories. Haagensen and Lincoln laid all this out in their book, *The Templars' Secret Island,* with a bewildering array of maps and geographical plotting that show the churches arranged in the pattern of a five-pointed star (or *pentagram*). But what if all those lines aren't pointing *at* the round churches? What if those lines get followed back to the center and the churches themselves point to a position that hides the Templar treasure?

Here's a tantalizing tidbit of Templar treasure temptation: Nearly 3,000 pieces of stamped gold ingots depicting a strange human figure have been found on the island, and no one can definitively say where they came from or who they depict.

Behage indrømme mig den skovl!

Rennes-le-Château, France

Ever since Michael Baigent, Richard Leigh, and Henry Lincoln published *Holy Blood, Holy Grail* in 1982, a stream of tourists have made their way to the tiny, out of the way, and hard-to-get-to village of Rennes-le-Château in southwestern France, on the trail of the Templars, the treasures of King Solomon, the Holy Grail, Mary Magdalene, and the Priory of Sion. In 2006 alone, the little hamlet was choked with more than 100,000 tourists. We talk more about this intriguing little village in Chapter 11, but suffice it to say, there's enough here to keep the average treasure hunter busy for quite some time.

Stuck between the Pyrenees Mountains in the south and the Cévennes Mountains in the north, the rugged countryside around Rennes has seen its share of bloody battles and rapidly changing landlords. One version of the story says that the Cathars who lived in the area actually had the treasure of Solomon's Temple, and the Templars moved in and took it from them.

Ruins from long-gone castles are everywhere, so you'll have plenty of places to dig. Just don't get caught. Between *Holy Blood, Holy Grail* and *The Da Vinci Code,* the town has been plagued by late-night digging and impatient, would-be Indiana Joneses setting off explosives to blast their way into what they believed were the secret hiding places of a vast fortune.

The best news for Templar treasure hunters is, thanks to the incredible high-speed TGV train system in France, you can get from Paris to this formerly isolated neck of the woods in just two hours.

Château de Gisors (Normandy, France)

This incredible fortress in Normandy has been tied to the Templars in a variety of sources, most notably in Gerard de Sede's book, *The Templars Walk Among Us.* Gisors Castle was built in the 11th and 12th centuries, and located about 40 miles northwest of Paris, in an area once known as the Norman Vexin. Built by the English who temporarily owned the property for a while, it was at the center of a struggle between King Henry II of England and Louis VII of France.

In 1158, the castle was handed over to the Templars for a while as neutral observers to keep the peace between the two kings. The castle later fell into the hands of the French and became a royal prison. It was reputed to have been the final prison of Grand Master Jacques de Molay in 1314.

The castle is an unusual round design that seems to rise up out of a cone-shaped mound of earth. Much of the building is underground, and a complex warren of subterranean tunnels and rooms exist. So it seems that an explorer back in 1946 claimed to have been doing some unauthorized digging down in the dungeon and struck pay dirt: 19 stone coffins and 30 metal boxes.

The story reemerged in the 1960s, and local authorities were compelled to do some digging of their own. They found nothing — or so they say. Modern authorities strongly discourage treasure hunters who are convinced that the Templar treasure is hidden at Gisors. The authorities say nothing is there. Who do you believe?

Switzerland

Okay, it's a small country, but it gets big when you're standing there with your shovel in your hand, trying to decide where to dig. As authors Alan Butler and Stephen Dafoe lay out in their book, *The Warriors and the Bankers,* Switzerland just appeals to common sense as the real haven for fleeing French Templars. It was close, it was friendly, it had lots of places to hide in, and in later years, it became world-renowned for international banking. Even its flag features the Templar Cross, in Templar colors, albeit in reverse: a white cross on a red field.

Switzerland was not a country, per se, in the days of the Templars. It was largely a smattering fiefdoms and dukedoms. But if you had to pick a spot to start digging, one town in particular jumps out with a suitably Holy Land–like, Templaresque name: Sion. High up in the Alps, it is the modern-day capital of the canton of Valais, and its medieval buildings are unique. Two enormous castles, both built around A.D. 1300, stand up on two opposing peaks in the middle of town: the Château Valère (home of the world's oldest playable organ, installed in 1390) and the ruins of the Château de Tourbillon.

If the treasure isn't there, you may be out of luck. Switzerland is known the world over for its strict laws of preserving the secrecy of its banking customers, and if somebody found it before you, you'll probably never know who it was.

Trinity Church (New York City)

If you saw the 2004 movie *National Treasure,* then you already know that Nicolas Cage has beaten you to the treasure. In the opening scene of the picture, a montage shows the building of Solomon's Temple, the Templars' discovery of its riches, their voyage across the Atlantic, and the revolutionary War–era Freemasons who protected the treasure. (We haven't spoiled anything yet — they do all this in the first two minutes of the movie. But stop now if you haven't seen it before, because we're about to ruin the end for you.)

In the end, the vast treasure of the Templars gets found at the bottom of a pit with an ingeniously designed 18th-century elevator, underneath Trinity Church in New York City. Trinity Church has an unusual history, and it sits on some of the most valuable real estate in the world, at the corner of Broadway and Wall Street, surrounded by massive skyscrapers and the New York Stock Exchange. With room in the church for just 550 members of its congregation, how have they been able to hold out for so long — since the 1600s — against what are undoubtedly lavish offers to sell the place? We know how — they're really financed by the Templar treasure. And all that loot underground in such close proximity to Wall Street and the center of commerce for the free world can't possibly be a coincidence.

Don't go digging in the adjacent graveyard — Alexander Hamilton is buried there, and he'll haunt you. He was the first Secretary of the Treasury and the biggest promoter of the U.S. government starting a national bank. With Templar gold perhaps?

Washington D.C.'s Rosslyn Chapel

We think we know what has become of the Templar treasure. It has never made sense that a group as shrewd as the fabled Knights would go roaming the countryside with trunks of gold and silver and burying it in a hole some-where, any more than Donald Trump or Goldman-Sachs would. Theory after theory has been concocted about locating the Templar's treasure, but to no avail. Many such conjectures involve so-called "sacred" locations and convo-luted claims of bizarre astronomical or geometric calculations, star charts and other such stuff and nonsense. Well, we've discovered the treasure. We know *where* it is, we know *what* it is, and it is hiding in plain sight.

Many books have been published over the years connecting the Freemasons mysteriously with Washington D.C., including Chris's own *Solomon's Builders*. But most people don't know that there is a neighborhood due west of, and across the Potomac from, the White House, called Rosslyn. It is named after the famous chapel in Scotland, and it is part of a larger bit of sacred geome-try of its own.

The Freemasons and the Templars are bound together in legend, and maybe even by a few facts (see Chapter 8). And *everybody* knows that the Freemasons were somehow involved in the building of Washington, D.C.

If you believe that, drag out your map of Washington, D.C., and start connect-ing the dots. Start at the White House and draw a line north up 16th Street to Rock Creek Park. Like the Rose Line in Dan Brown's *The Da Vinci Code,* the 16th Street meridian is believed by some researchers to be of mystic and spiritual origin — so much so that several "secret" societies and literally dozens of churches are built along it.

Follow 16th Street to the entrance of Rock Creek Park. It is a little known episode of history that, in the 1860s, there was a brief notion of the city plan-ners to build a new presidential mansion at what is now Rock Creek Park, because of the noise, smells, and general yuckiness of the swampland around the existing White House. The tradition of the original White House prevailed, the president's residence stayed put, the swamp got filled in, and Rock Creek Park is now a beautiful, rustic recreation area for D.C. residents. But, nevertheless, here are two potential White House spots located at either end of the "sacred" 16th Street meridian.

Now for the really clever bit. Draw a line straight west of the White House, just across the Potomac to the Rosslyn Metro station. Draw another diagonal line from the Rosslyn Metro stop up to the entrance of Rock Creel Park. Voila! Sacred geometry! A right-triangle that connects the two White House locations with a neighborhood named after one of the most enigmatic Templar locations in the world, Rosslyn Chapel!

So what, you say? Here's what. Just across the street from the Rosslyn Metro Station is *another* Rosslyn Chapel. And like its Scottish cousin, it is one of the most peculiar churches anywhere in the world. More important, its underground vaults hold a modern-day Templar treasure, one of the most valuable riches on Earth.

The Arlington Temple United Methodist Church is located at 1835 N. Nash Street, dead center in Rosslyn. And its treasure? It seems that the church elders decided in the 1970s that it would be good fiscal planning to have a steady income, so when the building was constructed, it was designed on top of a gas station. Its underground tanks hold several thousand gallons of gasoline, and with oil prices at what they are today, this modern-day Rosslyn Chapel has it made.

Index

• *H* •

Malory, Thomas *(Le Morte d'Arthur),* 229
Malta, 214–215
Maltese Cross, 102
Mamluks, 57, 123–124
Manessier's Continuation, 227–228
Manichaeism, 299
Manuel (emperor), 50
Manuel II (emperor), 31
Manzikert, Battle of, 40, 64
Marie (countess of Champagne), 225, 226
Marshal, 96
Martel, Charles (king), 37
Martin, Sean *(The Knights Templar),* 111
Martinism, 209, 210–211
Mary Magdalene (biblical character)
  arguments against marriage between
    Jesus, 275–279
  arguments for marriage between Jesus,
    273–275
  biblical account of, 234, 265–266
  church dedicated to, 240–241
  in da Vinci painting, 257–258
  as female disciple, 266–267
  Gnostic Gospel of Mary, 278
  Gnostic Gospels, 274–275
  Grail as metaphor for, 225
  legends of, 235, 268–269, 273–274
  Merovingian dynasty, 235, 236, 249–250
  as prostitute, 266
  Starbird on, 270–272
Mary of Bethany (biblical character),
  269–270
Masonic Knights Templar
  in American colonies, 198
  claims about, 5
  within Freemasonry, 200–201
  military costumes, 198–199
  original Templars, 202
  Rosslyn Chapel, 194
  symbols of, 199, 200, 201
Masons. *See* Freemasonry; Masonic
  Knights Templar
mass charge, 25

Mass, denying sacrament of, 143–144
Master and Commander, 95
Matthew 15:12–14, 193
Maximian (emperor), 294
McCall, Andrew *(The Medieval
  Underworld),* 144
meals, 92–93
*Memoirs: Illustrating the History of
  Jacobinism* (Barruel), 181
Menelik I (prince), 169
Merovingian dynasty, 235, 236, 249–250
Metropolitan Museum of Art, New
  York, 318
Middle Ages. *See also* 11th century;
  feudal system; knighthood
  Catholic Church in, 288
  knighthood in, 18
  "possessed by demons" in, 268
  religion in, 20–21
  warfare in, 76, 285–286
middle class, in Europe, 40
Middle East, Templar sites in, 321
military engineering, 195
military service, time owed for, 65
military tactics and knighthood, 18–19
millennial fear, 36–37
mode of recognition, 189
modern Templar orders
  Chivalric Martinist Order, 209
  Order Militia Crucifera Evangelica,
    204–205
  Order of the Solar Temple, 209, 211–213
  Ordo Militia Templi, 209
  Ordo Novi Templi, 207–208
  Ordo Supremus Militaris Templi
    Hierosolymitani, 176–177, 179,
    206–207
  Ordo Templi Orientis, 213
  Rosicrucians, 205
Mohammed (prophet), 47, 69, 117
monasticism, 19–20
moneylending, 43, 84, 108–109
Montségur, 305, 317–318

• T •

• *V* •

BUSINESS, CAREERS & PERSONAL FINANCE

0-7645-9847-3

0-7645-2431-3

Also available:
- Business Plans Kit For Dummies
  0-7645-9794-9
- Economics For Dummies
  0-7645-5726-2
- Grant Writing For Dummies
  0-7645-8416-2
- Home Buying For Dummies
  0-7645-5331-3
- Managing For Dummies
  0-7645-1771-6
- Marketing For Dummies
  0-7645-5600-2

- Personal Finance For Dummies
  0-7645-2590-5*
- Resumes For Dummies
  0-7645-5471-9
- Selling For Dummies
  0-7645-5363-1
- Six Sigma For Dummies
  0-7645-6798-5
- Small Business Kit For Dummies
  0-7645-5984-2
- Starting an eBay Business For Dummies
  0-7645-6924-4
- Your Dream Career For Dummies
  0-7645-9795-7

HOME & BUSINESS COMPUTER BASICS

0-470-05432-8

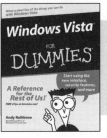

0-471-75421-8

Also available:
- Cleaning Windows Vista For Dummies
  0-471-78293-9
- Excel 2007 For Dummies
  0-470-03737-7
- Mac OS X Tiger For Dummies
  0-7645-7675-5
- MacBook For Dummies
  0-470-04859-X
- Macs For Dummies
  0-470-04849-2
- Office 2007 For Dummies
  0-470-00923-3

- Outlook 2007 For Dummies
  0-470-03830-6
- PCs For Dummies
  0-7645-8958-X
- Salesforce.com For Dummies
  0-470-04893-X
- Upgrading & Fixing Laptops For Dummies
  0-7645-8959-8
- Word 2007 For Dummies
  0-470-03658-3
- Quicken 2007 For Dummies
  0-470-04600-7

FOOD, HOME, GARDEN, HOBBIES, MUSIC & PETS

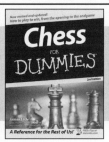

0-7645-8404-9

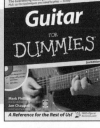

0-7645-9904-6

Also available:
- Candy Making For Dummies
  0-7645-9734-5
- Card Games For Dummies
  0-7645-9910-0
- Crocheting For Dummies
  0-7645-4151-X
- Dog Training For Dummies
  0-7645-8418-9
- Healthy Carb Cookbook For Dummies
  0-7645-8476-6
- Home Maintenance For Dummies
  0-7645-5215-5

- Horses For Dummies
  0-7645-9797-3
- Jewelry Making & Beading For Dummies
  0-7645-2571-9
- Orchids For Dummies
  0-7645-6759-4
- Puppies For Dummies
  0-7645-5255-4
- Rock Guitar For Dummies
  0-7645-5356-9
- Sewing For Dummies
  0-7645-6847-7
- Singing For Dummies
  0-7645-2475-5

INTERNET & DIGITAL MEDIA

0-470-04529-9

0-470-04894-8

Also available:
- Blogging For Dummies
  0-471-77084-1
- Digital Photography For Dummies
  0-7645-9802-3
- Digital Photography All-in-One Desk Reference For Dummies
  0-470-03743-1
- Digital SLR Cameras and Photography For Dummies
  0-7645-9803-1
- eBay Business All-in-One Desk Reference For Dummies
  0-7645-8438-3
- HDTV For Dummies
  0-470-09673-X

- Home Entertainment PCs For Dummies
  0-470-05523-5
- MySpace For Dummies
  0-470-09529-6
- Search Engine Optimization For Dummies
  0-471-97998-8
- Skype For Dummies
  0-470-04891-3
- The Internet For Dummies
  0-7645-8996-2
- Wiring Your Digital Home For Dummies
  0-471-91830-X

* Separate Canadian edition also available
† Separate U.K. edition also available

Available wherever books are sold. For more information or to order direct: U.S. customers visit www.dummies.com or call 1-877-762-2974.
U.K. customers visit www.wileyeurope.com or call 0800 243407. Canadian customers visit www.wiley.ca or call 1-800-567-4797.

SPORTS, FITNESS, PARENTING, RELIGION & SPIRITUALITY

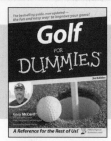

0-471-76871-5

0-7645-7841-3

Also available:

- Catholicism For Dummies
  0-7645-5391-7
- Exercise Balls For Dummies
  0-7645-5623-1
- Fitness For Dummies
  0-7645-7851-0
- Football For Dummies
  0-7645-3936-1
- Judaism For Dummies
  0-7645-5299-6
- Potty Training For Dummies
  0-7645-5417-4
- Buddhism For Dummies
  0-7645-5359-3

- Pregnancy For Dummies
  0-7645-4483-7 †
- Ten Minute Tone-Ups For Dummies
  0-7645-7207-5
- NASCAR For Dummies
  0-7645-7681-X
- Religion For Dummies
  0-7645-5264-3
- Soccer For Dummies
  0-7645-5229-5
- Women in the Bible For Dummies
  0-7645-8475-8

TRAVEL

0-7645-7749-2

0-7645-6945-7

Also available:

- Alaska For Dummies
  0-7645-7746-8
- Cruise Vacations For Dummies
  0-7645-6941-4
- England For Dummies
  0-7645-4276-1
- Europe For Dummies
  0-7645-7529-5
- Germany For Dummies
  0-7645-7823-5
- Hawaii For Dummies
  0-7645-7402-7

- Italy For Dummies
  0-7645-7386-1
- Las Vegas For Dummies
  0-7645-7382-9
- London For Dummies
  0-7645-4277-X
- Paris For Dummies
  0-7645-7630-5
- RV Vacations For Dummies
  0-7645-4442-X
- Walt Disney World & Orlando
  For Dummies
  0-7645-9660-8

GRAPHICS, DESIGN & WEB DEVELOPMENT

0-7645-8815-X

0-7645-9571-7

Also available:

- 3D Game Animation For Dummies
  0-7645-8789-7
- AutoCAD 2006 For Dummies
  0-7645-8925-3
- Building a Web Site For Dummies
  0-7645-7144-3
- Creating Web Pages For Dummies
  0-470-08030-2
- Creating Web Pages All-in-One Desk
  Reference For Dummies
  0-7645-4345-8
- Dreamweaver 8 For Dummies
  0-7645-9649-7

- InDesign CS2 For Dummies
  0-7645-9572-5
- Macromedia Flash 8 For Dummies
  0-7645-9691-8
- Photoshop CS2 and Digital
  Photography For Dummies
  0-7645-9580-6
- Photoshop Elements 4 For Dummies
  0-471-77483-9
- Syndicating Web Sites with RSS Feeds
  For Dummies
  0-7645-8848-6
- Yahoo! SiteBuilder For Dummies
  0-7645-9800-7

NETWORKING, SECURITY, PROGRAMMING & DATABASES

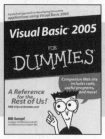

0-7645-7728-X

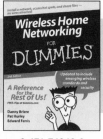

0-471-74940-0

Also available:

- Access 2007 For Dummies
  0-470-04612-0
- ASP.NET 2 For Dummies
  0-7645-7907-X
- C# 2005 For Dummies
  0-7645-9704-3
- Hacking For Dummies
  0-470-05235-X
- Hacking Wireless Networks
  For Dummies
  0-7645-9730-2
- Java For Dummies
  0-470-08716-1

- Microsoft SQL Server 2005 For Dummies
  0-7645-7755-7
- Networking All-in-One Desk Reference
  For Dummies
  0-7645-9939-9
- Preventing Identity Theft For Dummies
  0-7645-7336-5
- Telecom For Dummies
  0-471-77085-X
- Visual Studio 2005 All-in-One Desk
  Reference For Dummies
  0-7645-9775-2
- XML For Dummies
  0-7645-8845-1

HEALTH & SELF-HELP

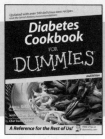

0-7645-8450-2

0-7645-4149-8

Also available:

- Bipolar Disorder For Dummies
  0-7645-8451-0
- Chemotherapy and Radiation
  For Dummies
  0-7645-7832-4
- Controlling Cholesterol For Dummies
  0-7645-5440-9
- Diabetes For Dummies
  0-7645-6820-5* †
- Divorce For Dummies
  0-7645-8417-0 †

- Fibromyalgia For Dummies
  0-7645-5441-7
- Low-Calorie Dieting For Dummies
  0-7645-9905-4
- Meditation For Dummies
  0-471-77774-9
- Osteoporosis For Dummies
  0-7645-7621-6
- Overcoming Anxiety For Dummies
  0-7645-5447-6
- Reiki For Dummies
  0-7645-9907-0
- Stress Management For Dummies
  0-7645-5144-2

EDUCATION, HISTORY, REFERENCE & TEST PREPARATION

0-7645-8381-6

0-7645-9554-7

Also available:

- The ACT For Dummies
  0-7645-9652-7
- Algebra For Dummies
  0-7645-5325-9
- Algebra Workbook For Dummies
  0-7645-8467-7
- Astronomy For Dummies
  0-7645-8465-0
- Calculus For Dummies
  0-7645-2498-4
- Chemistry For Dummies
  0-7645-5430-1
- Forensics For Dummies
  0-7645-5580-4

- Freemasons For Dummies
  0-7645-9796-5
- French For Dummies
  0-7645-5193-0
- Geometry For Dummies
  0-7645-5324-0
- Organic Chemistry I For Dummies
  0-7645-6902-3
- The SAT I For Dummies
  0-7645-7193-1
- Spanish For Dummies
  0-7645-5194-9
- Statistics For Dummies
  0-7645-5423-9

Get smart @ dummies.com®

- **Find a full list of Dummies titles**
- **Look into loads of FREE on-site articles**
- **Sign up for FREE eTips e-mailed to you weekly**
- **See what other products carry the Dummies name**
- **Shop directly from the Dummies bookstore**
- **Enter to win new prizes every month!**

* Separate Canadian edition also available
† Separate U.K. edition also available

Available wherever books are sold. For more information or to order direct: U.S. customers visit www.dummies.com or call 1-877-762-2974.
U.K. customers visit www.wileyeurope.com or call 0800 243407. Canadian customers visit www.wiley.ca or call 1-800-567-4797.